Classic American
Popular Song

Classic American Popular Song

The Second Half-Century, 1950–2000

David Jenness and Don Velsey

Routledge
Taylor & Francis Group
New York   London

Published in 2006 by
Routledge
Taylor & Francis Group
270 Madison Avenue
New York, NY 10016

Published in Great Britain by
Routledge
Taylor & Francis Group
2 Park Square
Milton Park, Abingdon
Oxon OX14 4RN

© 2006 by Taylor & Francis Group, LLC
Routledge is an imprint of Taylor & Francis Group

Printed in the United States of America on acid-free paper
10 9 8 7 6 5 4 3 2 1

International Standard Book Number-10: 0-415-97056-3 (Hardcover)
International Standard Book Number-13: 978-0-415-97056-3 (Hardcover)
Library of Congress Card Number 2005008175

Library of Congress Cataloging-in-Publication Data

Jenness, David.
   Classic american popular song : the second half-century, 1950-2000 / by David Jenness & Don Velsey.
       p. cm.
   Includes index.
   ISBN 0-415-97056-3 (hb : alk. paper)
   1. Popular music--United States--20th century--History and criticism. I. Velsey, Don, 1934- II. Title.

ML3477.J46 2005
782.42164'0973'09045--dc22

2005008175

Taylor & Francis Group
is the Academic Division of Informa plc.

Visit the Taylor & Francis Web site at
http://www.taylorandfrancis.com

and the Routledge Web site at
http://www.routledge-ny.com

in memory of Alec Wilder, 1907–1980

Contents

Acknowledgments

In preparing this book, we depended on the cooperation of dozens of songwriters, writers' heirs, performers, journalists, and other persons in the music business to recommend songs and often to send us copies. We cannot thank them individually, but they made vital and generous contributions all the same. It has been delightful to get to know a number of admired songwriters and performers by telephone and correspondence.

Over many years, we obtained copies of hundreds of songs through the courtesy and efforts of music librarians such as Wayne Shirley at the Library of Congress Music Division and Lisa Viall and Will Rhys at the Goodspeed Library of Musical Theatre, and from generous experts such as Marlene VerPlanck, Jackie Cain, William Engvick, Hugh Martin, Murray Grand, Mary Wolf Davison, and Andrea Marcovici. Also for providing songs, but, more important, for crucial guidance and support throughout this project, we need to thank, with special gratitude, Judy Bell of The Richmond Organization, Roger Schore, Robert Miles, "song-scout" Roger Crane, Bruce Pomahac, Glen Hunter, and Ronny Whyte. They saved us many hours of searching, and reassured us that we were doing something important. Those who gave invaluable advice on how to deal with the practical aspects of such a project included Michael Kerker of ASCAP, Donald Smith of The Mabel Mercer Foundation, scholars Allen Forte and Philip Furia, publisher Donald Lamm, writers Roger Kennedy and William deBuys, Ronald Prather, David Rosner, and Michael Feinstein. Knowledgeable encouragement was provided early by Max Wilk, Steve Ross, Berthe Schuchat, and Stanley Katz, as was insightful guidance on particular musical matters by scholars Howard Becker, Richard Peterson, Steven Feld, and Richard Sudhalter.

We are grateful indeed to a grant from The Mabel Mercer Foundation, Donald Smith, president, which offset some of the permission fees and computer preparation of examples in text. Bert Dalton, a fine jazz pianist and arranger in

Santa Fe, prepared the computer-generated musical examples throughout the book.

Professors Bruce Smith and Raymond Oliver provided timely guidance on aspects of poetics. Substantial portions of the text, in draft, were read carefully by David Lahm, Kenneth Hymes, and Victoria Velsey. Without their critical and informed, often challenging, readings, there would be mistakes and gaucheries beyond any acceptable limit. We can only regret our errors that remain.

Introduction

This book begins where Alec Wilder left off. In 1972, Wilder, with the assistance of James T. Maher, published *American Popular Song: The Great Innovators, 1900–1950*,[1] in which he examined, with great good taste, concision, and opinionated candor, some 850 songs from the first 50 years of the century. The book very quickly became the most important reference for those concerned with an important, many feel unique, musical genre; and so it has remained.

The appearance of the book renewed interest in the genre. In the 1970s, Wilder hosted a series of hour-long programs on public radio, bringing many of the songs in his book, together with newer ones meeting his standards, to the attention of a new generation of listeners. There had been a lull in the 1950s and 1960s as new kinds of popular songs became enormously popular. By the 1970s, a revival was apparent, partly owing to Wilder, but also to the continuing efforts of many fine singers and jazz musicians who had never stopped exploring what some have called the "Great American Songbook." A series of lecture-demonstrations at the YMHA in New York began in 1970, focusing on the work of the great lyricists, and still continues. Printed songbooks, arranged for piano and voice, were published, compiling hundreds of songs—including lesser-known songs—by the great songwriters, from Irving Berlin to Harold Arlen. Beginning in the 1980s, Robert Kimball brought together a series of books on the complete lyrics of Cole Porter, Ira Gershwin, Lorenz Hart, Irving Berlin, and others. Ella Fitzgerald's recorded "Songbooks" (of the Gershwins, Porter, Rodgers and Hart, Arlen, Kern, and Berlin), issued from the 1950s to the 1970s, had a clear celebratory cast in revisiting some of the finest songs from the tradition, the vast majority of them written before 1950. In 1984 the Smithsonian Institution issued an extremely well-annotated seven-LP set of "American Popular Song."

Since the mid-1970s, important scholarly books on the American popular song, considering the topic from the point of view of musicology, music history, or poetics, have come from major publishers and have received broad attention.[2] They too focus largely on the first half of the twentieth century, on "classics" or "standards." In recent times the term *classic pop*, referring to the songs from that period, has been adopted by journalists, writers on music, and record producers. All of this attention tends to mark off the first half of the century as a "golden age," another frequently used phrase. The result is that many take 1950 as the end of a tradition or genre, and assume that little or nothing of consequence followed. We disagree.

Part of the reason for the demarcation was numerical (1950 is a convenient benchmark) or actuarial. In 1950, Kern, Gershwin, and Youmans had died; Porter was 58, Irving Berlin 62, Arlen 45, Rodgers 48, Vernon Duke 47, and Arthur Schwartz was 50. But there seems to have been a deeper, more ominous, assumption. Maher, in 1972, said, "By 1950 the professional tradition in song writing was nearing its end." Forte commented, "[1950] marked the end of the careers of many major songwriters and lyricists of the Golden Era," an era whose beginning he dates to 1924. Furia wrote: "The lyricists I call the poets of Tin Pan Alley wrote songs in the years between World War I and World War II…."[3]

It is obvious, however, that the course continued to run.[4] It is our intention in this book to suggest reasons why 1950 has been taken as a terminus, and also to examine without prejudice the scope and quality of what came after. In fact, Porter was active until about 1958; Rodgers until the later 1970s; Arlen until about 1976. Some of the greatest lyricists of the classic era continued to do outstanding and successful work: Johnny Mercer until about 1974, Dorothy Fields until about 1973. This continuation might be viewed as a gallant last stand, a refusal of major figures simply to stop. But then, how to explain the outstanding careers of Frank Loesser, Cy Coleman, Jerry Herman, Bock and Harnick, Kander and Ebb, Jule Styne, Lerner and Loewe, and several other major figures? Where did Stephen Sondheim come from? How can we explain the fact that a number of the most successful Broadway musicals—among the very best, in the quality of the scores—appeared in the 1950s, 1960s, and later?[5]

And how can we explain the fact that major singers who were doing classic pop songs before 1950, or shortly thereafter, continued to record them, along with newer songs that they considered equivalent? These included singers of discrimination who helped establish the canon—Sinatra, Garland, Fitzgerald, Peggy Lee, Lena Horne, and others; a slightly younger generation, who started in the 1950s, such as Tony Bennett, Mel Tormé, Rosemary Clooney, Teddi King, Carmen McRae; or, in the 1990s, a new set of highly successful young singers, such as Diana Krall or Harry Connick, Jr., who clearly appealed to young listeners. The year 1950 seemed to be no barrier to them. What explains the fact that so many songs written after 1950 have been recorded by jazz artists such as Oscar Peterson, Bill Evans, Ellis Larkins, Erroll Garner, Teddy Wilson, Dave McKenna, Hank Jones, Tommy Flanagan, Bill Charlap, to mention only pianists?

The questions that need answers are these: Was the late work of the song-writers established in reputation by midcentury less good than their work before? Were the successful writers who then emerged working in an antiquated style? Were they perhaps working in styles reminiscent of the classic style, but significantly altered? Did they, on the contrary, adopt new musical and verse techniques, thus establishing a new genre? Are the post-1950 songs as memorable today as those that came before? Will they last as long, and mean as much? Finally, if indeed there is still "a great tradition," how vital is this tradition, as of 2000, in comparison with other types of songs and song styles of the later twentieth century?

The evidence on which answers can be based will be found throughout this book, particularly in chapters 3 through 8, as we examine particular songs, trends, and characteristics. In the final chapter we offer our own conclusions.

In chapter 1, we attempt to describe in some detail "the classic tradition" at midcentury. What are the defining features of the kind of songs that Wilder covered? However, intrinsic features alone are not sufficient when one is deal-ing with style history, extent of popularity, and cultural meaning. Thus, in chapter 2 we review some of the societal or contextual aspects—including demographic, sociohistorical, and technological features—that may be helpful in isolating some clear differences between that tradition and other streams of popular music.

Before continuing, however, we should describe our approach to the research and the presentation of this book. Wilder looked, at least glancingly, at some 17,000 songs from the approximately 300,000 songs that were copyrighted in the period 1900 to 1950 or shortly thereafter. Of these, he chose to mention some 850, treating perhaps 400 in closer detail, often with brief musical examples.

We have examined over four thousand songs copyrighted after 1950. We gave serious consideration to perhaps eighteen hundred, and in the end chose to include about twelve hundred songs for mention or analysis. Of these, we sup-ply musical or textual illustrations for about 130 of them. Like Wilder, we avoid reproducing the complete musical or verse text. In chapter 1, where we establish a pre-1950 baseline for comparison, we do show some complete songs for the sake of explication. In these songs, for ease of analysis, the songs are shown in C major, sometimes with reduced harmony. As with Wilder, our reference point for songs in chapters 3 through 8 is normally the first copyrighted published version; and where a musical example is shown, it is in the published key and harmonized as printed.

We wish to make our selection principles as explicit as possible. Wilder sometimes mentioned, but did not analyze, well-known songs that he found comparatively inferior. A reader using our book for reference will find that some very famous songs are mentioned only in passing or not at all. The usual reason is that the song is very widely known, and has been much recorded or written about. As for certain other songs known to audiences over the years, there are three explanations for their omission: (1) we missed the songs; (2) we may not consider them as "songs," in our terms (see below); or (3) we simply do not consider them, in an already long book, worthy of coverage. If the reader looks in the index for obvious titles and finds them missing, it is possible that we do not like them much.[6] In contrast, we occasionally spend time on relatively inconsequential, though never poor, songs, in order to point to an interesting feature or trend.

We touch lightly on songs from the very last years of the twentieth century because our main interest is in where we have come from, in the second half-century, not in predicting what the near future is likely to be. We also omit songs by non-American composers and lyricists, except for persons long resident in the United States. Finally, with great regret, we omit some excellent songs from the classic tradition that we or discriminating singers or musicians may know and perform, but which have not been published or recorded. We cannot justify writing about songs that the general public cannot locate.[7]

The presence of a musical illustration or lyric extract always signals that we want to direct the reader's attention to a feature or features we admire or find interesting. The converse is not true. There are instances of songs that we would have liked to illustrate, but we could not obtain permission from the copyright holder or could do so only with exorbitant cost or difficulty.

Unlike Wilder, we include, where possible, highly selective references to recordings of some of the songs that we discuss at length, especially songs that are not well known. In doing so, we give preference to versions that we find particularly illuminating, not the most readily available.[8] Additionally, we have limited ourselves to songs that have seldom been recorded, at least not well, and have thus been neglected.

Although our attitudes toward and appreciation of classic popular songs should become clear as the reader progresses through the analyses, we pause here to prefigure those attitudes and to make explicit our own values. Wilder, in his 1972 book, did not do this; but two-thirds of the way through his book we find this statement:[9]

> I should make clear that my criteria are limited to the singing line and include the elements of intensity, unexpectedness, originality, sinuosity of phrase, clarity, naturalness, control, unclutteredness, sophistication,

and honest sentiment.... Sometimes one is deceived by devices, in other words, cleverness.

We endorse all these aspects, but find the predominant attention to "the singing line" too limiting; there are other dimensions of songs that repay attention. In his two important books, music theorist Allen Forte concentrates, to a greater depth than other writers have provided, on the harmonically based structure of great songs. Of course he attends to the melodic line, and to rhythmic and verbal elements as well, but his unique emphasis is on the chords and chord and key changes, in their relation to the melody.[10] Philip Furia's stated topic is lyrics, and while he refers to harmonic movement or to characteristics of melodies, these are treated in relation to the words.

Both approaches are valid and informative, as is Wilder's largely melodic emphasis. But it makes most sense to us to claim that a great song has, simultaneously, *two or more* "predominant" aspects. We too give attention, sometimes minute attention, to specific elements—the horizontal contour that is a tune, the movement through time that is tempo or meter, the gait that is rhythm, and the color and vertical density that harmony provides. However, we are constantly sensitive to the gestalt, the integral essence, as we attempt the difficult task of describing in words the special memorability, the multiple creative achievement, that is a fine song.

Suffice it to say here that we think of the songs we value most as mysterious but recognizable amalgams of melody, words, harmony, all moving together in time. We do not give pride of place to any single element. A good song has a shape, a certain communicative weight, a density of verbal and nonverbal meaning. It is a verbal/musical form that is also a narrated set of events, an enactment of a mood, an attitude, an experience. Though all metaphors are inadequate, in our view an excellent song has "good bones": the melody line and the harmonic movement function as one. The words and music have the same pace and pointing. The "good bones" notion is grammatical in nature: it is a matter of how two formal systems, sound and verbal sense, relate to each other to make meaning. Given *this* musical move, is it plausible to say precisely *that* in the lyric? Does *this* harmonic event make *that* phrase semantically clearer? Does this *key word* coincide with a crucial *musical moment*?

Alternatively, a fine song is "shapely"—largely a matter of the interaction of melody and rhythm, which is to say, the complementary way in which movement through time matches the movement of the melody through tonal space. It is a coherent *gesture* in the soundscape, a figure of sound rather than a figure of speech. A shapely song does not meander, sag, or tie itself up in knots. It seems inevitable.

Beyond all these considerations, one can say, though still inadequately, that a good song has an emotional impact in the very moment of communication.

Meaning and feeling converge, and emotion is conveyed. One of the greatest songwriters, Harold Arlen, said: "Words make you think a thought, and music makes you feel a feeling, but a song makes you feel a thought."[11]

To be sure, when we say "an effective song" we have in mind a class of song that is fairly short, that has some degree of excursion (that goes somewhere, is not just a recitation or repeating loop), and is in closed form (i.e., comes to a clear-cut ending). For our purposes, "a number" may not be a song. *Rose's Turn* ("Gypsy"), *Jet Song* ("West Side Story"), or *Ascot Gavotte* ("My Fair Lady") are fabulous episodes in the theater. They are not, in our terms in chapter 1, songs. People often recall, with special fondness, a "number" or a musical sequence where, on re-examination, it turns out that the effect depended on some paramusical aspect: the uniqueness of its arrangement, its extraordinary style of delivery, or on the simultaneous occurrence of dance. We have in mind, for example, the *Steam Heat* episode from "Pajama Game" or the charming sung formula, "Thank you, thank you, please come again," with which the shopkeepers bid goodbye to their customers in "She Loves Me."

Nor is it solely a matter of theatrical embedding. There are songs that took on special meaning at a certain moment in American history or in a certain cultural context, which may or may not be worthy of attention as songs in our definition. Examples might include *Camelot,* or wartime songs, or *I Am What I Am.* Something similar can be said of novelty or special-purpose songs. Title songs from movies, like *Born Free,* generally fit this category, as do memory-commandeering TV commercials or amusing nonsense songs. For the most part, the criterion of quality—of tune and words working powerfully together—takes care of this problem.[12]

We also skimp on coverage of overtly comedic songs. Many such songs, especially where the words (often in multiple stanzas) must be at the forefront, have a merely serviceable structure: the song is the frame for verbal profusion. Many "list songs" by the great songwriters fall into this category; for example, Porter's *You're the Top.* Other comedy songs, especially those that come from musical theater, are fitted closely to a fictional or situational context, and do not work well outside it. *Sit Down, You're Rockin' the Boat* ("Guys and Dolls") or *You Gotta Have a Gimmick* ("Gypsy") are brilliant inventions in context, but one would be surprised to hear them included by an unknown singer on a new CD. By similar reasoning, many delightful, expert comedy songs are also topical or, in their verbal reference, tied to a bygone era.

Finally, we do not analyze songs from traditions such as blues, gospel, rhythm and blues, Western swing, rock, folk—except insofar as they can be seen as relating, by likeness or by contrast, to the tradition that this book examines.

How to Use This Book

This book may be used in several ways. Someone already interested in the classic American popular song in terms of style or genre, or who wishes to ponder more deeply the formal characteristics of a type of song with which they are only passingly familiar, will want to make his way through chapter 1. Someone who is interested in style history and the societal context for "popular" song since about 1950 may want to begin with chapter 2. Either reader could then review the final chapter to see how matters stood, in our estimate, as of about the year 2000.

Some sections of chapter 1 will benefit from familiarity with musical or poetic terms and concepts. Although we have tried to simplify and define these, some readers will find portions of the text hard to follow. They, and some other readers, may tend to use this book for reference—as a compendium of comments on some 1200 songs.

We hope there will be many such readers, because this book is not aimed only at the musically sophisticated or theoretically minded reader. Those using this book as a source book will be most interested in chapters 3 through 8. Even here, with regard to the illustrative excerpts, the discussion will mean most to readers with a rudimentary knowledge of musical notation, so they can follow the progress of the melodic line, recognize the indicated rhythms, and sense the nature of the harmony involved. However, it is entirely possible for readers without such skills to use the book. It is easier to make sense of the examples than a musically untrained person may think.

Chapters 3 through 8 are organized in primarily chronological fashion, by era or generation, with some excursions reflecting subtypes of songs. Within each chapter, we try to group the songs of a composer or of a lyricist and, further, songs from the same period of the writers' careers. Again, the organization is normally chronological. However, not all songs by a given writer are discussed in the same section: the reader should make frequent use of the indexes.

We do ask even the most casual readers to acquaint themselves with the section, "Special Usage and Conventions," pp. xviii–xx, and to follow cross-references back to certain locations in chapter 1 for fuller explication. There are two reasons. First, for efficiency in discussing hundreds of particular songs, we have summarized in the "Special Usage" section certain technical conceptions and usages that recur frequently throughout the chapters discussing specific songs. Second, we urge every reader to understand what we take to be "classic American popular song," and thus what kinds of songs are included. As we discuss at the beginning of chapter 1, it is not a simple matter to define that genre, and the rest of chapter 1 attempts to do so by enumeration, analysis, and example. There are also passages throughout the song analysis chapters that comment on what we believe to be general attributes, principles, or trends. Unless readers have a sense of our scope and our standards, they will doubtless search for songs that are not included, and may find the bases for our judgments arbitrary or capricious.

Notes

1. Alec Wilder, with James T. Maher, "American Popular Song: The Great Innovators, 1900–1950." (New York: Oxford Univ. Press, 1972.. Hereafter, Wilder.
2. These include Charles Hamm, "Yesterdays: Popular Song in America" (New York: Norton, 1979); Allen Forte, "The American Popular Ballad of the Golden Era" (Princeton, NJ: Princeton Univ. Press, 1995); Forte, "Listening to Classic American Popular Songs" (New Haven, CT: Yale Univ. Press, 2001); Lehman Engel, "Their Words Are Music" (New York: Crown, 1975); Philip Furia, "Poets of Tin Pan Alley: A History of America's Great Lyricists" (New York: Oxford Univ. Press, 1992; hereafter, Furia); Thomas S. Hischak, "Word Crazy: Broadway: Lyricists from Cohan to Sondheim" (New York: Praeger, 1991); Will Friedwald, "Stardust Melodies: The Biography of Twelve of America's Most Popular Songs" (New York: Pantheon, 2002).
3. Wilder, xxxvi; Forte, "American Popular Ballad," 3–4; Furia, ix.
4. Both Wilder and Furia recognized this. Wilder did cover a few songs of his "great innovators" written after 1950.
5. To cite just a few musicals from the third quarter of the twentieth century: "The King and I," "The Most Happy Fella," "Gypsy," "She Loves Me," "Cabaret," "The Music Man," "House of Flowers."
6. Another selection bias: we sometimes cover briefly a good-but-not-great song by excellent songwriters who published many songs, but omit a song of comparable quality by occasional writers. In the former case, we want to do justice to songs that have been neglected simply because the writers produced even better, or more famous, ones.
7. Strictly speaking, some songs from the 1980s or 1990s, say, have never been "published," in terms of a printed edition, although they are performed or recorded. The interested reader must sometimes check a writer's website to locate information about the song.
8. The reader may be able to find such a recording as a reissue (perhaps on a different label or with a different issue number), as part of a historical compilation, or in a library specializing in sound recordings. Occasionally we cite a uniquely fine version not now available, in the expectation that one day it will be with us again in some form. Other things being equal, we avoid original-cast versions of songs, which may not represent a song in what we consider its ideal or most widely accessible form.
9. Wilder, 355
10. Forte also gives more attention than Wilder to significant melodic *motives*, that is, brief tone-sets, as distinct from melodic lines as phrase-long entities.
11. Quoted by Stephen Holden, *New York Times*, January 30, 2002.
12. As it does for pop songs that swept the country for a time, made the Hit Parade, and then vanished—except from the recalcitrant memories of those doomed to remember them. We omit *How Much Is That Doggie in the Window?*

SPECIAL USAGE AND CONVENTIONS

Readers who refer to chapters 3 through 8 primarily for reference are urged to familiarize themselves with our conventions and terms. We also wish to direct readers to general discussions elsewhere in the volume.

Writers' names. Where a song has more than one writer, the composer's name is shown first; for example, Flaherty and Ahrens, or Styne — Comden and Green.

Dates. We give the copyright date, or the year in which a song became commercially known to the public.

Descriptors of rhythm and stress. We use several systems concurrently, including the standard note-duration names: whole, half, quarter, and so on. We sometimes use terms borrowed from poetics to suggest the rhythm or stress patterns of either a string of words in the lyric or a brief grouping of musical notes, or both; for example, iambic, trochaic, dactylic, and so on. This is just a convenience; when words are set to music, the principles of poetic scansion no longer apply well (see pp. 43–44). For a discussion of rhythm versus meter, see p. 43–44 also.

In popular music, the concept of an "up-beat" and that of a "pick-up" before a bar-line are often confused. We use both, and sometimes adapt the general term *anacrusis* to indicate an unstressed grouping of notes or words leading up to a bar-line or into a strong beat.

In quoting a string of words from a lyric, it is sometimes crucial to indicate the rhythm imposed on those words by the music, altering the normal speech rhythm. We use boldface to show actual stressed units; for example, Be**gin** the be**guine**. At times we need to indicate pauses or "empty beats" in such a string, again imposed musically. For this purpose, we use asterisks set into the line; the number of asterisks is roughly proportional to the number of beats: hence, When they begin ** the beguine.

In quotations from lyrics, whether in text or within illustrations, we try to preserve any essential punctuation. When a dash (—) or comma or period is shown within a quotation, it is probably from the original. When an elision (...) is shown, it is normally ours.

When single words or syllables of a lyric are italicized, we are making a technical point, often about rhyme or phonetic quality, vowel harmony, diction, and the like; the marking is not in the original.

Musical examples (extracts). When we excerpt a passage from a song, it appears in the key of the first printed publication (e.g., the copyright printing) or as otherwise approved by the songwriter. With rare exceptions, as in some explication in chapter 1, the original harmony and inner parts are shown intact. Small numerals above bar-lines reference the original measure numbers. The context should make it clear whether the verse or the chorus is excerpted. Musical examples may begin or break off in the middle of a measure or passage.

Tonality, scale position, intervals, and harmony. The context should show whether, for example, G refers to an absolute pitch or to a key. We refer variably to a key as G major or G minor, or simply G, as needed. G-flat, F-sharp, and the like refer to specific notes.

We generally prefer not to use absolute pitch names in analysis, but to employ more abstract notation systems, so that, for example, I is always the "tonic" or key-tone (at least in the major). We use Roman numerals I, II, III, and so on to refer to scale positions *along the bass-line*, especially as regards modulation or other major "moves" or organizing patterns in the tonal layout of a song. When we are interested in the specific sound of a *chord* or *chord progression* in a given key, we often employ lower-case roman numerals for particular scale tones, since chords built on ii, iii, vi, and vii generally involve minor triads.

When we refer to *melodic* or thematic *scale tones*, we use Arabic numerals to specify the tones in question; for example, "the tune begins on 7, goes to 8, drops to 5." Sometimes we will say, "a chord that includes tones 7 and 9," and we often refer to a "raised 5" or a "lowered 7" to indicate a half-step or a tone outside the normal scale. All this may seem peculiar, but it is efficient.

We try not to use complex symbols such as V^7 and the like, preferring to characterize the chord by its quality or function; for example, "dominant seventh." Ordinal nouns—third, fourth, ninth, etc.—always refer to intervals, the number of "steps" from one tone to another, or to a chord including those intervals importantly.

For background on some of these vexing notational but important theoretical, matters, see chapter 1, Figure 1.6.

For our distinction between functional, structural, nonfunctional, and "expressive" harmony, see pp. 30–31.

Song format. On pages 4–5 we discuss the importance of the organization of the sections of a song, in terms of their order and proportion. The reader will quickly understand such notations as AABA or ABBAC, and their more complicated variants, such as $A_1A_2BA_1$ or $A_8B_{12}A_8B_{12}C_8$.

Most songs are constructed out of modules, often in simple multiples. Thus the first A-section, let us say eight bars long, very often displays two subparts, each involving four bars. There may be a further natural subdivision into two phrases within each subpart. We sometimes use the term *period* to mean half of a unit, one musical-verbal "thought" or phrase.

In the text, we use m. and mm. with numerals to enumerate one or more than one measure.

Although we do not claim to have discovered the concepts, we do make use of some abstract analytical notions that are not commonly understood. For the meaning of *forward* or *anticipatory* syncopation, see p. 20; for *narrative minor*, p. 25. For the way in which rhyme can be phonetically exact but grammatically nonparallel, p. 296. For a distinction between *bridge* and *release*, see p. 5.

1
Classic Pop at Midcentury

Even the identifying phrases are troublesome. Alec Wilder's "American Popular Song"[1] claims too much because there are other American musical traditions of importance that he was not concerned to cover. All Americans know folk songs, nineteenth-century sentimental songs, or children's songs and musical games that are by definition popular.

Tin Pan Alley is a sociohistorical term that fits well only for part of the first half of the twentieth century. From the 1920s until after World War II, there was a large cadre of songwriters under contract as house writers to an oligopoly of music publishers and producers. Their job was to turn out songs for revues, for the recording–radio nexus, for home consumption on the parlor piano, or for public occasions. Most such songs were of little value, and vanished quickly. The most talented songwriters, including Ira and George Gershwin, Irving Berlin, and Harold Arlen, began in Tin Pan Alley. Eventually, as their talents were recognized, they became free agents, producing entire scores, sometimes on speculation, sometimes under contract for a show or film. To call the tradition we are concerned with *Tin Pan Alley* would lend an air of antiquation or an implication of routine to many good songs, especially of later decades.

A possible category name would be "American theater songs."[2] Many aficionados would accept this usage. For the period before 1950, calling the songs we (like Wilder) value most "theater songs" would involve only minor inaccuracy. Certain songs were not in fact written for theater or films; some were created for cabaret; some directly for the sheet music and record audience. Others were originally intended for shows or movies that did not in the event get produced, and became known only later by being performed in clubs, on the radio, or on record albums. The principal objection to our using this term in this book is that we cannot assume a priori that typical songs from the decades after 1950 will continue to have originated in the theater.

1

Forte and others use the phrase "classic popular song," or refer to "the golden era," by which they mean roughly 1920 to 1950.[3] This of course isolates that period from what happened after 1950, or implies that there is a fixed period of time after which good songs become "classic," like vintage automobiles. Beginning toward the end of the twentieth century, some commentators on popular music have simply called the genre "the Great American Song(book)," taking as a standard for reference the works established by midcentury.[4] This metonymic usage carries with it the implication that "they don't write them like that any more," an implication we examine in this book.

We shall be writing about songs from the theater, films, and cabaret; songs from the jazz realm; and stand-alone songs that got recorded. Depending on context, we use some of the terms cited above, but tend to fall back on "classic pop" or "the classic (American) popular song." "Pop song" is not just a compression of "popular song." "Popular song" is an enumerative concept: some songs are known to specialists, but "popular songs" are widely known in the general public, perhaps to millions. "Classic pop," however, refers to the conceptualization of a genre, an ideal type involving—as we discuss in this and the following chapter—certain intrinsic features and reflecting some external circumstances, settings, occasions, or cultural functions.[5]

The juxtaposition of "classic" and "popular" may seem inherently contradictory. Most of us differentiate "classical" from "popular" music, even though it is not possible to give tight definitions. However, in cultural theory, "classical" may also imply: formally ordered; a set of techniques or methods continuing for more than a generation; requiring formal training or skill. We believe these connotations to be valid. They are also historically accurate, in that the great songwriters of the 1940s through the 1960s— for example, Burton Lane, Frank Loesser, Jule Styne, and others—consciously followed the example of Kern and Gershwin and Berlin.

There is another useful meaning that the term *classical* suggests. An artistic or culture style becomes "classic" when it is attended to, endorsed, and economically supported by the dominant taste-making sector of a society. The songs in the great tradition, from 1920 to 1950, became familiar to the cosmopolitan urban elite and were valued by them *in preference to* the music-hall or parlor songs of the Victorian era. The latter genre was seen as old-fashioned, not stylish; the newer songs were up-to-date, appropriate to the Jazz Age and later eras. Many of them originated in the Broadway musical or in films, which in those decades were attended primarily by persons of the White urban middle- and upper-middle class. Great songs of the period are frequently alluded to in the fiction of the period, where they take on iconic significance. When the leading characters in the novel, "Tender is the Night," hear the song *Poor Butterfly*, one knows instantly what they are feeling—nostalgia for life in the United States—without Fitzgerald's having to say so.[6]

There is, of course, a considerable irony in the classicizing of this song style. The songs of Tin Pan Alley, certainly in the 1920s, were songs written by immigrants or the children of immigrants, for other immigrants. The songwriters, like the music publishers, were mostly Jewish, though the intended audience was broader than this. The first popularity for these songs was among relatively poor ethnic groups in the great American cities: part of the pattern of assimilation was to learn this aspect of the national culture. That the best early songwriters "made it" to Broadway and films ensured acceptance by the elites, so that the songs became "classic" in society as a whole.

We emphasize that "classic pop" refers to a stable *style*, not to some *level of achievement*. As is the case with all music, those who appreciate a style, broadly, listen to instances that range from routine to superlative. One hopes, of course, that those one thinks the best-made, the most inspired, will be the ones with the longest life and the widest fame, but there are lots of fine songs that are, after all, hardly known. Conversely, because a particular song is not very good does not mean that it never fitted the style category in question.[7]

Establishing something as "classic" involves a doubled process. Not only did these songs become validated by the upper strata of the society; by the same token, popular songs from other traditions, fully developed and widely known in the 1930s and 1940s—Black blues and gospel, country blues and fiddle songs, the old songs of the British isles still vibrant in the uplands of the American Southeast—were *not* thus validated, except by scholars. What is clear is that, as of about 1950, there was one song style known nationwide, by all middle-class Americans—by definition, one "classic popular" genre. These are the songs that Wilder discussed.

Times have changed, and knowledge and appreciation of valid American popular song traditions have vastly enlarged. In the next chapter of this book we take up some of the sociocultural factors that caused this enormous change. Whether the style on which this book concentrates remained *the* classic American popular song style at the end of the twentieth century, is a question we return to in our final chapter. We turn now to a more thorough description of that style in and of itself.

The Format of the "Classic American Popular Song," circa 1950

We use the term *format* to suggest something looser than a tightly specifiable form. Songs in this tradition are marked by a fairly stable set of features in common. At first glance, all these features seem easy enough to describe in layman's language, but if one digs deeply into any of them the details and boundaries become complex.

The song is, first of all, *short and compact*. The majority of songs are written in 32 bars, give or take a couple. They lie loosely within European ABA song form, in that their structure involves an opening section; a contrasting or at least different middle section; and a final section that is, normally, related to the opening one. It is thus a *closed* form: musically, the final section almost invariably returns to the melodic material, rhythm, key, and harmony of the opening (or of some earlier section). Much the same can be said of the verbal dimension: the distinctive phrase, figure of speech, or metaphor of the song occurs near the beginning, sometimes in the title, and it is then alluded to, elaborated on, or repeated thereafter, very often near the end.

The classic popular song tradition, however, tends to depart from the simplest European song form: statement, departure, and return. In the most common format, there are *four distinct sections*. There is an opening section, then a repetition or variation of that section, then a section that departs or contrasts—in character and usually in key—and then the closing section, recalling the beginning. The structural layout, in terms of measures, is typically $A_8A_8B_8A_8$. Often a degree of tonal closure, strong or partial, occurs at the end of each A-section. The final eight bars nearly always terminate with a complete cadence, a return to the home key. The verbal dimension is similarly organized, with the prototypical material—a concept or metaphor—stated near the beginning, a contrast of thought in the middle, and a sense of return toward the end. In terms of structural balance, the song tends to be *front-loaded* regardless of the exact proportions of the sections.

Simple symbol systems can convey some of the fine points. Thus, $A_1A_1BA_1$ indicates that the opening two eight-bar sections and the final eight bars are essentially alike. The sequence $A_1A_2BA_1$ indicates that the second section is like the first but breaks a certain amount of new ground, while the final eight returns exactly. The sequence $A_1A_2BA_3$ suggests that the first two and the final eight-bar sections are to some extent parallel, but that there is considerable variation among them. For example, the final A may have a conclusive or summative character, imparting more weight than the opening. That same purpose is served in a number of fine songs by repeating a portion of the final eight or by a short coda or extension in the same key that contains an afterthought; thus by accretion a weightier (or sometimes wittier) conclusion occurs. A schematic representation of a song with an extension or coda might be $A_8A_8B_8A_{8+2}$.

Another fairly common format is $A_1BA_1A_1$, or $A_1BA_2A_1$, or $A_1BA_2A_3$, meaning that the contrasting section comes earlier in the song, with varying patterns of identity or variability across the A-sections. Often (probably next in frequency to AABA), the song will take the form ABAB, involving alternation. Other formats are common enough: for example, even A_1A_2BC, where the final section represents a new path toward the close of the song. In Figure 1.1, the format of the chorus of *I Got Rhythm* is $A_1{}^8A_1{}^8B^8A_1{}^{8+2}$, while the Irish ballad *Danny Boy*, Figure 1.2, is $A_1A_2BA_3$, with no extension.[8]

Classic popular songs are also *compact,* not only in terms of number of bars and layout, but in tonal range and distribution of emotional emphasis. Most fine songs in this tradition involve a melodic range of about an octave, almost never more than an octave and a half, with a single point of emotional climax. Sometimes the climax, most often marked by the highest tone or tonal stretch of the melody, comes in the B-section, but in a structure such as $A_1BA_2A_3$ or A_1A_1BC, or ABAB or ABAC, the climax may come toward or very near the end. Such a song may be conceived of as *end-loaded.*[9] The emotional shape of the song depends in large part on the placement and nature of the B-section. If the B-section comes early in the song, or if the song ends with C, containing new material, the climax is likely to be found in the last section. In *Danny Boy* the climax is at the beginning of the final section. In the Gershwin song, the climax is placed, a bit unusually, at the point where the extension begins, with the penultimate sounding of "anything more."

While musicians often refer to "the middle eight" or "the bridge" or "the release" interchangeably, it can be useful to distinguish among these. The "middle eight" usage suggests that the B-section is a rather minimal way of introducing enough alteration to bring some degree of variety to the song as a whole. Calling the B-section a *bridge* suggests that something a little more venturesome occurs. At least a key change will mark off this section; and perhaps the climactic words and notes will be found here. Still, toward the end of those eight bars, the song will work its way back toward the material that began the song: the introductory material, musical and verbal, is *bridged* to the concluding material by some modest excursion. Calling B a "release" suggests something more remarkable: it suggests that the B-section is distinctively new and different, involving a radical key change, a markedly different rhythm, a new pitch zone, a greater or lesser degree of harmonic complexity, or new semantic content. Both songs exhibit bridges, in our judgment.[10] (The long middle section of the Arlen — Koehler song *Stormy Weather* is indubitably a release, as is the soaring middle section of the Kern — Hammerstein *All the Things You Are.*) Either a bridge or a release creates an overall *arch form* to the song, creating a going-away and coming-back (Figures 1.1, 1.2).

Where do the AABA format and the other arch-form variants[11] come from? The basic ABA form—statement, departure, restatement—is found in many musics of the world, in many eras and genres, both vocal and instrumental. In vocal music, the four-section format exists, though not predominantly, in classical *lieder* (the occasional Schubert song or Mozart work), in Baroque masque or music theater (Purcell), and in European operetta. Protestant hymns are normally AABA. The Elizabethan lute song *Fortune My Foe* is AABA, so are many Stephen Foster songs (e.g., *Beautiful Dreamer*), many songs that set verse by Robert Burns, or Irish-English songs such as *Flow Gently, Sweet Afton.*

Figure 1.1 *I Got Rhythm* (George and Ira Gershwin, 1930).

However, it is untenable to claim that the classic popular song format comes from "classical" or "European" music, since other genres of Western popular music show it also.

The open-ended, repeating ABAB format also has a long and variegated history. It is safe to say that this structure descends from stanzaic narrative or epic song structures of expansible proportions.[12]

As one might expect, given the prevalence of four-section song formats after 1700, the AABA format (with variants) is very typically seen in country music, Appalachian folk song, pop rock, gospel (itself a blend of African and European

Figure 1.1 *I Got Rhythm* (George and Ira Gershwin, 1930), continued.

Figure 1.2 *Danny Boy* (Old Irish air; words by Fred E. Weatherly, 1913).

elements), western ballads—in fact, in almost every Anglo-American tradition except the "pure" 12-bar blues. It is also the typical underlying format of a whole range of American jazz, from swing to bebop to cool and beyond—hardly surprising, since much instrumental jazz from approximately the 1920s to the 1950s was built on the basis of pop song "standards."[13] Thus the four-section format is distinctively, but not exclusively, a characteristic of the classic American popular song.

Words with Music, Music with Words

Now, regarding the layout of the song, what of the verbal element? There are those who say that they enjoy the nice tunes (say, played by a pops orchestra), but why are the words "so banal?" They do not really appreciate the classic popular song: it is rather like saying, I like Viennese waltzes, but they're all in three-quarter time.

While European classical song uses poetry as its text, it uses it in a very free way. Verbal phrases may be interrupted, deconstructed, stretched over long musical armatures; there may be a repetition of lines or portions of lines that the poet never intended; a single syllable may be sung on two or more notes. Moreover, the vocal demands of *lieder* or of cantata often require an alteration of the vowel sounds the poet called for. Thus the method toward emotional communication is words and phrases *fitted to* music, not organized as parallel tracks.

With the classic American song, things are very different. Whichever element a person attends to more in a particular song, a good song truly takes life *on both the musical and the verbal planes* simultaneously. Each word must be instantly recognized; each verbal phrase must make sense directly, as a unit. No word or phrase should be broken or shortened or elongated to fit the rhythm or melody line. Quite the contrary, not only must the verbal and musical aspects match point for point, but there should be some mysterious complementarity back and forth. That is, the tone and the import of the words must marry with the choice of rhythm, harmony, or tune.

An invariable feature of the good song is that, except for special effects, the metrical fitting of words and phrases to a given melodic contour follows the *natural prosody of spoken English*. It is one of the great joys of songs when this happens.

It is easy to find negative and positive examples of this principle. Many well-known pre-1950 songs set words like *melody* or *harmony* with the last syllable elongated so that the word comes out *mel-o-deee*. It is always a defect. Sometimes the chosen pitch of a word or syllable endangers or spoils the effect. Take as famous a song as *Some Enchanted Evening*, and sing it to yourself. In the second A-section of the song, the first phrase, "Some enchanted evening," follows the natural contour of speech, but the next phrase, "Someone may be laugh-*ing*" does not. Turning to a positive case, consider how perfectly Frank Loesser sets the opening phrase of *Luck, Be a Lady* from "Guys and Dolls" (Figure 1.3). The emphases are on the first word, *luck*, the grammatical subject, and then on the strong syllable of the word *la-dy*, which completes the first statement of the governing metaphor for the entire song: luck should be a good girl, not a bad one. The line could have had the emphasis: "Luck, _be_ a lady tonight," and the sense then would be, I've asked you before, but now I really mean it. Or it could

Figure 1.3 *Luck Be A Lady* (Frank Loesser, 1950).

have been: "Luck, be a lady *to-night*," probably with an upward-going interval at the end. In that case, the sense would have been: You've often come through, luck, but tonight it's really crucial. All this seems obvious after the fact; but the gifted songwriter makes the choice before the fact.

Good singers frequently report that they sing—convey—*words*; the music takes care of itself. In saying so, they mean that words, in and of themselves, have communicable meaning, while a melodic phrase or unit can indeed "communicate," but not with point-to-point "meaning." Good listeners report an interesting phenomenon. When you hear a jazz trio or pops orchestra play the music of a song you know—provided that it is played in more or less the way you are familiar with—the words come back to you unbidden. Even more interesting, you may experience simply the *sense* of the words. You may have forgotten some of the particular lines or turns of phrase, especially if the lyric is complex. But you recall the emotional character of the lyric (as simple, complicated, artful, direct): or that it is a lyric with lots of clever interior rhyme, or a delicate, rather than a passionate, love song. The import of the half-remembered words haunt the music. You will also retrieve, involuntarily, some personal history—the "standards" that you know exist in your memory as a skein of properties, some intrinsic to the song, some inhering by association with it.

The lyrics to classic popular songs are, like the nonverbal aspects, *concise*. They are invariably in a familiar mode, without fancy touches or straining after effect. They deal with common topics: either the experience that is common to all humans, or about topics that a generation or a group has in common. In songs as in life, there is a peculiar power to the well-timed, well-chosen cliché. The choice of which vernacular, which topical frame of reference, which calculated verbal style, varies of course from songwriter to songwriter and from era to era. The words to a Stephen Foster song are not those to a song by Stephen Sondheim.

Song lyrics also fit the AABA format and its relatives. The title, catch-phrase, or verbal "hook" of the lyric nearly always occurs in the first section, setting up a pattern, or in the final one, bringing the lyric to its pay-off. If the former, the writer arranges matters so that the rest of the lyric elaborates, in a nonpredictable way, the basic trope. If the latter, the lyricist contrives to make the listener wait for the end to "get the point."[14] Normally, the words in A$_2$ will offer another example of the proposition in A$_1$, or will amplify or in some way clarify that thought. The pattern will recur (perhaps with a twist) in the final A.[15]

As with the musical layout, *the words of the middle section will introduce something different*: sometimes a new kind of thought, perhaps a parenthesis, perhaps a contradiction or qualification, sometimes an emotional change. (An exception is the Rodgers — Hammerstein *People Will Say We're In Love*, which continues the rapturous mood of the preceding section.) The words may be in a new rhythm, may be fitted to a melody line that suddenly soars or flattens, or may sound over a denser or sparser harmonic foundation. The Arlen — Harburg *Over the Rainbow* has a strongly contrasting middle section, almost a negative "release": in contrast to the long-lined, large-interval, romantic A-sections, the middle section becomes childish, like a two-note mantra, up to the words "That's where you'll find me," which bridge back to the opening mood. Sometimes the words of the B-section will involve a new phrase-length. For example, if A$_1$ and A$_2$ have organized the tune and the words into brief units, B may offer one arching line and continuous thought; or vice versa. The Gershwins's *'Swonderful* is a good example.

On the musical level, a coherent song always involves a good deal of *parallelism or recurrence* from section to section. This is nearly always true also of a lyric. An obvious example is end-rhyme. Another way to pattern a lyric through parallelism is to repeat a single word over and over, often in the same position, that is, at the start of each line. This is a tricky procedure. The Gershwins's *Soon* works only because the sense of that word suddenly changes at the end; the Martin — Blane song *Love* works only because of the lavishness of lyric invention that follows the word in each line.[16]

A good tune recalls itself as it develops. It stalls if it sticks too closely to one tone, especially the tonic or another tone from the basic major triad (see Figure 1.6), unless a special effect is intended.[17] In the same way, and with exceptions, the use of the same word or phrase or even a restricted set of phonemes deadens a lyric, as when a lyricist uses one rhyme set (*more—for—bore—door*, etc.) too much. Just as a memorable melody line is recursive, so good lyrics use many forms of internal recall: exact repetition of the same word or phrase, short sequences of the same or similar vowels, words of the same length or the same vowel–consonant order, compound words with the same stress patterns, and various patterns of internal rhyme and off-rhyme, so that the listener's perception doubles back just for an instant without disrupting the ongoing progress of the line.[18] How all this works will be a strand of discussion as we examine individual songs in later chapters. The essential point is that comparable principles operate in different aural realms.

Before the Refrain

We have examined the format, a loose but useful term, of the typically 32-bar song, with regard to both musical and verbal aspects. However, the classic American popular song, in the Golden Age, had another, remarkable element. The main body of the song, the 32 bars, is called "the chorus," sometimes "the refrain." Preceding it, often, are a number of bars of introduction, called, rather confusingly, "the verse." The verse can be one of the unique glories of the classic popular song (Figure 1.4).[19]

Though excellent songs can exist without verses, or with brief pro forma introductions, a glance at Figures 1.1, 1.4, or 1.5 will show instantly the importance of the verse when it occurs. A verse provides a gradual introduction to a compact, almost terse, song body. It can set a mood; it can establish a sound or an attitude that the chorus will more fully express; it can introduce a rhythmic figure to be used in what follows. In some cases, the verse sets up a sharp contrast; for example, slow verse, fast chorus; or a meandering vocal line in the verse, then an angular tune for the chorus. Most often the verse is in the same key, or at least ends in the same key, as the A-section of the chorus. There are some notable and effective exceptions (see Figure 1.5).

Historically, in a musical theater piece or in a film, the verse provided a way to move gracefully from the unfolding plot, presented through spoken dialogue, into a musical episode. That episode may serve to express and deepen

Verse (*Rather freely*)
I was a stranger in the city
Out of town were the people I knew.
I had that feeling of self-pity —
What to do? What to do? What to do? —
The outlook was decidedly blue.
But as I walked through the foggy streets alone
It turned out to be the luckiest day I've known.

Refrain (*Brighter but warmly*)
A₁ A foggy day in London town
Had me low and had me down.
B₁ I viewed the morning with alarm,
The British Museum had lost its charm.
A₂ How long, I wondered, could this thing last?
But the age of miracles hadn't passed.
B₂ For suddenly I saw you there!
Extension or C And through foggy London town the sun was shining ev'rywhere.

Figure 1.4 *A Foggy Day* (George and Ira Gershwin, 1937).

Figure 1.5 *All the Things You Are* (Kern – Hammerstein, 1939).

character, but it is still an interruption, so it should not seem arbitrary. The verse permits a transition between normal speech and the heightened speech that is song. It can also supply a subtle rationale for why heightened speech is needed at this point.[20]

The verse / chorus pattern present by the midtwentieth century in the classic pop song evolved out of traditional patterns in British group or folk song or, later, out of the music hall, but it is unclear how. In the former pattern, a narrator/singer laid out a story in small units, interrupted every so many lines by a refrain, provided by the audience. Both units together formed one stanza of a strophic song. By the later nineteenth century, a singer in the music hall might perform both parts, still with a fixed repeating refrain (e.g., *After the Ball*). Still later, the first, expository part of a song became a single "verse" (now an illogical term), giving the background or setting the context. For its part, the refrain grew in number of lines and measures to be the main portion of the song, still called "the chorus" or "refrain," or, tellingly, in sheet music of the early twentieth century, "the burden," the place where the point of the song, the moral, was conveyed.[21]

The pleasures of the verse go well beyond utilitarian considerations. Good singers—and good songwriters and good listeners—love the verse because it provides the back-story, an insight into the character of the speaker/singer, and thus a shaded psychological fullness that the tightly structured song itself may not impart. As for the back-story metaphor: singers and listeners alike often conceive of the classic pop song as the analogue to a short story, not the O. Henry-like story that centers on a plot twist, but the Updike-like story that suddenly illuminates familiar experience in a new light. Consider *A Foggy Day* (Figure 1.4): Were the singer simply to begin by stating that she was in a strange place, "blue," and feeling at a loss, it would be like someone interrupting general conversation to turn attention to herself. But in the verse she takes the floor gradually, begins to prepare an anecdote: she was in London (with its particular associations), she was bored, and no doubt boring to others, but the most extraordinary things can happen! This is the way a good story-teller operates in conversation.

The opening line of the chorus of *I Got Rhythm* (Figure 1.1) is blunt, self-centered assertion. But with the verse present, something quite subtle and charming happens. The speaker says, Of course we all have happy days and high moods; but this just happened to *me*. That prologue makes the narrator seem ingenuous; it elicits fellow-feeling of the sort that occurs when a child states an obvious discovery for the first time.

In the famous song *All the Things You Are*, the narrator gives even more information, gets the listener even more on his side. He has felt alone in life, has longed for the warmth that only a soul-mate can provide, but now something quite special has occurred, and it all came about through *you*. Note how beautifully the verse leads into the chorus, by the repetition of that single word *you* with a minimal but oh-so-expressive half-step key change. Without the preparation, the lyric to the chorus might well seem pompous, despite the many musical beauties (Figure 1.5).[22]

In various ways, a good verse explores, defines, or enriches the situation within which singer and listener understand each other. It increases the intimacy and candor of communication that marks a fine song. It allows the singer (or the jazz pianist) to sneak up on the listener, to introduce herself. To be sure, some songs are just what they are, a neat propositional package: they do not need an introductory verse. This is particularly true of anthemlike songs or proclamatory, straight-ahead ones. A song that is intended as an "anthem" generally lacks a verse, or the verse drops out in performance; for example, *Climb Ev'ry Mountain, You'll Never Walk Alone*, both by Rodgers and Hammerstein. Conversely, there are fine songs that would hardly make sense in terms of their "action" were they not preceded by a verse: the Martin – Blane *The Trolley Song* is a good example.

The verse may be a teasing, not fully stated hint as to what is to come, or almost as long and verbally rich as the chorus, depending on what kind of mood-setting or situational information the songwriter wants to provide. Normally, it is in a more relaxed style and a more modest compass than the chorus that follows. The melodic range is generally smaller than that of the chorus. There is never a major emotional climax, for that would make it a complete song unto itself. In the verse in Figure 1.5, there is in fact a daring move, an extraordinary chord change at "touching your hand. . . . ," but it is momentary; it offers a foretaste of the emotional depth of the song to follow.

One type of classic popular song at its most elegant is the case where the bridge and the verse are related to each other. In such cases, the verse must be performed or the richness of association and the formal integrity are lost. The degree of connection varies widely. In *A Foggy Day* (Figure 1.4) the climactic phrase "Suddenly I saw you there," while musically unrelated to the verse, directly recalls the "age of miracles" reference in the introduction. Other examples of a relation between bridge and verse can be found in the Gershwins's *How Long Has This Been Going On?* and *Isn't It a Pity?* One of the great benefits of the development of the LP record was that finally, in recordings, the verse could be included.

Poetics and Performance Style

The Golden Age itself began in the early 1920s with the invention and use of the microphone. The microphone permitted an entirely new kind of singing style in public performance, even more with records and the radio. Now the performer could sing in a way that did not require "projection." She or he could use only as much voice as was needed for the intended communication, moment to moment. He could weight the voice subtly through an infinite number of gradations of loudness or urgency, according to the musical shape of the song and the import of the words. She could be "breathy" when appropriate, or use a very concentrated tone. He could achieve special local effects, delaying a syllable slightly, altering the color of a vowel, putting in a minute decoration of the vocal line, "bending" a pitch. Loud and exciting singing was still possible, of course; but even "belters" or singers putting over a big fast song remained vocally relaxed and in control, so that communication remained easy and intimate. The best singers no longer "sold" a song, but insinuated it into the listener's personal sound space. The singing style was idiomatic: the voice was the person. The finest singers managed to give the impression that they were standing next to you, singing into your ear alone.

The new style surely affected the possibilities of songwriting. The phrase could alter from soft to loud instantly, or change harmonically in a way that would not be perceived in a noisy public setting. A song could be very soft, very slow, and still keep the listeners rapt. The delivery could be long-phrased or short-phrased, emphasizing the overall line or more local eddies of motion and meaning. Most important, perhaps, each word would be heard, and with it the nuance intended by the composer and lyricist. No longer did a singer have to bite off consonants to define the words, or bang on the rhymes in order for them to be appreciated.[23] No longer did the singer have to land on the strong beats, ease off on the lesser ones, spit out short dotted notes, for rhythmic patterns to be clear. In general, lyrics became more subtle and flexible. Interior rhyme and other poetic felicities, such as implication, could now be appreciated. Vernacular touches could be easily apprehended. Now it made even more sense to perform a verse, whose off-the-voice casualness differentiated it from the body of the song.

Stated most generally, there was a change in *the distinct "registers" of popular song*. The term, to linguists, refers to a selection of a set of grammatical units appropriate to the communicative purpose. One does not use the same words, or even the same syntax, in public address, in expressing condolences, in making love. Prior to the microphone and recording, the registers of a lyric were limited. A lyric could be peppy, upbeat, but probably not at the same time sly, witty, cynical. A lyric could be sentimental, but not wistfully sensual. With the microphone, the classic popular song took on a richer and more variegated range of verbal registers, feelings and experience, gradations of meaning.

Writing of this change of subject matter and approach to more personal communicative level, James Morris comments:

> ... very few of these [classic popular] songs present a nineteenth-century fatalistic view. Rarely is all of life's meaning seen as residing in the past that can never be recovered or in some other unattainable goal closed off forever by an accident of birth, a youthful error, or the death of a loved one.... It seems only reasonable to assume that the array of possibilities, the sense of choice presented by these songs has both reflected and influenced the personal lives of Americans for nearly a lifetime.[24]

There is nothing Byronic or epic about classic pop songs. They are "about" longing, homesickness, stumbling into love, losing love, wanting to go to the city, wanting to come home, the fear of romantic failure, the memory of the absent friend, growing up, growing older, the irony of being free while wanting to be being connected (or vice versa), moving with the times, regretting change, waiting for a better day tomorrow. Classic pop song lyrics come in half-tints: charming, graceful, sly, slangy, mischievous, insouciant, wry, rueful, blithe, regretful, nostalgic, ironic. Songs are erotic or suggestive, but seldom aggressively sexual. They never reach tragedy, deep grief, agony, religious ecstasy.

Emotional extremes are absent.[25] A popular song does not convey anything approaching clinical depression. No songwriter or performer really wants the listener to break out in sobs, since someone sobbing cannot be listening. Similarly, while songs are never roll-on-the-floor hilarious, also for pragmatic reasons, some do go beyond amusing and witty to the elementally funny. We are suggesting here a distinction, common enough, between *funny* and *comic*. The former is more visceral, universal; the latter, more cognitive, contrived. When a song is downright funny, it tends to be a character song, as with Loesser's *Adelaide's Lament*. As for wit, it is the lyricist's job to be witty. A singer "being witty" seems to be self-satisfied, showing off, or trying too hard—except in cabaret, where this is an established tone.

The music hall song or the parlor song necessarily used a rather simplified public style of address or a sort of artificial diction.[26] In regard to poetic style of the song as a whole, the classic popular song is perhaps closer to the "art song" than it is to other forms of popular vocal music, in that the meaning of the song seems *personal* both to the listener and the singer. There is a level of confidentiality, a sort of me-to-you connection, which may be unique.[27]

However, the hallmark of the classic pop song is that singers (and indeed instrumentalists) do not keep to a uniform "vocal" style, employing always a centered tone and a constant resonance, but rely on a variable means, reflecting what the lyric calls for and what the song requires. To take one example, when Frank Sinatra, in his recording of *I'm a Fool to Want You*, lets his voice rasp and bend, almost break, on the word *fool*, it is a great moment in classic pop song; in *lieder*, it would be grotesque. There are not merely stylistic considerations, but structural as well. A fundamental reason why the melodic line of the classic popular song uses only an octave or octave and a half, except for the rare "big" song, is that it is unacceptable for the singer to change vowel sounds or alter her "production" because of purely musical demands.

In lyrics per se, there exists also a fascinating phenomenon having to do with the fictional situation, forms of address, and narrative stance.

When Ethel Merman sings *I Got Rhythm*, there is the singer, and that's it so far as dramatis personae are concerned. There is an *I*, and no evident *you* (or *him* or *her* or *they*). The lyrics offer information only about the speaker/singer. When Judy Garland sings the Arlen — Koehler *Get Happy*, there is no *I* but there is a *you* ("you better get ready for the judgment day"), which can be thought of as either singular, a particular *you*, or plural, a generalized you. (Only at the bridge does the pronoun *we* occur, once, which automatically includes the speaker/ singer in a first person plural.) When Bobby Short sings Porter's *You're the Top*, it is implausible that he is addressing this long set of elaborate compliments to a *you* who is listening, or to multiple individual *you*'s. It is understood here that the singer is addressing some third person, someone known to him, admired by him. In a case like this, the subject *I* is addressing a love object, known personally to the *I*, but not present.[28]

When Astaire sings, in the Schwartz — Dietz song, *I Guess I'll Have To Change My Plan* (which continues, "I should have realized there'd be another man"), there is no *you* in the song. There is the male speaker, another male on the scene—and some familiar wry circumstances involving romantic competition. Given the Astaire persona, and the construction of the lyric, the default interpretation is that he is singing a song in character, assuming a role we all recognize.

The situation is even more interesting in slower songs with sensitive lyrics sung in the most intimate, up-close style, particularly, but not exclusively, in the love ballad.[29] When Sinatra sings Porter's *I Get a Kick Out of You*, only the most naive 1940s bobbysoxer, or someone with delusions of reference, can believe that the singer is addressing her (or him) personally. What occurs in ballads generally is that we *identify* with the singer. The singer becomes, empathically, our surrogate. When he sings about *his* loved one, we covertly address *our* loved one, with pleasure or pain, happiness or regret, depending on the song. As our surrogate, the singer can voice things that we would never actually say to our loved one, since that would seem awkward or stagy. Similarly, in a somewhat more impersonal ballad, where the narrator tells a story (e.g., *A Foggy Day*, Figure 1.4), she tells a rather personal story to a *you* that is special to her ("suddenly I saw *you* there"). By transference, we could tell this story only to a *you* who stands in the same relation to us: to tell it to some other *you* would break conversational norms.

The play of identification, auditor to narrator, is endlessly complex.[30] For example, in songs that use plural pronouns, the play of identification can be quite loose. When one listens to the lyric of the Schwartz — Dietz *Dancing in the Dark* ("We're dancing in the dark…we're waltzing in the wonder of why we're here…"), it no longer matters exactly who is speaking to whom. The *we* out there can easily include some *you* and some *they*. As members of the same community, *we* share the same kinds of experience.

Elements of the Classic Popular Song

Rhythm and Tempo

With regard to tempo, some general trends over the decades can be discerned. From the 1920s on, songs were written in *up-tempo, medium,* and *slow* tempos, and were often so labeled.[31] There has always been a tendency, especially in nonvocal performance, for either the very fast song or the very slow song to drift toward something moderate. *I Got Rhythm* seems to call, in its very rhythm, let alone its words, for a fast tempo. But *Tea For Two* can be done fast, especially when several dozen feet are tapping in synchrony; or in moderate tempo, where it takes on a more charming character, appropriate to a two-person situation on stage or where a soft-shoe routine is employed. Some songs written as fast songs for a dance number work beautifully in slow tempo. *Nobody Else but Me*, written by Kern and Hammerstein as a very quick chorus-line number, is generally heard as a medium-tempo ballad.

The reason for this trend toward the middle of the road is twofold. First, complex lyrics cannot be comprehended when the song goes fast, especially when the accompaniment is correspondingly assertive (brassy, with heavy strong beats, etc.). Second, local rhythmic patterns can sound paradoxically more lively, more supple, when a little more time is taken. An example is the charming song by Rodgers and Hammerstein, *Many a New Day*, where every other first beat contains a graceful triplet (see page 22). The effect would be lost if the triplet were really fast. Conversely, with a slow song, the singer can avoid a tendency toward monotony or losing the beat if the song does not drag. Moreover, a moderate speed lets instruments delineate the rhythm with flexibility, perhaps with the full band emphasizing main beats, a solo instrument etching out smaller figures, or with the use of riffs (brief patterned instrumental interpolations) between phrases.

While up-tempo songs continued to be written, fast numbers in "specialty rhythms" became less frequent over the entire period from 1920 up to 1950. After the 1920s, the use of ragtime, the Charleston, or the soft-shoe tended to die out.[32] In general, the peppy number faded out of style; the 2/4 time signature, where the pulse is the quarter note, fitted most tempos.[33] On the other hand, in the 1930s and 1940s, "Latin" rhythms became prevalent in classic pop, Cole Porter being a prime exponent, as in *Begin the Beguine* or *I've Got You Under My Skin* (Figure 1.10), also a beguine. Again, a Latin beat—which, in the case of rhumba-like rhythms, plays with a 3-pulse and a 2-pulse in subtle juxtaposition—worked best at moderate tempos,[34] as do the samba and the tango. Too slow, and the intricacy of the rhythm is lost; too fast, and it becomes frantic.

Classic pop has used all the traditional rhythms and meters of the Euro-American musical tradition, although pure waltz time is relatively less common and march time and 6/8 were never common. (For a discussion of *rhythm* and *meter*, see the Addendum to this chapter.) One of the distinctive aspects of classic pop, however, is that virtually all traditional rhythms were altered in performance, and made less regular or precise. The ubiquitous European pattern of a quarter-note followed by two eighths ♩ ♫ became almost invariably rendered as an extended quarter followed by two shorter notes of flexible lengths: ♩. ♪♩ or ♩. ♩ ♪. Similarly, the sharp-profiled dotted rhythm of European music became softened: ♩. ♪ became more like ♩♪♩ or ♪ ♩ ♪. This was even true in waltz time, which took on a loping feeling involving one beat per measure, with unequal subbeats.[35] The modification is very subtle on the part of the singer, and may reflect the rhythmic or semantic grouping of the words. For example (see Figure 1.1): the opening of the verse of *I Got Rhythm* is notated as ♩ ♩ ♩ ♩ ♩. An idiomatic singer might render it something like ♩. ♫ ♩. ♩..

In sum, the pervasive tendency toward loose, relaxed patterns of unequal notes—brief, graceful, asymmetrical figures—is what we mean by "swing style."[36] Although swing style is normally not specified in sheet music notation, sometimes the performer will be instructed to "swing the eighths." It is just taken for granted, the way the Vienna Philharmonic understands how to prolong the second beat of a Viennese waltz. By the late 1930s, only songs in "specialty rhythms" or anthem-style songs did *not* swing.[37] The prevalence of swing reflected an instinctive sense of multiple rhythms under the surface. And it permitted other ways of compounding time: for example, a singer might keep the vocal line in fairly regular time over a strongly "swung" accompaniment, or keep the main notes of the bar in time while smaller notes went their wayward way.

The other very notable feature of rhythm in classic pop is the use of *syncopation* throughout entire songs or sections of songs.[38] Strictly speaking, syncopation refers to the absence of a note or chord on a strong beat. The opening of the chorus of *I Got Rhythm* is a textbook case. The all-important first word comes in just *after* the first beat. In addition, there is a syncope in between *rhy-* and *-thm*, and between *mu-* and *-sic*. In practice, the term refers to more than the absence of an expected element. The very common anticipation of a strong beat, by starting a word or phrase just ahead of it, can be thought of as a *forward* or *anticipatory* syncope: the expected stressed note or word arrives early. Holding a note past the next strong beat, where a previously established pattern suggests that there should be a new note or word, also sounds like a syncope: one distinctly hears the absence of something on the beat. Strong dotted rhythms, that is, involving note pairs of sharply unequal durations (like the "Scotch snap" ♪♩.) amount to syncopations. In fact, the swing figure itself is syncopation writ small and loosened up.

There is an analogue to syncopation, involving not the point in time but the pitch of a word or portion of a word. Looking again at Figure 1.3, we see that the first setting of "Luck, be a lady to-night" jumps *to-* to a higher note. This acoustic heightening has the effect of putting a strong stress at a somewhat weak rhythmic position; together with *night*, an important lexeme relegated to a very weak position, this device creates a kind of anticipatory syncope, although not entirely due to rhythmic means.

Once again, syncopation is not a mechanical device. If everything is syncopated, nothing is. In the chorus of an exceedingly tricky song by the Gershwins, *Fascinatin' Rhythm*, phrases quite regular in themselves are set so that successive stresses fall on noncorresponding beats; the effect is that of constant syncopation. It's a joy to hear—once in a while. When a tricky rhythm becomes a fetish, things can get tedious.[39]

Syncopation is often alluded to, by writers on classic pop or by musicologists, as one of the two main features traceable to the Afro-American tradition—the other being the bent or "blue" note. In fact, syncopation is prominent, in explicitly notated form and in performance practice, in much "classical" music, mostly notably the Baroque. It is also implicit in Renaissance motet style, in the folk song traditions of the British Isles, and in much other music from various times and places. But most of this older music does not "swing."

Neither swing nor syncopation was *uniquely* African in origin.[40] It *is* true, however, that, in the period 1890 to 1920 in the United States, strong syncopation lasting through entire songs, or entire sections of songs, was relatively less prominent in White country music (such as Appalachian or Western), and certainly in the sentimental or parlor song, than it was in Black music. One could hardly miss it in the blues and in ragtime. Probably Kern or Gershwin associated syncopation primarily with Black music, not with a European provenance. Over time, an entire complex of features—syncopation, anticipation (very common in blues), dotted rhythms, relaxed unequal triplets, and a growing overall emphasis on off-beats, which gives a song a buoyant, lifting character—all settled into the songwriter's and the performer's armamentarium.

It is also notable that Duke Ellington, the Black leader of a mostly Black band, and the most influential composer in the entire history of Black America, composed a number of songs in which he gave no great place to syncopation or even swing elements.[41] What made these songs "jazz" was Ellington's genius at instrumental color, chord voicing, and the uncanny balancing of solo passages against the ensemble.

As tempos and rhythms become less categorical, more fluid, the importance of *microrhythm* becomes relatively more prominent (see Addendum, p. 43). This is especially true where songs are concerned. While internal or local time patterns may serve a predominantly musical purpose, for example, by making a passage sound buoyant or angular, the primary relevance of local rhythm in song is that it sets short sequences of words, verbal phrases, in particular patterns of emphasis. It follows and supports the natural intonation contours and time units of speech—or, sometimes, counters or cancels them (intentionally or not).

A song that employs an unvarying rhythm can easily become deadly. *Tea for Two*, when performed without vocal or instrumental ingenuity, is a good example of dotted-rhythm boredom. Patterning stresses and note-values more subtly is what great songwriting is all about. It is what happens when superior lyricists and composers "work off" each other. The memorable effect of *Dancing in the Dark* comes from the repeated juxtaposition of a dotted-rhythm phrase ("Danc-ing in the" ♩.♪♩.♪) with a regular one ("dark" ᵕ♩), and again ("Till the"

♩. ♪) next to ("tune ends" ♩ ♩). Each element follows normal speech patterns: the song sings itself.

A comparable effect is heard in the Rodgers — Hammerstein *Many a New Day*. ("Man-y a new face will please my eye": ♫♩ ♩ ♩ ♩ ♩ ♩). Here, an "easy 3" nudges shyly up against the more common duple pattern.

Finally, it is obvious that some writers deliberately devise a song that is rhythmically distinctive. Cole Porter is said to have tapped out the microrhythms of *Rap Tap on Wood*, knowing that the song was intended for dancer Eleanor Powell, before writing either tune or words.

We will have occasion in our analyses of post-1950 songs to comment many times over on the correlation of word choice and microrhythm, together with related elements such as vowel value and rhyme scheme. For some detail on this realm of correlation, see the Addendum.

Melodic Pattern and Harmonic Movement

We treat melody and harmony together, almost of necessity. Wilder, quoted in the Introduction to this book, gives special weight to the way in which a melody unfolds: its intervals, recursiveness, pitch set,[42] and the like. But one can argue that no pop song melody is absolutely or intrinsically beautiful. It is the progression of harmony from point to point, in parallel with the tune, that makes it so.

In classical nonvocal music, there are many examples of relatively long melodies that in the actual process of their unfolding—in the very experiencing of their tonal excursion, their pattern of repetition, their choice of intervals—are unmistakably "great tunes," regardless of how they are harmonized. The same is true of certain folk songs, which may come to us with minimal or no harmonic underpinning.[43]

But classic pop song melodies move in rather short segments, and they are always accompanied. On the whole, the melodies occur in rather brief units, *motives*, instead of the longer melodic phrases of other types of song. Think of *Tea for Two* (Youmans — Caesar), or *Jeepers Creepers* (Warren — Mercer), or *I Got Rhythm*, in contrast to, say, *Shenandoah* or Schubert's *An Die Musik*.

A sensitive auditor will hear that *any melodic motive or line tends to generate its own implicit harmony*. The choice of successive pitches (other than simple repetition), a horizontal movement, creates vertical associations. Tones that occur several times within a phrase, or certain tones that are set with longer time values than others, seem to belong together. If one did not perceive them this way, one would not know what key the melody was in, where the fundamental tone lay. Listeners do sense this, and once it is sensed the implications of simple harmonic relationships come in train. Certain tones take on more functional importance than others. Conversely, in the listener's mental model, as it is built up through perception, some tones that occur only once, or rarely, take on a special expressive import.

In the *diatonic* system, once you sense the fundamental tone, 1 or 8, you also sense that nearby tones, such as 2 or 7, are notable insofar as they are "leading tones" away from or back to the fundamental (Figure 1.6)

Figure 1.6 Familiar Scales for the Classic Popular Song.

C major scale. The Arabic numerals above the notes give the position of the tone in the major mode, 8 being the same tone as 1 an octave higher. These numbers are useful in referring to the contour of the voice-line, the movement of the principal melody. The Roman numerals underneath refer, first, to the steps of the bass-line; in the figure these would be the lowest tones in the various chords. Roman numerals are, second, used to refer to the triads built on the corresponding steps. If one forms a triad on each successive tone of the C major scale, using only the white keys on the piano, a mixed sequence of major and minor triads results. The chords built on ii, iii, vi, and vii are "minor triads": the distance between the first and second tones of the chord, counting upward, involves three half-steps, while the distance between the second and third tones is four half steps (two whole-steps). In triads I, IV, and V, the relationship is reversed: the distance between the first and second notes involves four half-steps, and that between the second and third tones involves three half-steps (one-and-a-half steps).

As can be determined in the chromatic scale figure, from C to E (an interval called "major third") there are two whole steps, with three intervening half-steps, C-sharp, D, and D-sharp. Between E and G (an interval called "minor third"), there are two intervening half-steps, F and F-sharp.

For the diatonic major mode in classic popular music, designation by upper-case and lower-case numerals captures the essential difference between major and minor triads in the given key. However, in practice, any kind of chord (in principle) can be placed over any bass step. Within the song, if it is at all complex, there could be a C^7 chord built on I (involving a B-flat, not "in the scale"); a version ("inversion") of the C major triad on III, instead of a minor triad; and so on. (For an explanation of the chord labeled V^7, in this scale G^7, see p. 30.)

In this book, we use Roman capitals to refer to a bass-line step or position: for example, "a chord on III" simply means that in the bass-line III is the crucial tone. Sometimes we say "a iii chord," indicating that it is the familiar minor-triad-based chord for this position. In referring to a "bass-line progression," we refer to a sequence of crucial steps: for example, I, V, VI, IV, I. As a chord progression, however, the normal sequence might prove to be, for example, I, V, vi, iv, I, or some other pattern. In the minor mode, the notation would show different patterns. For the reader with little musical background, we simply emphasize that the melodic line and the bass-line are primarily horizontal conceptions, involving sequences of tones through time, while chords and harmonic implications are primarily vertical; see Special Usage and Conventions, pp. xviii–xx).

C minor scale. This scale begins with tone 1 over a minor triad that includes an explicitly lowered (flatted) tone 3 (in this key, E-flat). The two other commonly heard chords all involve the same flatted note, the same minor third interval: they are simply different versions of the minor triad on I. Western popular music uses any of the three sets of final tones, each shown beamed, to complete the minor scale. Each completion reflects a different ancient mode.

A minor scale. This minor scale is very closely related to C major: if the first set of three beamed notes is included, to complete the scale, there are no sharps or flats. The first tone, here A, can be labeled tone 1, which makes middle C tone 3, a minor third above the starting point. (The first tone, A, can also be labeled 6, its step in C major, which makes middle C "1," as in the major version.) Again, this scale may be completed in three different ways.

Chromatic scale. The key of C major has no sharps or flats ("black keys" on the piano) in its basic scale. Other diatonic majors do: for example, G major includes F-sharp. Additional sharps and flats, sometimes called "accidentals," are *chromatic* tones, since they add "color." A complete chromatic scale uses every white and black key in succession.

In the text accompanying Figure 1.6 we emphasize that songs in "the major" customarily use chords and intervals that are "minor," and vice versa. A song that uses mostly or entirely major elements is seldom persuasive in the classic American popular style. *Danny Boy* tends toward a consistent major-mode sound, and of course we show this song to demonstrate that in several respects it is not in classic popular style. In our discussions of particular songs later in this book, we often refer to a song's being in "the narrative minor." There is something about the prevalence of minor relationships throughout a song, together with the tendency to stay in the lower part of the octave, that is conducive to a confiding or casual story or attitude. Inherently, songs of this type are organized around a few intervals, such as the lowered 3 or the flatted 5 or 6, which, being smaller, mean that the inherent tension in the song is less. The singer in fact finds it easier to tune up such intervals, and may sometimes even adopt a sort of half-spoken, half-sung approach.[44] This "narrative-minor" aspect is also present in many *lieder*; we think we invented the term, but in any case some such concept is needed.

In Figure 1.7, we give the opening melody lines (without time values for the notes) of *I Got Rhythm* and *Danny Boy*, indicating with small vertical arrows the structurally most important notes.

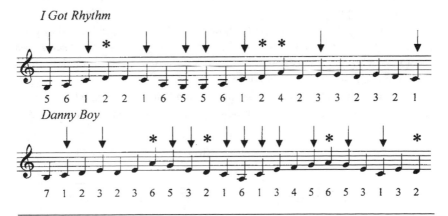

Figure 1.7 *I Got Rhythm* and *Danny Boy* vocal lines.

In *I Got Rhythm*, scale tones 2 and 4, marked with asterisks, serve an expressive purpose: they give the tune its distinctive profile. Tone 2 occurs often, tone 4 only once. In *Danny Boy*, the first use of scale tone 6 is largely expressive, primarily because its duration is short and the word is *the*. The next use of this tone, on a long, low note, seems to call for a chord change to mark its functional importance. A sustained tone on *-ing*, as weak as a syllable can get syntactically, must involve such a chord change, or the melody would simply stop in its tracks. In *Danny Boy* also, tone 2 has considerable expressive force.

Anyone will feel that the Gershwin tune is springier than the Irish ballad, which seems more lyrical. The Gershwin song uses shorter phrases; it uses fewer scale notes, and these more discontinuously (i.e., with wider intervals); while *Danny Boy* uses far more step-by-step movement (i.e., the interval of the second) and dwells on the notes of the triad (1, 3, 5) more persistently.

As the melody progresses, a "horizontal" pattern (e.g., in the Gershwin song, tones 5, 1, and 3) brings into being, perceptually, the corresponding "vertical" element, in this case triads built on the tonic. This is reciprocal: once established, the sense of "key" conditions the harmonic meaning of upcoming melodic tones. In this example, what we have called the "expressive" tones, 2 and 4, are defined by *not* being in the fundamental triad.

The written-out chords for these songs in Figures 1.1 and 1.2 are simplified for purposes of analysis. No musician would actually play such a clunky set of chords; but they are the minimal ones that make the harmonized tune recognizable. As predicted, both the Irish tune and the Gershwin song show a close correspondence between the most structurally important tones of the melody and the basic underlying chords. In both cases, the way the melody is fitted over a small set of basic chords is like the way modules of a roadway are fitted over the piers of a bridge. The piers may vary in height, as the road rises or dips, but the points of support come at regular intervals and in a regular sequence.[45]

There is one other scale besides the diatonic that has been rather widely used in classic popular music: the *pentatonic* (Figure 1.8). The pentatonic scale uses five tones. with one whole-step omitted, and without a tone leading directly to the tonic from below (as the 7 leads to 1 or its octave 8 in the diatonic system). This is perhaps the oldest scale in use in the world, and is associated with many "exotic" cultures: it can sound Chinese, sometimes Hungarian. When played in

Figure 1.8 Two forms of the pentatonic scale.

the order shown in (a), it can sound like a stripped-down major scale, with C as the fundamental; when heard in the order shown in (b), the hearer can experience tone A as the fundamental tone and the mode as a kind of ambiguous minor. Familiar Western songs in the pentatonic include *Amazing Grace,* or *Swing Low Sweet Chariot.* From the classic pop tradition, famous songs using the pentatonic prominently include Berlin's *Isn't This a Lovely Day* and the Gershwins's *Clap Yo' Hands.*[46] Some traditional blues use a form of pentatonic scale, which may sound like a simplified kind of diatonic minor. In classic pop style, most pentatonic melody lines are harmonized quite like the diatonic, in part because many of the songs turn out to *be* diatonic.

Most fine classic pop songs are not so simple as, say, *I Got Rhythm.* We offer, in Figures 1.9 and 1.10, selected A-sections of two harmonically remarkable songs. In *Words Without Music* (harmonically much simplified here) the very first, ear-catching note of the A$_1$ section of the chorus is set on a highly dramatic raised 4. The setting of *mu-* is also highly dissonant. The nominal key is C major; the perceived key for at least the first four bars is ambiguous. In the Porter song, we show the second A-section. There is an extraordinary series of chord changes near the end of this section, under "...resist when, darling, I know so well...." with momentary key changes on every one or two beats. This onset of sophisticated harmony is tipped off by the lowered tone, A flat, in m.21 and thereafter, a deviation from the corresponding moment in section A$_1$ that sets the song into a different harmonic course.[47]

We now see that fine classic pop songs do use any and all tones in the melodic line, and chords built on any tone of the scale. The density and colorfulness of the chords increases very dramatically, particularly with the addition of notes "not in the chord" and by the use of transitional notes "not in the key" that lead from chord to chord. In Figure 1.11, we illustrate how "jazz chords" supplied for *Danny Boy* (compare Figure 1.2) make the difference between a childish harmonization and a sophisticated one.

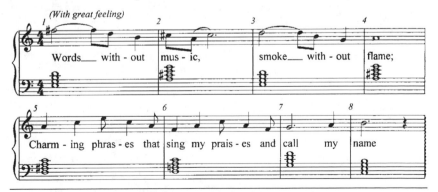

Figure 1.9 *Words Without Music* (Vernon Duke – Ira Gershwin, 1936).

Figure 1.10 *I've Got You Under My Skin* (Cole Porter, 1936).

In all contexts of diatonic (and pentatonic) classic pop, thirds are very important. The nature of the intervals of a third, in either the melody or the accompaniment, determines whether the song is in the major or minor mode (sometimes going rapidly from one to the other), and thus the sonic "mood" of the song. Using long ladders of thirds (e.g., C-E-G-B-D_1-F_1 and so on, involving tones 9 and 11 in Figure 1.6) yields a kind of "Debussy-esque" effect to the harmonic texture.[48] But employing a *chain of thirds* is not just decorative, but a common organizing device. In many songs, the very melody is built on

Figure 1.11 *Danny Boy* re-harmonized in standard jazz style.

a sequence of steps of the third. Rodgers was partial to this means, *Love Look Away* being an obvious example (Figure 1.12). In the melody, major and minor thirds (e.g., major from B down to G or A down to F, minor from G down to E, or F down to D) are so interspersed that the interval comes to sound neutral; the listener has no acute sense of the basic mode of the tune changing from major to minor.[49]

However, in classic pop song harmony, the *minor* third (one and a half steps) takes on a special importance. Partly owing to the dominating influence of jazz musicians in the performance of classic pop songs, a typical harmonization involves "jazz chords" that are pervasively *diminished*, that is, using minor thirds. (An example would involve: C-E-flat-G-flat-A-natural.) This tonal orientation is very obvious in the Porter extract above. In the Duke song, it is present in the stepping-down of the underlying chord from m.5 to m.6. Employing "lowered" tones and diminished chords permits a smooth, insinuating harmonic movement from transitory minor to major and vice versa. The tones of a diminished

Figure 1.12 *Love Look Away* (Richard Rodgers – Oscar Hammerstein, 1958).

chord tend to lie nearer to the tones of the next important major chord than to the tones of another major chord, so that momentary key changes are easier to effect. They are "passing chords," in the sense that they permit easy modulation to any of several keys.

We mentioned above that chords built with thirds are essential to *functional harmony*. The *dominant-seventh* is the most-used structural extension of the triad in classic pop style, as in all Western music of the past four hundred years (see the interpolated chord in Figure 1.6, top line). It is the normal means, in the diatonic system, to change between the keys built on the two most basic structural tones of the scale, I and V. If, in a song in the key of C, you choose to build the bridge of a song in the "secondary home" (i.e., dominant) tonality (involving the G-B-D triad), or come to the end of the bridge on that chord and want to return to "first home" (the tonic, whose main triad is C-E-G), all that is needed is to add one more third to the G chord, putting F now on top. The top three tones of the dominant seventh now move directly, by shifts of one note each, to the C triad, and you are back in C major. The underlying reason is that F is not actually a tone in the G scale (F-sharp is the true 7), but *is* a valid tone in the C scale to which you are heading. The dominant-seventh chord sounds as if it is working its way to the tonic key already.[50] Lowered-seventh chords in general are linchpins for harmonic movement; for example, the I^7 chord constructed (with lowered 7) on the tonic tone seems to want to effect modulation to IV (e.g., the transition of the bridge in *Lullaby of Broadway*).

Harmony is primarily a vertical concept: at a given moment or within a beat or two, what tones are heard under the melodic line? However, we claimed above (p. 22) that a melody line with any clear contour implies its own harmony, meaning that subsets of melodic notes, involving different zones of the main scale, seem to rest on implicitly chordal buttresses or piers: This is *structural harmony*. Think of how *Mairzie Doats* seems to begin in one zone, move to another, and return to the first. Normally the crucial set of tones involves the triad.

At the next level, analytically speaking, *functional harmony* can be thought of as involving transitional chords, inner voices (voice leading), and a more elaborate horizontal movement, under the melody line, that allows the composer to get from here to there, from main chord to main chord, or to shift keys for a section of the song. If the shift is brief, the usual concept is that of chord change; if longer, that of modulation. Chord changes also map closely on to rhythmic structure, since they occur at metrically significant points.[51]

What is sometimes called *nonfunctional harmony* does not counteract harmonic function, but brings in something additional, usually a particular color or stylistic reference. Thus, intervals of open fifths and fourths suggest an "American" sound; the addition of tones 6 and 2 bespeak a romantic or "French" style; certain other tones or modes may communicate an "Asian," or a purposely antiquated style like Renaissance or Elizabethan.

Finally, there is a level, in popular song, for which we need a term comparable to *painterly* in the visual arts. Here, harmonic layering would be the equivalent of distinctive brushstrokes. Some harmony brings a superadded value, where harmonic richness or distinctiveness seems to not only support but to saturate, or at least bleed into, the other musical elements, most notably the melodic line but also rhythm in the sense that a striking chord progression articulates rhythmic junctures. This is the legacy, largely, of the best jazz band music, with many instrumental lines and colors coexisting as "voices." A sensitive hearer appreciates such harmony for its own sake. By definition, this field of harmony is pervasive; it is not just a touch here and there. Perhaps this can be called *expressive harmony*. In recent songwriting, Sondheim is its master.

It is useful to distinguish, in popular song structure, between its harmony and what can be called its *tonal plan*. The tonal plan of the song refers more to its horizontal progress, especially in the bass, and to changes of key. The most useful symbol system involves labeling the tone of the scale that is perceived as predominant during some stretch of the song, using the symbols I-ii-iii...(Figure 1.6). One obvious example is the change from one "home key" to another. When a song moves, say, from a minor key in the verse to a major key for the chorus, that is a tonal shift. When it proceeds from, say, C major to the key of G major or F major (or some less common position) for an entire section, often the bridge, that is another example of tonal shift.

More subtle, but equally important, is that in a good song the momentary tonality shifts continually, though briefly, from point to point. The tonal base has to move a bit lest the song become boring. A song might start in C major, shift after a bar or two to D minor (one tone up from the starting point) or to A minor (a key very close or identical to C major in its scale), then move to G major, and so on, until eventually it regains C major. The important aspect is that "chord changes" happen frequently, last only for a few beats or a bar or two, and tend to involve nearby or adjacent movement in the scale. If the shift involves a farther tonal move (say, four to six tones distant), or if it persists for some time, it is heard as a modulation, a change of key.

When a musician says that a song "has great chords," it is quite unclear whether she means that the tonal plan is interesting or that the characteristic color of the tones under the melody line is pleasing. Musicians tend to analyze the tonal plan with special reference to the bass-line because the voice line may at any point involve an unusual tone—a flatted note or some other "accidental" tone (not one in the basic scale), or a series of half-steps forming a chromatic passage, for some expressive musical effect, perhaps to emphasize a syllable or word. Such tones may occur frequently, and may have a special import in the auditor's experience of the song, without disturbing the underlying sense of tonality.

We can now summarize what is characteristic about the melody–harmony complex in the classic popular song.

First, the melody line can and does use any tone of the diatonic major or minor mode, plus any of the intermediate chromatic tones. It may start on an uncommon tone (e.g., *Words Without Music*) and it may, as it proceeds, outline intervals that are unusual. In classic popular songs that do not stay within a simple diatonic framework, or that use more than the basic chord progressions employing I, IV, V, and V⁷, the concept of melodic "passing tones"—quick, un-harmonized tones of lesser significance in the scale—ceases to be meaningful, simply because they are so common. Second, the line reiterates certain pivotal structural or skeletal tones (I, IV, V) less tightly than does the nineteenth-century popular song, such as Stephen Foster's songs or *Danny Boy*. The melodic lines of later or more elegant classic pop songs tend to pull away from the obvious structural positions (compare Figure 1.10 with Figure 1.1). No longer does the listener perceive the melody to be pinned down, as it were, over the piers of a predictable sequence of chords. Nor does the melody alone appear to dictate only one set of *necessary* chords. Third, simply by virtue of passing through more tones of the scale, and by tending to equalize their importance, melodic lines can pass quickly from major to minor, or from key to key, even while the section of the song as a whole still "sounds" unambiguously in one key.

Correspondingly, the chord changes of the classic pop song are more complex than in nineteenth-century popular song, the hymn, the patriotic song, or the traditional folk song. They occur far more quickly; they alter at unpredictable beats. The harmonic underpinning adds remote or surprising tones to familiar chords. Similar discretionary transitional tones link successive chords, sometimes in elegant ways that create subsidiary "voices," inner lines that catch the ear but never compete with the main melody. A fluid and subtle current of melodic and harmonic movement serves the lyric well, since either can serve to support or underscore a fleeting but telling verbal moment.

One special characteristic of classic pop style is that *the melody moves along on top of the chords*. It is that element that one hears most directly. In this, it is like European *lieder*, cantata, and oratorio, and other vocal forms where the melodic line must always be distinct because the words must be heard. The role and prominence of the sung line are not the same in *all* American song: in shaped-note hymn singing, in barbershop, and in the "high lonesome" sound of some country music, the tune is in the middle of the chord, with a lesser descant on top.

Those who appreciate the classic popular song are, perhaps, those who respond most to a *middle-level of organization in song*; that is, a considerable degree of melodic freedom, a fairly rapid pace of harmonic change, a flexible but not bizarre metrical scheme, a well-crafted but not pretentious verse pattern. The beauty of classic pop may be that it offers an assimilable density or complexity within familiar boundaries.

Affinities

Those acquainted with European music are likely to recognize that the classic pop song is not something entirely unique. The flexible sinuous movement of the melodic line and the use of unusual (nontriadic) intervals are heard in Bellini or Chopin. A dense, quick-moving, complex underlying harmony, supporting the melody but not matching it point for point, is characteristic of the songs of Fauré, Wolf, Poulenc, or Rorem. The complex "jazz" chords one hears in Vernon Duke or Cole Porter are the chords one hears in the "stretched" tonal music of Liszt, Debussy, or Strauss. The pivotal dominant seventh chord has been pervasive in European music for several hundred years.

Some classic popular songs are, in effect, "art songs." Youmans's *Through The Years* or Kern's *The Song Is You* comes to mind. This is especially the case where the melody has a large arch to it (demanding a certain vocal prowess) and a rather traditional harmony. Other classic pop songs are like American folk, or folk-influenced, songs, such as *Shenandoah,* or like a long-lined country song. *I'm So Lonesome I Could Cry* certainly counts as one of the most evocative and beautiful tunes ever written: with different words, it could be Hoagy Carmichael.

What of the influence of African-American genres? As regards jazz, the relationship has been two-way. Some precursors of jazz —Dixieland, ragtime, stride—directly affected the classic pop style in the earlier period. But over the entire period of swing and the big band, extending well into the era of bebop with its smaller ensembles, and into the "cool jazz" movement of the 1950s, jazz and pop have interacted.[52] Jazz performance has often used the pop "standard" as its source. Even in bebop, with its heightened emphasis on radical improvisation, many numbers referred, obliquely or by brief quotation, to pop tunes. Much the same holds for the later phases of the big band which, one might say, continued the swing tradition while cocking an ear to bebop. Beginning around 1950, there occurred a degree of convergence of vocal and nonvocal approaches. Jazz trio cuts sounded like instrumental song,[53] while the best singers of classic popular songs often performed and recorded with small ensembles of instruments played in a softly swinging style and with jazz chords and voicings.

Henry Pleasants has commented that "Pop needs the jazz musician's instrumental skills and experience if it is to grow, and jazz needs the vocal and melodic innocence of pop."[54] In another illustration of the nonseparability of words and music in a pop song, Pleasants wrote that "Lester Young, one of the most eloquent of saxophonists, [said] that before improvising on any song, he first memorized the words."

Many of the style differences between jazz and pop at any era have to do primarily with parameters that are so basic that they can easily be overlooked. For example, length and loudness, jazz outdoing pop in both respects; or tempo, instrumental swing being typically played faster than a vocal pop song could permit. Especially determinative is basic sound color. The best swing bands had a set of timbres (e.g., strings plus sax or a dependence on contrasting choirs of instruments), which are different from the blended choirs and moderate loudness levels of recorded pop, or from the brassy theater orchestra. In swing, especially in bebop, the note attacks and the acoustic overtones of saxophones and trumpets and clarinets are distinctive, as is the phrasing of solos and riffs. By contrast, West Coast or cool jazz used a slowish, ultra-blended, luminous sound, with lots of guitar and winds, and a gradual attack quite distinct from the "speaking" quality of the pop band. Such differences are not absolute, of course, but they have a sonic signaling power that makes it clear what genre is involved.

One important affinity between classic popular song and big band jazz is the prevalence, in midcentury, of what is usually called the "walking beat." This refers to a medium-tempo, 4/4 meter, in which one hears a firm emphasis on each beat (beats 1and 3 still more prominent). It is the pulse against which "swing" can happen. It is typical of the 1930s and 1940s; it may have come about as an alternative to the "medium bounce" rhythm common in the 1920s. When present, the voice seems to float above, and be propelled, by it.

As regards the influence of blues, everything depends on whether one is talking about a blues "form" or simply blues elements. The classic pop song format and the pure blues are incompatible. The latter is shorter and more laconic: often simply 12 bars.[55] The classic blues is a very stripped down form. Its vocal range is smaller, and the pitches hover around the lower portion of an octave. There is never a contrasting middle section. The traditional Delta blues is bluntly narrative. It uses a four-bar A_1 and a four-bar A_2, both very terse, often with each segment seeming to bifurcate into two units of two bars each. A final four-bar segment sounds longer than it is, because it contains one continuous thought and phrase that move inexorably toward conclusion. An example is the opening of *Empty Bed Blues*:

I woke up this mornin' / with an awful achin' head
I woke up this mornin' / with an awful achin' head
My new man done left me just a room and empty bed.

The blues format is flat, not arched. Each phrase fades, relaxes downward, at the end, in terms of both diction and melodic contour; and the final descent is very final.

The blues uses fewer chords, and uses them in a relatively fixed pattern, with chord changes that often go directly from I to IV or IV to I; V is not the clear second home-key; and V⁷ is not a pivotal tone (see p. 30). The chords occur at fairly widely spaced intervals. They are blunter piers, relative to the melodic roadway above, than is the case in the popular song. However, the melodic line itself may be extremely melismatic and expressive. The rhythm of the blues is usually rather simple, basically a loping alternation of long/short. It should be pointed out that many early "traditional" blues do not exactly fit this normative pattern, especially as to length or tonal simplicity of the melodic line, sometimes as to rhythm.[56]

As one would expect, the words of the blues are terse, in vernacular diction, and organized into short parallel units expressing an accretional pattern: short A followed by short A, concluding in B. The ending thought is not a counterpart to the opening thought, but an intensification or elaboration of it. We tend to think of the words of "the blues" as expressing pain, lamentation, or dread, attitudes rarely present in popular song style. However, there are many examples of blues whose words express a defiant religiosity, or even a sort of determined aggressive happiness—especially with the rougher urban or Chicago blues, or with "evil blues," a style associated first with Robert Johnson.

With all these significant differences in mind, it is obvious that those famous popular songs that refer to or have the term *blues* in the title, like the Arlen — Mercer *Blues In the Night*, are not really blues.[57] There are, however, points of connection or influence. One is trivial: many popular song lyrics refer to having (or getting rid of) "the blues," a normal utilization of English slang. Moreover, the blues tends to sound as in the minor mode, and there is a long association in all Western music of that interval with such feelings as sadness or regret.[58]

The second, more important point of connection is the use, in both genres, of "blue notes" and "blue" intervals, owing to the presence of lowered tones. One of the diacritical features of the traditional blues is the way that the melodic/harmonic aspect seems to tend, even to press downward, toward the fundamental note or the essential interval, which is normally the minor third. The blues sound is built on a characteristic template of lowered (flatted) tones: tone 3, then 7, 5, sometimes 6. The classic pop songwriters of the Golden Age also used lowered tones, but more flexibly. But other influences were also at play, such as the traditional music of Eastern Europe with its lowered tones and minor intervals.[59]

There is an important difference between notated "blue notes" and the "bending" of sung tones used so frequently, and so expressively, by singers in *both* the blues and the classic pop genres. The *slight* flatting of important tones comes naturally to singers in both traditions, and has both musical and verbal significance. Flatting important tones, in the blues, expresses the overall downward-pressing character of the line to which we have alluded. In classic pop, it is more likely to be a form of decoration for expressive effect, a minute melisma or a "catch in the voice," underlining the momentary import of the word being sung.

The vocally bent note (and for that matter the subtly flatted notes in instrumental jazz solos) obviously passed from one genre to another via the work of magnificent singers of the 1920s and 1930s, such as Bessie Smith or Ethel Waters. Significantly, some singers of the day, like Mildred Bailey, a light-skinned woman of color, "sang black" or "sang white," depending on the song. With all the influence going from blues and jazz to pop in the early decades, it is not surprising that, not only did Billie Holiday or Sarah Vaughan bend notes, but so did Lee Wiley and Frank Sinatra. But the path of influence was probably a multiple one, reflecting not only Eastern European music but Celtic as well.[60] At a given moment, say shortly before 1950, you could hear identical vocal effects among gospel singers, pop singers, Appalachian and country singers like Hank Williams or Bill Monroe, and Western swing singers such as Bob Wills. Musicians listened to each other.

Co-occurrence and Coherence

Where styles and genres are concerned, it is possible to work through rather lengthy analyses of aspects and features, and still fail to isolate the essence of what is audible to all. Searching for contrastive features, that is, attributes that clearly mark off one type from another, somehow fails to attain the conclusive point. To illustrate this principle with regard to the classic pop song, we show one more song from just around the midcentury mark: Hank Williams's famous *Your Cheatin' Heart*. This is, of course, a "country song." But look at its formal attributes. It has 32 bars; it is in moderate 2/4 time; it is in AABA form; it has cadential closings at the end of each period; it shows some modest syncopation; its crucial chords are constructed on I, IV, and V (Figure 1.13).

Look back at the five songs we have examined in this chapter: Figures 1.1, 1.2, 1.9, 1.10, 1.13. On the page, at least, there is more variability *within* the category "pop song" than between pop, traditional Irish ballad, and country. In its short-

Figure 1.13 *Your Cheatin' Heart* (Hank Williams, 1952).

breathed phrasing and limited pitch set, *I Got Rhythm* resembles *Your Cheatin'
Heart* at least as closely as it does *I've Got You Under My Skin*. How is it, then, that
as listeners we *know* that this set of songs includes three pop songs, one sentimental ballad, and one country song? It cannot be melodic shape or complexity alone.
The most beautifully arched and balanced melody is in *Danny Boy*. The melodic
lines of *I Got Rhythm* and *Your Cheatin' Heart* are equivalently conventional
and square. The vocal line of *I've Got You Under My Skin* uses many repeated

notes and is relatively flat in contour, while *Words Without Music* contains the most unusual intervals, in its opening section and thereafter.

The melodic lines of the Duke and Porter songs can *only* be those of good pop songs—not country, not European concert songs. However, a country song like *Your Cheatin' Heart* could be a pop tune, except for two tiny details: stretching the word *rain* over the interval of a falling second (m.20), an expressive device that would carry over to some of the folk-rock of the 1960s, and the false rhyme, *rain/name*.

Length or format does not decide the matter. True, the Porter song is longer and more elaborate than usual, forming an AABCC design. But a European concert song might be structured in the same way.

What does matter is harmonic complexity, and the way in which subtle, rapid harmonic movement supports the singing line. This is particularly obvious in the Porter song, which changes key frequently (though momentarily), and goes in and out of minor/major. The Duke song, especially as fully harmonized (not evident in Figure 1.9), shows at least as much harmonic complexity, vertically speaking (i.e., in the density of individual chords), but less frequent key change.

As for tempo and rhythm, there are no absolute differences, except that the Porter song depends on a Latin rhythm that was often a feature of pop songs in the 1930s and 1940s. Again, the Gershwin and Williams songs are similar in the size of the basic motif and verbal unit, and they both need to move at a similar inherent speed. Somehow, however, a listener knows that the Gershwin song is in swing style, while the Williams song is not, a point developed below.

With regard to verbal style, it is also hard to generalize. The Gershwin song is unusual in that its chorus uses no rhyme except at the bridge. Otherwise, the differences are mainly those of word-choice. *Danny Boy* contains some touches of regional usage and bygone times. The lyric for *All the Things You Are* is slightly antiquated. The lyric for *Words Without Music* is consciously poetic; that is the governing metaphor. The Porter song is sly and suggestive. The Hank Williams song is most firmly in a vernacular.

So far, we must conclude that *every main formal musical element counts for something*, but none alone is definitive. Certain other candidates, however, remain. First, *topic or semantic field*. We have discussed at some length what pop songs, as distinct from blues or country songs, are "about." In this regard, *Your Cheatin' Heart* is not the most extreme choice of "country song." Without the dropped *g*'s, and with Jo Stafford singing, the song would move closer to pop. *Danny Boy* can be sung very nicely by an appreciative pop singer, but its subject matter will still not be that of a pop song. The song *I'll Be a Methodist Till I Die* is, a priori, unlikely to be anything but a "country" song. *Precious Lord, Take My Hand* has a wonderful, up-leaping melody, an arch format, and chord progressions that could make it a fine popular song. With its actual words, it is a gospel hymn.

Second is the significance of the overall *sound-color* of the song as it is performed; this is a matter partly of instrumentation. Hank Williams did his song in country guitar style. If Stafford were singing it in the 1950s, the arrangement, the whole sonic identity, would be different. If Iris DeMent were singing it in the 1990s, it would be different still. All the other songs "work" with piano alone, or piano plus strings plus some instrumental color. The Gershwin song works best with a brassy pit-band sound, the Duke with lots of coloristic voicings, and the Porter with Latin percussions; but note that these are sound-color choices *within* the pop genre. None of these approaches would suit *Your Cheatin' Heart* or *Danny Boy*.

Third is *singing style*, a dimension of phonology ranging from pronunciation to voice production to decoration of the voice line. *Your Cheatin' Heart* calls for a regional accent; in much the same way, *Danny Boy* gains something when sung by an Irish tenor. The three classic pop songs (with *I Got Rhythm*, primarily the verse) seem to demand an *acted*, at least an interpretive, singing style.

There is another critical difference, this one a matter of vocal emission. Singers in the tradition of blues, rhythm & blues, and soul do not "sing through" a melody line, and do not sustain tones in order to do so. Their actual pitch, note by note, may be quite approximate. The approach is rhetorical. It emphasizes particular syllables, and it tends toward something intermediate between singing and speaking. Singers in the various "country" traditions sustain tones, but do so by adding slurs, yodels, melismas, and other forms of very local decoration. They too do not go for "the long line," built on complete phrases, that classic pop singers normally seek.

Of all the aspects we have here examined as getting toward the heart of the matter, only harmony (or the melodic-harmonic nexus) is a musical-technical one. Everything else is a matter, really, of attitude, convention, range of semantic reference, and all these reduce largely to subcultural conventions and traditions. We commented above that the Gershwin song was in "swing" style, unlike Hank Williams's song. We know this, not from what is on the page, but as a reflection of style history. We recognize what kind of song we are hearing by what it deals with, how it sounds, and the way it is performed. Singing style, something external to what the songwriter provided, can be definitive. The fine classic pop standard from 1930, *Georgia on My Mind* (Carmichael — S. Gorrell), when sung decades later by Willie Nelson, has the plain tang of country; when sung by Ray Charles, the dark melismatic flavor of gospel. Which brings us back, once again, to the unspecifiable but necessary concept of "style." The argument is circular: we know that a song is in classic pop style because that is the way it is performed.

Those who love the classic American popular song, pre- or post-1950, and who may wish to claim that it is obviously "better" than other types of song, cannot point to one or two conclusive elements to prove their case. They love the songs, as we do, for their co-occurrence of melodic-harmonic distinctiveness, rhythmic subtlety, topical or semantic focus, together with their penumbra of familiarity and cultural associations.

We have now completed an examination of some of the formal and stylistic elements of the classic popular song, attempting an assessment of the genre as of about 1950. For illustration, we have restricted ourselves to songs written prior to, or very close to, that date. The reason should be obvious. As we analyze significant songs from the period 1950 to 2000, in the central section of this book, an underlying question will always be: Are these popular songs truly "like" those of the Golden Age? If so, to what extent, and in what regards? Is the American Songbook, post-1950, as good as what came before or are the songs good in a different way? Surely the songs of the 1920s were not, as a group, entirely like the songs of the 1940s: shouldn't we expect the songs of the 1970s to be different from those of the 1950s?

It has been necessary for us to spend some time and effort, and a certain amount of technical detail, on the period before midcentury, for two reasons. First, this preparation establishes a baseline for the comparisons that many will wish to make, in examining the whole sweep of twentieth-century American popular song: where it has been and where it might be heading. In our final chapter we take up some of these issues.

Second, assuming that comparisons across eras or generations are inevitable, we have tried to be fair and to be clear about the frame of reference we are using. It would be easy to bias comparison between the first and second half-centuries. By emphasizing, for example, ballads from the early period and up-tempo songs from the later one, or heavily chromatic songs set against mostly nonchromatic ones, or one linguistic register before 1950 and another thereafter, we could easily "prove" that the essential character of songs changed radically. Conversely, by selecting songs very similar in form and expression, we could argue that little has changed, or that "pure types" linger on.

Before we examine particular songs, however, there is a second kind of context or preparation that needs to be established. Songs are not just musical-verbal constructions out there in the ether. They are played or not played, with determinable frequency, in characteristic situations. They are published and recorded (or not), and reach listeners through identifiable economic and cultural pathways and markets. They are listened to at particular moments in time, by real people.

For that to be more than a truism, we need to give some attention to nonmusical changes in the culture, such as lifestyle, speech styles and verbal repertoires, technological development and obsolescence. It is relatively uninteresting to say that a particular song was written and recorded in 1934, another in 1972, and that they are alike or unlike, or a bit of both. It becomes more valid when one can say something about how prominent or how popular they were, how they were perceived as typical or atypical, who knew them, through what means. The question of how *good* they are may then follow. Thus we turn, in the next chapter, to a sketch of the cultural and historical context of popular songs, now with particular attention to the period around 1950 and the decades that followed.

Notes

1. Alec Wilder, with James T. Maher, "American Popular Song: The Great Innovators, 1900–1950." (New York: Oxford Univ. Press, 1972.) Hereafter, Wilder.
2. One of us engaged for over a decade in a project of privately recording more than one hundred songs with the overall title, "Forgotten Songs from Broadway and Hollywood." An indicator of the recent revival of interest in these songs is that a number of them had been discovered by others by the end of the decade.
3. Allen Forte, "The American Popular Ballad of the Golden Era" (Princeton, NJ: Princeton Univ. Press, 1995); Forte, "Listening to Classic American Popular Songs" (New Haven, CT: Yale Univ. Press, 2001).
4. See for example the lead article by Jesse Green in the "New York Times" Magazine, June 2, 1996, whose cover "teaser" read "Who Killed the Great American Song?"
5. Roy Hemming, "The Melody Lingers On" (New York: W.W. Norton, 1999), has used the term *classic pop* in this way.
6. This kind of direct emotional response is still experienced, and still helps define them as "classic." It is also still class- and age-linked. How many young or middle-aged American travelers, in the postwar decades, have wandered into a London bar or a restaurant in Rome, or even a park in some third-world city, and heard a Gershwin song being played, and have felt their hearts skip a beat?
7. Songs like *The Gypsy* or *Nola* belong in the category, even though they are not distinguished exemplars of the class.
8. *Danny Boy* may in fact be English in origin. The song is notated in 16 bars, but could be shown in 32 bars, using different note-values, without altering what we call the *format*. A careful reader may see that all the A-sections are much alike, but the final A might be considered a C-section. The B-section is also closely related; it gets a separate letter designation primarily because the "lie" of the pitch-set changes.
9. One example of an ABAB song is the Kern — Wodehouse *Till The Clouds Roll By*. An example of ABAC is the old James F. Hanley stride tune, *Indiana*.
10. In *Danny Boy*, because of the notation, the bridge is four bars long. More precisely, it begins with a three-note pick-up ("or when the") and ends on the long note for "snow."
11. If ABA is an arch, ABAB is an ogive, and ABABA is a double arch.
12. An excellent overview of song-form origins and types is given by Mark W. Booth, "The Experience of Songs" (New Haven, CT: Yale Univ. Press, 1981); and by Peter van der Merwe, "Origins of the Popular Style" (Oxford: Clarendon Press, 1999).
13. The tune, and especially the chords, of *I Got Rhythm* are claimed by experts to have been used as the basis for more jazz recordings than any other single source. One of the most famous, by Charlie Parker, lasts over twelve minutes.
14. With *Manhattan*, the point is clear by the third word. With Berlin's *I Used To Be Colorblind*, the precise point comes at the end, when falling in love suddenly brings the perception of color to the speaker's world.
15. Loesser was said to have advised songwriters to put the main idea or figure of speech first, as the engine, and then come up with a surprise at the end, as the caboose.

16. A few very good songs intentionally avoid overt parallelism, either by eschewing end-rhyme or by contriving to have each phrase, each thought, evolve out of the preceding one. An excellent example is the Bock — Harnick *She Loves Me*, where the last few words of one phrase lead conceptually to the first words of the next. No doubt such a striking effect would lose its force if used too often.

17. The Arlen — Mercer *Come Rain or Come Shine*, a great song, opens with twelve occurrences of one note in a row. The rest of the song shows that it was deliberate. Another example of deliberate repetition is the Rodgers — Hammerstein *Surrey With the Fringe On the Top*.

18. On this general topic, Furia's treatment is enlightening. Philip Furia, "Poets of Tin Pan Alley: A History of America's Great Lyricists" (New York: Oxford Univ. Press, 1992).

19. *Lieder* and other types of European songs sometimes have slow introductions to a faster main body, but that is not the typical case.

20. Obviously, the recitative/aria relation in opera is analogous.

21. Hamm outlines this evolution, but no one seems to have been able to pin down all the steps. Charles Hamm, "Yesterdays: Popular Song in America" (New York: W. W. Norton, 1979), 359ff. Early Kern songs often use the term *burthen*. See also the entry for *ballad* in Peter Gammond, "The Oxford Companion to Popular Music" (New York: Oxford Univ. Press, 1991).

22. Other songs where the final words of the verse lead directly into the chorus are the Lane — Harburg *How Are Things In Glocca Morra?* and *Can't You Do a Friend a Favor?* by Rodgers and Hart.

23. That singing style can be heard in the old records of Al Jolson or Sophie Tucker, who began their careers singing in raucous environments.

24. James R. Morris, "Introductory Essay," in "American Popular Song / Six Decades of Songwriters and Singers" (Washington D.C.: Smithsonian Collection of Recordings, 1984), 23

25. One reason for this is that music, including song, does not "express" clear-cut emotions of the sort that we are used to in literature or interpersonal life. Billie Holiday's recording of *I Loves You, Porgy* brings an irresistible emotional response, even a shock, to the hearer, but it would be impossible to say precisely what emotion is conveyed.

26. Remnants of this style can be found in early songs by Jerome Kern with Otto Harbach, in the use of such terms as *sequestered days* (*Yesterdays*) or *chaffed* (*Smoke Gets In Your Eyes*). For modern eras, the contemporary songwriter Dave Frishberg has said, "Good lyrics come up to the edge of poetry…and turn left." Quoted in Whitney Balliett, "American Singers" (New York: Oxford Univ. Press, 1988).

27. *Lieder* can be experienced in this way, partly because the intensity of the message creates a "personality" embodied by the singer.

28. The further complication here is that the grammatical subject of the song is the singer/speaker, the *I*, addressing an object person; but the person addressed is, semantically, the subject of the song. That is, "*I'm* the bottom, *you're* the top."

29. As with verse and chorus (see note 21), no scholar we know of has been able to trace how the term for a long strophic narrative form, *ballad*, came to indicate a slow intimate song.

30. An acute treatment of some of these issues, though not as they affect the classic pop song, is offered by Mark W. Booth. "The Experience of Songs" (New Haven, CT: Yale Univ. Press, 1981).

31. Especially in older songs of the genre, the tempo indication is often "medium bounce," meaning: moving along smartly but easily.

32. Ragtime was a sort of highly syncopated march. Soft-shoe involved prominent time divisions within individual beats. The Charleston was a distinct syncopated figure: see the words *rhythm* and *music* in A_1 of *I Got Rhythm*, Figure 1.1.

33. Jazz musicians often render classic pop standards in 4/4 time, trying for a more flexible time without frequent strong downbeats. As Forte, "The American Popular Ballad," 23, comments, this may change the vocalist's "pointing" of the line.

34. The Arlen — Mercer *That Old Black Magic* provides a perfect illustration.

35. For example, the Rodgers — Hart *The Most Beautiful Girl In the World*.

36. "Swing" also refers to a relaxed repetitive bass-line figure, usually four to the bar.

37. Kenneth Hymes points out that Latin rhythms, starting in the 1930s, sounded fresh because they were strongly syncopated but did not actually "swing."

38. A fairly common pattern is for the A-sections to be syncopated, but not the middle eight, or vice versa.

39. Berlin's *Puttin' On The Ritz* can sound this way.

40. This contentious topic is extremely well handled by van der Merwe, "Origins of the Popular Style."
41. Examples are *In My Solitude* or *Come Sunday*.
42. That is, a set of adjacent notes that cluster at a particular portion of the scale (pitch zone), or that reiterate a particular interval; see Alec Wilder with James T. Maher, "American Popular Song: The Great Innovators 1900–1950" (New York: Oxford Univ. Press, 1972).
43. As examples, *Blow the Wind Southerly* or *The Sally Gardens*.
44. Porter's *My Heart Belongs to Daddy* is in this mode, as is the Weill — I. Gershwin *The Saga of Jenny.* In rhetorical aspect, the blues is also often in "narrative minor."
45. In simple diatonic major, one can ordinarily construct the piers by I triads (in various positions), using tones 1, 3, 5; for softening, one can add 6 into the mix. Fight songs, college songs, and the like do little more than this. That is they are jerky, square, and almost indistinguishable from each other. It is the other tones, in both melody and chords, that give the song its distinct profile. If 1, 3, 5 are pier tones, 2, 4, 6, 7 provide degrees of freedom. The use of 6 in melodies is a stylistic feature in the pop genre. As a coloristic device, when overused it can result in a cloying "cocktail piano" style, which quickly wears out its welcome. The leading of tone 7 to 8 is crucial in much popular music, determining whether the melody sounds "Eastern European," Celtic, or modal (nondiatonic). Tone 4 (or IV of the bass) is important (like V) as a way-station for modulation, either briefly or for a section of music. Tone 2 is particularly important in pop style, because it allows one to construct a chord that departs from but stays near to the tonic. Many classic pop songs oscillate gently between tonalities built on I and ii.
46. In *I Got Rhythm*, the entire opening material can be heard as pentatonic up to the word *who*. In Berlin's *Always*, the opening sounds pentatonic until the middle of the second phrase—"with a *love* that's true"—and then refocuses in the diatonic.
47. Another way of viewing it is to say that the song darkens harmonically at m. 21, and then goes through a cycle of ii-V-I sequences until it regains the major.
48. The right-hand figure used often by jazz pianists to end a song with a sort of dying-away—1-3-5-7, sometimes extending to 9-11—is a related device.
49. Gershwin's *I Loves You, Porgy* is another superb example of a chain of thirds. Another is the Lane — Lerner *On a Clear Day*.
50. David Lahm has reminded the present authors that a feature of classic blues is that the perceived basic chord is the dominant seventh; it is not heard as signaling harmonic change.
51. A good example here might be the Loewe – Lerner *I've Grown Accustomed to Her Face*.
52. By contrast, "free" or atonal jazz beginning in the 1960s had no important relationship with popular song.
53. Especially in the hands of Ellington, Bill Evans, Teddy Wilson, and others.
54. Henry Pleasants, "Serious Music—And All That Jazz!" (New York: Simon & Schuster, 1969). "Vocal and melodic clarity" might have been a better choice of words.
55. There are also strophic blues, involving verse after verse with the same vocal line over a repeating chord structure. This kind of narrative "talking blues" or blues ballad, in the sense of a long tale, influenced a number of largely White genres, such as country & western.
56. W. C. Handy's *St. Louis Blues*, dating way back to about 1914, is in part a tango.
57. It is blueslike in its opening section, with three 4-bar units constituting the 12-bar span typical of traditional blues. Conversely, some pop songs, like Ann Ronnell's *Willow Weep For Me* have very blueslike chord progressions.
58. Whether, technically, a blues is in fact in diatonic minor, or invokes some other scale, is an interesting question best left to musicologists.
59. A topic thoroughly covered by Jeffrey Melnick, "A Right To Sing The Blues" (Cambridge, MA: Harvard Univ. Press, 1999).
60. See van der Merwe, "Origins of the Popular Style," chap. 3.

Addendum

The terms *rhythm* and *meter* are used quite differently in music and poetry, and can be confusing in either realm. Some literary theoreticians consider *meter* an entirely linguistic conception. Be that as it may, in musicology, what the layman calls the waltz rhythm or march rhythm is technically a meter: what is indicated is how often a main stressed beat occurs.

We consider rhythm to involve what is felt in the body; for example, where the main pulse comes, or how many pulses form a natural unit in time. Within a three-beat measure (i.e., meter), the waltz, the scherzo, the mazurka are each experienced as different rhythms. *Meter* is more a mental concept, involving calculation.

One may also conceive of a broader and a finer scale of analysis: major or macrorhythms, and local or microrhythms. The broader reduces to "time," as in "waltz time," "march time." The finer refers to specific patterns, such as Charleston rhythm, dotted rhythm, or cha-cha.

In writing about sung verse, use is often made of technical terms drawn from scansion analysis. This can be misleading.

A poet writing English verse first takes account of the built-in pronunciation, including both sound and stress aspects, called for in words as normally spoken. If he or she is writing verse that "scans," she can group syllables into recurrent patterns of stress and emphasis, into sets ("feet") of relatively stressed or unstressed syllables—for example, the iamb (unstressed-stressed, sometimes thought of as short-long); trochee (long-short, stressed-unstressed); dactyl (stressed-un-un-); anapest (un-un-stressed); and so on. Poets also use considerations such as vowel "height" (how bright the sound in normal speech) or articulatory force (e.g., plosives) in order to shape the sound of a phrase or line. The poet has much freedom of variation, in part because the inherent absolute length of feet—in fact, of most syllables—is roughly the same. In a given overall tempo: a "long" syllable" is not noticeably sustained in vocal production for a long time, nor a short one cut short in the breath.

The lyricist faces very different conditions. First, it is the composer who has chosen (or will choose) a meter—4/4, 3/4, 6/8, etc.—that will determine where the strong beats of the bar come, hence where relative stress will regularly fall. The composer also selects, sometimes, a distinctive rhythm to run throughout some or many passages of the song. If the composer chooses triplets, a dactylic pattern may be pretty much fixed; if a dotted rhythm, say a dotted quarter followed by an eighth, a trochaic pattern; if an eighth followed by a dotted quarter, an iambic one; and so on.

Moreover, the relative prominence or emphasis of a given word is partly determined by the lie of the melodic line. Other things equal, a note that is higher than its neighbors will be heard as bearing stress. So will the semantic importance of the syllable or word as understood in ordinary language. However, many fine songs deliberately place words such as *and* or *of* or *by* on higher notes, or higher/longer notes, thus giving them a special force that is rare in spoken language: think of *by* in the second phrase of the American national anthem. Finally, the pervasive occurrence of sung notes held far longer than would be possible in speech pretty much negates the relevance of the concept of metrical "feet." When a note is held a second or two, who can tell whether it replaces iambs or trochees, and how many? The same thing applies to designated rests, where the songwriter stipulates silence for longer than would be acceptable in poetry.

Although it is often handy to use "iambic," for example, to characterize a verbal rhythm in a song, it only applies part-way. Some music-specific terms, common in popular song, get one further, faster: downbeat, offbeat, upbeat, "swing style," and so on. These outweigh local rhythmic features, which in a song become less salient. For example, it is convenient to think of a string of notes and/or syllables before a bar-line as simply a "pick up." The Mercer words to a 1941 Arlen song, *This Time the Dream's on Me* begin: "Somewhere some day...," with three brief even notes leading to *day* on the downbeat of the first complete bar. One could analyze this as two iambs: some*where* some *day*..., with the second stressed syllable, *day*, greatly prolonged. Why bother? It is a lot more musical to think of the first three syllables as a pick-up, or just as a long, relaxed upbeat.

We should also mention here that the word *diction* means different things in the two media. In poetry, it normally means word-choice, and we follow this usage much of the time in discussing sung verse. In singing, sometimes it means clarity of pronunciation.

2

The Music Went Round and Round...

Wilder's title, "American Popular Song," with 1950[1] as the ending date of coverage, reflected a too-narrow but not inaccurate conception. Just before World War II, and just after it, one genre of popular music dominated. It was popular in the sense that it was familiar everywhere—at least to Whites from the working class and above in the social scale, and to some members of minority groups who lived in cities and went to the movies. This was the music that originated on Broadway or in New York, was used in films, was heard on coast-to-coast radio networks, and was issued as records by the major companies. It was the only popular music, other than patriotic songs and a few nineteenth-century songs, that had truly national exposure. It was also a genre that had a considerable degree of endorsement by tastemakers and "influentials" in the society. Although it was only twenty-five or thirty years old, it was thought of as settled in form, distinguished in quality, and worth taking seriously.

The title was nevertheless chauvinistic, even then. There were a number of other popular song traditions, older than that of Tin Pan Alley, also settled in style, self-renewing in terms of repertoire, and full of vitality: blues, country music of several types, gospel. But these were popular in specific culture regions of the United States or among nonelite groups. Otherwise, they were familiar only to musicologists and folklorists, and to some on the left who sought out the music of the "lower" classes or the racially oppressed.

Wilder dealt with the most elegant and "high-brow" level of classic popular song. The songwriters of Tin Pan Alley aspired to that height, but few came close to reaching it. In this chapter, we discuss popular music from that tradition as a style *aggregate*; that is, we deal with "pop," mostly quite routine, in relation to other broad streams of popular music of the society of the time. Even when we use the term *classic pop*, we refer to the broad stylistic category, not simply to the finest instances.

45

The coexistence of Wilder's kind of music with other genres, equally stable but of lesser status, is consistent with the dominant sociopolitical ideology of the United States., up to about 1950, which assumed a model of regional (or sectional) cleavage within a national identity. What has been called the Euro-American identity was based on the notion of a melting-pot process, most intense in industrial cities, on a model of pluralism within a single polity, and on public education as the crucible of socialization into one national citizenry. Foreign immigration had been largely suspended around 1923, and there had been time for the last immigrants and their children to acculturate to the national model. For a person born in Appalachia, or the Deep South, or the borderlands, familiar first with regional music, to come to know and love the national popular song genre as a teenager or young adult was part of socialization into the larger society. A child might first know, and always love, country blues, and only later, as she entered the larger society, come to know classic pop.

The social ecology of American popular music, however, changed markedly during the "long decade" from about 1947 to 1959. The change, which was irreversible, is traceable to two evolutions. The first is sociodemographic, and involves the movement, mixture, and interrelationship of large groups of people. The second is material, involving significant changes in the patterns and technology of communication.

Social Demography and Cultural Exchange

Population growth zoomed in the late 1940s and in the later 1950s, with the highest rate among Whites. The national economy also began to boom, reflecting a growth in the labor force and the consuming public, the technological innovations achieved during the war, and the expression of a pent-up level of consumer demand for domestic goods. Between 1947 and 1972, per capita income doubled. Spending on entertainment rose steeply.

What was also happening, clear now in retrospect, was a moving and mixing of peoples within the country. The historic northward migration of southern Blacks, interrupted somewhat in the Depression and the war, resumed, continuing until about 1965. By 1960, Blacks constituted 12 percent of the American population, close to a historic high mark. Equally important for cultural change, after the war young adult Whites fled the farm in massive numbers, migrating not only to the largest cities in the country but to rapidly growing sectional urban centers as well.

This level of internal migration set the stage for a degree of contact and mixing across social classes and ethnic groups (especially White ones) that was remarkable. Much of this class- and ethnic-based contact, together with some reciprocal exposure to cultural tastes reflecting regional and class patterns, had been prefigured among servicemen in the war, and continued in peacetime, with the

GI Bill providing access to higher education, and with the beginning of federal aid to higher education on a legally stipulated desegregated basis.

Participation in the nonfarm workforce and education were major carrier-waves for cultural exposure and mixture. An enormous sizing up of the entire K–12 system began by 1950 and lasted until about 1970: it included higher levels of participation by females, minorities, and poor children who no longer dropped out before the 9th grade.[2] As for higher education, growth in enrollment reflected, not just demographic pressures, but the economic boom, draft deferment, policies to encourage participation of neglected social classes and women, and the recognition of "human capital" as a prerequisite for a productive socioeconomic state.

For our purposes, the most relevant result of this fundamental sociodemographic alteration was the virtual disappearance of static, encapsulated cultural *enclaves*. This is not to say that preferences and allegiances in specific cultural regions disappeared. It simply says that exposure to the music of others vastly increased. That exposure began in the military in World War II. Clarke claims that, by actual tally, the most popular performer among the troops abroad was not Crosby or Sinatra, but the Appalachian-style fiddler and singer, Roy Acuff.[3] It ramified in higher education and in the workplace beginning in the late 1940s, and continued to grow in the coming decade, with the expansion of national media, a national highway system, and domestic air travel. We know from cultural historians and from literary memoirs of the period that the experience of encountering new cultural products and forms was enormously liberating.

Communications and Technology

We have solid information about a number of postwar developments involving the media, the entertainment industry, and communications technology. These factors can be looked at from the demand side, the supply side, and most fruitfully in their interaction. A key date here is 1956, the year that Elvis Presley first hit the top of the charts. But we focus first on the earlier era, the late 1940s to the mid-1950s.[4]

During the war, the "hot swing" touring bands had been suspended, vinyl for records had been in short supply, and radio had emphasized patriotic messages and music. In the early 1940s, owing to tensions between music producers and owners and the music unions, new recording by big bands (with or without vocals) had been proscribed for more than two years. So there was a backlog of demand among the young adult population for popular music, whether live, recorded, or on the new medium of television. To meet pent-up demand, to satisfy the new market, and to accommodate the now more variegated tastes for popular music, some major structural changes had to occur on the supply side.

At the end of the war, there were a few national radio networks (NBC, CBS, ABC, Mutual), heard across about one hundred local markets. Metropolitan radio stations, affiliates of these networks, got virtually all of their popular music programming from New York or Los Angeles. By and large, this programming was not record-based, but consisted of big-band broadcasts or "showcase" half-hours for stars (e.g., the Bing Crosby Show). Shows like Your Hit Parade, first on radio, then on TV, actually emulated records, in putting on the air their own versions, with new arrangements and contract singers, of the popular songs of the day. Which songs were programmed in New York and Hollywood, in turn, depended directly on highly constrained supply channels and cross-industry cartels. As of 1950, ASCAP[5] served the interests of a couple of dozen large music publishers. Sheet music publishers did not issue songs from outside the Tin Pan Alley (and Broadway–Hollywood) realms: no blues, rhythm and blues (R&B), country, or Latin. The record companies, for their part, issued middle-class pop for home listening by a White audience.

To be sure, a rival industry association, BMI,[6] had been created about 1940 to break apart this monopolistic concentration and batch-processing of style. BMI licensed and promoted sheet music and, indirectly, records representing regional (and by the end of the decade, "race") music, and had had some success in persuading some regional and local radio stations to feature such product. In 1947, the FCC, bowing to populist and entrepreneurial pressures, began to license new radio stations in small urban markets. By the early 1950s the number of local stations had quadrupled. The new stations did not depend on "feed" from the networks, but began to design their own music programming to suit local preferences. Thus they turned to records, in order to have a variety of pop music to play. In the early 1950s, the light vinyl 45-rpm format became available. Now record companies could send recordings cheaply and safely to stations all over the country, and thus could afford to issue "specialty" records, such as R&B or country music. These records were also suitable for jukeboxes, stocked to reflect local tastes. Sheet music ceased to be a major source of revenue for the publishers, being replaced by license fees from radio and TV.

Beginning in the 1930s, there was some Black/White mixing in organizations such as the Benny Goodman or Artie Shaw bands, both live and on record. An urban blues, using amplified instruments, had been created in the clubs of Chicago by Muddy Waters and others, mesmerizing not only Blacks but working-class Whites. Hank Williams and Jimmie Rodgers had made "country blues," with its blends of folksong and blues, a cynosure among some poor Whites. Bob Wills and others had fashioned a widely appealing form of fiddle-dominated Western swing out of blues, country, and jazz. But little of this music was nationally disseminated.

For a time, well into the 1950s, two patterns of product and communication coexisted. The larger networks, music publishers, and record labels continued in the White pop mainstream, while smaller producers diversified so as to fill smaller, more specialized market niches. The larger companies had close ownership and commercial ties with Broadway producers and the movies, and developed new songs and new performers from that "show-biz" realm.[7] Until the mid-1950s, the larger pop record companies—RCA, Columbia, Capitol, Decca, Mercury—sold 80 percent of the records, and had virtually all of the Billboard and Hit Parade top hits.

By the end of the decade, however, this share had dropped dramatically. Record companies aligned to BMI, such as Sun, Chess, Coral, Atlantic, had established thriving new subgenres and micromarkets. "Disk jockey" person-alities became the on-air proponents for these new forms of pop,[8] and small stations began to nurture new performing talent locally. The national "charts" revised their procedures to count jukebox plays and record sales, not just on-air exposure.

Thus a cat's-cradle of formats, product types, and means of dissemination, assembled from small nodes around the country, came to serve a multiplicity of like-minded audiences. It was not that classic American pop, the mainstream for thirty years or so, had died, but rather that many streams had surfaced.

What the Air-Play Figures Show

Since the main interest of this book is precisely in "classic pop" as a genre, we examine in more detail trends in popularity within that broad pop category. In Table 2.1 we list chronologically songs of quality that made the Hit Parade between 1950 and 1958.[9]

What is immediately obvious, to anyone of a certain age, is that most of these songs came to the Hit Parade from the movies. Some came directly from new Broadway shows. We have indicated those songs by *. Other songs had originated in Broadway shows in prior decades—for example, *Bewitched* or *I Could Write a Book*—but their most recent exposure had been in films. *A Dream Is a Wish* came from a Disney movie; *How High the Moon* was a jazz standard to which lyrics had recently been set. *La Vie en Rose* and *Autumn Leaves* were French chansons newly fitted with English lyrics; *Canadian Sunset* was a "sweet band" number also supplied with lyrics.

The preponderance of the charted songs were from musical films that had full "scores," either compilations of songs originally written for Broadway or sets of songs newly created by Hollywood songwriters. However, beginning in 1950 with *My Foolish Heart* and accelerating thereafter, a number of songs were either title tunes of nonmusical movies, recorded by a popular singer over the open-ing credits, or were single songs written for a particular moment in a dramatic or straight-comedy film. (A famous prototype for this usage had been *As Time Goes By* from "Casablanca.") They included *Three Coins In the Fountain*,

Table 2.1 Songs of Quality on the Hit Parade in the Transition Period

Title	First Appeared
I can dream, can't I?	January 1950
Bye bye baby *	February 1950
A dream is a wish your heart makes	February 1950
My foolish heart	March 1950
Easter parade	April 1950
Bewitched	May 1950
La vie en rose	August 1950
Nevertheless	October 1950
Thinking of you	October 1950
Dream a little dream of me	October 1950
A bushel and a peck *	November 1950
You're just in love *	January 1951
Use your imagination *	January 1951
If I were a bell *	February 1951
Too young	May 1951
How high the moon	May 1951
Wonder why	July 1951
Slow poke	December 1951
I could write a book	March 1952
I'll walk alone	May 1952
Wish you were here *	August 1952
September song	September 1952
You'll never walk alone	January 1953
How do you speak to an angel? *	February 1953
No two people	February 1953
Side by side	February 1953
No other love *	July 1953
I love Paris *	September 1953
Stranger in paradise *	December 1953
Secret love	January 1954
Three coins in the fountain	January 1954
Hernando's hideaway *	January 1954
Hey there *	January 1954
Whatever Lola wants *	May 1954
Something's gotta give	January 1955
(You gotta have) heart *	July 1955
Rock around the clock	**July 1955**
Love is a many-splendored thing	September 1955
Autumn leaves	September 1955
Love and marriage	September 1955
Mack the knife	February 1956
Mr Wonderful *	April 1956
Moonglow (Theme from "Picnic")	May 1956
Standing on the corner *	June 1956
On the street where you live *	June 1956
I could have danced all night *	June 1956
Canadian sunset	August 1956
Friendly persuasion	November 1956
Witchcraft	February 1958

Love and Marriage, Love Is a Many-Splendored Thing, Moonglow, Friendly Persuasion. Their popularity resulted from the hit status of the movie in question, or the appeal of the singer.

A list of Billboard Magazine's No.1 hits from 1955 to 1980 shows similar trends.[10] In the mid-1950s, a few movie songs such as *Love Is a Many-Splendored Thing* appear—in "cover" versions, that is, recordings by a pop performer intended for the mass audience (in this case, The Four Aces). In the late 1950s, a few songs appear that were revivals of pre-1950 classic pop standards, recorded by new-style groups or singers: *Smoke Gets In Your Eyes* by The Platters, *Blue Moon* by the Marcels in R&B style.[11] In 1964, Louis Armstrong's version of *Hello Dolly!*, an enormous "crossover" hit, appeared. And in the early 1970s, some movie songs sung over the titles, like *Raindrops Keep Falling On My Head* and *The Way We Were*, were new songs recognizably in the classic pop tradition.[12]

The Broadway–Hollywood Source

There were good reasons, besides shifts in taste, why songs from movie musicals died out. Traditional movie musicals virtually disappeared during the 1950s. Early in that decade the Justice Department broke apart powerful entertainment cartels that had linked production and nationwide distribution in theaters. From the invention of sound up to about 1950, musicals had been a cash cow for the studios, which turned out not only classy musicals (associated mostly with MGM) but also hokey ones that could be made in a few weeks with the studio's contract players and shipped out to the theater chains. The severing of the production–exhibition pipeline meant that distributors now could bid for the films they preferred, taking more risk but also keeping more of the gate. This in turn meant that the studios began to make fewer but more expensive films, which would need to be solid moneymakers all across the country to justify their production. Very quickly, movie songwriting teams such as Harry Warren — Mack Gordon lost their long-term contracts, a fate that soon afflicted musical performers such as Jane Powell, Dan Dailey, and the like. Even the major Broadway songwriters, such as Porter or Berlin, were no longer commissioned to create songs for a minor movie. In an earlier era, quite forgettable movie musicals had generated an impressive stream of wonderful songs, written direct for film, in memorable performances. Who now remembers the precise film provenance of (choosing only from the 1940s) *My Shining Hour* (Arlen — Mercer) or *Baby, It's Cold Outside* (Loesser)?[13] In sum, an entire stream of treasurable songs dried up.

The scaling-up of size and budget for the film musicals that did survive (for a time) did not always generate nationally popular hit songs. There were a few "big" musicals written directly for the screen, such as "Singin' In the Rain," "An American In Paris," but they used songs from the established canon. Some of the original songs written by Arlen and Ira Gershwin for "A Star Is Born" (sung by as commanding a figure as Judy Garland), by Porter for "High Society" (performed by major figures such as Crosby, Sinatra, and Armstrong), and those written for "Gigi" by the important team of Lerner and Loewe (with "My Fair Lady" already under their belt), became songs of lasting importance in the classic pop tradition. But none of them went to top of the singles charts, as had been the case in movie songs in earlier eras.[14]

Increasingly, producers filmed "presold" properties: highly successful musicals from Broadway. This approach was a mixed success, though some were big hits. After all, despite large Broadway audiences for musicals such as "My Fair Lady" or "Pajama Game," most Americans only had the chance to see them in their movie versions. But these versions did not always generate excitement within the film-going public. In many cases, the films were overblown, with "production values" added to such an extent that the original storyline or creative spark was occluded, or the songs lost in the decor and scenery. Others recast leading roles with superannuated or also-ran movie stars.[15] The studio orchestra sound tended to be bloated and crude, compared to that of the Broadway pit band. In other cases, it turned out that performers who were hugely successful on Broadway or on records didn't shine on the screen.

Interestingly, the big movie musicals that worked best tended to be those built around dance. Dance had always worked on film. More to the point, much of the pop music of the United States, in the 1950s and thereafter, was enlivened by new, exciting elements that called out for movement, notably Latin rhythms and rock modes. "Saturday Night Fever" (1977) was primarily a dance film with a contemporary story line, each aspect appealing to a new generation which no longer cared about "musicals" in the traditional sense.

If we refer once more to the Hit Parade roster (Table 2.1), one title jumps out: *Rock Around the Clock*, the first big commercial rock song. It was a rudimentary but catchy R&B tune with an irresistible drum track from a dramatic movie, "The Blackboard Jungle," concerned with juvenile delinquency and with urban gangs. On several grounds it was a precursor of things to come: a hit song from a nonmusical film, with a heavy dance emphasis, and attention to a new subject matter for mainstream entertainment, rebellious teenagers. Despite the fact that the song was primarily an envelope for dance, it became one of the biggest selling records of all time.

On an a priori basis, it would have been unreasonable to think that a new cohort would care about Fred Astaire (born 1899), or be interested in the romantic problems of Jane Powell. The trauma of Korea, the intensifying Cold War, and the beginning of enforced integration in the society altered everyone's range of concern, and accordingly the public's entertainment preferences and musical needs. With a vast new population of young adults (and, now, teens and preteens) constituting the mass entertainment audience, it was hardly likely that the typical popular songs would continue to express the sophisticated urban cosmopolitanism, or even the White middle-class cultural patterns, of the Broadway musical of the 1930s, with its emphasis on martinis, décor, and suave seduction.[16]

The Singles Market

Rock Around the Clock broke out in 1955. Elvis Presley came to fame in 1956. The landmark importance of Elvis, in retrospect, was that he was a nice rural White kid "singing Black"—and doing so in a musically compelling, exciting way.[17] Prior to Elvis, the market for "race music" was still segmented. Though it is not clear that all young fans of Presley were aware of more than his musical power and his sexy personality, the fact is that Elvis brought into the White audience and market the music of rural Black blues—to be sure, with a heavy admixture from country and even folk music. It was a style that Presley's big, natural voice fitted perfectly.

By the mid-1950s, teenagers were economically able for the first time to buy records in substantial numbers. The invention of the transistor radio allowed them to listen to the music they wanted, in private. Sociological studies from the period show that preferences between "hillbilly" and R&B were a function of geography and education level (and thus, indirectly, of race), while preferences within the pop and dance band world were strongly influenced by age.[18] Some young Whites certainly enjoyed, prior to Elvis, the music of Buddy Holly (Texas), Jerry Lee Lewis (Louisiana), Chuck Berry (St. Louis), Fats Domino (New Orleans), and other major figures of vernacular nonpop music—but they knew them primarily through direct culture contact. That is, they had grown up in the South, or they went to college or workplaces where the popular music of other demographic groups was to be heard. Just before rock & roll came in, young Whites were singing doo-wop. The fans of Presley and his successors could challenge the norms of the nuclear family, the values of middle (and midcentury) America, the authority of parents, the gender gap, the political inertness of the Eisenhower years—all this via radio, without actually mixing with Blacks. Neither young White working-class males nor teenage girls would have responded so unequivocally to Presley had he not been White.[19]

The Rudiments of Rock

In this book we will sometimes be looking at the relationship between rock-based and classic pop songs, especially in the period up to the mid-1970s, so it is useful to summarize briefly some elements of "rock" (of the first, 1950s to 1970s period) as a set of defining features. The reader may compare our summary of stylistic aspects of rock with corresponding aspects of classic pop, as described in chapter 1.

- Rock songs of this first period had a flattish melodic/harmonic profile. They do not show an arching or ABA structure. If there is a middle section, it tends to resemble the opening section moved up or down a tone or two. Verbal phrases, and the musical periods under them, are short and simple. A rock tune moves linearly through aural space, as if on tracks. In these respects, it is more like blues than classic pop.

- The pattern of chords is simple, often one to three chord changes over and over again. There is often a simple shifting of the chord from one step of the scale to the next, although movement from I to IV is common. Whatever the chord sequence, it often proceeds in the downward direction; a common one is I—down to IV—up to V—and up to I.[20] Many rock songs, including *Rock Around the Clock*, are built on a boogie-woogie pattern where the bass moves briskly through the entire octave without changing the key.[21]

- With repetitive chord patterns, the need for transitional chords (such as V^7) is minimized; so is the use of transitional tones as in jazz-flavored progressions. Most chords are in a fixed parallel position, with the root either on the bottom or on top. Blueslike, yes; classic pop, no.

- Rock is normally in a clear diatonic major or minor. In the latter case, there is of course a minor third interval, and there may be brief chromatic runs where other tones are lowered.[22] Rock style, while it may use a rough attack on crucial notes, does not employ the particular "bending" or "smudging" that is prevalent in blues.

- There is consistently a very clear rhythmic emphasis on beats 1 and 3, often combined with even a stronger "back-beat" on 2 and 4, a feature that came right out of swing and the jump-band style of the 1940s. The combined effect is that of the voice or lead instrument in cross-rhythm to the rest of band, especially drums and bass. The foreground pattern (1 and 3) can sound like the blues, but the background, in giving emphasis to the off-beats, is more reminiscent of country swing. The double-rhythm yields a push/pull effect, another term for which could be—rock and roll. Another common meter and rhythm is that of 12/8, with the machine-gun-like division of the main beats into patterns of three. There is little syncopation, and thus little of the "sprung" effect of jazz.

- Rock songs do not have intricate rhyme schemes. There is considerable assonance (near-rhyme), and much false rhyme at the end of phrases (*mind–fine, band–man*). The lyric in these respects is loosely like that of the blues. Classic pop almost always uses exact rhyme.

- The semantic content and verbal attitude of rock song words is overwhelmingly that of sex, defiance, juvenile acting-out—so much so that one can define "soft rock" or "pop rock" as that which is musically rock but verbally pop, probably involving young love. In this regard, rock style can be traced back to urban or Chicago blues, but probably not to traditional rural blues, whose words show a different register (p. 16), one maintained in rock-influenced gospel music. Rock lyrics in the first two decades were, in retrospect, less raunchy than early R&B. "Hard rock" lyrics, later, were more violent, misogynistic, and lurid.

- Rock, on multiple levels, is a tense music, partly due to its rhythmic insistence, perhaps partly to its normal tempo. No rock is majestic, like blues. Its words are forceful; its drum and percussion patterns are sharp and stinging, with hard rim shots, loud cymbals; its instrumental colors are distinct and assertive. Guitars (and other strummed instruments) and percussions are inherently short-breathed, with the sound dying quickly. Thus the sound palette is discontinuous, repetitively impactful over short time intervals. Early rock is sonically more like the brisk abrupt attitude of country music than like traditional blues, and not at all like classic pop.

One problem with the term *rock*, as of about 2000, is that the youth-oriented, hugely commercial music of the later decades has virtually nothing in common with the music we are discussing here. For example, the disco sound of the 1980s uses an unceasing four-equal-beat rhythm pattern that has more relationship to the ostinatos of *The Rite of Spring* than it does to swing or rock and roll.

The oppositions and contrasts we have put forward may read as if we are engaged in putting down rock in order to promote other genres of music. This is not our intention.[23] We think, for example, that *Shake Rattle and Roll, La Bamba, Whole Lot of Lovin'*, or *Good Golly, Miss Molly*, are pretty good songs, with a kind of innocent poetry in their lyrics. Their means match their goal, and serve a valid communicative purpose. But there is no gainsaying the fact that the rock song, in the acoustic rock era, was plainer, less complex, more in-your-face, in all its musical–verbal aspects, than what had existed before in any form of American pop music. Whether this was, in the end, a virtue or a defect is a matter of taste—and of ongoing cultural change. We understand those who would say, rock was vital, classic pop etiolated, even though we do not share those values.

Other Voices, Other Choices

Elvis and his successors tied back to traditional blues, with some admixture of "country"; the Rolling Stones and their coevals in electrified rock related more directly to the rougher strand of urban blues. Moreover, there was throughout the 1950s and1960s, at least, a continual pattern of crossing-over and borrowing among extant song genres. Bob Dylan's early music harked back to the folk-country-blues of Woody Guthrie and Leadbelly. The Beatles, incredibly, managed to blend American and British folk styles, skiffle sound, church vocal harmony, hillbilly and early R&B, English music hall, French chanson, even the tinny timbre of jingles, into a uniquely orchestrated compound—often, but not entirely, rock-based.

Early rock and the various other pop genres showed a constant urge to inter-breed, an inclination that produced often sterile offspring. In the realm of song, after the first rock shock, what the charts reflected (an important qualification: we speak here only of what reached national popularity) was a constant trend toward pop-rock: songs such as *Bye Bye Love, Chantilly Lace, I Can't Stop Lovin' You, Teach Me Tonight*.[24] Some of this represented a paler alternative to Black rock.[25]

The Beatles, the most brilliant innovators of the period, generated certain songs that were classic pop songs with a light rock instrumentation and a de-pendence on modal (nondiatonic) harmony. *Yesterday* is the obvious example. *Eleanor Rigby* is basically a folksong, *Let It Be* is gospel, *Michelle* is French chan-son, *When I'm Sixty-Four* is music hall. It all goes to show that strong melodies over interesting chords, together with a brash and cheeky attitude, will get you to a good song.

In the same period, the "folk revival"—from the Weavers to the Kingston Trio to Peter, Paul, and Mary—had its virtues, in terms of effecting a cultural revival,[26] but the versions one heard, well, they didn't sound like Woody, Lead-belly, Jean Ritchie, or the other originals. The typical approach of these groups was to reclaim a sound genetically linked to the string band or the jug band of the early part of the century. The cultural echo was that of upper South poor Whites, as distinct from either the Black or the Appalachian Celtic styles. The Weavers's *Goodnight Irene* is charming in this style; but Leadbelly's version had been a blues wail with slashing guitar.[27]

In the 1950s and early 1960s, the charts consistently showed a curious type of balanced dimorphism: a prevalence of two paired types of songs, each rep-resenting a process of adulteration. From the rock side, we have songs which were not so much pop rock as "prom rock" or "bubblegum rock."[28] From the pop side, the drift toward a bland center is a phenomenon we call "bleat pop": conventional pop infantilized musically and dumbed down verbally. *April Love* is perhaps the nadir of this dreadful genre. The pop tradition, from Tin Pan Alley on, had generated hundreds of sappy songs; but now songs of low quality consistently topped the pop charts (like Patti Page's *How Much Is That Doggie In the Window?* in 1953). Surprisingly, throughout most of the decade bleat pop did better commercially than rock. In 1956, for example, Doris Day's *Che Sera Sera* outsold *Heartbreak Hotel*.

We do not accept the notion that rock was a revolutionary occurrence that obliterated pop. We have said enough about blending and cross-breeding of styles to support the point that 1950s rock was more a sea-change in commerce and market focus than in the music itself. As we suggest below, a far greater discontinuity happened later, when hard rock and its affines came along.[29] We isolate some of the obvious trends, in part, because it will be our task, in the analyses of classic pop songs from the 1950s on, to judge whether similar tendencies are evident there. Was there a diversification of styles within the classic pop form, or more a pattern of a drift toward sterile compromises? We will address this large question in our final chapter.

...And It Came Out Here

Once could continue to outline sociohistorical, cultural, and economic trends throughout the later decades of the half-century, in order to provide a framework for points of contact or differentiation among styles. We do not feel obliged to do so. Most readers know that, beginning in the mid-1970s, the mood of the country turned darker. Boom times ended. The sizing-up of secondary and higher education reversed. The citizenry was suffering from ten years of civil rights turmoil, the murder of public figures, and the trauma of the Vietnam War. Black activism and the existence of a vital counterculture were, at the least, qualitatively distinct from, not mere intensifications of, racial awareness and teenage rebellion that had surfaced in the 1950s. Internal migration to the city had, in some respects, reversed, being replaced in the biggest cities by Latino immigration (which had, obviously, a major influence on popular music styles).[30]

The high point commercially for singles records was the late 1960s, when sales reached twice that of 1947. It was also, in retrospect, the beginning of a period of quite stable diversification, of largely separate markets, in popular music. Different audiences listened preferentially to Mo-Town, the LA sound, NY-Miami Latin, Tex-Mex, electric Dylan, Presley, the Beatles, the Stones, Peter, Paul, & Mary, Arlo Guthrie, Jimi Hendrix and Janis Joplin, Ray Charles, the gospel-soul of Aretha Franklin, a new country movement represented by Johnny Cash, the country-rock of Crosby Stills Nash & Young, the political songs of Phil Ochs, the pop rock of Neil Diamond. After some fifteen years of mixing and crossing, the White and the Black audiences were again fairly distinct.[31]

This niche pattern (though they were large-population niches) continued for the rest of the century. The result was that, while one could certainly say that the dominant popular music in the country was now "rock," it was incomparably broader and more stylistically diverse than had been the case around 1950, when classic pop still predominated and rock and roll was just surfacing. After about 1970, to be sure, there was a noticeable rapprochement between some guitar-based rock and the folk stream, and between rock and post-Miles Davis jazz.[32] This left "hard rock" and "punk rock" as a kind of heavily technologized residual, which at any moment appealed to a cohort of very new listeners, but did not create individual titles that lasted.

Sonic Boom

About 1970 technological developments occurred that sent all popular music genres along new courses that have lasted to this day. The victory of intensely amplified electric instruments, and the introduction of an electronic-based popular music, meant that rock became essentially different: not only louder but far "harder" and more monolithic. Not only was it now impossible really to hear verbal detail in the words,[33] the same was true on the musical plane. In early rock, a listener responded to individual touches: a pistol-like rim shot from the drummer, an inventive guitar riff between phrases, a smear from the horns, a leer or quaver in the voice. In the later decades, these effective momentary touches disappeared from recorded, and eventually from live, rock-based music. A "wall of sound," achieved by repeated overdubbing and mixing of tracks in the band, became the ideal, especially for hard or punk rock. Synthesis as a musical endeavor may have its persuasive aspects, from the point of view of aesthetic theory, but after a point it is simply synthetic. In our view, there came to be a sound, not a style. Texture replaced text.

The electronic revolution in music had a deeper significance. To put it bluntly, in earlier eras songwriters made songs; now, recording engineers made songs. In traditional classical popular song, the sheet music at the moment of first printing was its fixed, official form. Since songs, once they became popular, were recorded by many people in various arrangements, you went to the sheet music to determine the original tempo or key, to see what interpretive suggestions the songwriters might have made, or to clarify a rhythmic pattern or a sequence of words that, in performance, had become obscured. If you wanted the Platonic essence of a song, the sheet music was as close as you could come.

In later eras, you might still purchase a printed copy, but "the song" would have vanished: there would be only a minimal, ghostly set of notes, chords, words.[34] Now the canonical form of, say, a hard-rock number was the original recording where the aural/temporal creation was encoded. Similarly, in earlier times songs, once popular, became "standards" that other performers "covered"; that is, they offered their own approach to what remained, after all, the same song. In advanced electronic-based popular music, a number might be recorded again, but it was a new creation, not simply an alternative version of the same song. Radio announcers would remind the listener of the singer or group who first made songs hits, not of the songwriter, who was unimportant. While star performers remained vital to a record's success, the notion of a Diana Ross song or a Dionne Warwick song referred to the entire communicative effect. With generic rock, produced by music "factories" and by entrepreneurs who hired the engineers who created the song, the personality of the performer was cut to fit the sound bed.[35]

Viewed from a wide angle, rock was a vast tide. It did not submerge regional or class-linked styles so much as incorporate them as separate currents. In 1950, the typical listener, ignorant of regional or ethnic musics, might distinguish between taste levels: classic pop versus junk. By the 1980s, a discriminating popular music lover listened to a few genres—one or two types of rock, or "world music," or classic pop revival—and left the rest unheard.

But the Melody Lingered On

We have ignored, however, a major exception to our generalizations about the death of "the song." Even in the survey above, Bob Dylan would count in anyone's list of major songwriters. From the early 1970s on, a group of performers came to prominence who created remarkable songs, in a traditional, though not classic-pop, sense of the term. We refer, of course, to the singer-songwriters: Carole King, Judy Collins, James Taylor, Stevie Wonder, Paul Simon, among others. These pioneers were followed, throughout the rest of the century, by comparable figures such as Billy Joel, Randy Newman, and the protean Van Morrison.

They were important in a number of respects. First, they broke out of the commercial prison of the sound factories, and wrote interesting songs: the words were important, the words fitted the music, and a momentary detail—the sound of a guitar chord, a metrical fillip, an instrumental riff—counted for something. Once again, a "song" was not a bank of blended sound, but something narrative that provided a story, a vignette. These writer-singers proved that electrified instruments could be used to artistic purpose. In a sense they continued the artistic goals set by Bob Dylan, after Dylan himself went electric.[36]

Second, some of them, some of the time, achieved mass popularity among the rock generation and its immediate elders. At times their work was self-indulgent or obscure, but often it brought a newly topical, closely observed kind of intelligence and specificity of verbal reference back to the popular song. In the last decades of the century, the popularity of the singer-songwriters receded, except for the more pop-rock-oriented figures such as Elton John and Paul McCartney. The earlier generation, the troubadours, became "niche" artists: favored by listeners who had aged out of being rock devotees, or by listeners who had become deaf to (if not from) the Motown sound. Roughly speaking, their songs have tended to turn toward, or at least bring echoes of, country-music, urban-blues, or classic-pop prototypes.[37] In chapter 7 we will discuss them again, because they offer useful points of comparison to songs from the classic pop tradition of the same era.

Song as an Anachronism

With electronic music technology there came into the realm of popular entertainment an overwhelming impulse toward a new ideal of the *Gesamtkunstwerk*. "The sound"—the mixing of recorded tracks into an almost infinite set of aural compounds—was only the most obvious feature. There was also the matter of presentation. As far back as the Beatles, the design of the music album, the way the type was arranged, the cover art, became an essential aspect of the creative whole. Later, the music video became as important as the record. In the theater, the "rock musical" was no longer three hours of story line and moments of song: the main feature was "the sound": the beat, the orchestration. With "Hair," "Tommy," or "Grease," the book was minimal or nonexistent, and individual performances were less important to the total effect than the lighting, the sets, the sound system.[38]

There was also the further development of the dance-based musical. Beginning about 1960, Jerome Robbins, Gower Champion, or Bob Fosse presided over the realization of every aspect (the *Gesamtkunst*) of some of the most successful shows in Broadway history.[39] There was still room in the mix for songs per se—until true dance musicals like "Fosse," and "Contact" came along.

The more insidious challenge to the traditional musical theater came from another aspect of "total integration" as an aesthetic ideal. Despite the way in which successful Broadway creators had always sought to make the various elements work pleasingly together, the format had remained that of dialogue and stage action punctuated by "numbers" (choruses, dance episodes) and by songs. Both numbers and songs provided moments when the dramatic action stopped and, by some mystery of distillation, the feelings and attitudes of the characters enacting the plot were communicated. In the last quarter of the century, distinctions between book-action-dialogue-song-dance broke down. Music, together with movement, became continuous from the moment the curtain rose to the moment it descended. The pictorial elements in the seamless flow were at least as important as the enacted ones.

We have in mind here what some refer to as sung-through musicals—some call them pop operettas—the first of which was "Jesus Christ Superstar" (1971). Lloyd Webber (and other) spectaculars blurred the distinction between spoken and sung; there were few discrete songs as such, mostly a flow of momentarily heightened recitative or arioso. Fortunately, there developed quite another important approach to an integrated musical theater. In the case of Stephen Sondheim, even his most tightly integrated musicals included true songs, often brilliant and beautiful, though not necessarily in 32-bar form. Toward the end of the twentieth century, younger composers and lyricists were again attempting to write nongrandiose musical–dramatic works that felt rather like chamber operas (see chapter 8).

In the case where the sound event coming off a record prevents one from hearing the words as "a lyric," we, at least, no longer hear a song. Something comparable is true of music from the theater. One may hear, moment to moment, meaningful words set to a clear melodic line. But if those elements are not in some way organized in time into phrases and periods, into episodes with beginnings and endings—if, in other words, there is no clear syntax to what is ongoing—you do not have a *song*.[40]

An Exception to Gresham's Law

Sometimes technology allows the good to drive out the bad. There is one aspect of innovation, post-1950, that seems to have been all for the good. That is the advent of the long-play (LP) record. Looking back to around 1920, it is clear that the classic popular song would not have found an audience without the microphone. Looking back to the early 1950s, it seems equally clear that the classic popular song would not have survived, except as an antiquarian curiosity, without the LP. Certainly it would not have reached new, if select, audiences of younger people.

As the rock and roll era reached full spate, the 45-rpm record, later the cassette, became the delivery medium. New record production companies entered, then dominated, this mass market. The large, well-established companies also produced 45s, but quite soon came to angle the LP toward classical music, jazz, and to classic pop song, both old and new. Though there was overlap, kids bought 45s, adults bought LPs, and young adults bought both. With regard to classic pop, the LP ensured the perpetuation of pre-1950s "standards," which were no longer to be heard via radio or touring bands, and also the rediscovery and preservation of many superior songs that were in danger of fading from communal memory. Thanks to the LP, as listeners who had come to classic pop in the 1930s and 1940s began to disappear, others took their place in valuing the Great American Songbook. Pop LPs continued to out-sell rock and folk until the mid-1960s. Thereafter, rock sold more.[41] The point here is that the LP became the dedicated home for superior pop, show music, and jazz.

New pop songs, most of middling quality, continued to appear, of course, as singles, and those with staying power eventually made it to LP, sometimes in the "greatest hits" format. The LP also brought a new kind of collection: the easy-listening format, mostly instrumental versions of standards, recent hits, and show tunes. The important development, for those who cared about classic popular song, was that of the *album*, a rather old-fashioned term that had been used to refer to a deliberate collection of printed or recorded songs with something meaningful in common. The LP album permitted the best established singers and instrumentalists to present a set of fine songs: sometimes songs they themselves had recorded earlier; sometimes songs made famous by others but now performed in a different, perhaps more up-to-date approach; sometimes a florilegium from a thirty-year catalog of established value. Beginning in the mid-1950s, major exponents of superior pop songs, such as Frank Sinatra or Judy Garland, recorded series of albums, each album unified not only by quality but by using arrangements written by one person, like Nelson Riddle or Gordon Jenkins. These LPs, and those of singers such as Nat King Cole or Peggy

Lee or Fred Astaire, preserved not only the songs but the legacy of the performers. Ella Fitzgerald's "Songbooks" brought into focus the entire careers of most of the great innovators, as did Bobby Short's double album of Cole Porter.

The LP album also permitted compiling and reissuing as sets the irreplaceable versions, long out of print, of classic pop songs by jazz singers like Louis Armstrong, Billie Holiday, Dinah Washington, Anita O'Day. Ultimately, it permitted the recovery of the work of early singers such as Ethel Waters, Mildred Bailey, Lee Wiley, et al., who had strongly influenced the development of classic pop performing style, but whose recorded work had nearly disappeared. It gave good younger singers like Tony Bennett, Rosemary Clooney, and Mel Tormé a new security in their careers, and a new audience. Another benefit was that the LP permitted closer attention to the careers of the great lyricists, no longer simply the junior partners in songwriting teams.

The LP also fixed, probably forever, the most stable style of classic pop performance as jazz-based or informed by a jazz sensibility. The big swing band (or sweet band) had faded. Now, recording a song with a trio or a small group became commercially viable and stylistically exciting, not only for singers but for jazz players.[42] While the "show-biz" approach remained for a time viable, for Sinatra or Garland or Bennett, the sound of classic pop done in light (not "lite") jazz style has remained the representative style to this day.

The LP gave talented younger singers, who could never have competed for mass popularity, the basis for careers, as it did for cabaret and club performers and connoisseurs' singers, such as Mabel Mercer or Bobby Short. These were exponents of the classic pop song literature par excellence. Without the LP they could never have reached an audience of any size. This, in turn, enabled the careers of young songwriters who aimed neither at the mass pop market nor at the theater or television. Figures such as Dave Frishberg, Johnny Mandel, or Tommy Wolf and Fran Landesman, writing literate, melodically engaging, well-constructed songs, could expect that a new song might be taken up by a fine club singer, then find its way onto albums by a more famous singer or by a jazz musician of some réclame. By such steps, songwriters could reach devoted, if not huge, audiences. More important, by such steps new songs became accessible to new audiences without first appearing in shows.

The other obvious function of the LP, in keeping the tradition alive and vital, was the original-cast recording. Recordings of new Broadway musicals had been produced since the early 1940s, but they had been on 78-rpm discs: heavy, breakable, and expensive. The LP could contain, not just highlights, but virtually all the musical material—songs, transitions, dance music, crucial moments of dialogue—in a format approximating the real thing. Probably the Broadway musical would not, for economic reasons, have survived had it not been for the LP, whose audiences far outnumbered actual attendance in the theater.[43] Some estimable shows yielded respectable original cast recording sales, even though they closed after only a few performances.[44] One paradoxical result of original cast recordings of entire shows, however, was that it became relatively *less* likely that one or two songs would jump into the popular arena and become hits on the charts, then standards. Instead, a smaller, more specialized audience came to know the entire score.[45] At least for a time, the potential total revenues from a hit show were great enough so that the finest songwriters in the classic pop tradition aimed first and foremost at Broadway. There also grew up an intermediate form: the re-creation of musicals from pre-LP days, committed to vinyl in a theatrical style brought somewhat up to date. Without these splendid recordings, such as the famous series of Rodgers and Hart musicals produced by Goddard Lieberson in the 1970s, many wonderful songs from an earlier era would have eventually disappeared, not only from audience attention, but also from the ken of alert singers and musicians.

In sum, entering the 1950s, there was, with respect to the classic popular song, an established and widely successful creative tradition; a large audience in place; a number of effective means for dissemination—and a genre that was losing its exclusive national dominance. We have covered some of the changes, in social attitudes, in the demography of audiences, and in the technology of media, that ensued. But what happened to the songs themselves? What characterized their form, their style, their cultural frame of reference? This is the central subject of this book, to which we now turn.

Notes

1. Alec Wilder, with James T. Maher, "American Popular Song: The Great Innovators, 1900–1950" (New York: Oxford Univ. Press, 1972). Hereafter, Wilder.
2. The trend was weakest for minorities. Blacks did not stay longer in school or graduate at higher rates until well into the 1960s.
3. See note 4.
4. For the early period, there are excellent sources. We have relied most heavily on: Richard A. Peterson, Why 1955? Explaining the Advent of Rock and Roll, "Popular Music," 9 (1990): 97–116; Richard A. Peterson, "Creating Country Music: Fabricating Authenticity" (Chicago: Univ. of Chicago Press, 1997); Robert C. Kloosterman and Chris Quispell, Not Just the Same Old Music On My Radio, "Popular Music," 9 (1990): 151–64; and Donald Clarke, "The Rise and Fall of Popular Music" (New York: St. Martin's Press, 1995). A comprehensive sociological treatment of the various "streams" of American popular music, from well before World War II through at least the third quarter of the twentieth century, is: Philip H. Ennis, "The Seventh Stream: The Emergence of Rocknroll In American Popular Music" (Hanover, NH: Univ. Press of New England/Wesleyan Univ. Press, 1992).
5. The New York-oriented American Society of Composers, Authors and Publishers.
6. Broadcast Music Incorporated. BMI was created by station owners, and was oriented toward radio play for Nashville, country pop, and rhythm & blues.
7. On this base, Your Hit Parade, the Ed Sullivan Show, and others like them remained loyal to the pop mainstream for quite a long time. It was considered revolutionary when, in 1964, the Beatles appeared on the Sullivan show. In the 1950s, Rosemary Clooney, Tony Bennett, Johnnie Ray, Jo Stafford, Dinah Shore, Johnny Mathis, and other young performers went back and forth between radio shows, records, club appearances, or even movies.

8. Often, according to insiders, receiving monetary payoffs for their help. Disk jockeys were the key to success for the BMI system.
9. The list is adapted from Fred Bronson, "Billboard Book of Number One Hits" (New York: Billboard Publications, 1988). "Of quality" is our determination, but we have been set quite a low standard, omitting only obvious junk and the most fleeting kinds of novelty song.
10. Billboard hits were based on local radio and jukebox play, and tended to reflect the BMI stable of songwriters and publishers, that is, those not oriented toward Broadway and Hollywood, and performers who recorded songs written direct for records.
11. When the Marcels recorded *Blue Moon* as the B-side of one of their records, they knew the song only vaguely. They made an on-the-spot vocal arrangement, more or less making up their own bridge. It was a surprise hit; what Richard Rodgers thought of it remains unknown.
12. As we define that style in chapter 1.
13. Respectively, "The Sky's the Limit" (1943) and "Neptune's Daughter" (1948).
14. The 1964 film "Mary Poppins" (songs by Richard M. and Robert B. Sherman) was virtually unique in its decade in using an original score and yielding songs that showed up on the hit charts.
15. The intention was to attract viewers who couldn't care less about Broadway stars, for example, those who knew the name Mitzi Gaynor but not Mary Martin, for "South Pacific"; but it did not work out that way.
16. However, we are conflating a generational factor with a more complex sort of change of interests in the society. The audience of the 1950s did, after all, care about the dating problems of Sandra Dee. And the Broadway musical of the 1940s had, in some cases, been reoriented to a far more socially conscious "book."
17. Early Elvis records still used a "rockabilly" sound, without the hillbilly vocal timbre. Insofar as later Elvis "sounded Black" or seemed to understand the blues, it is significant that Elvis was brought up in the Southern Pentecostal church, in which there was much racial crossover. Elvis also had a remarkable intimacy with the microphone, comparable to that of Bing Crosby.
18. See Ennis, 1992, chapt.5; Gans (note 19).
19. This specific point is made well by Kloosterman and Quispell (1990). A good general treatment of age, class, and racial stratification, era by era, is offered by Herbert J. Gans, "Popular Culture & High Culture" (New York: Basic Books, 1999).
20. For an exposition of degrees of the scale, see Figure 1.6. A number of rock songs follow an Afro-Cuban chord sequence: I - ii - I - (lower) V - I.
21. The pattern ascends to I^7 and then directly back to I, in contrast to the V^7 to I relation in classic pop. David Lahm points out that, harmonically, *Rock Around the Clock* is a traditional 12-bar blues.
22. The rock song *Town Without Pity* shows this chromatic device at the end of its main phrases, but it is unusual.
23. For one thing, there are a number of rock-hybrid songs that have close affinities to classic pop. The John Davenport — Edward Cooley song *Fever*, made famous by Peggy Lee, was originally a rock song written for Otis Blackwell. All Lee did was to add additional lyrics of some sophistication, lower the pitch, and sing it softer. The result: it sounds like vaguely Latin pop.
24. The last of these is almost in classic pop format, with 8-bar periods, a bridge, and exact rhymes, but it has a rock tincture, mostly because of the lyrics and the 12/8 rhythm.
25. Ennis,1992, 245, forms an amusing comparison by calling Pat Boone "the good twin" and Elvis Presley "the bad twin."
26. It was a revival, of course, only to upper-middle-class urban Whites, not to those for whom the songs were still the mother tongue.
27. There was an alternate allele, a sort of hillbilly-folk subtype, performed by Tennessee Ernie Ford, Patti Page et al. While pleasant, it hardly matched the Carter Family.
28. Examples would include *Chantilly Lace* or *I Can't Stop Lovin' You*. The pairing of strong and weak forms of popular music continued throughout the century, with "elevator music" pop and "soft jazz."
29. The whole sweep of musical and cultural change in American popular music from 1950 to about 1990, with particular emphasis on racial–ethnic aspects, is brilliantly described in Martha Bayles, "Hole in Our Soul" (New York: Free Press, 1994).
30. Largely a welcome one, we feel. The first "Latin" number to sweep the charts, as early as 1955, was Perez Prado's delightful mambo, *Cherry Pink & Apple Blossom White*.

31. In a curious reversal, some Black music that had earlier cast its influence widely over adjacent genres now seemed to retreat to almost the rarefied status of "folk" music. Those who went to hear B.B. King did not, for the most part, go to Motown discos.
32. For example, with the group Santana and many Latin-influenced bands.
33. You could with Aretha Franklin, Al Green, or other soul-grounded singers.
34. The new generations of rock musicians would, revealingly, refer to a "chart," that is, a skeletal outline of a song, not a notated full representation.
35. The same was true, of course, of commercial pop in the 1940s and 1950s. The personality of Doris Day meant something to the listener, but it would have surfaced in almost any song she recorded.
36. In fact, Dylan continued, in all his phases, to revisit the traditions of blues, country, and early R&B.
37. This movement has continued in recent times, in such figures as Mary Chapin Carpenter, Bonnie Raitt, or Lucinda Williams.
38. This trend was not just evident in popular music, but in all areas of the arts and entertainment: the nonrock musical, mixed-media or mixed-style concert music and opera, public spectacle (stadium events), the visual arts, even in museums.
39. Jerome Robbins's had been, by the account of his own collaborators, the central creative vision behind "West Side Story" in 1957; by 1964, he was the director of "Fiddler on the Roof." Neither of these musicals, of course, was a "dance musical."
40. One might object that Wagner is songful or that birds produce songs. We simply make our assumptions explicit, as to what this book covers and why.
41. See Ennis, 1992, chap. 12; also Charles Hamm, "Yesterdays: Popular Song In America" (New York: W. W. Norton, 1979), 459.
42. The piano trio with voice format was pioneered in the early 1940s by Nat King Cole, then a jazz pianist, later a most popular pop singer. In the post-bebop, post-free-jazz era, after 1950, many jazz musicians were once again depending on classic pop songs for their material. Some younger listeners, in fact, began with a love of jazz, say of the Bill Evans variety, and then came to classic pop by discovering that the tunes they knew also had wonderful words. Moreover, the LP was the medium for esoteric "jazz singers" like O'Day, Chris Connor, or Chet Baker to build and maintain small but loyal audiences.
43. While the number of Broadway musicals produced each year was far fewer in the 1960s and 1970s than it had been in the 1920s and 1930s, the sale of original-cast albums produced an entirely new revenue stream that helped justify the far greater production costs.
44. A famous example is the Arlen — Capote "House of Flowers." Some long-running productions never made money in the theater, the most famous example being "West Side Story."
45. There were obviously exceptions, such as *I Could Have Danced All Night, Hello Dolly!, Maria*, and others.

3
Late Flowering from Old Stock

Among the living figures in the pantheon, as of 1950, Berlin, Rodgers, Porter, and Arlen kept on writing, Arlen and Rodgers at the highest level of quality. A number of other distinguished writers were productive for a decade or more.

HAROLD ARLEN (1905–86)

Arlen's songs from the very early 1950s are mostly negligible. An exception is *I Love a New Yorker* (1950, words, Ralph Blane), a blithe up-tempo song in the style of Arlen's early Cotton Club songs. It's a song in which a woman appreciates her guy, who's "bold, breezy and bright" and "out on the town ev'ry night." From 1952, *Who Will It Be When the Time Comes?* has a top-quality Arlen melody, an almost entirely diatonic line with one, expressive accidental—this over a bass-line that moves very plainly, mostly from I to IV up to a chromatic cadence at the end. The words (Blane and Arlen) are a little overplain. Arlen's best-known melodic style involves unusual intervals, minor tonalities, and "bluesy" touches, but there are also songs of major-key, mysteriously simple poise, like *This Time the Dream's On Me* (1941)—and *Who Will It Be.*

    With the Sun Warm Upon Me (1953) is an evocative song, with a crucial contribution from Dorothy Fields. The somnolent countrified words and the repetitive dotted-rhythm clip-clopping accompaniment threaten to bring the song to stasis. But Fields writes "...then I'm caught / I'm caught by the thirsty bees...." with a fine overlap between phrases and a nice specificity of diction. Just before the final A-section, Arlen writes a transitional set of chords that includes an unexpected step: one little touch adds a lot.

    Arlen and Ira Gershwin wrote the fine score for the 1954 film "A Star Is Born." *The Man That Got Away* is too well-known to need comment, except to point out that it has two climaxes, one at the end of the release ("And where's he gone to?") and another in the last A-section, with a dozen occurrences of the note D, the 6 of the scale. This is the famous Arlen style, chromatic, built on a vamp, with a Scotch-snap figure that becomes the norm so that the even rhythm of the release makes a contrast. Implicit in it is another Arlen trademark, the "smudge": one perceives, and a good jazz group will play, two tones a half-step apart, together, on the top tone of the first phrase.[1]

Other songs from the film are worth more attention than they have received. *It's a New World* is a very beautiful example of Arlen's radiant major-key gift, that radiance kept from becoming simplistic by a yearning chromatic release. This chaste song has also an extraordinary verse, where Gershwin, using only common words, brings in a touch of early-modern English poetry. The ballad *Here's What I'm Here For* is also lovely, and subtle in form. Within each section, the use of symmetrical double periods is perfect for the sake of words that just speak love. Arlen begins the final section, to the words "To share a journey that leads to heaven's door," on a raised 7, but makes us wait seven bars for the resolution. The song should be better known. A rhythmically irresistible, get-happy kind of song, *Lose That Long Face*, uses a strong forward syncopation and lends itself to a big two-beats-for-one Broadway finish. The Gershwin rhyme scheme is audacious, as in *panacea/idea*; only he and Ogden Nash took such groan-producing chances and got away with it. This is most apparent in the 32-bar verse, which is as brilliant as the song.

Also in 1954, Arlen reached one of the summits of his career with the Broadway musical, "House of Flowers," which yielded any number of songs that rank at the very top of his lifetime output. The words are credited to both fiction writer Truman Capote, who wrote the book for the musical, and Arlen; they employ the flavor of Southern Creole/Black English without going so far into the vernacular as to make the songs too "regional" for use outside the show. A possible exception is a driving, calypsolike number, *Two Ladies In De Shade of De Banana Tree*, one of the best up-tempo songs Arlen ever wrote. It repays close attention to a specific vernacular (e.g., the omission of *to be* verbs "When you flyin' too high / Like birds sweepin' de sky." The message about the joys of life couldn't be clearer.

There are two exquisite ballads, *I Never Has Seen Snow* and *A Sleepin' Bee*. The former, particularly, uses devices, beloved by Arlen, that are hallmarks of the strand of a Jewish–Black affinity so important in classic American popular song. One is the vocal glide, in which the singer moves from one tone to another in a continuous adjustment of pitch. It happens in this song on the two last syllables of the title phrase, again on "Like my love is," and again on the word *took* at the end of the release. The other special expressive touch is the smudge. Instrumentally, this is often a very quick half-step appoggiatura ("grace note"). Vocally, it involves hitting the main note a tiny bit flat or sharp, and instantly adjusting. It's a common feature of blues and jazz singing, often heard from Billie Holiday and others. It occurs here on "with my love."

I Never Has Seen Snow begins with a marvelous verse in vernacular language. It draws a character and sets up a story, starting with "I done lost my ugly spell" and ending with the utterly charming, "Feelin' fine and full o' bliss / All I really wants to say is this," fastened over a series of chiming open chords on a tonic pedal tone. The chorus, in its A-sections, alternates in-the-scale declarative phrases, such as "I never has seen snow," with chromatic phrases of commentary or elaboration: "(Snow) c'ain't be so beautiful like my love is," the last two words done with glide. Thus the opening phrases address the auditor, while the latter phrases show the speaker's thought turning inward. These A-section opening periods are in regular time. The wonderful release, shown here, provides a fine contrast Figure 3.1). The dotted rhythms of the voice line move the

Figure 3.1

narration ahead, and the sense of two strong beats to the bar has the same effect up to the end, where using four beats to a bar slows down the pace for the transition back to A. The voice line is full of Arlen's altered intervals (the G-sharp on *near to me*, the B-natural in *horizon*), these two chromatic moves are also, in effect, vocal glides, like that on *took*. The song has a fine vowel pattern: the verse uses every vowel, mixing dark and bright, short and long, while the chorus restricts itself to mostly dark vowels for the first A, mostly bright ones for the second A. The A-sections are set over the simplest possible chord progression, I-ii-iii and back, with just one harmonic surprise. It could be rock and roll, but not with this melody and these words.[2]

This long song, with its 16-bar verse and 48-bar chorus and its complex narrative, presses up against the boundaries of classic American pop, and can be considered a sort of aria. This is not the case with the other marvelous ballad, *A Sleepin' Bee*, one of the greatest ballads of the half-century. The opening strain of the chorus doesn't sound immediately like Arlen; it's a Rodgers-like chain of thirds. But there is a tiny noodling figure in the right-hand accompaniment at the end of the first eight bars, with altered 7 and 9, that couldn't be anyone else; a bass-line descending by half-steps over the next seven bars, right out of the jazz string-bass tradition, and a giveaway glide in the voice at the end of the second eight. And in the verse, the slurred upward seconds in the voice, over extended-dominant chords, would tell one. This ABAB song has an extraordinary glowing quality, achieved by the most minimal means, like raising by one step the highest tone of the voice line in the second four bars, as compared with the first four.

There are other unexplored treasures in this score. *Don't Like Goodbyes* should be a standard. This dramatic ballad uses more or less standard speech. It has the familiar upward glide, on words that convey yearning; for example, the last syllables of "Don't like goodbyes, tears or sighs...." There follows a verbally confiding bridge in shifting narrative rhythms, and a stunning ending employing repeated notes on, first, the lowered 7, then the pure 7, before ending on the octave.

The 1957 "Jamaica," with lyricist E.Y. Harburg, gave Arlen his last hit show. It too contains many excellent numbers, but the dramatically integrated, consistent Afro-Caribbean flavor of the songs, though ebullient, worked against their becoming well known. The songs, in that vernacular style, might sound contrived or condescending were it not for the loving wit and good taste of the lyricist. In some of them, Islanders gently mock the obsessions of European civilization. The amusing *Push De Button* concerns the amazements of urban mechanization, in a complex rhythmic pattern labeled *moderate beguine* ("From de television come de Pepto Bismo with baritone").

In a more intimate register, the delightful *Little Biscuit* is an example of a light-hearted, major-key, 16-bar blues, in the A-section, plus another brief blues for the bridge, and a conclusion where the moral of the story is conveyed. The lyrics are affectionately clever: "Sweet little sweet potato I'm your pie." The long, ingeniously worded, calypso-style *I Don't Think I'll End It All Today* gets almost giddy in its verbal invention; it also has a middle section in contrasting regular trochaic rhythm that prevents sameness. *What Good Does It Do?* is a bigger song in a blueslike tempo and rhythm, with a wonderfully sinuous vocal line, featuring lazy double-turns on the raised 6 and the 7, constructed over a bass that could not be simpler: a long section on I, another on IV, and a blues chord progression joining them. Harburg outdoes himself throughout, as in "...there are birds and bees / Composing beautiful Calypsos in de Eucalyptus trees."

A sweeping, beautiful ballad, *There's a Sweet Wind Blowin' My Way* (cut from "Jamaica"), is top-rate Arlen. It's a long song, more than 60 bars, in which the speaker registers that a new love is on the horizon, sensually anticipates, and then exults. All the A-sections are long, and all begin in a solid C major, with Arlen's minimalist harmonic delicacy beneath, an inner voice that moves in half-steps. All develop slightly different melodic contours, in the same rhythmic pattern, but the A$_3$ is set, ending the song, in a strongly affirmative G major. The release is special, with very strong syncopated triplets (an unusual effect) against duple-time in the bass, and a passionate vocal line: "And lately from lazy azalea and daisy come rumors like crazy...." Harburg's vowel harmony is evident throughout.

Perhaps the finest song in the show is the ballad *Cocoanut Sweet*. Like *Little Biscuit*, its images of love are put in naturalistic terms, here mostly botanical. The lyric is very fine, but in this song it is Arlen who surpasses his normally high standard. The format of the song is A$_1$BCA$_2$, each with 8 bars. The final A is closely related to but varied significantly from the first A. The B- and C-sections are marked *grandioso*, but, though solid, are not grandiose. The B is set low in the scale; the C is raised up to the top of the octave, and beyond. They are certainly not bridges, and they amount to something more than a release. Together, they make a large, directly communicative unit in the center of the song, around which the A-sections form lighter, more verbally allusive brackets. Thus the song, though in arch form, has an unusually broad top to the arch.

There is more of interest than simply the proportions. Arlen keeps the entire song basically in the tonic C, using quite rapid chord progressions that step down or up a tone or a half-tone at a time. One never has the sense of actual modulation. Moreover, the voice line, across all four sections, moves almost completely in adjacent steps of the diatonic scale, 3 and 4 being infrequent. The song opens (a) with a lazy turn, touching on the upper key-tone but moving right away again; in fact, the entire first A consists of such turns (see Figure 3.2). The neighboring-tone pattern continues in the B-section (b); what is different is that there are additional repeated notes, though still a turn on "sugar plum." In the C-section Arlen introduces a couple of accidentals, which adds brief instants of tension into the melodic line. (Figure 3.2c).

Figure 3.2

Figure 3.2 Continued.

The most memorable effect comes at the beginning of the final A, where Arlen unpacks the melodic turn into a series of four caressing, arching phrases, eventually overleaping the upper key-tone (Figure 3.2d). Suddenly, the melodic line, which began very small, becomes expansive, though for the end of the final A the composer reverts to a set of turns.[3]

Cocoanut Sweet is a stunning song. It illustrates a gift that Arlen had beyond the other great composers. A theorist might call it, *development by variation.* Except in fast stanzaic numbers, Arlen, in his vocal lines, tends to begin with just a few notes, in a small figure, and then spins them out into longer or slightly different or more extensive patterns, usually with the addition of a few new tones or by introducing brief local rhythmic changes. He does this throughout the A-sections of his songs, and sometimes, as in *Cocoanut Sweet*, throughout the whole song. The technique is especially noticeable when large-scale harmonic movement in the song is absent or minimized. Many songwriters use restricted sets of tones with lots of repetition (e.g., Styne) or integrate their songs with accompanying vamp patterns (e.g., Coleman). With Arlen, the materials, as they effloresce, are inventive in all their manifestations, so that one gets both the feeling of recursiveness and that of growth.

In 1959 Arlen teamed with another preeminent lyricist, Johnny Mercer, for the Broadway show "Saratoga." This was a period piece, rather like a nineteenth-century popular opera. There are many fine songs, including one called *Love Held Lightly*, but most were too specialized to have a life outside the theater. The song *Goose Never Be a Peacock* is demanding, with an eloquent vocal line and a typical vamplike bass chord pattern. The message: Be yourself.

With Harburg, for an obscure 1962 film, Arlen wrote one of his big moody ballads, *Paris Is a Lonely Town*. It is a powerful song with a big range, with long high notes set dramatically on out-of-the-scale tones, the voice then descending through lowered tones in a pop-blues pattern down to the key-tone. It should have been a hit.

In the 1960s Arlen worked mostly with new or younger lyricists. With singer Peggy Lee, there is *Happy With the Blues* (1961), in pop-blues style. This one is proficient, but slight in emotional impact—in a sense too Arlenesque to be that interesting. There were two unproduced scores with Martin Charnin. An effective song, *That's a Fine Kind of Freedom* (1965), in a fast vamp-and-blues style, reverts to the style of "Bloomer Girl" (1944) with Harburg, but is a bit pallid. *I Could Be Good For You* (1964) has a strong tune and a Broadway-jazz rhythm, very like what Coleman was writing. At least one superb big-blues ballad with Charnin, *Why Do You Make Me Like You?* has never been published, so there may be more of quality still unknown. Perhaps the best of the published late songs is *So Long, Big Time* (1963). It is signature-style Arlen, and it has a good faster-tempo interlude. The words are by Dory Langdon, who wrote in conventional pop style with André Previn, and subsequently went on her own to write interesting songs, both words and music, in the singer-songwriter mode. Here, Langdon writes like Ira Gershwin, with short phrases, neat rhymes, and a dapper sense of diction.

COLE PORTER (1892–1964)

Porter's late career proved a disappointment. It's not that he had no hits after 1950—*I Love Paris* was a huge hit, though to us it's a bore—but there is little distinguished work. However, an overlooked movie song from 1948, *Love of My Life*, has the Porter melodic sweep (with a voice line almost entirely in adjacent steps), the soft rumbalike underlying rhythm, the big climax, and superromantic words. It also has a fine wistful verse in a big arc that makes a short song in itself.

The first Broadway show of the new decade was "Out of This World" (1950), not much of a show but one with lots of songs. There are a number of comedy numbers, all good, none brilliant. *Where Oh Where* is a pretty, fast waltz, really a scherzo, with a good climax. There is also one beautiful love song, *Use Your Imagination,* a 60-bar AABA song with a good opening bass-line (I-raised IV-IV-III) and a very pretty melody. The bridge is satisfying in the way it works toward a conventional dominant-seventh before the final A, and the words are also strong: "Behind ev'ry cloud there's a so lovely star," the *so lovely* word order unusual but persuasive. There is another gorgeous melody in the show, the opening strain of *No Lover,* which is set in a big portamento that sounds like a moment of sexual bliss, and a release whose last phrase repeats the effect. The other words are a bit arch, but the song is salvageable in the right performance. The best-known song, *I Am Loved,* is indeed cold Porter.

A famous song, *From This Moment On,* was dropped from the show. It's effective, but seems rather strenuous, perhaps because the down-going setting of the title phrase, at the end of four-bar periods, is hard to sing. Porter thought another dropped song, *You Don't Remind Me,* one of his best; the words are indeed direct and attractive, and the song has a fine close.

One of Porter's finest songs was copyrighted in 1966 and published even later, but *Why Don't We Try Staying Home?* actually comes from a 1920s show. Here Porter keeps the melodic line very simple, the rhythm very regular: the words take the spotlight. The song is about a couple of sophisticates who are tired of the social swirl, but there's nothing satirical about it: the pace is deliberate and the lyric touching. "What if we threw a party or two, and asked only you and me?" Some of the charm comes from the compacted rhyme (*why/try*) of the title phrase, which always happens on narrow intervals on successive downbeats. On the last occurrence of the title phrase, Porter stretches the phrase to the higher key-tone, for the final *home,* somehow imparting emotional importance to a simple triad. The words at the end of the main phrases are set on a legato third interval, so that, for example, *home,* one syllable, gets two notes. There is something inherently caressing about this device. The chorus is elegant, but the verse, with two sets of words for two stanzas, is a marvel. It's long, a 32-bar song in itself, and full of complex rhymes, like *incomes/gin comes,* and *fly by/bye-bye.* The verse moves quickly, but with an emotional ritard at the end. The distinction of the song may well be in its reversal of the usual verse–chorus relationship of tempo and tone. Normally, a verse is slowish, ruminative, while the chorus moves ahead declaratively. Here, the opposite obtains. It's a dream of a Porter song—but it was written decades earlier.

We simply record our opinion that the famous Paris-oriented songs from "Can-Can" are bottom-of-the-barrel Porter. The title song, to be sure, is quite persuasive: the off-beat *can-can* is perfect, and the brilliant compound rhymes, especially those that hug the off-the-beat rhythms, are mighty satisfying, even when you know it's an easy with a rhyming dictionary. The songs from Porter's last big Broadway hit, "Silk Stockings," are no better—though *Stereophonic Sound* is a hilarious "big number." The well-known *All of You,* quite like *It's All Right With Me* from "Can-Can," is accomplished and has a characteristic sinuous melodic line; but they are both just smutty songs. *High-Flyin' Wings On My Shoes* from "Les Girls" is one of Porter's good dance-rhythm songs, though the lyrics are tired. Finally, from a television production, "Aladdin" (1958), there is a bizarrely funny song, *Come to the Supermarket In Old Peking.* Porter must have been on some great medication or thinking of Beatrice Lillie when he wrote this one.

IRVING BERLIN (1888–1989)

The case of Berlin is less clear-cut than that of either Arlen or Porter. Berlin was 62 in 1950. Unlike his peers in the Golden Era pantheon, Berlin had always published lots of trivial songs alongside some of the greatest songs ever written, so it isn't surprising that his post-1950 output was variable. From the 1953 film "White Christmas" came a honey of a song, *The Best Things Happen While You're Dancing*. Berlin wrote dozens of great songs about dancing in his career; this is one of them. The song opens with a leisurely version of a Charleston rhythmic figure, a dotted quarter (for "best") followed by an eighth-note tied to a very long note ("things"). Already the song is in motion. Then comes a delightful little break figure on a descending scale (Figure 3.3): Can't you just see the dimpled tread of the feet of Fred Astaire for that dance-down? The bridge is also a winner: "Even guys with two left feet/come out all right if the girl is sweet." The climax comes on the 3 above the upper key-tone, for *dancing*, with three chord changes under it before the song gets to a I chord in anticipation of ending. What a sly-boots, Berlin!

Figure 3.3

Another good film song from the same year is *Love, You Didn't Do Right By Me*, conventional but ineffably charming, probably because of the lavish use of slow triplets to set relaxed, conversational words; for example, "To send me a Joe who had winter and snow in his heart ** wasn't smart." Going back to 1949, the Broadway song *Falling Out of Love Can Be Fun* is a winner, owing to the intricate rhythmic élan with which Berlin treats an unusual take on romance. The words develop a sexual innuendo sort of like your Uncle Charlie's kind of humor, amusing and unobjectionable.

Berlin's songs for the hit musical "Call Me Madam" (1951) were not all top-drawer. *It's a Lovely Day Today* is a charmer, especially at the end with its

chromatically widening intervals for "...except it's a lovely day for saying...."
The most accomplished song in the show is *The Best Thing for You*. The tune
begins as a phrase stretched out in third intervals in a seventh chord; then, coming down, there is a surprising lowered tone. The auditor doesn't perceive the
main key until the fourth eventful bar. This kind of tantalizing opening, when
well done, gives you the feeling that the song has been ongoing for some time;
you're just tuning in at an interesting juncture. The release is short and jubilant,
in the major, and the song ends with no fuss: q.e.d.

You're Just In Love is a contrivance, a duet that works perfectly, and "a rub-
down with a velvet glove" is priceless. The song is technically neat in the way the
two good tunes fit together, the more syncopated into the more regular one, but
it's ultimately banal. It doesn't undercut the genius of Berlin to admit his hokey
side. From 1953 is a charming, naive song, *Sittin' In the Sun,* in casual dotted
rhythm, which manages to concern both the appreciation of nature and the love
of money. The lyric brings these together at the end, in a metaphor for the moon:
"There's a silver dollar in the sky shining down on me."

Berlin wrote for many more years, so it's probable that there are some fine songs
still in the trunk. May the best emerge—and may the lesser ones stay hidden.

RICHARD RODGERS (1902–79)

Richard Rodgers enjoyed some of his greatest success in the second half of the
twentieth century. Some of that success seems to us artistically doubtful, but a
number of late Rodgers songs are among his finest.

To begin with the negatives, some find Rodgers's later songs with Oscar Hammerstein II disappointing: sententious, bland. We concur that there is an honor-
able but heavy quality to much of it, especially rhythmically. And yet this attitude,
songs as conceptually persuasive statements, has always been a part of what the
American popular song spoke to. Big churchy songs like *Climb Ev'ry Mountain*
from "The Sound of Music" (1959) are so well known that we can simply leave
them to their admirers. Another solemn song from that show, the title song, is
hard (though possible) to resist. The tune is commanding, the words more than
competent (despite lines like "a lark that is learning to pray"), the climax at the
end of the release effective. If we don't like it much, it's because the very end is
limp. More a problem to us are the saccharine songs: the faux-folk *Edelweiss,*
the irritating *Do-Re-Mi,* and the so-naive *Sixteen Going On Seventeen.* Even here
we have to admit there are nice touches, like, in *Sixteen,* the portamento phrase
in the last A-section ("telling you what to do," *do* set over two notes) and, at
the end of the song, the two upward sixth intervals, the second set a half-tone
below the first, for "I'll take care of you," again with *I'll* and *care* given two notes.
The lyrics to this song, including a graceful verse, are entirely suitable, though
you can call them condescending if you fundamentally object to the idea of the
song. One can also dislike *My Favorite Things* for its enumeration of rather twee

items like kittens and mittens, and the somewhat abrupt final rhyme; and yet the words, "When the dog barks, when the bee stings," have a nice Elizabethan echo to them. More important, the tune is interesting, obsessive, with lots of notes in each phrase landing lightly on two strong beats per measure, starting as a sort of whirling minor and ending in the major. The perpetual-motion, looping aspect of the tune has appealed to some superlative jazz musicians.

For the film version, Rodgers wrote both words and music to *Something Good.* It's inconsequential verbally, though touching, but his melody is pure Rodgers: graceful, with a buoyant rhythmic surprise at the midpoint of the second eight bars (where a four quarter-note extension replaces the expected long note), and a single out-of-scale note, a raised 4, that brings a special color.

Only a churl could object to the songs from "The King and I" (1951). The cultural police might gibe at the Orientalist theme, but the music is sumptuous. *Shall We Dance* feels like a spinning top, its underlying forceful rhythm an unusual kind of ecossaise or polka. The last period of the song, beginning with "On the clear understanding that this kind of thing can happen," is terrific. *Getting to Know You* also dances, with the striking quick-triplet, multisyllabic upbeat figure (as on *get-ting to*) carried into the brief bridge. Hammerstein is at his best, with phrases like "... all the beautiful and new * things," with the polysyllabic word fitted to those triplets. One can admit that the rhythms of these two songs are very regular, more in the European operetta tradition than the American swing one, but they are elegantly handled. *Hello, Young Lovers* manages to be both deliberate in its main beats and light owing to the dotted notes, as in "**All** *my* good **wish**-*es* are **with** *you to*-**night**," where the boldface indicates the stresses, and the italics the quick notes. In general, Rodgers's late rhythmic approach is to eschew syncopation and strong dotted figures in favor of a larger pattern of sets of quick notes mixed with long notes; in this he is close to his contemporary, Frederick Loewe. All these songs use a small range, no more than an octave or so.

Far more intense is a fascinating ballad, *Something Wonderful.* The meter here is essentially one beat per verbal unit, which gives the song a courtly feel. Rodgers also uses an exotic mode for the melody, with the Lydian raised 4 tone contrasting over and over with the normal 4 of the diatonic scale. A formalized quality results. It is a distinctive Rodgers technique, to use the simple scale with one conspicuous altered tone (an obvious example is *Bali Hai,* again with the raised 4 tritone). If you think it works (we do, here), it is spectacular; if not, it seems forced.

Finally, there are two great love songs, *We Kiss In a Shadow* and *I Have Dreamed.* The former has a fine release, in a surprising key that saves the song from hymnlike stodginess (there is indeed a resemblance in harmonic layout to *We Gather Together to Ask the Lord's Blessing*) and a great melodic leap, a secondary climax set daringly on the third-from-last word, in "Behold how my lover loves me." Even better is *I Have Dreamed*, which attains ecstatic heights near the end, and then finishes with a peculiarly satisfying "I have loved being loved by you." Love ballads featuring a big sweep and a big vocal range don't get better than this.

The other shows from the 1950s were a let-down. From "Me and Juliet" (1953), the big song, *No Other Love*, has boring lyrics, but the tune is very strong, with a proud habanera rhythm. *Keep It Gay* has a good pace and interesting rhythm. "Flower Drum Song" (1958) showed Hammerstein at his most preachy. *I Enjoy Being a Girl* has a nice scampering tune but dreadful words: the "feminine rhymes" *female/free male* and *hairdo/air do* are not technically bad, just deplorable in their reference. By contrast, in *Don't Marry Me*, Rodgers reverts to his 1930s 2/4 verve rather than his 1950s 4/4 regularity, and Hammerstein responds with a Hartlike brashness. *Sunday* is a classic American nostalgia song, in absolutely the right time-honored step-and-drag rhythm. A nice touch is that the second eight-bar period ends four beats early (at "breathing the hours away"). The use of irregular phrase lengths in a basically eight-bar-unit song produces an effect that is a kind of large-scale syncopation. The middle section then begins with a new, equally danceable rhythm. Hammerstein uses simple alliteration very well in this song.

Love, Look Away is the finest. The chorus opens on what proves to be the leading-tone, the raised 7 of the main key; in retrospect, that's what gives the yearning quality to the song, along with the resigned slow-two feel, even though the song is written in 4/4. The "leading-tone" leads nowhere, except into a pattern of chains of thirds (p. 28), over and over, playing around the key for a very long time: the tonic note is withheld until m.8, on *sea*, but even here, it is not perceived as the tonic, owing to the harmony (Figure 3.4). It's a remarkable effect:

Figure 3.4

one keeps hearing the highly dissonant opening tone as the "home" tone of the song. It is what gives the song its wistful, ambiguous feeling. After all, the song is overtly about a longing that love leave the speaker alone, which conveys an inherently double message. An exceedingly graceful, grave bridge is set right in the same vocal range as—and with a rhythmic pattern comparable to—the A-sections, so that it all seems like one unbroken line. The end of the bridge leads scalewise right back to the potent unstable tone that begins A. The song ends beautifully, with a sounding of the basic scale, up over the tonic, then down below it, for repetitions of *look away*. The lyricist's contribution is impeccable. One way in which the song attains a calm, resigned feeling is that Hammerstein sets his rhymes unusually far apart: "Love, look away," starting a phrase at m.1, sounds against "Call it a day," starting the phrase at m.9. It's a great song.

Hammerstein died in 1960. In 1965, Rodgers worked with Stephen Sondheim on the show, "Do I Hear a Waltz?" We find the title song memorable. It's one of Rodgers's fast waltzes, really a scherzo. There is an arresting rhythmic feature at the beginning (Figure 3.5). The title phrase occurs first with a conventional stress

Figure 3.5

pattern, an upbeat to *I* as the one strong beat (with an understood shortened third beat for a waltz lilt). Then there is an interjection, and the next *I* begins on a weak beat, which in turn gives *hear* an unusual stress. Anyone else would have left the second beat in m.4 blank, set *but* as another upbeat, and brought *I* again to the strong position. We think this kind of Brahmsian ambiguity, with a three- and a four-metric in effect at the same time, stimulating, though some listeners could find resetting the meter awkward. The release to this song is irresistible, with Rodgers playing happily with a string of chromatic alterations around tone 5 of the key of the release, and Sondheim obliging with giddy words:

> Magical, mystical miracle! —
> Can it be?
> Is it true?

Things are impossibly lyrical! —
Is it me?
No, it's you!

The rest of his lyric hovers on the edge of losing control (*impossibly* is the telling word), giving the entire song an amusingly hysterical tone. The song would end too abruptly, were it not for the way in which the writers again reset the meter by inserting "Oh, boy!" before the last time the title phrase is heard (that "save" occurs in the score, but not in the separate sheet music, alas). This song is rather like the title song to "She Loves Me," in that both title songs from the same era are almost manic in their drive. We like them.

The Rodgers — Sondheim show included a good big ballad, *Take the Moment,* in which Rodgers achieves a typical "sculpting" technique. In some of his songs this means using one unusual tone. Here, it means building the melody on 8 (the upper tonic), 5, and 3—the most basic three tones in the scale—and momentarily lowering or raising each one a half or whole step. The song has a wide range, a bridge that ends gracefully, and a slow, seductive quasi-tango rhythm in the voice line. The lyrics are restrained, for a carpe diem theme: they use parallelism judiciously, notably in the sequence of verbs *take, hug,* and *hold,* each beginning successive phrases.

A song for three women (singable by one person), *Moon In My Window,* is lovely. It too begins on the raised 7, avoiding the tonic for a long time. The proficient lyric shows the transition from trusting love to a state more skeptical and then resigned: "You'll be back tomorrow—I can wait," and then "Come again tomorrow—I will still be here." Finally, a medium-tempo number, *We're Gonna Be All Right,* is worth looking up. As heard in the show, it is run-of-the-mill, with competent words in a moderately positive mode. The original words, however, involve several stanzas of spectacularly mordant lyrics, with a dark view indeed of long-term relationships.[4]

We have left until now the songs from the 1962 Broadway show "No Strings," which not only had a number of good songs but lyrics written by Rodgers himself. The best-known song is probably *The Sweetest Sounds*, which employs a fast four-beat meter without seeming frantic. This is another looping tune beloved by jazz musicians. Rodgers's lyrics here are at least as good as what Hammerstein might have achieved for the subject matter. *Look No Further* is interesting in its rhythm, with very deliberate single or double stress coming immediately after "empty" beats; the effect is not that of syncopation, but of a stylized dance form. These stresses occur for words that can be heard as interpolations, such that the melody would make sense if they were all removed. It is another Rodgers chain-of-thirds tune. *Maine*, in a leisurely clip-clopping rhythm and with references in the lyric to sleighs and horses, seems like a wintry version of the

Surrey With the Fringe On Top. The words are all charming (e.g, "Far away, 'cross the bay / Goes an old train: Mainly I do like Maine.")

There are also two medium swing songs with words that express unusual attitudes—for popular music. In *Loads of Love* the speaker "just want(s) money, and then some money, and loads of lovely love." The tune, however, is merry, with a striking use of the raised 5, and a Stravinsky-like disjunctive quality to the voice line. Even odder is a bitter song, *An Orthodox Fool*, in which the speaker admits to being a disaster at love, in vehement terms: "I'm a young victim of senility / I am destiny's tool." It's not funny, but it's not actually unpleasant, because the music is jaunty in its tune and tempo. It is interesting to speculate where this verbal tone came from: it is certainly not Hammerstein, but it's not Hart either. Smack in the middle of the song, the singer switches to 16 bars of the great ballad from the show, *Nobody Told Me*, which adds to the psychological complexity of the song.

That ballad is a beauty, with another of Rodgers's memorable melody lines "sculpted" by the well-placed use of strong accidentals, contoured so that they are gratifying to sing and easy to really "hear." After a calm and entirely diatonic verse ("Night is the only time / With no one to sing to"), the chorus begins (Figure 3.6).

Figure 3.6

Here again we have the deliberate rhythm, the hurrying-over of the tonic note (D) in favor of the out-of-scale D-sharp, and a powerful chromatic ascent. The song is ABAA, with a rather muted, almost pensive, climax halfway through the final A ("No, not even you"). However, the B-section, though shifted up a tone—striking in itself, because it brings a contrasting key into play abruptly— uses the same melodic phrase shape and rhythm as in the A-sections. Thus the entire song seems one long interior monologue, managing to be big in impact within the compass of an octave plus half-step. Rodgers, at this stage, seemed to be at his best with love ballads of renunciation or loss, like this one and *Love, Look Away*.

Rodgers also wrote words and music to a very pretty song, *Willing and Eager*, for a 1962 film. The melody begins liltingly with an unusual chord and a melody tone leading to V, and then does it again in the second bar with a different harmonization. The words are fine.

Rodgers's career dropped off after 1965, with a number of failed shows and songs that are mostly unpublished. Nevertheless, of all the first-rank Golden Era composers active after 1950, he had the largest output of excellent songs, comparable to those of Arlen but more numerous. If one likes the songs with Hammerstein, Rodgers stayed on top of the heap after midcentury; if not, he is still right up there.

ARTHUR SCHWARTZ (1900–84)

Although he wrote such well-known standards as *Dancing In the Dark* and *You and the Night and the Music*, Arthur Schwartz is seldom mentioned in the same breath as the other top-tier composers, still active in 1950, like Berlin, Porter, or Arlen. One reason surely is that his songs, many written with lyricist Howard Dietz, were often better than the shows he wrote them for. In fact, like Vernon Duke and Burton Lane, Schwartz at his best provided some of the finest writing in the classic popular song literature.

An almost completely overlooked show, "Park Avenue" (1946), slightly predates the time-frame of this book, but should be mentioned because of some fine songs with lyrics by Ira Gershwin. *There's No Holding Me* is a happy song of young love. It's in E flat major with a 22-bar verse, followed by a standard 32-bar chorus. The verse is marked *leisurely*, but the words are confident and up-beat, indicating a sort of Park Avenue approach to enthusiasm. That confidence reaches its peak in m.11 of the verse, from which high point the notes of a major-seventh chord descend on the words "put me to the test." The chorus, although marked *slowly*, moves along as a rather jaunty ditty, using mostly the first five tones of the scale, and reverting often (perhaps too often) to "There's no holding me / If I can keep on holding you." The chorus words are fine, but the conceptual "hook" is somewhat obvious.

For the Life of Me has a quite talky verse that is lyric-based and plot-specific, but the chorus in ABAC form is a musical romp. It starts right in with melodic enthusiasm on a big upbeat figure and doesn't stop for reflection. Gershwin cleverly plays on the song's title words as both a modifying clause, equivalent to *By golly!*, and as a predicate (*life* as *lifetime*), and there are many nice turns in the lyric ("I look at you and then / I pinch myself again. . . .").

These two songs are blithe. Schwartz changes the mood with *Goodbye to All That*, from the same show. It is a heartbreakingly beautiful song, the melodic range of which complements the emotional range, constricted to an octave. The 16-bar verse is a gem of understatement. The melody hunkers down over only small intervals, matching constrained, chill words (Figure 3.7a,b). Following a brief, mournful vamp at the end of (b), the chorus begins, using the same lim-

(a)

(In a leisurely mood)

Don't look now, but sum-mer's o-ver; The North Wind is here.

(b)

you can't fight Cit-y Hall.

Figure 3.7

ited range. Phrases alternate quickly between major and minor (Figure 3.7c). Gershwin gives us a particularly touching lyric in mm.17–24: "The years ahead / We *never will* share / Our golden anniversary / Melts *into thin* air," with sad slow triplets as indicated. The valediction of the song tries to be in major,

(c) *(Smoothly and not too fast)*

The things we planned, Good-bye to all that.

We built on sand, Good-bye to all that.

Figure 3.7 Continued.

but fails. There are few songs that describe love lost as poignantly as this one. There is a second stanza of touching words.

In the early 1950s Schwartz's collaboration with Dorothy Fields produced some good songs that ranged from the comic vaudevillian, to the wistfully amusing, to the dramatic theater ballad. In the 1951 film, "Excuse My Dust," there is an amusing little love song, *That's For Children,* with some priceless Fields lines. The chorus has a childlike nursery-rhyme motif of repeated notes to accompany a sweetly cynical take on (very) young love. The release is wonderful: "Pressing flowers and April Fooling / Holding hands while the fudge is cooling * I may start drooling."[5] There is also a wistful small song, unpublished, from 1950 called *Where Do I Go From You?* It has a conventional eight-bar opening with two contrasting four-bar phrases, which sounds like a normal A-section, but then a contrasting eight-bar section in a remote key that eventually leads back to A. The A-sections have different sets of words, the B only one: thus, $A_1BA_2BA_3$. The song is about disappointment in love: "It isn't fun, so neatly ended...but I won't be befriended...." It's slight and odd, but sweet.

The Broadway show "A Tree Grows In Brooklyn" (1951), also with Fields, is one of Schwartz's best scores. Wilder found the ballad *Make the Man Love Me* "a gem of tenderness and warmth." We concur. The verse is unusually musical, and the release, in a new key, is beautiful and quite passionate. Another ballad from this show, *I'll Buy You a Star,* has similar qualities, but whereas the former song ends on a hopeful but quiet note, this song is expansive and self-assured, with a big finish: "But I won't stop until I buy the moon." This fine score also included three songs that allowed Dorothy Fields to kick up her lyrical heels. *Look Who's Dancing,* in fast cut-time, has an infectious music-hall beat and big, bold intervals in both verse and chorus. Much of the time there are crisp words set to four stresses to a bar in strict time, which works up a palpable drive. *Love Is the Reason* is similarly boisterous, with funny, down-to-earth words of sweet bawdiness ("Love was the gleam in poppa's eye"). The printed music allows it to be done as a duet, two voices in canon. Stephen Sondheim has listed as a favorite the amusing song, *He Had Refinement,* for which Fields wrote one of theater's best comic lyrics: "In the water at Coney Island was our first embrace / When my water wings flew off and hit him in the face. He introduced himself before he put them back in place / He had refinement."

"By the Beautiful Sea" (1954) was another Schwartz — Fields collaboration. The light-hearted songs in this show outnumbered the serious ballads and included the sassy *Old Enough To Love*: "I wouldn't let you sleep upon my shoulder ** if you were older." *Happy Habit* is a friendly little song that includes the only instance we know of the use of the word *indefatigable* in lyric writing. *I'd Rather Wake Up By Myself* is a fine example of Fields's genius for encapsulating a situation in a few words: "That fresh air fiend was healthy, but not too bright /

My wifely duties would have been very light / Inhale, exhale, was all we'd do all night." From the same show, *More Love Than Your Love* is a soaring ballad, somewhat slowed down by the frequently repeated main melodic line—nicely tempered, however, by key changes here and there. The song has an odd interlude with words from Shakespeare's "A Midsummer's Night Dream" set to a musically stiff melody, as if it were the verse to an old-fashioned operetta.

The memorable song from this show, however, is the magnificent ballad, *Alone Too Long.* If the Schwartz — Gershwin *Goodbye to All That* is a great elegiac song, the Schwartz — Fields *Alone Too Long* is a great exultant one. First it expresses the fear of seeking love; then, in the bridge, it gathers courage (musically, if not verbally); and in the last A-section, it knows that the loved one understands. The main tune is a big lyrical arc, cresting first on tone 2, then 3, then 5; and at the climax of the song, at the very end, it reaches to 6 (Figure 3.8). Part of the beauty lies in the simplicity of the vowels in key words that rhyme or chime: *dared/scared, known/alone/flown, afraid/faded,* together with some "crunchy" monosyllables like *talk/walk.* The lyric is an example of very simple language with enormous impact. A sensitive singer will use a lot of *rubato* for this great theater song.[6]

The film "Dangerous When Wet" (1952) saw a rare collaboration of Schwartz and lyricist Johnny Mercer. *I Got Out of Bed On the Right Side* is a long song packed with energy and good humor. It's in the form $A_1A_2BA_1A_2$, with the second A_2 extended to accommodate a series of high notes. The unmistakable Mercer style is evident in the B-section, in phrases like: "...eggs are beamin' sunny-side

Figure 3.8

up ... coffee's steamin', money- side up." Schwartz's tune takes right off with successive phrases that step up one note each time, getting out of bed on "the right side," then "the bright side," and then "the light side," until a high point is reached and the melody tumbles down in a favorite Schwartz device of intervals of thirds to the words "I'm havin' a wonderful day." It's a happy song, reminiscent of the Schwartz — Dietz *A Shine On Your Shoes* (1932).

From the 1963 show "Jennie" we can recommend the touching song *Where You Are*, with lyrics by Dietz. The knowledgeable reader will have noticed that we have skipped over the 1961 show "The Gay Life." Wilder extensively discussed this marvelous score in his book; and we fully agree with his views. Three songs from the score were *For the First Time*, *Something You Never Had Before*, and *Why Go Anywhere At All*. The last of these is one of the great ones, with fine élan, but they are all first-rate.

VERNON DUKE (1903–69)

Another great melodist whose songs were well known long before 1950 was Duke, whose lyrical gifts were first-class and whose harmonic sophistication was unexcelled. Although he wrote up-tempo or decisively rhythmic songs such as *I Like the Likes of You*, *Taking a Chance On Love*, and the Caribbean-flavored *Island In the West Indies*, Duke's great achievements were in romantic ballads that combine memorable melodies with delicately luscious chords, as with *April in Paris*.

Wilder overlooked a 1944 song, *The Love I Long For*; a pity, since it has a fine tune in the A-section built on intervals of the third, which gives the words by Howard Dietz ("The love I long for I've no right to demand ... is a thing set apart") a deliberate, contemplative character. The song opens in D major, but the bridge keeps moving to F sharp minor and B major. Rather daringly, the return from B to D major at the opening of the last A-section is unmodulated: the tone D sharp simply moves to D natural. It is a device familiar in Schubert, not in popular song.

One of the most beautiful songs of Duke's career, *Ages Ago*, was an incidental song used in a production of a play in 1957. Duke supplied the words for this song: they are generally fine, but sag in quality in the final six bars. That is a minor blemish in this extraordinarily beautiful song. It opens with a statement of nostalgia so delicate that it avoids any suggestion of bathos (Figure 3.9). The verse and all the A-sections of the song use only the occasional, telling rich chord, and avoid the marked chromaticism of much of Duke's work, an avoidance that is appropriate to this situation of love recollected in tranquility. The release, however, is full of rather daring harmonic movement, appropriate to the speaker's sudden contrasting pang of longing. There are many subtleties. In this AABA song, the first A is slightly shortened, the final A slightly prolonged.

Figure 3.9

The striking inflection of the melodic line (the redoubling of *ages* at mm.5–6) is matched, in its effect, in the final A by an asymmetrical rhyme (*change* / *dang*-er). The climax is set on 3 above the upper key-tone. As with *The Love I Long For*, modulation is not effected between phrases or in "empty" (voice silent) bars, as is normally the case in classic popular song, but is either inconspicuously done in the middle of a long phrase (from C to E major in A$_2$), or directly (from the use of a C-sharp to a C-natural), as the A$_3$ begins. This is a great ballad that should be well known.

For a Broadway revue, "Two's Company" (1952), Duke wrote some songs with Sammy Cahn, a serviceable rather than an inspired lyricist. *It Just Occurred to Me* is a medium-tempo cheery song about Spring, marred by some too-cute rhymes (*fancy turns/dancey turns*; *rhymable/sublimable*), which seems to be a hazard in Spring songs (cf. the DePaul — Mercer *Spring, Spring, Spring*). But the release is elegant. For this show, Duke also used previously created work with the fine verse-writer and lyricist, Ogden Nash. One of their songs, *Just Like a Man*, has a witty set of words, but it's a rather rudimentary tune; the song was obviously special material for the star.

There was, however, a great Duke — Nash ballad in this show, *Roundabout*. It is perhaps his finest melody. The song is interesting in having a very difficult, constantly modulating, highly chromatic verse (too difficult for most theater singers) that leads into a perfectly simple, poised vocal line for the opening of the chorus. That line, reflecting the phrase *round about*, simply uses (in the key of F) adjacent steps of the scale, first in the upper octave, then below the key-tone. But these conventional intervals are so wreathed with appoggiaturas, notes a half- or whole-step distant, that the entire line becomes a sequence of slow, graceful turns. (We count six essential tones before the first half-cadence, but the actual line uses 26 notes.) Once again, Duke effects the key change for the release subtly, sneaking it in within the last phrase of A$_2$. That B-section is a winner, moving the song smartly ahead, with piano arpeggio underneath, in a sequence of keys modulating smartly from A to F major with quite wonderful chords, for example, under *danc*-ing (Figure 3.10). It is a typical Duke pattern—a poised, conventional opening melody, combined with a highly creative release—that makes his best songs beloved by good singers.[7]

Duke's *Who's to Blame* (words and music, 1951) is as harmonically and melodically elegant as *Autumn in New York*, which it resembles at the end of the verse. The chorus, basically in C, opens over a ii chord, a distinctive Duke touch, and for half its length tries to go to D flat and then D minor, all of it over a beguinelike rhythm. The speaker reports that the world "... seemed hopelessly tame, and it's you who's to blame." A rapturously sad song, oddly unknown.

There are some delightful songs from "The Littlest Revue" (1956). *You're Far From Wonderful*, with Nash, begins with a typical lavish, wandering verse that is already undergoing modulation when the voice line comes in. The verse concludes with a classic Nash rhyme: *churlish* with *girlish*. The chorus begins with a strong syncopated figure (for "You're far ** from wonderful"), and that dipping, dancey feeling lasts throughout the song. The bridge starts conventionally, but ends on a surprising tone of the scale. Nash's words are charming, a bit goofy.

Figure 3.10

This is a little-known song that is better than most standards. There is a gem of a little song, *Madly In Love*, about a young girl with a yen for an older boy. It begins irresistibly, with a silly Nash couplet ("His name is Davey, his hair is wavy") and with a typical Duke harmonic surprise, the first vocable (but only the first) set right on the dominant of the main key. The rhythm is also notable: there is only one strong beat per bar in the A-sections, two in the release.

For a 1963 revival of the much earlier musical, "Cabin In the Sky," Duke wrote words and music for a neat song in Gershwin-swing style, *Livin' It Up*. It's an uncomplicated joy ("Mister Gloom is leaving town...."). Some of the words echo the Ira Gershwin lyric for the 1936 Duke classic, *I Can't Get Started*.

Finally, there is an elegant unpublished song, *Small World* (1955). It sounds melodically and harmonically conventional as it begins, though there is a graceful triplet bracketing the key-tone in m.2. As it goes on, harmonic felicities come in, and the song ends with one of Duke's superb extensions, involving a new melodic figure over a touching chord sequence (Figure 3.11). Duke's was among the finest talents in the genre. There should be a Duke Songbook.

Figure 3.11

BURTON LANE (1912–97)

Like Arthur Schwartz and Vernon Duke, Lane had a gift for tunes, like *How About You?*, that speak with poise and simplicity. His harmonic style was different. One could call the chords of Schwartz or Duke chewy or chunky, and their chord progressions luscious. Lane used a plainer style, suiting his personality: his harmonies have an open ring to them, and his songs bespeak a benign view of human nature.

Although his career was thriving by the early 1940s, Lane continued at a high level after midcentury. Wilder singles out *Too Late Now* (words, Alan Jay Lerner) as a great ballad. From the same 1951 film, "Royal Wedding," there are other good songs. A song for Astaire, *Ev'ry Night at Seven*, is a buoyant joy, with a fine verse and a brilliant transition from the release back to the final A. *You're All the World to Me* is a list song, but a blithe, superior one, with a great syncope at the start of A-section phrases. From a 1953 film, "Give a Girl a Break," came *Applause, Applause*, written with Ira Gershwin. It also is light weight and falls into the crowded category of show-biz numbers, but the treatment is droll, almost wacky, with Gershwin supplying terse rhymes to Lane's short phrases. Gershwin stars with *In Our United State*. It's a basically silly song, punning on marriage and politics, but it's funny and has a good release. In a marital counterpart to taxes, "You can't withhold on me, I can't withhold on you."

Together with Dorothy Fields, Lane wrote a delightful rhythmic tune, *Have Feet Will Dance*, for a television production. The concept of the song is young-at-heart and charming, about a young lover wanting to sweep his or her date away: "…all I need is a chance: have arms, have eyes, have feet ** will dance."

In 1965, Lane and Lerner created a marvelous score for the Broadway show, "On a Clear Day You Can See Forever." The show was peculiar, owing to its odd subject-matter—ESP, reincarnation, and the like—but it gave these writers the chance to produce some highly distinctive songs, virtually all of them wonderful. To begin with, the title song is one of the irresistible, sweeping title songs of the post-1950 period. Title songs don't have to be memorable, but it's good for everyone when they are, like *She Loves Me* or *Do I Hear a Waltz?* On the page, the opening device of a pure chain of thirds is one that has been used many times, often by Rodgers, and it happens all over again in mm. 8–11 (Figure 3.12). That

Figure 3.12

might get boring, but then one hears the extraordinary richness of the C-with-lowered-7 chord, m. 3 (a chord that could move the song to another key, but does not, it just deepens the spectrum of the main key) and the slight chromatic alteration of the first note of the second phrase, and one knows that this is already a special song. The bridge is short, only eight bars with two graceful eighth-note turns; the final A is eight bars with a slight extension for finality. The climax of the song is in that last section, and is achieved by the simplest of means: the apex notes in the first A-sections have been A and D, now the line goes up to E. On the page, also, the words seem unexciting. But when voiced, *clear day* and *see* are pure vowels totally appropriate to their referent, and in the bridge the pattern, within two bars, of *hear-near-heard* has an enticing playfulness.

There is also an uncomplicated minor-mode waltz, opening (once again) in a chain of thirds and then stepping up that figure a fourth higher. It's a song addressed, several times over, to an eponymous *Melinda*. It all ought to sound banal, although the rareness of *Melinda* would help overcome the curse of "name" songs. But it doesn't, it's beautiful, and when the song opens, at the release, into a glorious relative major, the song becomes memorable. The words are unremarkable but just fine.

Both those songs have a grave, deliberate quality that takes them somehow beyond their innate elements. By contrast, there are stand-out songs from this show that are strongly rhythmic-comedic. Listening to *What Did I Have That I Don't Have?* is like watching the classiest woman you know do a bump-and-grind routine: it comes out sexy, sweet, and adorable. It's built on a vamp of deliberate triplets plus a dotted figure (the bump) and a syncopated grind. The release wails: a single note held to lung-busting length over a flaunting pattern of absolutely in-time triplet drumming: "Where **** can I go to repair / All the wear and the tear ****?" The lyric is wonderful, with rhymes like *track of / lack of / knack of,* set 8 and 16 measures apart, respectively, like a gong sounding in the distance. The only similar song that's this much fun is the Styne — Sondheim *You Gotta Have a Gimmick.*

Even more endearingly bizarre is *Hurry! It's Lovely Up Here!* This is another big-finish number, sung by someone who discovers she can talk to plants still below ground. (Don't ask, just enjoy; Figure 3.13.) In this long, rhythmically irresistible piece, the opening strain of each phrase corresponding to (a) ends with a strong double stress, permitting equivalently strong far-apart compound rhymes: *compare with / share with / ev'rywhere with.* After some delicious rhyming ("Come give at least a / Preview of East-a," or, in another stanza, "Push up, azalea / Don't be a fail-ure"), the big finish of the song starts with a vaudeville-style "break" (b), and eases into a last "Hurry! it's love *** ly *** here—," the final three syllables stretched over six arms-out-wide measures. Like *What Did I Have?* it's hokey, it's funny, and it's wonderful.

There is one other rollicking song from the show, called *Wait Till We're Sixty-Five*, a funny little comic scherzo and a fine example of music-hall style. It's a paean to the joys of old age: "If you ever thought you had fun**at twenty-one**wait till we're sixty-five." The chord structure is simple; the whole song can be heard as being in the tonic key, C major, with only a brief bridge. That bridge is slightly unusual in that it is pitched below the level of the rest of the song, on the lower dominant. There is thus a slight relaxation to the bridge instead of the more usual stepping-up of tension.

The distinctive rhythmic feature occurs right at the opening (Figure 3.14). The two reversals of stress on *thir-ty* and for-*ty*, with the two higher notes counteracting the two verbal trochees, the way *then* comes too late, off the beat,

Figure 3.13

while *wait* comes, too soon, on the beat—these touches give the song such an off-balance, complex rhythm that one never quite knows where one is. The song is lively partly because it is *not* consistently syncopated. The lyric has many droll moments, including the immortal "If the children never mature / What the hell, the bonds will, so we're secure."

Ten, twen- ty, thir- ty___then we're for- ty, wait till we're six - ty five

Figure 3.14

One more good song from this show is *Come Back To Me*, a strong tune with a rather Latin rhythm and an eccentric point of view: "Tell your flow'rs you will phone, let your dog walk alone...."

It would be hard to match this score, and that did not happen. Lane and Lerner did create a fine song, *One More Walk Around the Garden* (1979), another instance of the fervent simplicity we have alluded to in Lane and Lerner. It is a gravely beautiful stanzaic song about the end of life. It opens with a strain of musing: "That old April yearning...I have a longing to wander." This long section has a melody with a pure, waltzlike sound in the minor; but it's in slow 4/4 time, and the reflective words are grouped with an extra beat giving space between them. We then move into the parallel major, from E minor directly into a radiant E major, for "One more walk around the garden...until I dream no more...." Then once more back into a minor and then its major, for "one more rose before I say goodbye and close the garden gate." The majesty, and pathos, of this poignant song are in how it winds its way through these alternating sections. This is not a pop song, it is valedictory Schubert.[8]

HARRY WARREN (1893–1981)

Another fine songwriter active after 1950 was and remains underappreciated. Rather, everyone knows Harry Warren's songs—*I Only Have Eyes for You, Lullaby of Broadway*, or the sublime *The More I See You*—but few know who wrote them. No doubt this is because many of his songs were film songs, incidental even to the films they were in.

With his long-time collaborator Mack Gordon, Warren wrote some good songs for a 1950 musical, "Summer Stock." *Friendly Star* may be a bit trite in concept, but it is a lovely song, with a melting release, an elegant transition at the end, and a sweet coda. *You Wonderful You* (words, Jack Brooks and Saul Chaplin) seems at first like a standard 2/4 "light bounce" number, but the bounce is real, the tune is graceful, the bridge is a joy, and the tap dance "break" in the final eight bars is delightful. A 1952 movie song with Leo Robin, *A Flight of Fancy*, has a pleasing though square opening melody, followed by a remarkable bridge that moves with minimal preparation into the minor, then back to major for the last A-section. This abrupt harmonic movement is also a feature of the transition into, and out of, the bridge of *Why Is Love So Crazy*, an exceptionally fine song written with lyricist Arthur Freed for a 1950 film. Basically, the song is all A-sections moved around tonally. The opening melody starts on 2 of the scale (always graceful), and uses only tones 1, 2, 3 over chords that also change only from I to a nonmodulating V^7 for the first eight bars. The second section introduces accidentals into the voice line, and the chords move all over the place (Figure 3.15). The lyric is more than competent. A song like this places Warren into the first rank of classic pop composers. Had he always had lyricists of the caliber of Mercer (see below), his songs from this period would surely be well-known.

Figure 3.15

Going back a bit in time, there is a film song from 1947, *Spring Isn't Everything* (words by Ralph Blane). It's a very good ballad, whose message is "If you're together / Life is a golden ring." Once again, the bridge goes right to your emotions. A 1949 song with Ira Gershwin, *There Is No Music*, is a minor-key beauty whose opening strain sounds quite like Ann Ronnell's *Willow, Weep For Me*. The lyric is understated and subtle, closing with "Salty tears glisten, all night I listen / But there's no music for me."

Warren's last important score was with Johnny Mercer, for the 1951 "The Belle of New York," an Astaire film. It's full of charming work. Warren's tune for *Baby Doll* is catchy, to say the least, in a lilting four-beat meter. The tune is full of lifts (like the last vowel of *baby* set on surprising accidentals) and empty-beat pauses (e.g., "I'm taking you off * the shelf / I'm showing you off * myself"). In the fine verse, Mercer shows off his skill at compound rhymes (*platitude/attitude/gratitude*): they register not as studied, but lovable. *Naughty But Nice* is full of period references, has a saucy tune, and is a tour de force for Mercer; for example, rhyming (Eva) *Tanguay* with *gangway*.

The Warren — Mercer song that should be a "standard" is the marvelous *I Wanna Be a Dancin' Man*. It is classier than Warren's *Lullaby of Broadway*, a similarly dance-focused, far more famous, number. The tune is highly rhythmic, basically medium-tempo but so sharply contoured that it can rev up to high speed or slow to a soft-shoe without losing quality. The basic notion is that of a dancer: "Gonna leave my footsteps on the sands of time." Along the way, the songwriters show lots of moxie, at the end of the song by prolonging an important word (*sands*) and extending the phrase beyond its predicted number of beats, separating *rhythm* from *and rhyme* (Figure 3.16). The song is a joy, and ought to be known to all who love—well, song-and-dance.[9]

Figure 3.16

JOHNNY MERCER (1909–76)

Throughout this book, readers will find many references to songs written by this gifted man with any number of composers, some important, some less so. It is not necessary to argue the point that the lyricist is as important as the composer in writing superior songs. Here we cover some songs not elsewhere treated.

With Hoagy Carmichael, Mercer wrote the famous film song, *In the Cool Cool Cool of the Evening* (1951), it is very offhand, but the little-known verse is more venturesome than the chorus. In 1962, Carmichael and Mercer, for a film, wrote *Just for Tonight*, which has a lovely, relaxed melody. With Gene de Paul, Mercer did the complete score for "Seven Brides For Seven Brothers" (1954). Most of the songs are, by intent, cornpone in flavor, but impressive for all that. *When You're in Love* is a short, pretty, naive song in slow cut-time. There are a couple of good songs in 3/4 time. *June Bride* has an excellent melody, and Mercer invokes "by the light of the silvery moon" and "Mendelssohn's tune." *Wonderful, Wonderful Day* is a waltz that works up a fine momentum; it has exultant, nonfancy words, very deftly set at the end of the bridge so as to provide a natural ritard before the final A-section. *Spring, Spring, Spring* is a formula song about that season, with a standard strong dotted rhythm; Mercer's lyrics are tongue-in-cheek, involving an "antelope who feels that he can't elope," and so on in that delightful vein.

Also with de Paul (1919–88), a talented songwriter, is *Namely You*. The composer used a graceful vocal line, a steady medium beat, and a mostly narrow range to throw emphasis on the title phrase (and variants thereof), and it works better than one might imagine. (I Wish It Could Be) *Otherwise*, also from "Li'l Abner" (1956), is a slight ABAC song with a striking opening motif, made from a spread-out dominant seventh chord (Figure 3.17). The B release is a beauty, with a carefully offhand-sounding Mercer lyric,

The song *Drinking Again* (1962, music by Doris Tauber), would captivate just by its title, but the writers were smart enough to keep the song away from bathos: life does go on after the lover leaves, but somehow it feels better to be "Drinking again / And thinking of when you left me." The tune uses a lot of short

Figure 3.17

chromatic lines with jazz progressions underneath. Mercer also supplied lyrics (1962) for Michel LeGrand's song, *Once Upon a Summertime*, a slow waltz with a good tune about fondly remembered love (it was "as if the mayor had offered me the key to Paris!"). The title phrase actually begins the verse, fairly unusual in this genre, though it comes back at cadences in the chorus.

Mercer wrote a number of songs by himself, of which *Dream* (1945) is perhaps the most famous. It's a very simple ABAB song with an immaculate lyric that seems to make its way directly into memory as the kind of minimalist song that might have been written as far back as 1890. Almost as well known is *Something's Gotta Give*, written for one of Astaire's last films, in 1955. It has an intricately syncopated voice line that amounts to little more than a series of noodlings, with lots of repeated notes, set at various points of the octave. Verbally, the charm comes from the use of rather high-falutin' polysyllabic words like *irresistible, immovable, implacable*, which don't slow down, in fact they point up, the metrical precision of the voice line—perfect for a light-voiced singer like Astaire. The song sounds terrible when "belted."

I Wanna Be In Love Again (1964) is a bouncy, sly number; *be in love* is certainly a euphemism for stronger pleasures. The words are Mercer at his wittiest (e.g., "...the chills again...the million porcupine quills again," with lots of interior rhyme). He is also responsible for *I Fought Every Step of the Way* (1950), one of those "musical-comedy" songs, amusingly off-color but not raunchy, where the girl knows, in the sexual battle, to admit defeat. The tune is fine; the lyrics are top-of-the-line (e.g., "He was pretty shifty...and he could shift with either hand.")

A song dating from 1962, *If You Come Through*, is interesting: it is by Mercer and Rube Bloom, the composer (with Mercer) of *Day In, Day Out* and other excellent songs going back to the 1930s. It is not one of Mercer's best lyrics, and the song has trouble ending, but is worth knowing. From a briefly visible Broadway show "Foxy" (1964), with music by Robert Emmett Dolan, there is a rollicking number about the joys of being (newly) rich, *Rolling In Oil*; a moderate, rather banal ballad, *Talk to Me Baby*; and a very strong song, *I'm Way Ahead of the Game*, a medium up-tempo ballad with one of Mercer's excellent lyrics, two stanzas for the chorus plus a fine verse.[10] Mercer's collaboration with Dolan went back to at least 1946, with *And So To Bed*, an evocative song about remembering a loved one ("The moon descends...the music ends"). It has a pure melodic quality, in both verse and chorus, like a Christmas carol. From the 1949 show, "Texas Lil' Darlin'," there is a pleasant ballad, *A Month of Sundays*, whose A-section bass-line moves up steadily in half-steps. Best of all, with Dolan, is *Chimney Corner Dream* (1951). The lyric includes "Oh, gee, how corny can you get!"—and that's the charm. The song opens with an example of the voice line figure toying with intervals almost in the major triad, over a minor chord built on ii. It's a naive song of great charm.

Hoagy Carmichael and Gene de Paul

Carmichael, a famous and distinguished composer (most famously, *Star Dust*), wrote relatively little after 1950. A film song from 1951, *My Resistance Is Low* (words, Harold Adamson), is a medium-fast waltz with a release that has a pretty progression of step-down chords. Also with Adamson, from 1957, is *Winter Moon*, a slight but appealing song about being unloved and lonely. It's in the minor, with raised 7, and the tune recalls Matt Dennis's *Angel Eyes*. The concept for *Serenade to Gabriel*, written with Vick Knight, 1957, is that great jazz players resident in Heaven play nightly on the celestial radio station. What with Bix Beiderbecke, Bunny Berigan, Eddie Lang, Fats Waller, and others, "…think what's in store for little ole me and you." A nice conceit, and a long, loving song with great chords in a relaxed loping rhythm; inevitably it reminds one of Dave Frishberg's *Dear Bix*.

A well-known song by de Paul with Sammy Cahn, 1954, is *Teach Me Tonight*. It's a good example of a suggestive but naïve song, in light rock&roll style, expressing the persona of a very young girl, and lends itself to a noncondescending vocal approach and a jazz piano treatment with barrel-house left hand.

JIMMY McHUGH (1894–1969)

Another veteran songwriter, comparable to Harry Warren in distinction and even more famous, was Jimmy McHugh, the composer of songs known by everyone, like *On the Sunny Side of the Street* or *Exactly Like You*, both written with Dorothy Fields. For a 1955 film, working with Harold Adamson, an often pedestrian lyricist, McHugh wrote the delightful up-tempo song, *I Just Found Out About Love*, the completion of whose title is "and I like it." McHugh had the gift of opening a song with a new twist. In this case an oscillating sixth-interval figure incorporates an out-of-scale tone on the first long note (a C-sharp in the key of G). The opening rhythm is likewise distinctive. The routine songwriter would have set *I* as a pick-up, and *just* on the down beat. Here, a slightly prolonged *I*, together with a strong agogic emphasis on that word *just*, is enough to "sell" the song, but the writer also contrives a big finish in high-stepping style.

McHugh and Adamson also wrote the 1950s teenage love standard, *Too Young to Go Steady*, a nice ballad despite its sappy-on-purpose words. A ballad with a fine tune, *Where Are You*, predates 1950, as does the delicate *Let's Get Lost*, this one written with Loesser. *Reach For Tomorrow* (1960), with Ned Washington, is another verbally rather obvious song, as is *Warm and Willing* (1959), written with Ray Evans and Jay Livingston.[11] This fine composer hadn't lost his touch, at the end of his career, but he deserved better collaborators.

JIMMY VAN HEUSEN (1913–90)

Wilder mentions a number of good post-1950 Van Heusen songs, mostly ballads, singling out *Here's That Rainy Day* (1953, words by Johnny Burke) for special praise. He omits an excellent up-tempo song with Burke, also from "Carnival in Flanders," *I'm One of Your Admirers*, which has an unusual ABABCBA format. The A vocal line is sturdy and straight-ahead, mostly in on-the-beat half notes. The eight-bar B-sections, by contrast, use highly compressed, almost overlapped, phrases of syncopated quarters and eighths, with a lightly mocking set of words ("You may have a few faults, you drop ashes. . . .") that contrast with the opening title phrase. It's a very neat effect, and enlivens the song as a whole. Another song with Burke that Wilder omits is the lovely *But Beautiful* (1948), which has been much recorded.

Wilder also has high regard for *Call Me Irresponsible* (1962, words by the reliable Sammy Cahn) and the restrained and moving *The Second Time Around* (1960, with Cahn), which has a fine release, curving down at the end (citing how "love is wasted on the young") and a gently terraced close. The Van Heusen — Cahn *My Kind of Town* (1964) seems to us more strenuous than swinging.

We suspected that a general coarsening of Van Heusen's style after midcentury might be due to his working mostly with Cahn, a lyricist who, though proficient, was not distinguished in terms of a distinct poetic style. The case is not clear. With Cahn, in the 1950s and 1960s, Van Heusen wrote a number of more-than-effective fast-tempo songs. *The Tender Trap* is a winner, with its striking dotted A-section phrases built on oscillating half-steps, and with a perfect contrasting release. The opening A figure is a kind of textbook case for popular songs that play with half-steps like a puppy worrying a bone: you can almost see one eye cocked—it's such fun, please don't make me stop! (quintessential examples are the Spence — Bergmans *Nice 'N Easy* and the Kander — Ebb *How Lucky Can You Get*). Equally bouncy and delightful is *Love and Marriage* (1955), with its corny music-hall flourish at the end. *Come Dance With Me*, with a big-band sound and brash lyric to match ("Hey there, cutes! Put on your dancing boots. . . .") is undeniably swinging. These are all commercial, but just fine.

Further inspection shows that there are also good ballads from this period. The daringly strong chromaticism of *The Last Dance* (1959) makes it highly effective; there is a wrenching climax; and the lyric is excellent, although, characteristically with Cahn, there is a lapse at the end of the bridge. *Only the Lonely* (1958) also depends on a chromatic note for the first syllable of *lone-ly*, and a slow dotted-rhythm pattern for the entire word. It's a big song, but slow and quiet. The Cahn lyric slips in the release ("fun-time" rhymed with "one time"), but he does a nice change at the end: having used *lonely* many times, he uses *loneliness*. Good singers perform *All My Tomorrows* (1959) effectively. *I Couldn't Care Less* is a charmer, with a melody line that Kern would have envied; the Cahn lyrics, again, are imperfect, but the idea for the song (couldn't care less "unless you could care once more") is a good one. *I'll Only Miss Her When I Think of Her*, from the 1965 show "Skyscraper," is another good-concept song: the kicker is, "I bet I'll forget her completely—in about a hundred years." Also from this show is *Everybody Has the Right to Be Wrong*, an up-tempo song in 2/4 with a snappy rhythmic and melodic device, featured in mm.8–9 of the chorus, in which there are syncopated chromatic jumps of a sixth: for "dunce-like" (E-flat to C), and "once-like"(E-natural to D-flat). The verse is a demented little waltz with very clever lyrics, according to which the word *wrong* has "...tremendous allure because it's preceded by *you're*," while it's rare that "*wrong* is preceded by *I'm*."

Saying that songs display a good conception or idea is in a way faint praise, suggesting that the realization is not extraordinary. Yet these are still fine commercial songs. So where is the problem with Van Heusen — Cahn? Well, there is also a long string of crass songs from the same period: *High Hopes*, *All the Way*, *Come Fly With Me*, and others. They are obvious or self-regarding. What seems to have happened is that in this period, Van Heusen and Cahn became house composers for Sinatra in his least attractive aspect.

A pretty Van Heusen song, written with Mercer, is the casual, medium-tempo ballad, *Empty Tables* (1976). It too is a concept sort of song, built on an extended metaphor of an entertainer singing to "a gallery of ghosts," but it's a good concept. Another is a 1963 song with Mack David, called *Where Did Ev'ryone Go?* (Figure 3.18). It should be a favorite for jazz pianists as well as for singers, who will be reminded of the story line of the Arlen — Mercer *One for My Baby*. It has a bluesy vocal line, with "smudge" accidentals throughout, and chords that

Figure 3.18

Figure 3.18 Continued.

move continually but subtly. The song is beautifully integrated. The verse (a) and the chorus (b) begin in essentially the same way: The chromatic last portion of the first period of A_1 (c) provides the springboard to the second period, while the end of the second period modulates to go back to the beginning. It's a highly professional bit of songwriting, and more.

Notes

1. The craft of Gershwin's lyric, including the importance of the pronominal "that," is well ana-lyzed by Philip Furia, "Poets of Tin Pan Alley: A History of America's Great Lyricists" (New York: Oxford Univ. Press, 1992), 151. Judy Garland's ardent, bronzen approach is famous. But there is an equally valid way to bring out the beauties of this song: do it quietly, leaning on the half-step dissonances, as in a beautiful instrumental version by Bill Charlap and trio: "Written in the Stars," Blue Note CD 7243527291. A revelatory vocal version is Audra McDonald, "How Glory Goes," Nonesuch CD 79580.

2. Performance: Weslia Whitfield, "Until the Real Thing Comes Along," Myoho Records, 128 Bayview Circle, San Francisco CA 94124.
3. Performance: Sylvia McNair and André Previn, "Come Rain or Come Shine," Philips CD 446818.
4. They can be heard in all their blistering brilliance on "Sondheim: A Musical Tribute," Warner Brothers LP 2705.
5. Performance: Blossom Dearie, "Arthur Schwartz Revisited," Painted Smiles LP 1350.
6. Performance: Susannah McCorkle, "The People that You Never Get to Love," Inner City (MMO) LP 1151.
7. Performances of several of these songs: "Dawn Upshaw Sings Vernon Duke," Nonesuch CD 79531.
8. Performance: "Michael Feinstein Sings the Burton Lane Songbook," Nonesuch CD 79243.
9. Performance: "Robert Clary Sings Harry Warren and Jule Styne," Original Cast CD 6040.
10. Performance: Sandra King and Richard Rodney Bennett, "Making Beautiful Music Together," Audiophile CD 268.
11. Performance: The most persuasive case for these songs is made by Wesla Whitfield, "Let's Get Lost," HighNote CD 7065.

4

Indian Summer
of the Classic Popular Song

FRANK LOESSER (1910–69)

Loesser was the first to secure a top-tier reputation after 1950, and proved to be one of the most gifted and individual of American songwriters. He began, in Hollywood, by supplying lyrics for others, but by 1943 he had already written, alone, a great ballad, *Spring Will Be a Little Late This Year*. The tune is constructed around intervals just smaller or larger than the octave, which moves it along by avoiding any predictable resting place—an effect reinforced by the absence of time-out rests in the voice line.

The printed music for his movie hit, *Baby, It's Cold Outside* (1949), shows Loesser's sensibility. The two voice lines are labeled *The Mouse* and *The Wolf*, and the interpretive instruction is *Loesserando*. Loesser's attitude was funny, slangy, brash, urban-American.

Loesser's first Broadway score, in 1948, was "Where's Charley?" *Once In Love With Amy* is one of those easy, dancey tunes in soft-shoe two-to-the-bar, drag-and-skip rhythm that lodge in memory. The second period of the A-section reverses the dotted rhythm on the second beat, from long-short to short-long, for an irresistibly jaunty effect. The brief bridge uses yet another dotted rhythm, and contains a funny set of words, about the "fickle-hearted rover, so carefree and bold...(who) just quits cold." An unpretentious song that couldn't be nicer.

From the same show, *My Darling, My Darling*, with its patter of triplets, is almost as buoyant. There is also the charming long duet, *Make a Miracle*, an affectionate period piece (set in 1893). It's more than a duet: it has two parallel streams: one speaker natters on about the wonders of the oncoming twentieth century ("Someday they'll have horseless carriages that fly"), while the other is more focused on romance in the here-and-now. *Lovelier Than Ever* is inexplicably neglected. Its melody and harmonization could easily be Jerome Kern, it has a built-in lilt owing to its simple dotted half-note rhythm, mm. 3-4 and thereafter, and its climax in the final A-section is delicately set, where Spring is said to be "devastatingly clever * and lovelier than ever."

The year 1950 marked the production of "Guys and Dolls," one of the greatest scores in Broadway history. Here we select for discussion only some songs that are relatively unappreciated. The love song, *I've Never Been In Love Before*, is less performed than *I'll Know* or *If I Were a Bell*. The vocal line has an almost Handelian purity, and the entire song has an uncanny simplicity and poise. The form is a perfect AABA. The melody lies within an octave and a third, except for a single climactic note. Every tone is within the diatonic scale, except for only two accidentals. In the A-sections the key-note, a much-sounded B flat, tends to lie at the top of the vocal line (Figure 4.1a), with phrases encompassing the intervals of the sixth arranged in descending order. At the bridge (m.17), for a mere two bars, the melody line shifts above the key-note (Figure 4.1b), but the phrase shape stays the same, now with intervals of upward sevenths instead of downward sixths. At the song's climax, Loesser again raises the line above the upper key-tone, on the word *love*, before proceeding to the final cadence. Thus does the singer manifest her strange new feelings.

Rhythmically, the same economy of means obtains throughout the song. There is one rhythmic feature. Long (three-beat) notes occur always at the beginning of a measure, as in m.1; they are followed by one-beat notes at the end of

Figure 4.1

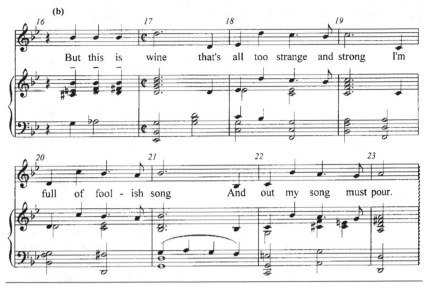

Figure 4.1 Continued.

the measure, providing a pick-up to the next bar. The pattern is sustained, but in compressed form, in m.2 and corresponding locations. This gives a graceful propulsion to each verbal phrase, which invariably comes to completion on a long-voiced word.

Loesser saves his most expressive chord changes for the strong-stress words on the third beats of the faster-moving measures (e.g., mm. 2, 4, 6). He always links the melodic tone in that position to the following, phrase-ending, long note (e.g., *love/fore*), which reduces the relative prominence of those third-beat notes. By keeping the quarter-note downbeats (*been, all, you*) light, he presses on toward the second half of his phrases. Thus he avoids what might have been a singsong stress pattern: not, "I've **never been** in **love** be**fore**," but "I've **never** been in **love** before." He lends importance to the opening of the bridge by using, not one but three quarter-notes, and thus three stressed syllables, as the upbeat figure—and does the same before the final A-section.

In terms of poetic aspects, Loesser, in the A-sections, sticks to plain and placid words, sometimes old-fashioned (*forevermore*), sometimes slightly slangy (*knew the score*). The antiquated word-order inversion of "out my song must pour" reinforces the Handelian aspect. But things change: At the bridge he uses words expressing bewilderment, and some bright vowels not heard before, *wine, strange*. The sense of surprise carries over into the final A, with, for example, *helpless haze*.

Altogether, a textbook-perfect 32-bar classic popular song, whose individuality is achieved by using: one dotted rhythm, two accidentals, a couple of extended upbeats, one big surprise in the melodic line (where *wine* leaps up over the key-tone), and a slight change in verbal register at the bridge. Songwriting doesn't get better than this.

This song has no verse. In the score it follows and is musically linked to an arioso, *My Time of Day*, in which the leading man quietly acknowledges some unfamiliar feelings. It is a stunning, loose-metered accompanied recitative, which in effect acts as a verse for the ballad that follows. In 22 bars it changes key ten or twelve times, mixes heightened poetic diction with vernacular, changes meter and rhythm constantly, uses extraordinarily expressive intervals including augmented fourths and fifths, and ends without a cadence on what may be considered tone 7 of the upcoming key that transitions into the next number. It is a mark of Loesser's integrity that he would have created something so fine primarily for a limited dramatic purpose.

There is another seldom-performed song in the same show, *More I Cannot Wish You*. This is a glowing song in 3/4 meter that does not for a moment sound like a waltz. Wilder chooses this song to conclude his survey of superior popular songs from the first half of the century. He calls it "very special... shining with tenderness...."

The title song is well known, but not performed as much as it should be. It's an utterly delightful tune, with sassy, urbane lyrics. The tune begins with a nice example of what we call forward syncopation. "When you see a guy," with *guy* coming ahead of the next strong beat and thus instantly resetting the metrical clock. In m.3, for the phrase "stars in the sky," Loesser sets *in* on the highest note, which also displaces the felt rhythm by shifting the stress away from the first beat, and brings *sky*, rhyming with *guy*, in ahead of the downbeat. With touches like these, the song bops along. There is no real bridge; the form is bipartite, AA, or $A_1A_2A_1A_2$. Partly because the song is so compressed, it works up a fine momentum by the end, where the song just stops short. The terrific words are slangy-urbane, with references to a *John* and a *doll* and a *mouse* that don't date.[1]

In "The Most Happy Fella" (1956) Loesser attempted something more ambitious, a musical theater piece mixing conventional popular song with extended "arias" and ensembles, and employing both spoken and sung dialogue. We examine only a few of its numbers, in classic pop form. There is an extraordinary "big ballad," *Joey, Joey, Joey*, requiring lots of voice and a commanding style. The 20-bar verse personifies the wind as a "perfumed woman" singing to "one of her ramblin' kin" (i.e., the speaker), thus giving voice to his ambivalence about staying "too long in one place." This introduction is musically intense, with the voice line coming to rest on 7, straining for the octave; with one of the writer's trademarks, the use of a medium-fast triplet for relaxed narrative; and with a stunning dominant seventh with added 9 at the pause before the main body of the song begins. That main body can hardly be called a chorus. It's 70 bars long, an expanded AABA plus coda. The A_1 and A_2 sections sit on a sustained tonic "pedal" tone for virtually their entire length, except for a modulation to III at the end of each. The first time, this leads to a distinctive nonvocal chromatic interlude that moves right back to I. The second time, the chromatic figure takes the song into the middle section, not a bridge but an interlude, which stays basically in the same key as that for A.

In effect, the entire 90-bar song is in one simple major key, with an inexorable accumulation of force and intensity. Somehow Loesser manages to avoid monotony, simply by using the 7 tone often, and by the use of one prominent accidental, a raised 5, a mere five times. The song ought also to be monotonous in that *Joey* (or *Joe*) is repeated three to six times at four places in the main part of the song, and *time to go* is also heard frequently. Looking back, we see how crucial it was for Loesser to frame this song in terms of a speaker reporting what the wind says to him, for messages that come on the wind are incantatory. Then too, the diction in the middle section is different: here the speaker drops the spoken-on-the-wind register and tells us candidly about himself, that his bunk "gets to feelin' too soft and cozy," and that he's had all "the ladies in the neighborhood." Without this change in word-style, which only lasts about 10 bars, the song might be insufferably grand, wanderlust without the personal touch. Instead, the song ends up as very large in scale and import without being pompous.

There remain to be mentioned two more normally constructed ballads. *Somebody, Somewhere* is marked *plaintively*, but is not morbidly so. The wistful quality of the song comes, perhaps, from the pronoun/adverb indeterminacy at the beginning expressed by a melodic turn around the tonic note, a feature that is always sweet. The song builds to a heartfelt climax: the entire final A-section is actually an extended climax pitched at the higher end of the octave. The format of the song, a little longer than customary, is unusual: either there is no real release, in which case the form is AAAA (with internal variation), or possibly $A_8 B_8 A_8 B_8 B_8$, with the B-sections very like the A-sections but with three quick key changes in each, and a minute rhythmic change. The latter feature is subtle, but results in some striking forward syncopation.

The luminous ballad, *Warm All Over*, is a hard song to sing, with very dense harmonies that could lead a singer astray and with accidentals (as in m.4) and an augmented seventh interval (m.6) chosen to emphasize crucial syllables. Especially lovely is the way the introduction, with its mostly short questioning phrases, slides right into the main song by means of an elegant slow triplet, a rhythm that will recur most gracefully in the short release (Figure 4.2). The highest tone in the release is only one octave higher than the lowest tone in the song, but that highest tone is approached chromatically, and then retreated from in the same fashion: one senses a huge arc.

Figure 4.2

The harmonies in this song are exceptionally rich. The chorus opens with a beautifully voiced open triadic chord with the voice on 6, inherently an untethered tone of the scale, for a Schumannesque effect. Then come a series of almost dominant-seventh chords, but with subtly altered tones. For example, the complex chord on the first *o-ver* is built on a lowered 6, a tone not in the scale, and includes a half-step dissonance, F-sharp against G. The harmonization is mysterious; for example, the voice line in m.8 comes back to the key-tone, but there is no sense of having regained the tonic.

The words are wonderfully well controlled. The "high" vowel of *smile* is followed by a series of long dark *o* sounds, connecting introduction to chorus (*glow/so/know/o-ver*), before *smile* is heard again. There are then no more bright vowels until one word, *feel*, in the release, and its affine, *feeling*, at the very end. Added to this control is a miraculous attainment of an innocently sexual tone in the title phrase, as sung unconsciously by a naïve young woman. For the auditor, picking this up is like not hearing the key-tone (m.8): you recognize it, but don't stop to think about it.

The songs from "Greenwillow" (1959) are smaller in scope and ambition. The nicest song from this show is *The Music of Home*, which is short (the chorus has 20 measures) but must be performed with the verse, which is twice as long. It is an Irish ballad in character, simple but very well composed within the scope of an octave plus one tone. The lyric here, especially in the long verse, is the element to admire most. Loesser is writing here in a folkish voice that is older than the classic American popular idiom but not incompatible with it.

Never Will I Marry is a big declarative song, dark in tone ("Born to wander 'til I'm dead"), dramatic in shape. The phrases are all very short, incisive. The vocal range is very wide, an octave and a sixth, which adds to the defiant quality. The song stays basically in one key, with an ostinato bass-line figure that moves constantly in whole steps along the scale. Like *Joey, Joey, Joey*, it's an uncompromising song, suitable only for a performer who can sing big but not belt.

The songs from "How to Succeed in Business Without Really Trying" (1961) are tricky to appreciate as songs. It was Loesser's last produced show, and a funny and quick-moving one. The songs in it have consistently the subliminal flavor of spoofing. It is as if Loesser said, I'm going to write a show for the tired businessman—and contrived the songs so that they appeal both to the tired businessman and to the more sophisticated listener. A song like *I Believe In You* is a catchy medium-tempo song, with a great beat and neat words. *The Company Way* is a driving ensemble number, with smarty-pants lyrics. *The Brotherhood of Man* is a rousing showbiz-gospel creation. All the same, there is something distanced about them. The irony implicit in *I Believe In You* makes for a brilliant moment in the theater, when the auditor realizes that the hero is singing this song of love and devotion to himself, in a mirror. But if one tries to sing the song outside this context, it sounds contrived. At one level, *Happy to Keep His Dinner Warm* is as delightful a song as Loesser ever wrote, and affectionate in tone. But it's about a housewife who does her bit while her guy "goes onward and upward"; outside the show, it would either sound dumb or convey a rather condescending satirical attitude.

Loesser's unrealized last show, "Pleasures and Palaces" (1965), concerned the life and loves of Catherine the Great. There is an air of self-importance about it, as if he wanted to reestablish himself on the slopes of opera, as he had done with "The Most Happy Fella." One song, *In Your Eyes*, has a simple and elegant melody, with rhythmic octave chords underneath. It is lovely, but it sounds a bit worked-over, as if intended for theme music for an epic film.

Loesser died young. He seemed to be groping at the end; but his best work is at such a high level that he takes his place as one of the great American popular songwriters of the twentieth century.

JULE STYNE (1905–94)

Any discussion of Styne's songs should start with an appreciation of the man's boundless enthusiasm. His prolificacy (some said, profligacy) was a legend in the business. James Lardner once said of him, "He can write like a hack in the company of hacks, or like a genius in the company of geniuses." Wilder mentions Jule (pronounced *Julie*) Styne only once, calling a 1947 song, *Time After Time*, his best. However, his early songs include standards, such as *Saturday Night Is the Loneliest Night of the Week* or *I'll Walk Alone* (both 1944, lyrics by Sammy Cahn), that would earn Styne a permanent place in the popular music catalog. The latter starts with a flip little verse: "They call, no date. I promised you I'd wait," but then becomes a nice, wistful chorus for the lover left behind.

The film "Manhattan Melody," also 1944 with Cahn lyrics, introduced two songs whose style presages the later, more sophisticated writer. *And Then You Kissed Me* has a release that brings a surge of musical happiness (Figure 4.3). *Some Other Time* (not to be confused with the Bernstein — Comden and Green song) uses interesting rising chords that start after empty down-beats in mm.3-4 and 11-12, and features another buoyant release in which the same eight notes are repeated three different times, but with harmonic changes. Repeated notes are sometimes problematic, but in this case the lyric, concerning obsession, could hardly work otherwise.

I Fall In Love Too Easily, from "Anchors Aweigh," (1944), has a short 16-measure chorus with a very simple clear melodic line. Cahn's lyric is short and sweet: "I fall in love too easily. I fall in love too fast." *Guess I'll Hang My Tears Out to Dry*, 1944, is the finest of the Styne — Cahn torch songs. The chords of

Figure 4.3

the chorus move so as to avoid the tonic chord for an entire eight measures, and the melodic line features some astringent accidentals, the lowered 2 and the conjunction of a lowered with a natural 7, which gives it a keening quality. In keeping with the novelty of the title phrase, the verse, with some gliding upward-sevenths, cleverly compares the Statue of Liberty to a torch-carrying jilted lover.

There's also a charming 1947 film song with Cahn, *Brooklyn Bridge*, a nice medium-swing song with smart lyrics ("I love to listen to the wind through her strings, the song that it sings. . . ."). Not great, but better than a lot of better-known songs about New York.[2] The last film song to mention is *It's Magic* (1948). It has a very good verse, the first measures of which move through dominant-seventh chords to a main-key major seventh chord. The chorus, with its descending slurred notes ("You sigh, the song begins. . . .") is less interesting.

The post-1950 development of Styne's style makes him into a more important figure. Styne's only successful Broadway show with Cahn was "High Button Shoes" (1947). Two songs move away from the danceable pop character of their

Hollywood work. *You're My Girl* is a sweet song with an interesting first eight measures that sound like a waltz forced into 4/4 time: "You're my girl, the boys all know; You're my girl, I've told them so." *Can't You Just See Yourself* uses repeated notes in the melody with accompanying chords that change in chromatic steps up and down, giving the song a strong sense of movement.

Bye Bye Baby, from the 1949 musical, "Gentlemen Prefer Blondes," with film lyricist Leo Robin, is written almost entirely in quarter- and eighth-notes, marching along with a tiny syncopation. *You Say You Care* has a pleasant verse with a chord progression reminiscent of Noel Coward, and illustrates how writing for the theater started to bring out the very best in Styne.

For the 1951 Broadway revue "Two On the Aisle," Styne, working with the proficient Comden and Green, wrote two good theater songs. *So Far So Good* is a fizzy song that chronicles, in 34 bars, no verse, a long-term relationship. A first meeting is outlined in snappy, pronounless one-bar phrases in the A-section. That is followed by emotional and melodic flux in the B-section. Equilibrium is attained in the last A-section: "Happy we've come so far **** so far, so good," with the first *far* on the apex note of the song. *How Will He Know?* is a touching song, with a yearning emotional quality. The verse is an evocation of romantic anticipation: "Tick tock, Punch the clock...." The 64-bar chorus introduces a yearning melody, stretching over an octave in the first A-section. The chords in the first A change from I to IV to a pivotal I⁷, coming to rest on a minor seventh on ii. The release has a wailing quality, and then a wistful fall, on, "...the love and kissing that I know I'm missing," followed by a transition back to A by one step. The song ends with a nice homonym: "...No, No, No, No / he'll never know."[3] There's also a comic gem called , *If (You Hadn't But You Did)*, in which the mordantly funny Comden and Green lyric includes a gunshot. Styne's melody, using phrases starting with the accented *if* on the down-beat, followed always by a suspenseful rest, makes perfect rhythmic sense for the lyric, right up to the looping, manic ending.

"Bells Are Ringing" (1956), with Comden and Green, had three excellent songs, two of which became standards. The famous *Just In Time* has an unusual verse. It's a rather peculiar, but amusing, character-defining recitative, starting with the deadpan, "I was resting comfortably face down in the gutter...." The chorus is a happy contrast, starting with the title on a swinging three-note phrase, D, C sharp, D, and noodling with these three notes five times before a new note is heard. The song is a favorite of jazz pianists, because of the incisive opening pattern and the clear chord progression, which combines stepwise motion with a chain of fifths and fourths. We think it's a better instrumental than vocal piece, since the very strong melodic figure can sound obsessive, like a *device* for a song. Gershwin or Coleman would have set the opening as a syncopated figure or on the off-beat.

The other well-known song, an elegiac ballad, *The Party's Over,* deservedly became a hit. The chorus is an elegant, understated melody which fits the poignant lyric: "Now you must wake up, all dreams must end...." The melody line here is an example of the power of accretion. The title phrase is five syllables (and notes), ending with *o-ver* set on two adjacent tones. The next phrase is seven syllables, with the two-note step-down becoming a four-note turn. The third phrase concludes with an 11-note figure, beginning with the turn and finishing with a longer turn including one altered tone (on "taken the moon away"). Technically, the line develops by lengthening an appoggiatura to a mordent to a double-mordent.

The third song, *Long Before I Knew You,* is not so well-known, but it may be the best of the three. The message is tender but shy. A somewhat indeterminate verse leads to a gorgeous chorus, the A-sections built on parallel phrases stepping down one tone at a time (Figure 4.4). The B-sections, with piquant raised 2, work through some tonally remote chords.

Figure 4.4

From the 1958 "Say Darling" is another song with Comden and Green that is minimal but exquisite, *Dance Only With Me.* It comes near to being an all-A-section song, in that each eight-bar unit is built on the same rhythmic and melodic pattern. It's a slow waltz, in which each section opens with a monosyllable set one to a bar, each on a different pitch: *dance* on 6, *dance* on 3, *love* on 6, *dance* on a flatted 7. The first of these onsets is striking because it is set on ii, which gives it a mysterious floating quality. The last of them is an especially telling accidental, since it is the highest tone in the song, and only occurs once, so that this one note forms the climax. Thereafter, the melody line descends in undeviating half-steps to the key-tone. The lyric is as plain as could be, perfect for this plangent song.

In "Gypsy" (1959, lyrics by Sondheim), Styne reached his peak as a theater composer. *Everything's Coming Up Roses* heads any list of commanding theater songs. *Some People, Together Wherever We Go,* and *You'll Never Get Away From Me* are all rousers. The last of these is the only one in standard 32-bar length. The simple but effective melody rises from the tonic B-flat through the first six notes of the scale before dipping to the lower A and returning to the key-tone. The "dipping" is both melodic and rhythmic, which gives the line a great lilt wherever it occurs. The bridge is a variation of the same motive, using the same notes in a somewhat different and descending order, which gives this song unity and a sense of order. The determination of the music is perfectly matched to that of Sondheim's lyric: "True, you could say 'Hey, here's your hat' / but a little thing like that wouldn't stop me now."

All I Need Is the Girl is a terrific song in cut time in which the A-section melody builds in four-note chromatic phrases. In m. 7, the line comes to rest, with the word *girl*, on a striking accidental, permitting a modulation into the second eight. The song (really a "number") has great rhythmic élan in a time-honored vaudeville/Broadway style that demands show-off drumming. The song starts with a strong sense of four beats, even though in "cut time," with a forward syncope every other fourth beat. As mentioned, the entire first A and the first half of the second A use almost nothing but upward-leading half steps. That gives an almost tick-tock inexorability to the opening of the song. Mm.12–16 in the second A, however, constitute a kind of "break," and the strong beats are clearly two to a bar, a metrical compression by a factor of 2 (Figure 4.5). It's like old movies

Figure 4.5

where Dan Dailey or George Murphy danced up a staircase a step at a time, and then danced down. Then a third A starts up again, same half-step motion, but all of a sudden the voice leaps a sixth to a high E on "for a *whirl*." There's another staircase break; then a fifth down on *tweed*, and a third up on the rhyming *need*, and that's the song. The one large interval into *whirl* gives enormous emphasis to this one word, which is really the climax of the song, an occasion for a pirouette. The sheet music unfortunately omits the almost maniacally informative verse ("Once my clothes were shabby / Tailors called me "cabby" / Now I'm the cat's meow—my wardrobe is a wow!"), which contains some of Sondheim's best invention and semantically foreshadows the words of the chorus.[4]

A gentle song that emerges shyly amid these show tunes, *Little Lamb*, quite cleverly uses discordant B-naturals in the bass, amidst F major triads for the tune (at "my birthday is here at last") to suggest the singer's uneasy transition from childhood to adulthood. The melodic line uses the inherently wistful upward-sixth interval very effectively. *Small World* has a direct but satisfying melody based on a move up from a B-flat to the tonic E-flat on the repeated disyllable *fun-ny*. The four-measure bridge shifts into D flat for a neat setting of the words "We could pool our resources by joining forces….," in which the last two measures descend chromatically over a sequence of luscious chords.

Make Someone Happy from the 1960 show "Do-Re-Mi," with Comden and Green lyrics, has been much recorded. The song's basic melodic line, for "Make someone happy, Make just one someone happy," has a bass-line that moves up chromatically one half-note at a time as the melody builds, giving the song the straight-ahead exuberance we are accustomed to in Styne's music. Nevertheless, we think *Make Someone Happy* is in the wrong rhythm. As it stands, there are rather a lot of empty beats ("Make **** someone happy") and it takes seven bars for the first interesting chord change to occur (on "sing to"). The song would have been tighter in a brighter "jazz-two beat" rhythm.

"Subways Are for Sleeping" (1961) had two pleasant songs. *I'm Just Taking My Time* is a catchy Styne — Comden and Green song of self-reliance. *Comes Once In a Lifetime*, more interesting musically, is a jaunty medium up-tempo number with deft, amusing words and a complex urban rhythm. The message is right up-front in the repeated phrase, "Ev'ry day that comes, comes once in a lifetime…." The syncopated break between the two *comes* energizes the vocal line. The bass-line steps up as the melody line steps down to create a "Chopsticks"-like line of dissonances. The song is 32 bars, plus a six-bar extension that sounds as if Styne got a bit bored and didn't take pains ending it.

Great success was to come once more in 1963 with "Funny Girl." Bob Merrill, an excellent composer in his own right, was the lyricist. *Who Are You Now?* is a tender song in B flat. A two-bar repeating melodic phrase starts on F, then moves down to start next on E-flat; but the next phrase lengthens, and begins on C-sharp, so that the song already expresses an introspective vulnerability. *The Music That Makes Me Dance* has a verse that hints subtly at the melody of the chorus to come. The first bars of the chorus are simply the notes of the C major triad plus 7 spread apart linearly: "I know he's around when the sky and the ground...," a melody pattern then repeated on different notes in a textbook instance of a chain of thirds. In what could be designated the B-section, Styne turns this motive in on itself, in a downwards direction. The song comes to a beautiful climax with "more him" set twice, first over an E minor seventh and then a C diminished chord before coming to a C major finish. Verbally, the song has an appealing conversational quality.

Don't Rain On My Parade is another of Styne's propulsive cut-time theater songs. The song has a striking, disjunctive opening strain, with intervals quite hard to sing, and then a real release, which moves into a brassy Broadway beat and a more connected tune that allows the singer to wail for eight bars. There is, alas, a rather frantic ending. Styne's endings tend to be the least satisfying part of his songwriting. Sometimes they depend on use-worn formulas, as in *Comes Once In a Lifetime*; sometimes on forced repetition, as if insistence will carry the day. *People*, from "Funny Girl," also ends desperately.

A very interesting song from the show "Hallelujah Baby" (1967, lyrics by Comden and Green) has a rather experimental sound to it. *Being Good Isn't Good Enough* uses unusual harmonies, and discordant but effective intervals. It is a long way from the predictable melodic phrases of the Hollywood Styne. The key signature is G major, but F's are much more often natural than sharped. The main melodic motive is a simple seven-note phrase set to "Being good isn't good enough," repeated with variations. The song builds dramatically to mm.31–37, whose key is A flat but which introduces E naturals, emphasizing by discordance the last words in the phrases "That's the way it's got to be" and "There's no other way for me." Another song from this show, *When the Weather's Better*, is based on a melodic phrase of seven notes. There is a lot of repetition during the 62 bars, which some may find tedious. On the other hand, the strong opening syncopation, with the weakest word, *the*, set on an out-of-the-scale tone, hence emphasized, is bracing, as is the use of eventful interior rhyme. The lyric for *My Own Morning* concerns the universal need for individuality. The hoping quality of the words ("I want a bed that belongs to me... (I want to) wake up in my own morning") is projected by the use of repeated notes, in this case also repeated triplets in the melody, and a simple bass-line that underscores the urgency felt by the singer. The song has a range of only one octave. The childlike simplicity of the lyric surely contributed to its frequent use on "Sesame Street."

The first and only collaboration of Jule Styne and E.Y. Harburg gave us the marvelous score for "Darling of the Day" in 1967, though the show did not "run." The song, *That Something Extra Special*, is indeed just that. It is perhaps the most tender song Styne ever wrote, with a melody so simply constructed to words so well-considered that the whole song imparts the feeling of inevitability. What could be simpler than the way Styne uses the E-flat major scale to build the main melody? He organizes it in a lapping pattern, like a shy person stepping forward and back. The A-section opens with a partial use of the scale in the first five measures. It resumes in the very next three measures, ascending the six tones from E-flat up to C and repeating each one (Figure 4.6a). It is only at this point that the harmony moves out of the main key, to a transitory dominant seventh, and it is right here that the melodic line becomes memorable with one

Figure 4.6

note, a D-flat on "makes life more *liv*-able. That single tone accomplishes a lot. It is consonant relative to the bass-line progression, but dissonant with regard to the main scale of the opening. We cannot think of another song that pivots so remarkably on one tone and syllable. What then follows, in mm.10 through 16, are simply sections of the E-flat scale descending in reverse: "We walk along the river, and through his eyes I see, a world of things I never thought could be." The release (Figure 4.6b), marked *Cantabile espressivo*, is also simple, and carries the loving and quiet tone of the song, via an aching turnaround with accidental

Figure 4.6 Continued.

(on the first syllable of *ban-ish*), into a repeat of A. The last A uses the ascent in the main key scale up to two momentary hang-ups on D-flat, before a descent to final E flat cadence: "And isn't that what love is all about?" Well, it's what good songwriting is all about.

There are two other fine songs in the show. *Let's See What Happens* is a long, lyrical waltz with a marked "dip" in the rhythm. It's in AABA form, but the B is so well integrated that you almost miss it. Harburg uses vowel repetition or assonance masterfully, as in "*Mu*sic can do the most un*u*sual things." In the phrase "**Let's** give the **waltz** a **chance**, Let's **dance** and **let's** see what happens," the nice effect is the way that stress is imparted to, and then withheld from, *let's*. The words *chance* and *dance* rhyme at noncorresponding points in their phrases, always an elegant touch, and a line like "let us carouse while Strauss caresses the strings" uses off-rhyme and verb parallelism to brilliant effect. Even better is *That Stranger In Your Eyes*, which can be found only in manuscript at the Library of Congress Music Division. This lyrical 80-bar song in B flat has the same simple and tender approach to melody as *That Something Extra Special*. Styne's publishers should make this fine score known.

Later songs by Styne have not much interested us, except for three. The first is *Hey Look, No Cryin'* (1981), a long song with lyrics by Susan Birkinhead. There is an incipient rock beat in the rather thin verse, which prepares a rhythm in the chorus with strings of repeated eighth notes in almost every measure. From the same year is a lightly atmospheric ballad with Birkinhead, *It's Sunday*. It's a pretty song, romantic and sexy ("Talk away the morning, read the papers, misbehave...."), and it ends on a floating setting of *Sunday*, on tones 5, raised 5, and 6.

Killing Time is a short, pessimistic ballad dated 1983. Although the lyric, by Carolyn Leigh, is about lost love, what makes this song even more poignant is the fact the Leigh died at a relatively young age the year it was published. The melody line, in very short phrases, feels tightly held-in, as if the singer cannot trust herself to control her voice, and is limited almost entirely to one octave. The lyrics say it all: "... feeling old / Matching socks and hatching plans and catching cold." The repetitions of the title phrase at the end fade out as if "killing time" is going to go on for the rest of a lifetime. It's a powerful and moving song.[5]

Styne cherished his lyricists, and worked with a number of great ones—and others not so great. Despite some falling-off at the end of his career, Styne was, with Coleman, the most irrepressible, exuberant, and prolific composer of the last half of the twentieth century.

FREDERICK LOEWE (1901–88) and ALAN JAY LERNER (1918–86)

No Broadway musical of the half-century following 1950 enjoyed a greater réclame than "My Fair Lady" (1956). It was not only extraordinarily good, as a show, but it had "prestige" value: it was based on Shaw, had a well-loved plot, a well-made book, and was, by definition, literate. It appealed in general to those who liked "show music," but especially to adults in the middle and professional classes with traditional musical tastes. Much the same applies to "Camelot" (1960) and to the film "Gigi" (1958). The former was based on British legend, as retold by the best-selling novelist, T. H. White; the latter was based on Colette, with its Belle Epoque story "presold" in other media.

To us, the songs of Loewe and Lerner now seem to represent a high-quality dead-end. Many have observed that Loewe's music was "operettalike" in style. Insofar as that comment applies to melodic structure, it is not a conclusive criticism, since there are any number of songs by Kern, Gershwin, Lane, or Arthur

Schwartz that fit that description in terms of the shape and range of the tune. Insofar as it applies to harmonic style, it is true that Loewe's chord structure tends to operate in an uncomplicated diatonic–triadic mode, without much chromatic alteration and without the rich complexity of voicing that forms the distinctive American classic popular song style. But again, the same is true of certain fine songs in "musical comedy" style by the American masters. The criticism is perhaps most forceful as it applies to rhythm. Loewe wrote in established, undeviating European rhythmic patterns: the waltz, scherzo, gavotte, the medium fast 4/4. When Loewe uses syncopation in the opening strain of *The Night They Invented Champagne* (from "Gigi") or in *With a Little Bit of Luck* ("My Fair Lady"), it is big-gesture syncopation, like Offenbach or the English music hall, and it remains predictably so throughout the song. Loewe and Lerner songs have few surprises: the beginning predicts the end, and the craft is in getting to the end without boredom.

This is not to dismiss, but to praise with some stylistic reservations. The songs may be a little remote from the American mainstream, but they are not formula songs, and melodically, and in terms of basic harmony, they are excellent. The "character songs" in "My Fair Lady" are beautifully constructed; for example, *I'm an Ordinary Man*, and the numbers devised for a dramatic point, like the ebullient *Show Me*, are as effective as a plot-specific song could be. Most of the songs from this musical need no analysis from us, but we will comment that *I've Grown Accustomed to Her Face* is a beautiful love song, all the more beautiful for having a lyric that expresses reluctance. The very evenness of the setting of the opening, title phrase—a long stepping of eighth notes ending in one long note—is naturalistic, close to the way one would speak. The same is true of "Her smiles, her frowns, her ups, her downs," which follows perfectly another common speech pattern. The halting series at the end of the song—"her looks…her voice…her face"—is touching because it is totally in character and prosodically perfect. *On the Street Where You Live* has a commanding range, a great romantic tune, and a release with even more sweep. *I Could Have Danced All Night*, of course, is full of verve, but for us the effect is due primarily to the rushing string-tremolo accompaniment, which brings a sort of clang-association effect in music. Its greatest moment is "I only know…," set on even dramatic strokes with accompaniment suspended.

The songs from "Camelot" tend to be very verbal, with neat but rather inhibited-sounding musical setting of overcomplicated words. Lerner tries too hard. Numbers like *I Wonder What the King Is Doing Tonight*, while amusing, seem to strive to modernize or lighten up the fictional source, a rather self-defeating approach. The title song is nicely poised, with its **one**-two-three-four pattern; but it keeps lapsing into discontinuous units (for *in Camelot*), and it is "bitty" in its lyric. Indeed, much of the score sounds oververbalized and semantically coy. Rhyming *pedestal* with *better still* might be charming in a more ironic style, but sounds forced here. *If Ever I Would Leave You* is a success as a big romantic ballad, but is of course somewhat artificial in the word-order of the title phrase and overfamiliar in its verbal plan, involving the cycle of the seasons.

In the film "Gigi," the song *I'm Glad I'm Not Young Anymore* strikes us as a technical success; we like the grouping of units of two words and two beats within its overall fast-four momentum. The title song is very singable, and we like the pattern that reiterates the girl's name tersely, and then follows that with a very long phrase.

The Broadway shows that brought Loewe and Lerner to prominence were "Brigadoon" (1947) and "Paint Your Wagon" (1951). Lerner had been writing on American (or mythic) subjects with a displaced Berliner, Kurt Weill, and now wrote, respectively, an out-of-time Scottish fantasy and a settling-the-West story with Loewe, a classically trained German of Austrian background. The results were mixed. The best songs from "Brigadoon" are well-known, and very good in their style. *The Heather on the Hill*, with its delicate rhythm for the chorus (and the "Scotch snap" for **heath**-*er*) and its pretty verse, is completely successful. *Almost Like Being In Love* has a fine tune, a powerful short bridge, and a very good close, paid out in two short, then one long, phrases. This may be Loewe's most "American"-sounding song, harmonically. Actually, the entire score, while Scottish in flavor, is not that far from a score that Rodgers and Hammerstein might have written. *Waitin' for My Dearie* is a delight, with maybe the prettiest tune Loewe ever wrote and with a finely judged approach to Scottish vernacular. *There but for You Go I* is a big ballad, a bit too big for its content, with a long-held high-note climax, operetta style. *From This Day On*, however, is a placid but deeply felt ballad. It uses basically the same melodic tone set as *Waitin' for My Dearie*, but in a smaller, more deliberate compass. The two periods that constitute the A-section are joined seamlessly, so that it sounds like one long statement with a modulation halfway through, an effect achieved by starting the second part of the vocal line (m.5) with, not the first measure again, but the second. It is a kind of near-parallelism that avoids predictability. The delicate Lerner lyric begins with a positive assumption; it ends with almost the same words, but invoking a reference to loss.

From "Paint Your Wagon," *They Call the Wind Maria* has a Hollywood-western tune, not bad, and faintly ridiculous words. *I Talk to the Trees* is also absurd, though again the tune is better than serviceable. *I Still See Elisa* is lovely, with short, lapping phrases, very delicate, and sweet sad words. Despite its being a "name" song, which may limit its appeal to performers (who is Elisa, what is she?), it deserves to be remembered. *Another Autumn* has a fine lyric by Lerner, with a heartbreaking conclusion ("...time has shown if you're alone when autumn comes / You'll be alone all winter long"), but we find the beguine-style musical setting peculiar.

These comments on much-loved songs may seem condescending. Many of the Loewe — Lerner songs indeed have "good bones," an attribute that we discussed in our Introduction; and *I've Grown Accustomed to Her Face* seems to us a great song. But the overall style was inevitably a bit old-fashioned, a bit nonindigenous, compared to the styles we like best in American classic pop. Combining these two observations, it is not surprising that we like the songs best in jazz or otherwise modified styles.[6]

HUGH MARTIN (b. 1914)

This fine composer was born just too late, in that his best work did not come to attention until the 1940s. He also, perhaps, suffered from working a lot in Hollywood early in his career, so that he was taken for granted. The same career pattern describes Loesser, but Martin wrote in a narrower range that we would label as tender: both his fast songs and his ballads have an innate loveliness, literacy, and poise, a respect for the singer and the audience, which make him quite special. His penchant for unusual intervals in the vocal line and his rich harmonic sense are reminiscent of Vernon Duke, though the harmony is one degree plainer. His gift for melody lies close to that of, say, Burton Lane, being direct (save for some extraordinary intervals) and innately singable. His lyrics—he often wrote his own—are of high quality, disclosing a sophistication reined in for the sake of the song as a whole.

Wilder mentions a few post-1950 songs, the sweeping and well-known ballad *You Are for Loving* (1963) and a film song *An Occasional Man* (1955, lyrics by Ralph Blane). There's an equally good song from the same film, "The Girl Rush," called *Out of Doors*. The verse is verbally complex—dealing with "...life as the city leads it...Who needs it?"—and harmonically restless, moving from the dominant of F to the dominant of D to B major to E flat major, thence to a simple C major for the chorus. It's a clever setup, complexity leading to plainness, since the chorus has a tune and a harmonic underpinning of great simplicity. The first period is plain-Jane C major, with the standard pop additions of tones 2 and 6. The second period is exactly the same save for a mere two measures including the lowered 3 (Figure 4.7). The bass-line underneath stays invariant, yielding an ambiguous effect in m. 6. It is an example of a parallel-minor relation, quite common in classical concert music, rare in classic pop. The evenly spaced chords and the plain words together give a measured, chiming quality to the song, which persists all the way through. The auditor doesn't decide whether the emotional import is banal or sincere until an eight-bar coda, in which the narrator provides a sly, sweet twist: "No matter just what you have in mind, It's bound to be better, you will find, If you try it out of doors." A great song? No. But one of the pleasures of American classic pop lies with songs that teeter on the edge of the

Figure 4.7

falsely naïve without falling. There is another good song from that film, *At Last We're Alone*, not memorable musically but with a delightful lyric by Martin and Blane together ("Don't holler for help / No, not even one little yelp").

From another MGM musical, in 1954, came *Love Can Change the Stars*, with Blane. It's a superromantic melody. There is a curious feature, unusual for popular songs: the A$_2$ section modulates up by a minor third, for no structural reason except, perhaps, to emphasize the breadth of lyrical feeling.

Wilder rather downgrades Martin's late 1940s and 1950s Broadway shows, and here we disagree. From "Look Ma, I'm Dancin'!" (1947), there's an irresistible song about dancing. It's called *Gotta Dance*, and it's a lot of fun. Martin's lyrics limn the dilemma of a boy who grew up wanting to dance (in the sly-boots verse: "…they could never love me with my arms above me in the fifth position"). But this kid loves every kind of dance, and sums it up thus: "Love to swap my bus'ness clo'es for my dancin' pants / Anyone who knows me knows I'm a guy who's gotta dance!" The tune is as direct and engaging as Berlin's dancing songs. The show also included *Tiny Room*, one of the great, passionate ballads.

"Make a Wish" (1951), with lyrics by Martin himself, has a title song of great playfulness, the voice line skipping around the entire major scale (though in singable intervals) in an irresistibly cheery fashion. The first two short phrases are syncopated at their onsets; so is the third, but it is twice as long without a "hitch" in the middle, which produces the paradoxical effect of a negative (i.e., absent) syncope. Much the same plan applies to dotted rhythms throughout the

A-sections of the song: present in short phrases, absent in ones that push ahead. The words are fine, including that effective rhyme scheme in which the paired elements occur at slightly different points in the lines: "...you'll make it happen / the break will happen for you" (note that exact repetition is experienced sometimes as rhyme).

If the title song has drive, the big ballad, *When Does This Feeling Go Away?*, has melodic sweep. The verse is too long; it even includes eight bars in a contrasting tempo. The chorus opens beautifully, with an arresting title phrase set on notes bracketing the key-tone; but this is one of those effective songs where the key-tone is not definitively perceived until the final cadence, a technique that always gives a song buoyancy. There is a rhythmic lilt, just a little dotted figure, built into mm.2–3. The song is ABAB in form, with a nice little bonus measure, an interpolation built on two juicy chords (the bass note goes down a half-step, the voice line goes up), as a transition from B_1 to A_2. Martin again tucks his rhymes (e.g., *go away/stowaway*) into nonobvious spots in the phrase. This is a superior theater song that works just as well on its own.

I Wanna Be Good and Bad is fun. It's one of those "suggestive" songs that depends on word play, in this case words that repeat with a twist: "I wanna be chaste ... chased by men," and so on. *That Face* (not the Spence — Bergman song) is even better, the words and the tune fitting like a glove ("that darlin', snarlin' face...that jazzy, snazzy face....").

From 1964 comes the score to "High Spirits," an adaptation of Noel Coward's play, "Blithe Spirit," with Timothy Gray as co-lyricist. It produced a strong set of songs. The best-known is *You'd Better Love Me*, which is direct and swinging, and a natural for jazz-style performance. The modal grammar of the opening phrase, "You'd better love me while you *may*," bothers us a bit, because there seems no good reason for it other than for the sake of later rhymes. But the off-the-beat rhythm of the song is persuasive. *Was She Prettier Than I* is conventional but pleasing: for once, a torch song without heavy breathing, just a sigh of regret. And its bridge is lovely, with another of those simple, dotted-figure lilts that Martin provides. *Something Tells Me* could be Cole Porter in a beguine mood, but the release is more interesting, with its minor-chord progressions. In this song, what is being (fore)told is that "tonight is the night." One does get the feeling, with some of these songs, that composer and lyricist are writing down, somehow; there is a certain "twee" feeling, perhaps deliberately chosen for a Coward play.

But this reservation is swept away by the best song in the show. *I Know Your Heart* sounds like a piece for the Basie band. It opens with a stunning apostrophe to the loved one, set to an equally powerful chord progression (Figure 4.8). Not only is the opening vocal phrase set off the beat, for a kind of strong syncopation in retrospect (that is, you don't know it's a syncope until the second bar), but

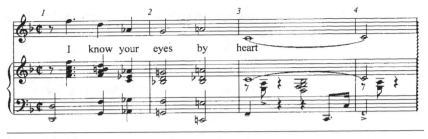

Figure 4.8

the voice line starts on the key-tone while the chords underneath disguise that: they start as if involving the dominant of the key of C, but the A flat plus 7 chord moves the series toward the true key, F. That single chord on an unstressed word (*your*) does its job instantaneously: such a chord is sometimes called a "passing chord" to indicate that it slips in, makes a big effect, and gets out of the way. All told, the effect of the opening is to make you feel that the song has been going on for some time; you just dropped in at a choice moment. The entire song is both lithe and exultant, which is interesting in that the lyrics (the best in the show) are ambiguous: "...when (your smile) is this naïve, there's something up your sleeve" and "so clean, so neat, so deceitfully sweet." It's a supersophisticated song, and a great one.

The last memorable Martin song we know is *I Have Something to Say to You* (Martin's words and music, 1992). The title phrase promises metrical stiffness or semantic pomposity, but it is not so; the phrase is perfect: *I* set on a long note, *some-thing to* on a slow triplet, *say to you* on a dotted figure. The whole phrase, which uses only four notes in the lower part of the octave, spins gently like a snowflake in air. It's in AABB form, with the A-sections set low, the B-sections raised, with the occasional gentle accidental at the onset of phrases, and with Martin's distinctive, silken harmonic touches, delicate as fingertips, throughout. There is a long excellent verse, itself in AABB form, which deepens the import of the piece as a whole. There is something very moving about this song. It ends in the most satisfying way: what wants to be said, finally, is "I love you."[7]

Martin's output, both before and after 1950, was small but choice. Any songwriter who can remind you simultaneously of Harry Warren and Noel Coward had a unique talent. The hallmark is an easy grace, a shapeliness, at any tempo. The other remarkable thing about Martin is that the words fit smoothly, whether they are by Blane or Martin himself, and whether they are technically elaborate or very simple. They fall on the ear like speech that is sometimes, in fact, called "musical"—meaning, full of nuance, plasticity. Such speech catches one up, makes one really think about the meaning of what is being said, as opposed to getting the drift. So too do Martin's verbally aware melodies.

A Note on Noel Coward

In contrast to Martin's songs, Coward's are, almost by definition, "salon" songs. That is what he wrote. He was of course English, and thus outside the scope of this book. However, Coward wrote two shows for original American productions. From "Sail Away" (1961), *Something Very Strange* is a fine ballad, and from "The Girl Who Came to Supper" (1963), *I'll Remember Her* is reminiscent of earlier Coward songs, a reminder of the understated, sophisticated bittersweetness for which he was well-known.

MARC BLITZSTEIN (1905–64)

Blitzstein and Leonard Bernstein were of the same generation and the same background. They were friends, collaborators, and rivals. Both were highly trained, highly gifted composers of concert music, as well as musicodramatic works in a distinctive American style. That distinctive style combined, in each case, influences from nineteenth-century European classical music, American classic pop and slang, Jewish folk and Weimar jazz, Weill and Krenek, the music hall—every mid-twentieth-century influence acting on alert American composers, except for Anglo-American folk music and Black traditions (though each could do a mean concert-style blues). Blitztein also wrote in a politically hortatory, street-music style, which marked his first great success, the proletarian stage work "The Cradle Will Rock" (1936), and some wartime patriotic cantatas. His operas and his concert songs lie beyond the limits of this book.[8]

Blitzstein wrote his own words. The songs are basically tonal, melodically romantic, harmonically eclectic, rhythmically alert, and *composed*; that is, in piano-vocal presentation, the piano part is carefully specified. They are in a sense art songs in a convincing popular layout and attitude. From "The Cradle Will Rock" there is a driving, 2/4-time ABABAB number, *Nickel Under the Foot*, an effective, hard-bitten presentation of the low economic motive in society: "But first be sure / the nickel's under your foot." Musically, it is a pop-blues, and shows a preference for "direct" modulation, a quick, short-lasting shift to a nearby tonal center, without conventional harmonic preparation (an aspect also of some Bernstein songs) and a layout that alternates fairly long, arching lines with short staccato phrases.

From about the same time is a free-standing song, exceedingly beautiful, called *Stay In My Arms* (1936). There is a long verse, which moves from dark diminished to achingly open chords made from thirds, and which modulates in a lovely IV-V-I just as the chorus begins. The words are those of increasing discontent, from "In this great city is there no peaceful, pretty spot?" to "...the mad existence of our time." Then the main melody begins, in big chords with very traditional harmony; it could be a Rachmaninoff song. The chorus is in perfect AABA. From the onset, the harmonic choices, the rhyming of *lazy* and *hazy*, and the grave pauses on the first beats convey acceptance or contemplation more than distress. The vocal range at first is small. But at the release (Figure 4.9), the voice line climbs, the downbeat cesuras drop out, and the tonality becomes unspecifiable, evolving constantly upward, full of dissonance until it *almost* reaches the dominant of the main key, which the final A-section then resumes. This middle section has a big range, and is full of conflict and pain, verbally and harmonically, but the final A is again simple, resigned, tender. In the second stanza, the song ends with the despairing phrase, "The world's insane, dear / So stay in my arms." This is an amazing, touching, great song.[9]

Figure 4.9

Another fine, tender song is *In the Clear* (1939), in which the speaker imparts the pains and joys of growing up. This song also has a long and complex introduction, but a rather short and simple main section; together, the format is a large binary one. The words are direct also, without anger, ending with the reassuring, "There are no fanfares to hear / you're just in the clear." The melody line ends with a caressing lowered 3 on *in*.[10] The musical show "Reuben Reuben" (published 1955) included a short, consoling song, *Never Get Lost*, and the big, blowzy *Monday Morning Blues*, a song of sexual braggadocio with just an undercurrent of desolation. It's not a blues in structure, and it consistently flats only tones 6 and 7. The song reaches completion, a cadence to the tonic, only on the very last note of the song. It's a terrific song.[11]

From "Juno" (1959), *I Wish It So* has a sort of Celtic radiance; it's another song of intense yearning on the part of someone with a pure heart. The melodic line is made mostly of single steps in the scale coming to rest very briefly on beautifully placed thirds and fifths; it is a melody that one might ascribe to Richard Rodgers. The lyrics are plain, with a lot of word and vowel repetition, lending an air of ingenuousness to what is being said. The finest feature of the song is the relation of the verse to the main body of the song. The verse, with a loose 6/8 meter and hesitant rhythms, sits low in the main singing octave, and the words speak of anxiety and confusion. The words of the verse open eloquently, "I've an unrest inside me...." and end "...I think I'll go mad." As the chorus begins, now in common time, the lie of the line moves to the upper part of the octave, and the words simplify into a pure, innocent form of desire: "For I wish it so! / What I wish I still don't know...." The chorus concludes, as expected, with another "I wish it so," the last word at last resting on the tonic tone (m. 35). But it isn't the last word. The singer returns, as if haunted by fear, to the opening notes and words of the verse (m.38): "It's the unrest inside me...," with *inside me* set on an aching set of intervals resting on a sixth chord above the dominant.[12] Of such expressive touches are great songs made.

To us, Blitzstein's songs seem more personal, more authentic, than the far more successful songs of Bernstein's later (post-1950) songwriting career. In subtle ways they prefigure some aspects of Sondheim's approach to song writing. When the balance is perfectly struck between musical venturesomeness and accessibility, the songs deserve to be far more famous than they are.

LEONARD BERNSTEIN (1918–90)

Counting all its versions and exposures, "West Side Story" (1957) gained probably the widest audience of any musical theater piece ever produced. Part of the overwhelming impact of the score as a whole was its eclecticism, its almost flaunted demonstration of the musical versatility of the composer. The score draws on swing, Latin, Weimar-style "jazz," operatic lyricism, street cries, the Gershwin symphonic-vocal synthesis of "Porgy and Bess," Stravinskian motoric rhythms, Broadway up-tempo, and other styles. As we listen to it today, much seems dated. In particular, eclecticism as an *ideal* seems pretentious. The fit between the music and Sondheim's words varies widely, being sometimes brilliant, sometimes embarrassing. The element that holds up best is the orchestral writing: It is this stratum—this superaddition of internal rhythmic verve, this coloristic lavishness, this wealth of lively inner melodic figures, of intricate key relationships—that makes "West Side Story" an impressive achievement.

About the songs as songs, we have mixed feelings. The tune, harmonization, and tonal format of *Tonight* seem essentially European, something that Frederick Loewe could have written. The melody is quite square, and the bridge simply raises the pitch of the basic material, though the *meno mosso* ending with its climb to the high key-tone is beautiful. What makes the song exciting is the propulsive, peremptory accompaniment figure that entrains the auditor's attention. It is the Tchaikovsky-to-Borodin rhythmic underlay that proves compelling. Sondheim's lyric is good: at the bridge, the stepping-down of linguistic level, from the high-falutin' metaphor of "Today the world is just an address" all the way down to the slangy comment, "No better than all right," is psychologically acute.

Somewhere as a tune, again, is boring—Beethoven with an echo of Copland, ending in Puccini high notes. Its best feature is the striking opening seventh interval, and the nice ambiguity of "There's **a** place," with the article stressed so as to suggest a specific vision in the singers' minds. The brass-heavy ascending two-note motif for the word *somewhere*, heard often throughout the score, becomes tiresome. The famous *Maria* foregrounds, in its setting of the name, an interval that Bernstein used throughout the show, the raised 4 (for the second note), and then again for the oh-so-expressive (and unconvincing) finish. Toward the end, the song becomes incoherent, both musically and in terms of the words ("music playing...almost like praying"), and with the mawkish repetition of the name. The accompaniment for this song chooses a timeworn "classical" figure, including plucked strings. Why? The best of the romantic songs is *I Have a Love*, which has a fine melodic ascent, but it is something of a fragment.

The fast songs are a lot better. *America*, with its intricate mambolike rhythm and its constant tension between duple- and triple-meter, is a triumph. It would sound frantic without crisp lyrics; as it is, the words are slangy but exact, and capture a 1950s register of ethnic self-mocking with affectionate humor. The saucy, cha-cha-like *I Feel Pretty* is also irresistible. (*Maria* is actually a slow cha-cha, when one listens carefully.) Sondheim has suggested that his lyric is faulty, in that a young *barrio* woman would not sing to herself, "A committee should be organized to honor me." But might not such a girl assume such cultural attitudes as she might try on a too-fancy dress in front of a mirror? And it's nice when the lyricist shifts the adjective *pretty*, heard repeatedly at the end of the line, to another syntactic function, in "pretty wonderful boy."

The best number in the show may be the rushing, syncopated *Something's Coming*, with its nonsyncopated middle section ("Around the corner....") and the calm slow triplet on "maybe tonight," built on the mottolike tritone. Why this suspended ending works in this song, and not in *Maria*, is ultimately mysterious. The word-choice in this song is right-on, informal, punchy.

It is quite possible for someone to argue that what we hear as incoherent in these songs was intended that way by the extremely sophisticated writers for a specific dramatic purpose; stated differently, that the creators chose to avoid making a musical play, after all an adaptation of "Romeo and Juliet," that was merely a collection of individual songs. That argument cuts both ways. Yes, the repetition toward the end of *Maria* is dramatically effective, but it is destructive of the song. We can only assert that, as songs, many of them seem today more like compositorial curiosities than living communicative entities.

That is not true of a number of Bernstein songs from other periods. Bernstein first became famous as a songwriter with "On the Town" (1944), lyrics by Comden and Green. The songs are fine. The exuberant opening, *New York, New York*, is irresistible, and the roisterous comedy numbers like *I Can Cook Too* played to Comden's and Green's ability to write "character" songs that are genuinely funny, even out of context.

There are three memorable ballads. *Lucky to Be Me* is in conventional AABA form, with wide intervals in its sweeping opening melody, which outlines an octave and a third within the first six bars. The release, by contrast, is built entirely on half-tone steps and a new key for each bar. Curiously, this melodic line, covering only six steps of the scale, seems "bigger" than the A-section melody, probably because the half-step motion gives it an urgent quality. The A-sections stake out a vertical space, the B-section releases a horizontal thrust. And the words in the B-section are exultant: "I am simply thunderstruck / At this change in my luck...." At the end of the song, one expects the title phrase once more, for the final cadence, but the lyricists sneak in a surprise, an extra short phrase "I could laugh out loud," which gives an immediate lift to what otherwise might be predictable. This song also boasts a reflective, out-of-time verse, which avoids foreshadowing the tune of the chorus; also has a big range; sets the scene ("I used to think...."); and defines the character of the speaker: "I thought that it would be a pleasant surprise / To wake up as a couple of other guys."

In the wistful but calm *Some Other Time*, the words are judicious, what with the use of the interjection, "oh well," the interesting near-rhyme of "gone to / want to" toward the beginning, and of course the pathos of the title phrase. There is a gentle verse that ends on a harmony that sounds peculiar until the chorus begins. The other big ballad, *Lonely Town*, is also well known, a favorite of jazz groups, probably because of its subtle, constant modulation from minor to major and its unusual chords. Vocally it is demanding, requiring a lot of voice and exact intonation. The song ends in a strong major (with added 6), yet manages to sound minor in flavor.

From 1950 there is a pretty song, *Who Am I?*, written for a version of "Peter Pan," lyrics by Bernstein. The tune is conventional, but there are some momentary, unprepared key changes that are striking. Cut from the same show was a more ambitious number, *Dream With Me*. It is AABA in form, with a number of modulations by one tone, so that the A-sections sound like C major transported up or down. The words are rather banal, The song is published with cello solo and obbligato, and is nowadays performed primarily by concert singers.

The songs from "Wonderful Town" (1953), again with Comden and Green, have been somewhat forgotten, unjustly. As with "On the Town," the score is full of brilliant production numbers with raucously funny lyrics. They are strongly dance-based, drawing on 1940s popular rhythms (as in *Swing* and *Conga*), or taking off more genteel styles, like *Christopher Street* and portions of *Pass That Football*, which are approximations of gavottes, funny owing to antiquated music with very up-to-date words.

There are also some winning ballads. *Ohio* is a ballad in an old-fashioned sense, simple and diatonic with no complex chords, a short 18-bar song in brief sections: ABABA(coda). The A is set, musically and verbally, as a near-palindrome; the B (from m. 5) is also a line that turns lazily on itself, in relaxed triplets (Figure 4.10). Comden and Green are generally thought of as writing "serviceable" lyrics, a fair overall assessment. But some serviceable lyrics are still worth

Figure 4.10

detailed study. Note the parsimonious vowel selection here. The whole song uses, almost entirely, repetitions of the long *i* and *o*. With this as the baseline, a later combination such as *wander/yonder*, with its contrasting lax vowels, directs the attention to a nice play of meaning, the bright vowel gives "leave" a distinctive force, and the occurrence of the word *maybe* at the very end of the song conveys a new class of thought (a logical conclusion). This kind of poetic control helps a song to be sung well, for the singer can keep the long line going, altering the vocal "production" only for the occasional special verbal effect. The sense of a pervasive vowel harmony (with telling deviations), together with a simplicity of word-choice and the composer's almost hypnotic recursive melodic line, gives a little song like *Ohio* permanent life. Perhaps its memorability comes from its being, subliminally, a parody of turn-of-the-century parlor songs, the kind of tune you find yourself harmonizing in thirds.

Another deceptively simple moderate-tempo song, *A Little Bit In Love*, is longer and a bit more complex in its A-sections, but has a rather long and unusual release that moves the song ahead and gives the impression, by short casual phrases like "I don't know...but I know...." of the speaker's working out a problem as she sings—and finding the solution just as the last A begins. *It's Love!* is a more exultant ABAC song. The climactic moment, as C begins, is followed by almost throwaway brief phrases that end the song with a nice vernacular touch: "Well, I see it * I know it * it's love!" Finally, there is a haunting, reflective slow ballad, *A Quiet Girl*, once more with minimal but well-chosen words, a beautiful brief minor-mode bridge, and a simple four-bar coda. It is a very poised, reflective song, with a hint of the folk ballad.

The Bernstein songs from the 1940s and early 1950s are distinctly different from the run-of-the-mill, although they use standard formats and direct language. The composer often uses one note that is "out of the scale" in a way that gives a special expressive touch to his melodic line. *Some Other Time* slips in and out of the mixolydian mode (heard first in the eighth word, *haven't*), but this passes without a lot of fuss; it simply brings a delicate tinge of pathos into the line. *A Little Bit In Love*, for the most part purely diatonic, uses an "odd tone" (a tritone) to get from the release back to the opening strain. The songs from this period also, like some of Blitzstein's, use direct modulation, typically to a nearby scale position (e.g., at the start of the middle section of *Lucky to Be Me*). The average listener will sense that a sophisticated writer is at work, without stopping to ponder whether or not the songs break new ground. The style is familiar, the handling creative within that style. The songs in "West Side Story" are more obviously "advanced." We hear the earlier ones as superb songs, but without all the fuss.

Toward the end of his career as a songwriter, there is a pretty, wistful song, *My New Friends* (1979), but Bernstein's words are enigmatic, and rather clumsy in any case.

In retrospect, Bernstein seems a highly gifted musical polyglot. Early in his career he mastered the conventional comedy number or love ballad of the Broadway musical, bringing something fine to them, in the same way that he would master the coloratura concert aria like the spectacular *Glitter and Be Gay*. In midcareer he assimilated songs to the demand of complex musical drama, at a certain cost. In late career, the weakness of the songs he wrote for chamber operas, or even for what were nominally Broadway shows, demonstrate that his true interests and commitments lay elsewhere.

ALEC WILDER (1907–80) and Friends

In his 1972 book with Maher, Wilder covered with discrimination the "great innovators" of the genre up to about the midtwentieth century. He omitted from coverage one important figure, however: himself.

Wilder was eclectic, in the best sense of the term, which probably cost him wide popularity. He was an important composer of concert chamber music, especially for wind, and of "jazz suites" for various musical combinations. With Arnold Sundgaard and others, he wrote a number of delightful children's or folk operas. He also wrote, throughout his career, art songs to texts by such figures as Gerard Manley Hopkins or Christina Rossetti, many of them very fine.[13]

Though he wrote for the stage and films from time to time, most of his popular songs were written independently, to be given life by singers and instrumentalists. Because of that, and because they are so various, though always personal in style, it makes sense to organize them with reference to the lyricists he worked with, often across several decades. However, early in his career, Wilder, supplying his own words, had two major commercial successes, *It's So Peaceful in the Country* (1941) and *I'll Be Around* (1942). The latter is in a clearly "commercial" style with, nevertheless, an exceedingly lovely, altitude-gaining release. The best section of the former song is also the middle section; otherwise the notable feature of the singing line is the difference between a major and minor seventh interval. The bass of the A-sections is built on a line that descends by half-steps over six bars, while the harmony remains in the main key. This chaconnelike underpinning is unusual in American popular song; it sounds to us a little willful.

After these early successes, Wilder seemed to attempt more poetically demanding lyrics and to adopt a more chromatic approach to the melody line, using intervals that some singers couldn't hit and some listeners couldn't hear. Among songs for which he also wrote words, the effective, mostly minor-mode *Trouble Is a Man* (1944) has an Arlenesque touch or two. A later song (1968), *Night Talk*, seems like a draft of a better, later song with McGlohon, *A Long Night*.

Occasionally, Wilder wrote a lyric to another composer's tune. One such song is Edwin Finckel's *Where Is the One?* (1948). The tune is superromantic, and the words are apt. Even finer is *A Child Is Born* (1969), music written by jazz musician Thad Jones. It is Wilder's best independent lyric, fitting Jones's exquisite melody perfectly; it's a pity the song is heard most often as an instrumental (Figure 4.11). The crucial notes are the ones, all low in pitch, that start successive long phrases: here D, later E-flat, D, E-natural, F: they occur low in the range, like a cello digging in. The highest tones in each phrase are mostly near-octaves, and sound like a woodwind obbligato. There are thus two vocal registers in the song, pinned together by "accidentals." Correspondingly, Wilder's words

Figure 4.11

use sounds that chime in a slightly oblique way; for example, *now* and *new*, and, later, *warm* and *morn*, and only a few vowel sounds, all of them relaxed.[14]

William Engvick (b. 1914)

The first important lyricist collaborator is Engvick, who wrote mostly with Wilder, although he also did the words for *Song from "Moulin Rouge"* (music by Georges Auric, 1953) and other non-Wilder songs (see below).

Their first success together was *While We're Young* (1943), to which Morty Palitz also contributed. The quality of the lyric is very high, with the longer or darker vowels set as one-syllable words on high notes so that they soar emotionally. The moderate waltz tempo and rhythm is arguably a bit rigid. If sung with strong downbeats on each measure, it sounds a little old-fashioned; displacing some of the words to the second beat would give it more of a lilt. The song sings perhaps better in a loose 4/4 meter, though Wilder deplored performers who took such liberties. There are twice as many measures as normal, but its proportions are ABAA, with the final A stretched so as to act as a coda. The bridge comes early, which gives the song an urgency, with high notes ascending from a surprising A natural to a B flat and then a D. About 16 bars later, there is a pitch-memory effect, as Wilder stretches one more half-step to the high E-flat. By that means, the climax of the song, at m. 50, seems to reach back over a long arc and complete the B-section (Figure 4.12). Note how the phrase shapes in the excerpt, together with the word choices and the triple rhyme, outline the emotional curve that brings the song to a poignant close. The first phrase is exclamatory, with a big upward interval and only a slight retreat thereafter. The

Figure 4.12

second expresses emotional self-assessment, where *all* can refer back to *blue skies* and also forward to the verb *shines*. The third phrase begins with the concluding verb, *shines*; the pitch is that of *young* at the cadence, but first comes the oddly rapturous phrase, "before our eyes."

Who Can I Turn To? (1941) is a stunning AABA song, its only weakness being a slightly pedestrian (for Wilder) release. Its memorable feature occurs in mm. 3-4, where the composer creates a stepwise line (with one crucial downward leap), the line strongly chromatic but including two dissonant accidentals. Quite unusual in popular song, the space between the first and second four-bar periods is not marked by a rest but is filled, so that one hears one extended phrase. The words are, "How can I face it alone...now"—*now* coming as a distinct surprise. Later in the song, Engvick extends other phrases, such as "star...how" and even "parade...oh," with *oh* not sounding contrived because it leads right into the next phrase. This joining device gives the song a continuous long line.

Another beautiful ballad is *Everywhere I Look* (1943), in ABAB form with lovely material in the B-sections and with odd, evocative words. *Ellen* (1954) is an exquisite, deeply enigmatic song. Written in 32 bars, it is not really sectional in nature, but sounds as one long unit, like a lyrical solo for horn or clarinet. It opens on an unusual tone of the scale, an unstable 4, and immediately wends its way through unusual intervals, using often the expressive, innately dissonant, raised 7. Song lyrics that give prominence to a name generally backfire, because the direct address becomes annoying. This does not happen here: *Ellen* is fitted into the discourse in natural syntax. The words in general are slightly mysterious:

"Ellen walks in shadow streets that never were...." (not "shadowed"), and they gain great intensity at the end of the song, where they are set as run-on phrases containing one long thought: "Don't tell me I'm lonely, and don't tell me I love you unless you let me find you some day." Who *is* Ellen, who lets the speaker know that he loves her? Some dream figure, apparently. It's an amazing song, though difficult.

More conventional is *Listen to Your Heart* (1957), a short, attractive song with a long and excellent verse. Most of the Wilder — Engvick songs do not have substantial verses; this one is communicative. Another song with a fine verse is *The April Age* (1956), whose concept is fine—falling in love for the first time is like coming from Winter to Spring—but whose realization in the chorus is a bit disappointing. Engvick's lyrics for the verse are, by contrast, exceptionally satisfying, a nice mixture of echoes of English poetry with everyday language—and wit.

> You tell yourself it's a winter world,
> A leafless world well lost,
> And the golden fall doesn't dazzle you at all.
> Even summer is a frost.

I Like It Here (1961) is a perfect little song with a distinctive Scotch-snap rhythm: why it didn't become a hit recording is anyone's guess.[15]

A late, curious song, from a children's television program, is *It's a Fine Day for Walkin' Country Style* (1955). As the title suggests, it's folkish, with deliberately naive words and abrupt shifts to and from the dominant. It's perhaps a little precious, but it has a lovely arching close in the melody line, for the words "Isn't it amazing how the miles go by?" In 1958, Wilder and Engvick did another television show with original score, "Hansel and Gretel." It included some delightful songs. *What Are Little Girls Made Of?* is a version of sugar and spice, snails and puppy-dog tails. A charming brief query, serving as a verse, in a free rhythmic pattern, leads into a lilting chorus, featuring the Scotch-snap figure at the end of mm.4 and 8. The bridge is nothing but one note sung like an incantation: the last four bars lead with good chords through a quick circle-of-fifths. Basically the song is 16 bars, though there are stanzas and an interlude. The words remind one of Victorian poetry; for example, "a silken gown and a silver crown, a flirt of an angel's feather." There's also a stanza about boys: "A stone to throw and a frog or so in slightly used condition." A more driving song is *I'm Much Too Happy Dancing to Care*, whose main idea is quite like that of the Gershwins's *I Can't Be Bothered Now*. The title phrase is set especially well: it's impossible not to sing blithely. Again, the basic pattern is short, but there are multiple stanzas. The very brief bridges end with a time-worn chromatic riff for an interpolated phrase ("Don't give into it!"), leading into the last eight bars in a time-honored way.

The integral score (rare for Wilder) to a film from 1964, "Open the Door (And See All the People)," produced a batch of wonderful songs with Engvick. *Unbelievable* is an amusing, throwaway sort of song, deadpan.. There are two stanzas, one relating unbelievably happy events, the other, unbelievably bad ones—though the latter end happily. Wilder disliked songs that he called "notey," meaning a melodic line with lots of even-time notes setting lots of words. That exactly describes this song, but it works. There's also a sly 1960s Brazilian flourish at the end.

The charming AABAA *That's My Girl* is in big-band swing time, with Engvick at his slangiest. In the second and the final A-sections, he manages to dovetail the last word of one phrase with the first word of the next; for example, "Laughter in the *wind / wind*ows in the *sun / Sun*day in a quiet town." Only a few popular songs use this technique (e.g., the Bock — Harnick *She Loves Me*); it's fun when done with élan. *Remember, My Child* is a winner, a not-fast waltz with a built-in lilt. It opens on an out-of-scale appoggiatura, kicking the line into motion. It is ABAB in form; B reverses the direction of the melody line and the main rhythm of A. There is a minute rhythmic surprise at the end of the first B, and again at the end of the song, where there is, in addition, a stunning chromatic turn just before the last note. Once again, Engvick provides tiny alterations to what is expected: he writes, "Dragonflies *in* their paper wings," instead of the more obvious *with*.

The knock-out song from the film is *Mimosa and Me*. If we had to choose one among all the Wilder — Engvick songs to be universally known, it would be this one. It is fey, but *big* in its reach and effect. We sometimes comment how problematic are songs with person's names in the titles. *Mimosa* is an exception to the name-in-the-title problem, owing to its loose-limbed, jaunty character.[16] Who is Mimosa? Dunno, but she must be a peach. The song begins (Figure 4.13) with a unique pattern of syncopation: a set of brief three-note, three-syllable figures, separated by all-important eighth-note rests. The first one of the figures has been truncated to be a carefully specified pick-up. Some singers try to change these figures to a "swung" pattern of dotted-eighth plus sixteenth, but the way Wilder set it is more loping, more eccentric, and more buoyant.

The words throughout the song are casual and fond, with dropped consonants, and colloquial terms like *bumpety-thumpety* and *racketty-packetty* that nevertheless avoid being cute. And there is the wonderfully observed line, "Spring is here again, When you're in love it's mighty likely to be." It's a vernacular lyric to rank with the finest ones by Johnny Mercer. The song is not harmonically advanced, but the B-sections go through seven decisive chord changes in four bars (as at m. 9 and again at m. 25), while the underlying key stays in F, as at the opening, and the verbal rhythm retains short clauses. The

Figure 4.13

final B (mm. 24-28) amounts to a playful, likable coda. Leading into m. 25, the
line bursts its bounds: the phrases are still short, but the singer traces big arcings
of joy: sevenths butting up against octave leaps, set over a descending bass line
ending with a bluesy flatted VI–V–I progression. And it isn't over yet: there is
the endearing tag, "Oh my!" with the same flat-6 tone included in the chord. If
ever the end of a song expressed pure joy, this is it.[17]

In 1993, for Jackie Cain and Roy Kral, Engvick did a quite brilliant lyric to fit an early Wilder tune, and called the resulting, ebullient song *Watch Out for Sharks, Dear*. The speaker cautions his loved one that pretty much everything is risky—except him. Musically, it's a quick noodling treatment of chains of thirds with one strategic diminished chord set on a lowered 3. The striking rhythmic feature is that the title phrase and its counterparts enter strongly on the second, weak beat, a reverse syncopation that sets up a succeeding, longer note to produce a strong stagger effect. All three stanzas have amusing words ("No hocus-pocus, Just focus on me!"). A crisp jazz trio and a sassy singer could do a lot with this fine song. From the 1940s, there are two excellent unpublished songs with Wilder: *The Result Was Dad* opens with a mock anthemlike verse, then swings into a 32-bar, AABA chorus built on jazz chords and syncopation. It's a "suggestive" song handled with finesse. Engvick's words in this instance are in a class with Harburg's or Ira Gershwin's, being light, tasteful, and constantly surprising.

> There's ladies in our fam'ly tree the fellas couldn't lay off
> No minister! Bar sinister! Pop was the pay-off!
> MacGregor wooed a bonnie lass and covered her with plaid
> And very indirectly, the result was Dad!

Another amusing one is *It's Monogamy*: ("What has four legs and kisses? Mister, It's monogamy."), which may fall into the category of special material.

Engvick with Others

Gordon Connell, an actor and singer in New York, is also a composer of some good songs, alas, little known. Some were written in the 1990s with Engvick, in a style that uses harmonically advanced "jazz" chords. They sound a bit like Mandel or Strayhorn ballads, and Engvick's evocative, delicate lyrics match them beautifully. *In the Middle of the Night* is a pretty example, as is *Open the Door*, with intervals using tones a half-step below or above the triadic tones. Even better is *Or What?* in a sinuous Latin rhythm and with a lovely vocal line. The words are an expression of love, with just a hint of cajoling. ("Are you the one, the one in my number-one spot—or what?") *Number 25 Mariposa Drive* is a little waltz, with some piquant touches, about the joys of family and home.[18]

For his part, Wilder wrote some occasional songs, reflecting his respect for talented peers, with other lyricists. *Rain, Rain* (1955) is a haunting tune, full of ninth and eleventh intervals and prominently placed, lowered 2 and 7 tones that yield a sort of mixolydian mode. As with so many of his songs, the release is a complete surprise, longer-phrased and calmer in emotional temperature. The excellent lyric, by Marshall Barer, ends with an unexpected, vulnerable tag, "...till my baby comes back to me." With Ben Ross Berenberg, Wilder wrote in 1955 a moody song, *The Winter of My Discontent*. The tune is beautiful; the words are perhaps too "poetic," over and above the Shakespearean echo to the title phrase. The actress Judy Holliday wrote artfully quiet words to *Welcome Home* (1976), which has a tender melody with great chords at the climax, four bars before the end. It's a charmer.

Finally, with the inestimable lyricist Johnny Mercer, Wilder wrote two touching songs. One, *The Sounds Around the House* (1976), uses a very simple tune and ordinary chords to go with the deceptively plain lyric. In fact, the lyric alters vowel color subtly and uses rhyme sparingly, at one place concealed (*best/nest*ing). We intuit that the breath-catching moment in the song began with Mercer: out of nowhere comes the calm interjection, "Small boy," set twice to even half-notes. At this moment, one realizes that the song is a fond salute to a younger persona no longer present. Also good, perhaps a bit faux-naïve, is *If Someday Comes Ever Again*, from the same year. It is a sweet not-fast waltz, which starts elegantly (with the A of the major triad of the key, F) over a G-minor seventh chord. Both writers shift gears nicely for the bridge. In his lyric, Mercer reflects that "The straightest roads turn and life is run mostly by chance," the latter phrase involving an attractive ambiguity. He also chooses an antiquated word order for the title and last phrase. The technique is effective when used sparingly.

Loonis McGlohon (1921–2002)

Wilder's other major collaborator on popular songs, also over several decades, was Loonis McGlohon, from North Carolina. McGlohon was a pianist, arranger, and musician who wrote music, but, with Wilder, mostly lyrics. His verbal range was not so wide as Engvick's (whose diction extends from the poetic to the silly), but he had perhaps more of a feeling for jazz and pop-blues moods, judging by the number of such songs the two men created.

An example of role reversal is *I Wish I Had the Blues Again* (published 1986), where McGlohon, as composer, created a song whose A-sections are made out of a fast right-hand piano riff. The light blues feeling comes from flatted 3, 5, and 6, and a repeating pattern of I-IV-ii-I chord progressions. The B-section is trivial. Wilder's words are efficient in getting across the notion that having the blues is worth it—since it means one is in love again. A better song from the same period, with the two men in their customary roles, is *Turn Left at Monday* (published 1988), where McGlohon reassures us: "If the rain comes down on Sunday...turn left at Monday." Wilder's melody line is distinguished by quick harmonic movement, achieved by using two different chords with added tones (discordant to the main key) at the start of the first and second bars, under *rain* and *Sun-*, and by very brief key changes for the "empty beats" (without words) at the conclusion of the two A-sections. The song ends abruptly; but the idea of the song is a good one.

Blackberry Winter, from 1976, is an unusual song, a sort of understated torch song, very original in the way it represents the flexible pacing and contours of ordinary speech. The actual word choice is fairly standard, casual English; the Southern vernacular term forming the title sets a rural American tone (Figure 4.14). Almost any other songwriters would normalize the speeds of the individual verbal phrases, setting them in the default scansion pattern: "**comes** with-**out** a **warn**-ing...." Here, phrases of several words are intended to run quickly, as one might speak in conversation. The same patterns are used in the bridge. This is

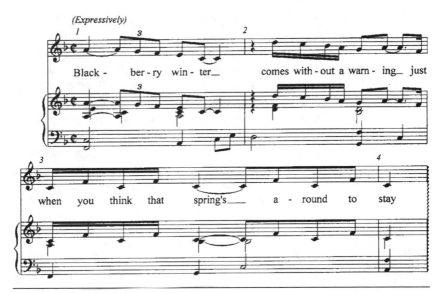

Figure 4.14

the distinction of this song, together with the way Wilder uses quick-repeated intervals ("when you think that") for the same naturalistic purpose. There is also a fine seamless transition from the middle section back to A.[19] There is no inherent reason, in the literate American popular song tradition, why this kind of attention to spoken speech-rhythm over a stretch of words should not be rendered more often. Of course, all good lyricists set short phrases naturalistically, and pay strict attention to accurate fitting of words, especially in up-tempo songs. But for songs at moderate tempos, the only other important popular songwriter in the second half-century who has shown this kind of avid regard for the speech-rhythm aspects of song "discourse" is Sondheim.

A Long Night (copyright 1981), recorded by Sinatra, is in urban-blues style, like Arlen. As with *Turn Left at Monday*, Wilder opens forcefully with two harmonically complex chords, followed by a normal move to the minor tonic. McGlohon's lyric is organized, in the A-sections, in very short mournful phrases, as in "The barrooms...and the back streets...dead end," which tell a familiar sad story tersely. In the B-sections, the verbal phrases become longer, more propositional. The trochaic motto-rhythm of the A-section, followed by a loose triplet, is appropriate to the short-winded, down-turning words of a blues, and the layout of the 48-bar song, ABABAB, has the repetitive quality of a blues. The B-sections use the device of descent by half-steps in both the melody line and the bass, reminiscent of big-band jazz of the 1940s. In all, a striking song, lessened only by the whiff of banality that comes from a lyric idea structured around depression and booze.

More venturesome, but unknown, are two other blues-flavored songs from the 1970s. One is *Walkin' Sad*, whose opening lyric is also in a typical blues pattern of two very short statements followed by a longer one: "Walkin' sad...movin' slow...goin' nowhere fast." This song has both a long and fascinating 14-bar verse, almost a song in itself, and a compelling story in the faster-moving, less bluesy, B-section of the chorus, where the words come in longer lines and more complex syntax. It is a song whose words take primacy over the music.

The same can be said of *'Sgonna Be a Cold Cold Day*, which has a similar layout and a similar pattern of, first short, then longer verbal and musical phrases. The elision in the title phrase is all-important for setting the confidential tone of the story. The words are all good; we provide the A-section ones:

> Look for winter weather
> Next time we're together
> 'Sgonna be a cold cold day.
> Caught you cheatin', lover
> If I share your cover,
> 'Sgonna be a cold cold day.

These are two songs that male singers really ought to be performing.

The last known song Wilder wrote, with McGlohon, is *South—To a Warmer Place*, 1980. It concerns getting a cold shoulder from a lover, and then heading on out. It's notable for an anticipatory syncopation at the end of the first phrase (and in corresponding places thereafter): in "I'd be glad to stay right here with you," *you* comes an eighth-note early. This allows the composer to change chords, for brisk harmonic movement, on the empty beats right after a phrase, not while it is going on. McGlohon alone wrote a fine ballad, *The Wine of May*

(1975), which uses out-of-scale notes wistfully at the end of phrases and has a well-knit-together lyric.

To true lovers of the American popular song, Wilder is an important figure, for his book as well as his songs. For the general listening public, a few of his songs, like *I'll Be Around*, may be familiar—but not as Wilder's. A comment often heard is that Wilder's songs are "too good to be popular." That does not explain much. Many great writers wrote songs that are too difficult or too subtle to be big hits. But they also wrote hits. Wilder was not a great stylistic "innovator." He was so good at every aspect of the music of song that his work is not recognizable for any one cardinal attribute, although he was specially good at middle sections and endings (especially in the songs with Engvick) and mightily respectful of words. His songs are, in a sense, taciturn, making their effects subtly. They are often long, but they're seldom "big."

You can recognize a Rodgers tune, a Berlin attitude, a Coleman rhythm, Duke's harmonic color, the integration of words and music in a Sondheim song. Wilder did everything well, except perhaps for strongly accented "bounce" songs, which he could do but mostly did not (*Mimosa and Me* being a memorable exception). Some maintain that Wilder's songs are so "tasteful" that they don't reach out and grab one. So be it. If good singers would perform them, it wouldn't take much before he reached the reputation he deserves.[20]

Notes

1. Performance: "Blossom Dearie, "Soubrette," Verve LP 2133
2. Performance: Barbara Lea, "The Melody Lingers On," see Barbara Lea website.
3. Performance: "Blossom Dearie Sings Comden and Green," Verve LP 2109.
4. Sondheim's clever words for a female singer can be heard from Annie Ross, "Gypsy, the Jazz Version," World-Pacific LP 1808.
5. Performance: Maxine Sullivan, "Together," Atlantic LP 81783.
6. We recall with pleasure the famous André Previn — Gerry Mulligan — Shelly Manne trio recording of the "My Fair Lady" songs, Annie Ross or Susannah McCorkle singing *I've Grown Accustomed to Her (His) Face* with relaxed irregular phrasing, Shirley Horn or Oscar Peterson delightfully swinging *Wouldn't It Be Loverly?*
7. Performance: "Michael Feinstein Sings "The Hugh Martin Songbook," Nonesuch CD 793142.
8. In the early 1950s, Blitzstein enjoyed fame, but as the translator of a new American text for the enormously popular "Three Penny Opera," by Weill. He died before he was able to reestablish himself as a composer in public awareness. Blitzstein's life and works are well covered in Eric A. Gordon, "Mark the Music" (New York: St, Martin's Press, 1989). In 2002, Boosey & Hawkes published a three-volume compendium of his songs, in various styles.
9. Performance: William Sharp, "Marc Blitzstein: Zipperfly & Other Songs," Koch CD 3-7050.
10. Performance: Dawn Upshaw, "I Wish It So," Nonesuch CD 79345.
11. Performance: Sharp.
12. Performance: Upshaw.
13. Some art songs and some that lie between genres are published by The Richmond Organization (New York, no date) as "25 Songs for Solo Voice," with intelligent commentary on style distinctions by Robert Wason of the Eastman School. A useful biography is: Desmond Stone, "Alec Wilder In Spite of Himself" (New York: Oxford University Press, 1996).

14. Performance: "Marlene VerPlanck Sings Alec Wilder," Audiophile LP 218.)
15. Performance: Irene Kral, "You Are There," Audiophile CD 299.
16. In its rhythm, its wide vocal intervals, and its apostrophe to an oddly named woman, it reminds one of, and would fit nicely with, another exception, *Evalina*, by Arlen and Harburg.
17. Performance: Jackie Cain and Roy Kral, "The Alec Wilder Collection," Audiophile LP 257.
18. These and other Connell — Engvick songs can be requested from the The Richmond Organization.
19. Performance: Teddi King, "Lovers and Losers," Audiophile LP 117.
20. The publishers of most of Wilder's songs, even unpublished, are generous about sharing them. Contact The Richmond Organization, New York.

5
Restocking the Songbook

In the 1950s and during the next three decades, there came to prominence a number of exceptionally talented songwriters who were not completing, but starting, fine careers.

CY COLEMAN (1929–2004) and CAROLYN LEIGH (1926–83)

Like Styne (chapter 4), Coleman showed an impressive joie de vivre and fluency. Each was able to write not only scores, but individual songs that made it to the Billlboard charts. In Styne's case, these hits were mostly songs from films. In Coleman's, certain Broadway songs became widely popular, but also a number of stand-alone songs, often written with Carolyn Leigh.

In part, this overleaping of categories was owed to performers such as Tony Bennett, who especially appreciated Coleman. But in part it was simply the ability to write well in different styles. Leigh was particularly gifted in this regard. No one was more sophisticated than she in show songs, but she also came up with concepts for songs that attracted the general public. Coleman was also fortunate in working with the consummate professional, Dorothy Fields (below), who wrote as slangily and brashly with him as she had written formally and lyrically with Kern or Schwartz.

There are clear differences between Styne and Coleman. Styne wrote rhythmic, "swinging" songs, while Coleman wrote jazzy ones, often integrated by vamp or riff figures and sometimes using complex rhythms quite difficult for the average singer or player. Partly reflecting their lyricists' input, Styne's tunes were often catchy, direct, and upbeat, while Coleman's can be said to be insouciant, urban, and hip. Most significant, some of Styne's songs sound like great ideas needing a second draft, and a few are pretty poor. Coleman's most inconsequential songs are polished. Styne is like Berlin, Coleman like Gershwin.

There are a number of wonderful Coleman — Leigh songs from the 1950s not associated with shows. The opening section of *I Walk a Little Faster* (1957) plays with tones 5 and 6, below and above the tonic, with the intervals nicely etched as dissonant sevenths arranged os that the key-tone is skipped. The end chords on all phrase endings are forms of seventh chords, returning to I for A_2 and to IV for the B-section: the means are time-honored, the effect utterly fresh. The melody line begins with big downward intervals; the lovely confiding bridge, opening with "Can't begin to see my future shine as yet" and then rhyming "sign as yet" and "mine as yet," inverts this with up-intervals. Another fine touch is that the title phrase is always set on a pattering repetition of one tone, with one step up for the last syllable: it is a perfect expression of someone taking rapid steps forward. Most of last A-section is set this way, so that the speaker now seems to be rushing without hesitation to his goal. The lyric includes a smart example of enjambment ("stronger/castle") in the last eight bars.

From the same year is a lazy boogie song, built on very simple chords and with an open triadic harmonization, *My, How the Time Goes By*. Harmonically it's plain, but the format is unusual: it could be analyzed as $A_1A_2A_1A_2A_2A_1$, where the bridge is a version of A_2. The verbal phrase lengths are irregular, the melodic line, basically a little riff, uses lots of slow triplets, the vocal range is small (matching the narrowness of the boogie chord pattern), and the important word *time* is set on a strong accidental. The lyric has a sweet country feel: "Hoot owls cry…clouds made of cotton…my oh my."

It Amazes Me (1958) has a reverential, love-struck character. The verse begins the musing mood. The opening melodic strain of the chorus contains everything fine in the song. There is the delicate turn figure, touching just lightly on tone 5 and avoiding the key-tone (it's in the bass); the slow triplet expressing wonder; the yearning accidentals; and the poised dotted rhythm pattern etching the most expressive syllables (Figure 5.1). The chords are rich and beautifully arranged; bringing a slight dissonance on down-beats, then clarifying. The final A-section is mesmerizing in the way it combines small melodic turns with one large interval (on *fazes*), then climbs delicately up the chromatic scale to the final

Figure 5.1

upper key-tone. The lyric is masterful: the exact rhyme, *dazes/praises*, occurs 10 bars apart, but in between Leigh uses *ways* and *praise* (and *dazzles* right next to *daze*), keeping the listener always alert. This is a great song.[1]

You Fascinate Me So (also 1958) couldn't be more of a contrast. It's a fast, snappy song with double-length A-sections, except for the last. Each period in the A-sections opens with a missing beat, but ends with a strong forward syncopation in the last bar, a Gershwinesque pattern. The song is made of lots of short words, set on long strings of eighth notes. The important feature is that they are in strict time; they are not "swung," but strung like pearls on a line. The song is remarkable in being a patter song without a moment of musical tediousness or verbal contrivance.

One of the best-known Coleman — Leigh songs was written as early as 1951. *The Best Is Yet to Come* is an extremely striking song rhythmically, using the Scotch- snap pattern (short-long, with stress on the short) all the way through, except in the complex bridge, which mixes new material with old in an innovative way. This basic rhythmic figure gives the song an exultant, off-balance feel. The vocal line, sounding like a keyboard riff made into a song, is given a strong contour by the use of two-note slurs at the end of all the phrases (except at cadences), which has the effect of stabilizing each off-balance phrase just in advance of empty beats between phrases. The striking opening vocal strain simply lays out the half-tone scale in strong sculpted intervals, oddly like Chopin's Mazurka, op. 24, no. 4. The song modulates all over the place. It's most effective rhythmically when not sung too fast, in which case it sounds like Berlin on speed.

Two other fine Coleman — Leigh songs are *Firefly* (1958), which mixes long and short phrases, has delicious words ("she radiates moonglow"), and involves some great syncopation, and *Witchcraft* (1957), with a fine boogielike vamp and bass. The latter shows Leigh's ability to use colloquial language that remains just a little obscure: "It's such an ancient pitch / But one I wouldn't switch...." (Another good song named *Witchcraft*, from the same era, is by Michael Brown.) *Doop-Do-De-Oop* is a nonsense song that worms its way into your memory. It's built on a vamp, and is organized around rhymes like *noodle/doodle/bet your boodle*. A torch song, *On Second Thought* (1961), has excellent lyrics that tell of someone giving up a lover, and regretting it. It opens with "It seemed a good idea at the time"; the eponymous second thought occurs well into the song. Minor-to-major alternation throughout the song is a simple, effective, expressive device. There is a subtle interior chain of rhymes toward the end: "It's terrible / how many small wonderful things you recall / on second thought, After you're all / alone!" Finally, *The Rules of the Road* (1961) has Coleman's and Leigh's distinctive accented rhythmic bounce. Here it springs from a clever vamp between phrases, and from the fact that there is virtually no bridge. The lyric is dry without being bitter: "The brighter (love) glows, the longer you burn."

Coleman's and Leigh's first Broadway show was "Wildcat" (1960), whose theater songs are actually less demanding than the earlier stand-alone songs. We think that *Hey, Look Me Over* is subliminally a spoof of band music, heavy on the tuba. The title number, little remembered, is also bandlike. It's an up-tempo, fast-four number using an old query-response formula: "Who's the greatest at getting her man?" (answer: "Wildcat"), and it sounds like a sly homage to *Take Me Out to the Ballgame*. The words are a lot of fun; for example, "Who is the cat who is ready to pounce? / Who's the cat with more pounce to the ounce?"

In some respects the most interesting song is for male chorus, but it could also be a moody solo. *Tall Hope* has a steady slow, clop-clopping, beat and a definite cowboy flavor to the words—and a tune as placid as a lullaby. The harmony moves back and forth between a radiant diatonic and a darker, blueslike color. The words are calm, phonetically pure, and hopeful, with a tinge of resignation: "I'm ridin' that tall bright hope right now!," the minute extension *bright* allowing more time for a crescendo. It's hard to forget this song, once heard.

Two other songs are at the opposite pole from country-western. *One Day We Dance* is in three-quarter time, but sounds in two, with an undeviating stressed short, unstressed long rhythm that gives the song a sort of possessed quality. The melodic line also has an underlying wildness, with nothing but disyllabic units set on upward intervals that widen to the midpoint of each phrase, then narrow. There is no bridge, just a two-bar out-of-time interpolation, so that the song is an unusual AAAA design. The opening melody is strong but subtle (Figure 5.2).

You've Come Home is a beautifully unified ballad, whose phrases get longer

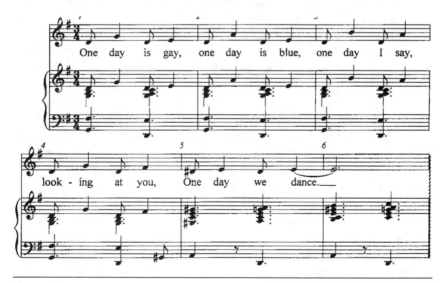

Figure 5.2

and longer until they double back to the opening figure. Partly because of this recursion, the final climax is very powerful. The first important word, *home*, is set indeed long, on the unstable, yearning tone 6. When this three-note figure occurs three bars later, *home* is drastically shortened, so that the phrase moves on to a more complex thought. This song is in ABAB form, plus a climatic extension. The two last-mentioned songs have a sweep that reminds one of the aching simplicity of Loesser in "The Most Happy Fellow."

The funny show "Little Me" (1962) reveled in a Broadway revue format. Its best-known song was *I've Got Your Number*, so syncopated that it levitates until the B-sections tie it down. It's so syncopated that it would become monotonous were it not for the precision of the words.

Our favorite song from the show is the delightful *Real Live Girl*. It's a waltz with a jazz feel, especially when one combines the second and thirds beats into a dotted figure, as one inevitably wants to. The tune is simple, the harmony elementary, the vocal range tiny. What makes the song are the words, which illustrate song vernacular at its best. It would be impossible to write verse not set to music about a horny guy just off the farm and discovering girls, and keep it inoffensive: "Strayed off the farm with an actual armful of real, live girl" (note the hidden rhyme, *farm*/*arm*-, and the verb whose remote homonym is *straight*); or, "Dreams in your bunk don't compare with a hunk of a real, live girl." In a song, the tale is endearing, smile-inducing. There is also one tiny musical feature that makes a big difference. In mm.3–4, you hear, on the first level, dactylic units (e.g., **nev**-er done **this** with a) (Figure 5.3). But subliminally you hear a trochaic overlay, such that it takes on another stress pattern: **nev**-er **done** this

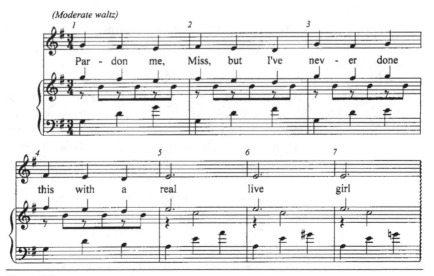

Figure 5.3

with a (then back to **one**-two-three for "real ** live ** girl"). It's subtle, but it's there, and it's wonderful.

From 1964 there's another famous self-standing song, *When In Rome*, which is a beaut. It has a great, loose salsalike rhythm, and spectacular words, including some in the longish verse ("errant mate department...State Department") worthy of Cole Porter).

Early on, Coleman had written with others besides Leigh. In 1952 came the well-known *Why Try to Change Me Now*, with Joseph McCarthy, with a haunting setting of the title phrase; and in 1955, with McCarthy, the ballad *I'm Gonna Laugh You Out of My Life*, which has a fine opening title phrase and a "hook" at the end of the song. Coleman and McCarthy also created *The Riviera* (1957), a delightful number with a scampering congalike rhythm and lyric about love and life that are "zany and free." *Sweet Talk* (1964), words by Floyd Huddleston, is a delightful jazz waltz in the narrative minor; it's deliberately "talky" since it's about romantic shining-on: "... if you don't mean what you say...You better go home right away."

In the 1960s, Coleman wrote several occasional songs with the singer, Peggy Lee. The modal-sounding *Then Was Then and Now Is Now* is short and slight, but haunting. Even better, and underappreciated, is *That's My Style* (1963). It's Coleman at his airiest, and the Lee words are eccentric and clever, including a rhyme sequence about a smile that's "wicked and crooked...and it's got me hook-ed." A neat song.[2] There is also a fine song with Tommy Wolf words, called *Here I Go Again* (1987). The lyric is muted and powerful; the song has a big range and a passionate release, and requires a big singer.[3]

Carolyn Leigh died relatively young. By 1972 Coleman was working with the old pro, Dorothy Fields, on the songs for "Seesaw." Fields, less dazzlingly brilliant than Leigh, was perhaps a better colleague for "book" musicals. *Nobody Does It Like Me* is a textbook "show song," by definition self-regarding, offering what amounts to a list of examples by a speaker who does admit to frailties, but finds them all endearing. *We've Got It* is also selves-centered, a paean to falling in love. The words are clever ("...the girls I've kissed are duller than a laundry list"). Both these songs are rather tick-tock in rhythm. *I'm Way Ahead* is better. It mixes narration on quick eighth notes with summation on longer ones ("I'm way ahead...Well said, well said"). It opens on a harmonically unmoored set of pitches, and stays away from a clear I chord until the very end. The end is powerful for that reason, and because only here does the voice go to the top of the octave—as the speaker thanks, but says goodbye to, the lover. That song concept is normally treated lugubriously, but this is clear-eyed.

The best-known song, *It's Not Where You Start* (It's Where You Finish) is old-time vaudeville, including a humorous bridge made for a tap break. The finesse of the song comes from the way the writers handle the prosody. The title phrase, for example, does not follow the normal speech pattern, with *not* receiving extra stress and length, but uses absolutely even notes so that the first important stress falls on *start*. That gives the beginning of the song a unique flair. *My City* is an understated, atmospheric song about New York, with a nice flexible rhythm for the vocal line, over a nearly constant, bluesy vamp. The melody to the main part of the song is entirely pentatonic, which gives it its nighttime, alone-in-the-city sound.

Deleted from this show, probably because it is difficult, is an unusual song, *You're In a Highly Emotional State*. This has a complex story line involving two emotionally frustrated people trying to help each other. Verbally it's vehement, as opposed to sympathetic, and the most striking part of the song expresses this almost violently (Figure 5.4). This figure, the second half of the A-section, is a complete contrast to the first half. It recurs many times, as if the speaker were

What dy 'a gon-na do? What dy'a gon-na do? What dy 'a gon-na do a- bout it?__

Figure 5.4

taking the interlocutor and shaking some sense into her: it begins first on B, later on D, and at the end, on the series B, C-sharp, D, and F-sharp (the tensest note in the scale), before the speaker relents and ends within the tonic triad. It's an aggressive song, perhaps hard to apprehend out of dramatic context.[4]

In 1965, and then 1968, came the hugely successful show and film, "Sweet Charity." The most famous songs were *Big Spender*, with its jazzy rifflike opening and bluesy ending; the driving *If My Friends Could See Me Now*, in "strut tempo," another great show-stopping number that begins with an attention-grabbing verse; *There's Gotta Be Something Better Than This*, with its vehement ("I'm gonna get up / get out / get up. . . .") big finish; and a neat, fast New York song, *My Personal Property*. The Fields lyrics for all of them are just right, slangy, low-life, and brash. Less well-known is the loving and lovable *It's a Nice Face*. Coleman uses his typical mixture of short and long phrases to match Fields's colloquial words; for example, "His eyes? Clear . . . His ears? They're ordinary ears. . . ." The end is most appealing in its simplicity: "But it's a very, very, very nice face." *Very nice* is verbiage that would be dreadful in a poem; it's charming here. A delightful song, *Pink Taffeta Sample Size 10*, was cut from the show. In the midst of this jangly, urban score, this is a short-story song, very sweet, about a young girl from the sticks and her often-absent father. The Fields lyrics are a dream of lightness and sentiment.[5]

A slight (although double-stanza) song, but one we are fond of, is *Baby, Dream Your Dream*. It uses the oldest bass-line vamp in the book, includes a few bars of Charleston rhythm, and extends each A-section by a four-bar "break" that cries out for the *ka-ching* style of drumming. The tune is not remarkable, but fits Fields's short phrases and surprising scansion like a glove. Her final couplet pairs a familiar phrase, "Life will be peaches and cream," with the last occurrence of the title phrase. But, in fact, she writes "Life will be *frozen* peaches and cream," which is not only a nice surprise but catches the way the speaker has moved from hopefulness to outright fantasizing.

Where Am I Going? is famous, but so extraordinary that we want to comment on it. It is long, 42 bars; it's built on an unremitting vamp; it sets natural speech rhythms perfectly, using exact quick rhythm for a cumulative impact (no "swing" rhythm here, it's all hard-driving momentum); and it modulates constantly. Except for a couple of very brief contrasting, six- then four-bar units with triplets. which slow the pace for a moment, it's basically the same material throughout, varied in small but powerful ways. Only a few strategic bars are syncopated, and they make a huge effect. It's Coleman at his best, complicated but accessible. The title phrase suggests a rumination, but the Fields words (and the ferocious music) are remarkable in expressing self-anger without self-pity.

> Do I keep falling in love for just the kick of it?
> Staggering through the thin and thick of it,
> Hating each old and tired trick of it.
> Know what I am, I'm good and sick of it!

Surely, *good and* should be *goddamned*. There are no rests written into this long song. It just keeps pounding, but it also intensifies, closes up on itself. In the middle of the song, the opening rhythmic pattern returns, with altered vocal line (mm. 29–30). Measure 31 brings in a distinctive syncope (Figure 5.5). Mm. 32–33 includes the triplet meter; but m.33 goes back to the opening tone set, which had been in an entirely different rhythm. What is happening is that all the elements of the song are jammed together or overlapped in a few bars, something one is used to hearing in Beethoven symphonies, not popular songs. The ending is similarly concatenated. This is perhaps Coleman's most memorable dramatic up-tempo song. Here, and with some others like *I've Got Your Number*, one can raise the question: are such songs so strong, so unremittingly driving, that they pass beyond the limits of classic popular song? We don't think so, but they may intimidate some listeners.

The 1978 show "On the Twentieth Century" had lyrics by Comden and Green. The only memorable song is very fine indeed. *Our Private World* is certainly

Figure 5.5

an "art song," in its deliberate pace, its calm regular rhythm, its long-phrased cantilena, and in the way it is placed over a pattern of broken chords, like a song by Mendelssohn. Like an art song, it comes in nonstandard periods. The first A theme is four bars, beautifully balanced, with a kind of deep, heartbeat rhythm. The second period grows rhythmically out of the first, but goes to six bars, so that the thought is extended. It is a B, but also a variant of A. The second A-section (illustrated, Figure 5.6, to show the lovely D-flat leap in the voice line)

Figure 5.6

is again four measures; but then comes a mere two-bar transition on the dominant, leading to an entirely different eight-bar C-section, vigorous, urgent, in 12/8 meter. Only in the last two bars does the song touch back on the A theme. C is thus not just a coda, but a forceful final section, as in many *lieder*. All this may sound contrived for a popular song. However, the "plot" of the song and the elaborate lyric develop in one sustained, complex figure of speech: a private world is "a play about a pair of lovers," who enter, find stage center, and share the "(spot)light of love." The ending lyric brings it all together: "Night after night, day after day / living our private two character play...." It is one of the deepest lyrics Comden and Green ever created. Musically it is not recognizably Coleman: the fact that he could write a "classical" song perfectly is another aspect of his talent.

In the late 1970s Coleman wrote with lyricist Michael Stewart. The songs are curious. *I Love My Wife* (the title song from a 1977 show) is a pretty waltz, playing with an upward fifth interval, first in major, then minor, but the words are "adult" in a crass way: "a lady jiggles" and "got the hots" are samples. *Hey, There, Good Times* is a Broadway strut, very catchy, an extreme all-about-me song, multistanza, with some good words, some not so good. *By Threes* is amusing, if specialized ("Between the sheets it's lovely to spot an extra pair of knees"). *The Colors of My Life* (from "Barnum," 1980) is a pleasant ballad with a buglelike opening vocal figure, while *Out There* is a big song about existential angst. One gets the impression that Coleman, here, was supplying songs by category: just between us guys (*I Love*), Broadway show-stopper (*Hey, There*), risqué cabaret (*By Threes*), naïve lyrical (*Colors*), philosophical (*Out There*).

Though Coleman seemed to be experimenting after 1980, it was admirable, venturesome work. In 1989 Coleman and David Zippel did the interesting show "City Of Angels." It was constructed so as to be fluid and cinematic, with on-stage equivalents of quick- and cross-cutting. Not surprisingly, the copious music tended to sound like underscoring for a film. Its melodic-harmonic flavor was that of, say, Elmer Bernstein, and it seemed to comment on the actual events and on the emotions of the characters, rather than representing them. However, *With Every Breath I Take* is one of Coleman's great tunes. It begins very low in the voice, in a film-noir sort of narrative minor: "There's not a morning that I open up my eyes / and find I didn't dream of you." The middle section clarifies into a more deliberate pace and a more open harmony. It's one of those very effective songs where the title signals the story, but the lyrics tell it. *You Can Always Count On Me* is a superior example of that long line of songs sung by a woman who always chooses the wrong man: in this case, "I crashed the junior prom and met the only married man." Like many such songs, it's in a jaunty, rhythmic style that reveals how the woman in question is actually rather proud of her predicament.

My Unknown Someone, a song from the 1991 "Will Rogers Follies," written with Comden and Green, is an elegant if conventional ballad, whose opening strain ties satisfyingly to the closing measures.

Coleman's hallmark was rhythmic buoyancy and deftness. He built songs on "now hear this" riffs and rhythms that startle, but prove compelling. His was the most unusual combination of complexity and accessibility among the composers of the half-century.

A Note on Dorothy Fields (1905–74)

We have occasion, at several points in this book, to speak with affection about the lyrics of Dorothy Fields, who wrote with an extraordinary variety of composers. Part of her merit is that she did not need to write brilliantly in order to write well. An unusual collaboration was with Sigmund Romberg, the operetta composer whose career began before those of Berlin and Kern. In his last Broadway show, "Up In Central Park" (1945), Romberg wrote prettily. The verse to *Close As Pages In a Book* is fluttery, but the chorus is a knockout of good plain writing, with some daring chord changes. Fields provided words just this side of florid, appropriately enough for a superromantic ballad, and included a memorable pun in the last A-section, which brings both a smile and a pang. From the same show, *April Snow*, without a verse, has a sweet gravity that is most satisfying, and the words are delicately considered; for example, "...the early Spring's an impermanent thing, a delicate string to cling to," which might sound overrhymed, were it not for that word, beautiful to sing, *impermanent*. A single word, later in the song, *meager*, has an inexplicable, but lovely, shine.

In 1950, Fields did a show, "Arms and the Girl," with Morton Gould, a distinguished composer and arranger of concert music and ballet suites. *Nothin' For Nothin'* has the falling-off-a-log rhythmic force and melodic profile of a Berlin song. *There Must Be Something Better Than This* fizzes melodically and lyrically, and has a nervous, springy rhythm, especially at the end—uncannily like some of the work that Fields did later with Coleman.

Writing with Albert Hague in 1959, for a show called "Redhead," Fields came up with some droll words for a rather routine tune, *Look Who's In Love*, that lift that song to a higher level ("Who was surprised? We were! Well, weren't we?").

JERRY BOCK (b.1928) and SHELDON HARNICK (b.1924)

Sheldon Harnick is one of the very few lyricists for whom "brilliant" is not just a convenient adjective. He writes impeccable but venturesome lyrics in all formal and emotional styles. Jerry Bock also was equally gifted as a composer of love ballads, character songs, or comedic numbers. (Bock seems to have stopped writing about 1971.) Together, they amount to the most accomplished and memorable songwriting team of the second half-century.

Harnick's and Bock's huge success on Broadway was of course, "Fiddler On the Roof" (1964). "Fiddler" is a Jewish operetta, if such a thing is conceivable, a historic and cultural panorama of the world of Sholem Aleichem and Marc Chagall. Some have dismissed the show as "ethnic kitsch," but the same aesthetic objection can be raised against "West Side Story," or, when you think of it, "My Fair Lady." The show is full of "Jewish" music—combining the penta-scale, parallel major/minor shifts, klezmer clarinet, fervent choral numbers. Most of it lies outside our purview, since there are few songs from the score that have an independent life. *Sunrise, Sunset*, with its pure minor strain and piercing raised 5, is a great choral number, and *Matchmaker, Matchmaker* has an irresistible gypsylike verve, with its propulsive triplets within an overall duple time. Both have nonostentatious words, respectful of character. *Far From the Home I Love*, with its grave major/minor alternation expressing the dilemma of love against tradition, is beautiful. But none of these is really in American classic popular style.

The Bock — Harnick show that preceded "Fiddler" could not be more different. "She Loves Me" (1963) has lots of Hungarian, or at least between-the-wars Central European, touches. Though far from "pure" stylistically, it is one of the most exuberant, tuneful scores of the half-century. *Days Gone By* is one of those insouciant waltzes that sneak up on you, owing to one startling accidental (m.12) and the perfect octave skip at the final cadence. *Ilona* is a sort of Hungarian habanera, starting with a proud minor feel in the voice line over an irregular accompaniment pulse, and ending triumphantly major. The lyric plays with *only* and *alone* (to go with *Ilona*); but Harnick uses a lot of unrhymed phrase ends, which imparts naturalness to the thought as it progresses. The vocal line mixes intervals of the fourth and the fifth, but avoids tones 4 and 7, giving it a pentatonic sound until the end.

Grand Knowing You is a brisk, strongly syncopated song in music-hall style; it has a sly sarcastic lyric that may make it untransportable from the show. ("It's a small pleasure but I'll treasure each warm intimate snub.") The memorable *Tonight At Eight* is in a classical quick-dance rhythm, with a nervous profile involving long strings of fast eighth-notes, punctuated by empty beats and very brief asides (i.e., the title phrase, split into two disyllables). The A-section uses only adjacent steps. The first portion of the middle section (not a bridge or release, but an interlude) maintains the fast-note patter, but goes through a modulation underneath, a very unusual technique; then there is a contrasting brief section on even quarter-notes, so that the interlude amounts to B_1 and B_2. The A material comes back for 16 bars; then there is a return of B_2 sweeping inexorably into a repeat of the opening A. The entire song is 60 bars, but it seems to go like a shot. There are two stanzas of spectacular words. Not only are there wry little jokes about romantic anxiety ("More and more I'm breathing less and less"), but the entire lyric is patterned with extremely complex inner rhyme and repeated abrupt consonants,

> I'm nervous and upset because this girl I've never met I get to meet....
> I haven't slept a wink I only think of our approaching tête-à-tête....

all of this on unbroken eighth notes. At the end, the nervous lover is so excited that he forgets his approach-avoidance mood, and bursts out (in the second B_2),

> Two more minutes, three more seconds, ten more hours to go....

The whole effect, musically, has the speed and crispness of diction of *I Could Have Danced All Night*—but with even better words.

And then the ballads, which are lovely. *Dear Friend* is a perfect slow waltz. It avoids being saccharine by using one out-of-scale tone, the raised 4, in the vocal line. That line begins with a gracefully dotted pattern; but then the voice soars on an urgent string of eighth notes over a span of a tenth, before the waltz theme resumes. This is one of those songs about romantic longing and fear intermixed: the pattern of yearning and anxiety is made clear by the contrast of rhythms and apparent tempo in the first eight bars of the song. Added to this, the harmonization of both strains, especially that of nine consecutive eighth-notes all on the same high note, imparts a zitherlike quality to the song. The ending is one of those simple but startling achievements, where the voice line leads up to a B, then to C, then to D, and then back to C, the key-note. The song could perfectly well end here, but it reduplicates itself, leading on again to D, stretching to E, and then, most movingly, coming down to C by means of two half-steps. Harnick's lyric is beyond praise. At the final cadence, he has the courage not to rhyme phrase ends. The long verse is masterful in its ratio of sounds that "chime" and sounds that don't: "a-gleam/a-glow"; "music is muted...lighting is low." As it ends. Harnick pairs *low* with "so * depressed," which is not only funny but plays into the vulnerable duality of mood of the chorus.

Even more beautiful is *Will He Like Me*. Once again, successive eighth notes convey a naturalistic thinking-out-loud, while phrases with longer notes break in as an emotional outpouring. The release is exceptionally lovely, and uses warmer vowels than the opening A-section of the song, which sticks to the bright (and slightly anxious) *he, me, meet, see, be....* The climax the first time through ("Will he like me? / He's just got to") is muted, coming to rest on a wafting coloristic tone 2. By contrast, the final climax comes to the tonic chord, with added 6 (a feature throughout the song), but puts the voice on the major 7, the most exposed cry of appeal possible. It is a great song.

Figure 5.7

So is the title song. It strides, dances, floats, and pirouettes. Have you ever seen a dancer leap and click his heels together? That happens in this song. And yet it is very simply made. A big step from tone 5 of the scale up to the 2 above the key-tone, then the heel comes down on the tonic. Then a very little step up, only a whole tone, and the same little descent (Figure 5.7, 1–11). This first three-bar segment includes two forward syncopations, stopping the phrase in advance of the normally strong third beat, here absent, thus creating a rumba figure as distinctive and buoyant in this song as the opening Charleston rhythm in *I Got Rhythm*. The first short phrase is a stride; the second one is a footwork step, in which the first four notes form a springy upbeat to the third bar. In what follows, the stride elongates into leaps, as the opening interval, a fifth, stretches into a sixth and then a seventh. The vocal line continues to arch higher, first to C and then to D, in the succeeding four bars. Just following a scale can have a huge impact.

Perceptually, the middle section of the song begins a bar early: the singer is so jubilant, he jumps the gun. It uses the rhythm of mm.2–3, but the pattern reverses, the upward leaps coming last, seeming to cartwheel into the next phrase (Figure 5.7, 16–26). The singer rights himself just in time to be carried by his own

Figure 5.7 Continued.

exuberance into a great traveling lift on a three-bar-long *Ah!*, the voice steady over bracing discords When you're this ecstatic, what can you sing but *Ah?* (a similar effect occurs in *I Got Rhythm*.)

The lyric is the full, virtuoso partner in this dance, passing from being exuberant to droll to delirious. Did anyone ever rhyme *Bah!* and *Hah!* and *Ah!*, and get away with it? More subtly, notice how the verbal phrase endings in mm.3 and 7 do *not* rhyme, and how the whole sentence in the first seven measures circles around, playing with who loves whom and who loves what. This is a brilliant example of verse-writing where the semantic units do not coincide with line length: "to my amazement" is not the end of a complete thought—the sense leads on across adjacent phrases. The first complete phrase-end rhyme does not occur until the end of A$_1$.

In the A$_2$ section, the singer is so excited that he begins to repeat himself, launching one phrase from the words of the last. Here, in stanza two, words begin to fail, as the speaker interpolates "What the heck does that mean?" or inserts "That's because it's cold out." The two features together convey the sense of someone's finding the words of the song he is singing as he sings it.

The 54-measure song ends, as it must, with a contrasting C-section whose rhythm becomes an insistent, driving pattern. There are two whirling turns with a tiny separation (between *discovers* and *that*), then one sustained *fouetté* as the spin becomes continuous—and finally the final lift up to the zenith of happiness, supported here by adding a 6 to the chord, a cliché in song endings but perfect here.

Bock and Harnick made their first big impression with two Broadway shows that were period American: "Fiorello" (1959) and "Tenderloin" (1960), both concerning New York politics of bygone eras.

"Fiorello" has a triumphant score. The comedic song, *A Little Tin Box,* about how machine politics are greased, is one of the funniest ensemble numbers ever written. The Harnick lyrics are justly admired (they include the risible fragment, "...up Your Honor bit by bit"), but the tune is also a marvel, beautifully springy yet predictable, vaudeville with a touch of barbershop.[6] *Politics and Poker* is as witty; here the words take precedence.

There are quieter songs as well. *When Did I Fall In Love* is one of the great medium-tempo theater ballads. Following an excellent verse, the 32-bar chorus builds up like the gradual accretion of love it describes, from tentative questions—the title phrase, plus two short phrases, "what night? which day?"—to a rapturous affirmation: that it doesn't matter "as long as I love him now." The harmonic pattern also moves from tentative and complex to an exultant major triad at the end.[7] *Till Tomorrow* is a well-known song, no doubt because it is one of those immaculate, slow-waltz tunes that are instantly memorable. More power to them for writing a simple song so beautifully.

A song cut from the show, *Where Do I Go From Here?* is worth discovering. It has an appealing tune, built on very short phrase sequences, and Harnick uses pure rhymes placed unexpectedly—one element at the end of a phrase, the rhyming element advanced to the next-to-final position of the next line. The opening of the song is musically notable for beginning with a close. That is, the first five voice-line notes, setting "He doesn't love me," provide a set of tones that would ordinarily end a song (Figure 5.8). Only the chord on the downbeat

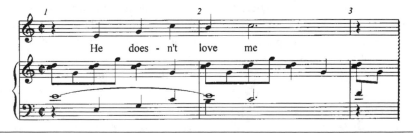

Figure 5.8

Figure 5.8 Continued.

of m.3 signals that the line is moving forward. It's a striking device. The release, mm. 33-40, has a strongly contrasting rhythm, strings of fast notes punctuated by pairs of slower ones like a tambourine shake.

Finally, there is a superb character song that also works outside the dramatic context. (I'll Marry) *The Very Next Man*. The lyric is incredibly good, both in the Loesser-like verse, revealing the speaker's personality in brief telling strokes, and in the chorus, with its intricacies of rhyme and stress: "I'm through being wary, I'll marry the very next man." It's a song about a woman who's been waiting too long. To a melody sounding like a bugle call, the first words of the chorus are, "No more waiting around," and this no-nonsense attitude carries through all the savvy lyrics: "Waiting for ships that never come in a girl is likely to miss the boat." The tune is brilliant, the title phrase set insinuatingly to half-step turns. The song recalls Loesser's *Adelaide's Lament*, but this woman is a lot smarter than Adelaide.[8]

"Tenderloin" includes the cheery *The Picture of Happiness*, in which the debauching of a young woman brings joy to all. It's in English music-hall style. *Artificial Flowers* is a send-up of a turn-of-the-century parlor song, about a poor little flower girl: It's ridiculous, and totally endearing. A more ambitious song is *Lovely Laurie*. The lyrics are ambiguous: is the song about someone who has died? But the A-section tune is piquant, with a clash between a raised 4, inserted discordantly into a major triad, and a lowered 4 as part of a dominant seventh chord

The very first Broadway show from these writers was "The Body Beautiful" (1957), which contained a delightful up-tempo tune, *Just My Luck*. It's a quick song in the minor, with a sneaky opening chord that suggests more than one underlying key, and a strong bridge that connects inexorably to the last A-section. The song is rhythmically very forceful, with each A-section opening using three equally stressed syllables ("just my luck"; "my true love"; "lightning struck") that keep the song spinning.

Among later work, from shows that were not very successful, the ballad *What Makes Me Love Him?* from "The Apple Tree" (1966) is a stand-out. The tune is plain but poised, starting with a triad on the key-tone, and then going through two very rapid circle-of-fifths changes within the first six bars while the vocal line stays within the original key. The impression is that of an art song with a restless but conventional harmonic motion—until m.10, with a discordant note. The lyric has been proceeding without oddity, until the phrase, "[his singing] sours the milk," with *milk* set on the sour tone. The whole song is a paradox of the affectionate and the sardonic; for example, with "plain man" set on the richest chords of the piece. It's a perfect example of pop song writing that is kept just apart from banality, while using banality for its own effect.

From "The Rothschilds" (1970), *In My Own Lifetime* is a simple, dignified, and eloquent anthem. Using a distinctive "Eastern" mode with lowered 7, it could be a more musically satisfying inspirational song for special occasions than many songs thus used.

Bock and Harnick stopped working together, a real loss. But each has written with others, or alone. In the 1950s, Harnick was writing memorably, both words and music, for revues, and cabaret. In this category, *Gus the Gopher* is perhaps the only good, noncute shaggy-dog song ever written, in this case about a love-sick rodent ("His suits and ties were fabulous / His pants were neatly pressed / And in his buttonhole he wore a rose"). *Merry Little Minuet* is in mock Elizabethan folk style, but with a mordant twentieth-century message: "The whole world is festering with unhappy souls / The French hate the Germans, the Germans hate the Poles...." It sounds like Tom Lehrer at a higher artistic level, and it's priceless.[9] Quite well known, one of the best cabaret numbers ever, is his *Boston Beguine* (1952), about repression loosening—to spectacular effect. Musically, it has a Latin zaniness. Dating from 1950 is *The Shape of Things*, a strophic number in mock English-ballad style about a love affair that has gone badly wrong, recounted in hilarious deadpan. Any stanzaic song, since it is inherently predictable, must have wit and audacity to succeed.

For his part, Bock is the writer, with Larry Holofcener and George David Weiss, of the truly swinging song, *Too Close For Comfort* (1956). It's commercial, but it's a good tune with a great bridge, and words that stick in your mind ("Be wise, be smart, beware my heart"). *Without You I'm Nothing*, also from "Mister Wonderful," is jaunty and fun.

The work of Bock and Harnick is interesting to ponder, because it raises some conceptual issues about the definition of classic American popular song style. Some Bock — Harnick songs are in an established American musical comedy or music hall style. Others are set in an exotic time or place, or have a "classical" European flavor. While he uses dotted rhythms and syncopation, Bock seldom writes in "swing" style, nor does he use a vamp as a rhythmic basis. He often sounds angular or percussive, but not "jazzy." The basic rhythm patterns could be those of London or Paris or Berlin during the second quarter of the century. Similarly, the harmonic structure is Euro-American, using scales and chords with added or altered tones, but without much use of complex chords or telling inner voices.

Since we have said that rhythmic profile and harmonic richness are definitive features of the classic American style, why do we find Bock and Harnick so satisfying? For one thing, their songs are in the compact format, with an arch or ogive shape, that we have emphasized as a crucial aspect of American popular song style. Bock also has the gift of devising truly captivating tunes, with harmonic implications that are part of an international style that developed under twentieth-century American popular *influence*. In this regard, he is like Loewe. Harnick, however, has a more clearly American voice, as a lyric writer, than Lerner—brasher, less literary in range of reference and diction—and Bock has a more energetic, piquant melodic style than Loewe. In the end, a truism: first-rate melody combined with first-rate words yields wonderful songs.

HARVEY SCHMIDT (b. 1929) and TOM JONES (b. 1928)

Rather like David Shire and Richard Maltby, in the next professional generation (chapter 8), Schmidt and Jones are a long-established team, they are successful, their work is solidly "American" (Shire and Maltby more urban, Schmidt and Jones more regional), and they are men of the theater. Their work reflects the goal of a musicodramatic whole, whose integrity comes before the commercial portability of the songs. Most Schmidt — Jones songs are not in the Gershwin-to-Arlen line of pop blues or jazz, nor are they in the swing tradition that carried on into the work of Coleman and Styne. Rather, like Bock and Harnick, they show a basically Euro-American feeling in terms of melodic contour, musical and verse rhythms, and international-style harmony.

Their approach has yielded some fine songs. Their most famous song, *Try to Remember*, from the 1960 off-Broadway hit "The Fantasticks," is one of the great tunes of the entire period, one of those mysterious achievements that, once heard, are never forgotten and never pall. (Others from this period include Jerome Moross's *Lazy Afternoon*, Michael Leonard's *I'm All Smiles*, and Bock's *Till Tomorrow*. Not by accident, three of the four are in 3/4 time.) Much of its memorability comes from the lyric. The elegant compound rhymes and off-rhymes (*mellow, yellow, fellow, hollow, follow*), each of these set on paired eighth-notes, make the tune seem like a cat's-cradle of phrases. These sometimes far-separated "echo" rhymes are powerful binding devices. Part of their force comes from the fact that they are not all syntactically parallel: they mix nouns, adjectives, and verbs unpredictably. Serving a similar binding effect is the frequent exact repetition (*try to remember; deep in December*), each used several times. This is especially important, because musically the song is a ballad in the older sense: it has only the most minimal bridge, which is itself related to the A-section material. It all ends up hypnotic, not soporific.

Other admirable songs from the 1960 show include *Much More*, a song about a craving for life experience that begins with a long lyrical vocal contour and, as the emotion intensifies, moves into a kind of flamenco rhythm. Two ballads, in the contemporary sense, that became almost as famous as *Try to Remember* are *Soon It's Gonna Rain* and *They Were You*. The latter song, a "pristine" waltz in the writers' specification, also has a tiny bridge, mostly an occasion for introducing some enriched chords; otherwise, the melodic line is one of those amazingly appealing contrivances made out of chains of thirds plus the introduction of tones 6 and 2.

Soon It's Gonna Rain is, for us, the finest. Verbally, it has an opalescent quality, as if one is looking through a rain-streaked windowpane. There is a beautiful verse, with strong imperative verbs opening the first few phrases (*hear/see/smell*). It is set on what proves to be the dominant of the key of the chorus. There is a marvelous transition to that key with a progression of major and minor seventh or bitonal chords, lovely stinging discords in the final "Where we can stay," and then four bars of a vamp that introduces the key of the chorus. This chorus does have a full release, a fine sweeping one, with a new melodic line and rhythm. The opening rhythm of the chorus in the distinctive pattern ones hears often in Sondheim (e.g., *Take Me to the World*). It is a sort of stepping, then pause, figure: a series of equally stressed quick notes, followed by a stressed long note: ♩ ♩ ♩ ♩ ♩. The even, quick notes begin on the first beat of the measure, but they act as a long anacrusis to the third, strongest, beat—a rhythmic figure with a gestural effect, like a Renaissance court dance.

Their next show, "110 In the Shade" (1963), was a more ambitious work. *Gonna Be Another Hot Day* served as a kind of theme song, setting the tone for the whole musical play. It is a fine piece of work, achieving an unusual country blues feel, but it is essentially a choral aria. *Too Many People Alone* is in mainstream pop-jazz style, in terms of its harmony, and has a melody worthy of Rodgers. The transition out of the bridge is notable. The message of the song—don't pass up affection—is a bit preachy, but the words go lightly. By contrast, the show "I Do I Do" (1966) was very small dramatically, a two-character piece. The score is not miniature, however. The best-known song, *My Cup Runneth Over With*

Love, is a curious paean to marital love with a lot of musical and verbal repetition and a very marked iambic rhythm. Again, it is a strictly stanzaic, old-style "ballad," constructed in very short units. We admire the formal clarity, but the song seems tight, contrived.

"Celebration" (1969) included a long, ambitious song called *Under the Tree*, which immediately reminds one of *Try to Remember* in its use of widely spaced compound or off-rhymes: *billow/pillow/follow*. The opening melody is daring, in an occluded A major but with a prominent raised 2, often repeated. In the vocal score, a long middle section introduces a more conventional, hymnlike style. It serves to bring weight to a song whose A-sections consist of short, ambiguous phrases—but at some cost, since the lyric of the central section is overblown.

Schmidt and Jones are musical playwrights first, creators of songs second. But some of their songs are among the finest of the period.

MEREDITH WILLSON (1902–84)

Willson tends to be condescended to now as "corny." His achievement is broader than that. As far back as 1941, Willson wrote a gently swinging, affectionate song, *You and I*, associated with the Glenn Miller band. It sounds like the kind of accomplished tune that Loesser was writing about the same time. The A-section melody line uses every note in the major scale—altering just one, the raised 5—but features a minor seventh leap jumping off from that one out-of-scale tone. With one tone, one interval, a light jazz chord underneath the latter, and a medium swing tempo is a good commercial tune constructed. Alas, this good song became better known as the Maxwell House commercial.

When one turns to Willson's smash hit musical, "The Music Man" (1957) and considers the famous *76 Trombones*, one finds also an opening that uses every note of the major scale, (one omitted and with no altered tones); a leap of a seventh; a march rhythm; and totally triadic harmony. Examining the lovely ballad, *Goodnight, My Someone*, one finds the very same tone set as *76 Trombones*, in a different tempo and meter and with a slightly richer harmonic ambience. All three songs mentioned so far open with strong pickup figures, and have the same overall melodic contour: downward, with a leap up and then a slight recession to the end of the phrase. This versatility, within an economy of means, should put to rest the notion that Willson wrote in plain diatonic, regular-meter style because that was all he could master.

There are, of course, many famous songs from this show. *Till There Was You* has a perfect, pure melody, notable because its phrases lie in all parts of the octave (plus one leading tone below the key-tone), imparting an evenness and poise even though the up-going intervals still create local interest; and notable also because the writer uses only one tiny alteration of the scale (on "hear it *at* all") and no complex chords. The plangent release is marvelously shaped melodically. *My White Knight* is a similarly pure, affectionate ballad; why should a simple octave be so moving? *Lida Rose* is an irresistible nineteenth-century barbershop choral piece. At the up-tempo part of the spectrum, *Gary, Indiana* is a textbook illustration of matching musical and verbal rhythmic stress, and *The Sadder-But-Wiser Girl* is simply a perfect vaudeville-style number, with neat words. When you add into the list the famous *Ya Got Trouble*, a tour-de-force patter song, to put it mildly, we see again that Willson was technically accomplished: he chose to write plain.

Alas, the songs from Willson's later shows range from earnest to dreadful. He started his career in radio, as a music director, someone who is expected to write copiously for all sorts of purposes. Perhaps this background prevented him, as a theater writer, from knowing just when and how to rise to the occasion. We find it hard to explain why his best work is so good, but why there is so little of it.

CHARLES STROUSE (b. 1928)

Strouse is perhaps best known for his very popular Broadway shows "Bye Bye Birdie" (1960) and "Annie" (1977). From the former came *Put On a Happy Face*, the quintessential show tune in 2/4, with a melody that skips up and down in the octave, omitting tones 4 and 7. The jaunty melodic line—"Gray skies are gonna clear up"—perfectly fits the cheerful lyric by Lee Adams, with whom Strouse has worked most. Strouse replicated that cheerful approach with *Tomorrow*, from "Annie," with lyrics by Martin Charnin ("The sun'll come out...."). You can bet your bottom dollar that infectiously happy songs of this kind have a lot of appeal, and Strouse knows how to write 'em. There are other toe-tappers from these shows. From "Birdie," there's *Kids*, with a chorus marked "Charleston tempo," perhaps the last successful instance of that tempo as the wave of rock crashed in. *A Lot of Livin' to Do* appealed to a public beyond Broadway for its four-beat, proto-disco rhythm and snappy lyrics. "Annie" also featured *You're Never Fully Dressed Without a Smile*, a jaunty tune with a Rockettes kick rhythm, and the very good *Easy Street*. It's marked "nice and mean." The 16-bar verse, with one vamp figure, sets up the 16-bar chorus, with its own vamp and a tune in an aggressive lowered 7 mode, a sound appropriate to its words of advice from a dear-departed but cynical "sainted mother," about finding a place where you can "sleep 'til noon."

Strouse had done another comic-strip show with Adams, "It's a Bird, It's a Plane, It's Superman" in 1966. Three songs from this effort deserve mention: *You've Got Possibilities* is a verseless song that depends on a finger-snapping, syncopated four-bar musical phrase that moves through three keys, as the thought alters, from the terrible taste in clothes of the addressee, to "Baby ** you're improvable," to the conclusion in the title phrase. *You've Got What I Need, Baby* is in the tradition of rousing show tunes in 2/4. It's unusual in format: it can be seen as four A-sections, no bridge, but with the last four bars of A_1 and A_2 providing a brief "break" figure and the end of A_4 a big-finish coda. *We Don't Matter At All* is a lyric-driven song with clever Lee Adams alliterations ("... what are we? A pair of puny primates"), internal rhyming ("We muck things up in the same destructive way"), and wry wit ("What am I? Some phosphorus and water, I've heard chemically speaking worth a dollar eighty-three!").

There is another side to the songs of Strouse and Adams, evident in some of the ballads from these shows. From "Birdie," the mellifluous *Baby, Talk to Me* has long romantic melodic lines, with supple up-gliding seventh intervals. From "Annie" the wistful little song *Maybe* catalogs an orphan's hopes. From "All American" (1962) come two fine songs. *Once Upon a Time* is a lovely, sweeping tune, quite well-known. The lyric evokes images of a faraway place and time, and a yearning for youth and young love. The song has no verse. The bridge is also very modest, going to the dominant only briefly at the end (on a graceful fall for the words "Where did it go?"), so that the basic melodic strain is kept unclouded. Songs have the ability sometimes to express loss and happiness together: the music forms the amalgam.

From the same show is an overlooked song we like even better. *I've Just Seen Her* (As Nobody Else Has Seen Her) is a 32-bar song, no verse, in the form ABAA, in an easy-four rhythm. Something quite wonderful has just been revealed to the speaker, who tumbles headlong from one tonality to the next to tell us about it, in words expressing an artless enthusiasm. We tend to admire songs that begin in medias res. This one opens (Figure 5.9) in midmodulation, with a sequence of enriched dominants over a bass-line chain of fifths that reaches the main key, B flat, only in m.6, and then only for a moment, since we move immediately through more fifth-relationships to G minor (relative to the main key) to begin the B-section.

Sometimes this effect has a vertiginous effect; here, it is one of off-balance exuberance. There is a strong melodic unity to this song. Even though the character and rhythm of the vocal line of the B-section is a marked contrast to the A, the actual voice line is very similar. Furthermore, by the sixth bar of this eight-bar section the tonality is already on its way back to that of A_2, via a half-step alteration in the voice line over some juicy chord changes. The climax of the song comes at the very end of A_2, but is sustained into the opening of A_3, by means of one vocal note held over another satisfying chord progression (mm. 23-25). There is nothing more effective in song-writing than this kind of enharmonic change; that is, where a single sustained note belongs to different successive chords (and keys), so that there is movement underneath stasis. This song is superb.

Figure 5.9

"Golden Boy" is one of the richest musical scores of the last half of the twentieth century, with songs as fresh today as they were when introduced in 1964. One of the finest is *While the City Sleeps*, a paean to New York after midnight. Several types of nocturnal, urban American music have become aural icons. One is the lonely sound of wide-spaced chords, as in Aaron Copland. A second is the edgy rustle of Latin rhythms, darting riffs, and a bed of complex percussions, as with Leonard Bernstein. A third is a song in the minor mode, with flatted notes and "stretched" intervals and (typically) a saxophone wailing a countermelody, which has become the canonical style for movies and television. The Strouse — Adams song is this kind of film noir ballad. It is not "bluesy"; it lacks the structure or the melodic weightiness. It also moves right along ("with a good swing") and has a sophisticated smartness in the lyrics, a recognition of secret thrills that night affords. Rhythmically, it has a soft Latin feeling, but is subliminally hard-driving. All this together invests ordinary nighttime events with mystery. "Put a Stan Getz record on; Send the judge for pizza, When the last anchovy's gone, then it's dawn," but also, "While the city sleeps, When the air is still; Life can bring you that secret thrill!" It ends with a wail of B-naturals against B-flats.[10]

Night Song aches with a sense of longing to know what one's place is in the world. The rhythm (marked *Languidly*) seems to drift along and rock as gently as a lullaby: "Summer, not a bit of breeze…." The song opens with an almost pentatonic, slightly "spacey" motif, with some very delicate harmonic tensions underneath (as on the word *someone* in m.13). This is no pastoral idyll, but a city with "neon signs" and the "squeal of brakes." It's a long, 64-bar song; in the center is a release with urgent triplets ("Where do you go, when you feel that your brain is on fire?"), followed by an extra eight-bar interlude relating to the opening strain.

All the songs for "Golden Boy" are infused with a sense of New York, with all its gritty reality but an overlay of expectation and hope. *Can't You See It?* expresses the latter. It's a moderate-tempo "rhythm song" in 32 bars, no verse, and the harmony is without any strong altered notes. Adams's lyrics are perfect. The question in the title is posed in the first two measures; the answer comes in the next two bars, "It's as clear as it can be!" The same emphatic phrase is repeated in mm.3–4, accompanied by an upward surge in the melody based on the C major triad. The release is a real pleasure, with references to soot, and cops, as well as Bing Crosby and Fred Astaire.

Lorna's Here is a song about tenacity of love: "Try to lose me honey, just try." This is a song, in style slightly like Porter, which could have been a torch song sung by a tough woman who sticks by her man. But instead, it's a song of almost maternal reassurance. The melody is mostly expressed in quarter-notes. The principal motives have a range of only four tones, basically the same pattern moved to different pitch zones in the octave. There is no middle section, and no vocal climax: eight bars before the end there is a rhythmic pause and a big piano arpeggio, after which the song resumes as it began. This is a restrained, emotionally deep song.

The show's title song, a quiet reflection on the fact that life may not always turn out as we hope, is another beauty in a still different style. Melodically, it reminds one of Kern. It's in the form ABAC, with C being very close to, perhaps a version of, A. The first A-section is in B flat, but the bridge starts in G minor and then wanders slowly into D flat, so that the second A sounds in this key, giving the song a huskier sound. The melody has a range of over an octave; in fact the first three notes encompass a full octave on *golden boy*, including a questing seventh interval. The vocal line dips down to notes like low bells, as on the words *try* and *lost*; each is followed by a leap up of a tenth. These adjacent depths and heights work beautifully to engender mixed emotions—of possibility and uncertainty. The emotional force is that this mix is not resolved. Adams masterfully expresses, in a few words, a case where the older speaker understands more than the character being addressed: in the B-section, "The things you want you want too much, The love you need you need too much; So when you're hurt, it hurts too much, I know."

Perhaps the most interesting song in "Golden Boy," *I Want to Be With You*, is not a fully rounded ("closed" form) song, but a musicodramatic incident set to music. There is a striking bitonal four-bar invocation: a voice line that sounds in F minor, omitting tones 2 and 4, underscored by a rumbling tremolo in the bass on notes that also belong to the true key, E-flat, for the words, "Lorna, Lorna and Joe, Somehow it seems so right...." The "refrain," which proves to be truly that, not really a "chorus," opens with a cry of longing (a), repeated twice (Figure 5.10).

Figure 5.10

The song then moves into a more normally contoured line set in a much lower register, as if a "chorus" were just now beginning, with phrases that turn back on themselves (b). But then within seven bars comes a new arching motif, a new cry (c), a motif repeated four times with almost no variation, high in the octave. In the next bar, seamlessly, we are back at (a); from there on, the song mixes (a) and (b) material freely, coming at last to (a) twice, ending on an up-in-the-air 5. It now appears that (a), which originally seemed to be an introductory fragment was indeed the main strain, the end as well as the beginning. But the last measures provide no real ending. The song simply stops, and the listener takes away the feeling that (a), with its incisive gestural profile, could repeat endlessly.

This particular song is something of a landmark. It ignores the usual two-, four-, and eight-bar modular design. While it has musical-textual cohesion in form, perhaps analyzable as ABCABA (starting from the "refrain"), still, in its free mixture of musical-verbal gesture and rhetoric, it goes beyond the format for the classic American popular song that we describe in chapter 1. Loesser had stretched that format. Strouse and Adams here anticipate the style of later Sondheim (or "City of Angels" by Coleman) by two or three decades. They also move toward the fluid, open-ended style, the scene rather than the song as the unit, which came to dominate in musical theater later in the century.

We find no single recognizable Strouse style. Strouse, a trained musician, seems to seize his opportunities as they present themselves, bringing fresh invention to the lyrical demands of a chamber opera, "Nightingale," to Broadway ballads or rhythm songs, or to intentionally blatant "numbers," as in "Annie."

From "Charlie and Algernon" (1980), with lyrics by David Rogers, comes a sad, beautiful ballad, *Whatever Time There Is*, AABAA in form. The minor-mode melody of the A-sections begins with the title phrase and a dramatic jump of one note more than an octave, after which it moves downwards phrase by phrase. The release moves into the major, with a bittersweet variation on the main melodic theme.

> Forget about the future, we'll make it
> Live through it somehow.
> Today is all we're given, let's take it
> Live our whole lives now!

There are several extraordinary chords as the song nears its end (Figure 5.11). It is a lovely, lucent work.

In 1983 Strouse collaborated with Alan Jay Lerner on an ill-fated musical, "Dance a Little Closer." The title song as well as a song called *There's Always One You Can't Forget*, are good romantic ballads with the kind of long melodic lines that would feel at home in a Loewe and Lerner score. In 1986, Strouse and Stephen Schwartz collaborated on "Rags," an interesting New York folk opera

Figure 5.11

about immigrants. (It included ragtime sequences, predating the decade-later show, "Ragtime.") *Blame It On the Summer Night* from this score is graceful, but its time-worn minor to parallel major melodic structure has an "ethnic character" that may limit its appeal. In a completely different style is *Pals*, a friendly little song from "Lyle the Crocodile," an animated TV production (1987) for which Strouse wrote his own lyrics. The melodic motive is really a series of syncopated little riffs which all end on the phrase, "we're pals."

"Nick and Nora" (1992), lyrics by Richard Maltby, Jr., had a very good score. It's undeservedly obscure, perhaps because many songs are plot-specific, but Maltby's lyrics suffuse it with his usual tender sophistication. *Is There Anything Better Than Dancing?* is a verseless song that starts right in on a pick-up to eight bars of delirious gliding triplets: "When the orchestra's packed up and gone / but the music's still working its voodoo...." Good songs about dancing (as with Berlin's many examples) tend to be utterly delightful, and this is no exception. In response to the title-phrase question, some room is left for the notion that "If there's more on your mind, darling, you'll have to give me a clue." It's a superlative song that brings the pleasure of hearing that good old word *darling* sung, and that only hints at sex. *Look Who's Alone Now* is a short song that amounts to a conversation the singer is having with himself. Maltby packs it with some wordly wise lines: "Was she talking while I slept? / There's some line I over stepped. / We'll get over this, except Look who's alone now." The song clearly is related, in origin, to the *Dancing* song: the opening vamp is taken from that song, and both are in the same key. There may be nothing better than dancing, but later developments can be troublesome. They'd make a nice medley.

Married Life is Strouse and Maltby at their sentimental best, reminiscent, in theme at any rate, of the Old World waltz, *Marriage,* from the Kander — Ebb "Cabaret." This is a gently swinging song, with a springy dotted opening figure, and some sweet words. The loping, playful melody conveys in music a comfortable banter between a long-wed couple (Figure 5.12). In its familiar terms, it's a song that could hardly be better.

Although Strouse's versatility may have clouded his individuality, as perceived by listeners, we know of no songwriter who wrote over a larger range, from the very commercial to the dramatically specific, including an impressive number of fine, varied songs in between.

Figure 5.12

JOHN KANDER (b. 1927) and FRED EBB (d. 2004)

Kander, the composer, and Ebb, the lyricist, had a long and very successful career, creating songs almost always together. Their most famous songs have permeated present-day culture to a greater degree than is true of any others in their generation, though Jerry Herman comes close.

In this book, we give relatively little attention to songs that became big hits, on the grounds that, for the most part, such songs need little analysis. This is fortunate, since in the case of Kander and Ebb we do not like them much. The reason has to do, essentially, with rhythm. Their songs are often called "jazzy." Close attention to context suggests that such a term reflects mostly nonmusical attributes: urban or "adult" subject-matter, Fosse-style dancing (boys in raked hats, girls in long black stockings), brassy orchestrations, high-contrast lighting. As for the "jazz" nature of their songs, we would liken it to the way nonhip audiences clap on the beat.

It is impossible to define the "jazz" quality of American popular songs. Some songs draw on the Charleston, stride, or other 1920s rhythms; some use a swing inflection, like many of Styne's; some draw on diminished harmonies and lowered scale tones, like Arlen; some make use of boogie-style vamps, like Coleman; some employ complex Latin patterns that are inherently polyrhythmic; some have a bebop sensibility, like Frishberg or Dorough. A pure, hard-jazz style is generally inimical to songs, since it compromises subtle or interesting words.

But most up-tempo songs, and most songs with a strongly rhythmic profile, at least try for a lightness, a springiness of beat and verbal inflection, that constitute the quality "swinging." In the first half-century, we had Gershwin and Berlin, "jazzy" in a now-bygone style—and we had songs like Warren's *Lullaby of Broadway* or Gershwin's *I'll Build a Stairway to Paradise* (another aspect of Gershwin), which were just show-biz. Kander and Ebb seem to have followed in the latter stream. They entrain their hearers by a rhythm that is actually very square, with a stripped-down pattern of heavy down-beats and insistent syncopated or dotted figures that feel big but not light. It is a hard-sell approach that is useful in the theater, in that it raises the emotional temperature at desirable intervals, but as the second chorus ramps up the strut sags, the swash buckles. They give us the old razzle-dazzle—but all *what* jazz?

In fairness, the lyrics of such otherwise oversold songs as *All That Jazz* are often sophisticated and technically clever, as is *New York, New York* (1977) or *Cabaret* (1966), especially in its verse. With the latter song, true, the rinky-tink nature of the chorus is appropriate to the period and the setting. With the former, it's musically all in the vamp.

"Cabaret" (1966), which marked the beginning of their pumped-up style, included two songs worthy of attention. *Perfectly Marvelous* lives up to its title; it's a funny and driving show song in a forceful dotted rhythm. *Why Should I*

Wake Up? has a good melody, and a neat concept, but the song would have been better with less obvious harmony.

The movie song *How Lucky Can You Get?* (1975) has an insidious, honky-tonk quality, with its opening noodling of repeated half-steps, which hooks you, and some good lines ("You could circle the globe with my circle of friends"). *Maybe This Time*, added to "Cabaret" for film (1972), is a persuasive song of perpetual hopefulness: a fine idea for a song and a strong realization, with the bridge a near-continuation of the opening sections so that the whole song seems tightly knit. From "Chicago" (1976), *My Own Best Friend* seems to us a very good song, straight-forward but not strident. It uses the figure of a relaxed triplet followed by a long note that is one of the nice features of popular song story-telling, as in "I've always **known** **** I am my **own**...." It has a pretty set of chord changes right at the beginning: I to II (with 7) to ii (with 7) to V to I. The entire vocal line, except for the brief bridge, hovers around 3 and 6; only at the end does it rise, impactfully, to the upper octave tone. The song insinuates itself when sung in a relaxed, conversational mode.

There were several good songs from "The Rink" (1983), including a rather Sondheim-like ballad, *We Can Make It*, which has an opening A-section in two clearly contrasted periods, the first with a bass-line that moves by half-steps in the chord, the second using a circle of fourths and fifths. *All the Children In a Row* is an effective paean to the counterculture of the 1960s and 1970s, a bit megaphonic in approach. But *Colored Lights* is a complex, effective song whose message involves nostalgia for a purer, happier time. It opens with a restless, soft-rock narrative, with three verses of specific recollection, and then moves into a simple, waltz-time refrain with a pretty tune emphasizing the wistful 6 ("Where are *my* colored lights...?") Other Kander — Ebb shows from the 1980s and forward produced no songs that impress us, except for *Dear One* and the sweeping *Marta*, both of these from "Kiss of the Spider Woman" (1993).

Back in the 1960s, Kander and Ebb were doing another kind of work. There are a number of very pleasing songs from their first hit show, "Flora, the Red Menace" (1965). *A Quiet Thing* has a lovely, wistful opening melody ("When it all comes true") on a Bernstein-like progression, 1-2-3-raised 7–8. It's a pretty song entirely, in a moderate four beats: love doesn't come with trumpets or bells, but "...happiness comes in on tip-toe." One would like to hear this song more often; the same for the up-tempo comedy duet, *Not Every Day of the Week*, which shows two very average people considering romantic possibilities. The tune and the vocal rhythm pattern are good, though not venturesome, again relying on the strength of the relation of leading tone to upper octave tonic note, but with a nice surprise, since the phrase doesn't end on the upper tonic but drops down again to end on the floating 6. The entire lyric is clever, amusing without going for high wit, which would not fit the situation.

Sing Happy is interesting: it shows the songwriters testing their more grandiose style. Like many effective songs, it starts ruefully, wistfully, and ends big and belting. It's mostly built on open triadic intervals, but avoids the tonic tone in a clever way. There is a nice touch, where "no lyric, singing of *Stormy Weather*" invokes notes from that famous song. The title is odd, syntactically; one wishes the songwriters had done more with that oddity.

"The Happy Time" (1968) was also full of good, graceful songs. The title song is a pleasant, old-fashioned, purely diatonic waltz, remembering how home felt when one is young. *A Certain Girl* is a light bounce tune, almost soft-shoe, with some nice rhyme and rhythm surprises ("…swishing her skirt / walking a cert ** ain way"). *The Life of the Party* is a comedy song in a fast four, also showing the writers' nascent "show" style. The rhythm is very marked, on the beat, but the title phrase is always set as a syncopated appositional phrase. *Without Me* is another comedy song depicting a naively boastful person. It's an ensemble number, but would make a funny solo. It's in a strong four, almost a march, with a catchy dotted rhythm for the third beat. Finally, a poignant song is *Seeing Things*, a ballad in which a lover faces up to incompatibility, leading to the conclusion, "I love you very much—goodbye."

The adjective we keep coming back to for these early songs is *nice*. This is not really faint praise: many good classic pop songs are charming, insouciant, just-between-friends. These songs are among them; some, like *A Quiet Thing*, are more than that.

JERRY HERMAN (b.1933)

Herman is of the same generation as Kander and Ebb, and has also enjoyed a big success. We have a bit of trouble with Herman also; though some of his work is admirable, there is much that is obvious or sentimental. This is not a defect in technique: Herman is happy to be an old-fashioned writer. His tunes have easy-to-grasp melodies that go where the listener expects them to go.

I Am What I Am, the gay anthem from "La Cage Aux Folles" (1983), we dislike because it is a bombastic anthem, and thus wears poorly. There are other rather overbearing songs, easy enough to forgive. *Hello, Dolly!* has a certain loopy majesty. *Mame* has a good strut. The trickier problem with Herman is sentimental verging on mawkishness, a weakness that is more detrimental in his words than his music.

Herman often avoids this. *Song on the Sand* from "La Cage," is certainly sentimental, but it is not cloying. It opens with a sort of verse in conversational words ("Do you recall that windy little beach we walked along?") and meandering "notey" musical material suitable for a narrative-style verse. Then, starting with m. 9, comes a strong tune, just right for nostalgia, groups of three notes on one beat. It's a concertina kind of tune, and Herman simplifies matters by devising a lyric for it that simply goes "La dadada dadada." Slowly the song comes into focus. After eight bars of purposely banal material, the speaker breaks into a couple of contrasting interpolations: "something about sharing... something about always." The point is that the speaker can barely remember what love amounted to: he knows that it was built on the occasion and the setting, on someone playing a tune—but it *was* real, and he *was* in love. The last two bars of the song make that point clearly, with one of the few strong accidentals in the entire voice line. The "point" of the song, and the musical climax, is contained in that one tone, a raised 5 for the word *and*. (Popular song is perhaps the only verse genre that can make something subtly important out of *and*; see p. 44.) The song would have been unbearably banal had it not been "framed" so as not to be.

Another song from the same late show, *With Anne on My Arm*, is comparable in that it is an utterly conventional lyric about a boy and a girl, set in a simple diatonic style. Yet there are some propulsive half-steps to the vocal line, and a dancey rhythm for the fourth beats; in all, it's graceful and catchy.

Herman's biggest hit show was, of course "Hello, Dolly" (1964), and in it one finds a number of songs that more than suit the purpose. *Before the Parade Passes By* has a strong tune that maintains energy by avoiding the upper tonic note. It also uses multiple pick-up notes very effectively in a propulsive 6/8 meter: four quick launching notes before the first strong beat ("before the pa-**rade**"), or three before a double stress ("Saturday's **high life**"). The mixed two- and three-beat rhythm makes for a vivacious song, even with rather lame words (e.g., the too-predictable compound rhymes, like *high life/my life/by life*) and an overassertive ending. *Put on Your Sunday Clothes* has the same rhythmic verve, the same kind of alert tune—and the same overdone ending. The pretty ballad, *It Only Takes a Moment*, has a strong Interlude, and Herman nicely uses the word *instant* as a relief from *moment*.

The songs from "Mame" (1966) are similar musically to what came before, but the lyrics are a bit more accomplished. The marchlike *Open a New Window* overlaps phrases in a surprising way. There are signs of a deepening emotional power in *If He Walked Into My Life*. The fairly routine verse is needed, in that it clarifies to whom the song is addressed, a first love. As the chorus opens, Herman uses one of his long anacruses ("Did he need a stronger **hand**?"), giving an entire bar to the main word *hand* set as a floating 6. The next phrase is withheld until he can move his opening half-step-laden melodic figure into the accompanying tenor line, a graceful way to integrate two tonal registers in a song. The melodic figure, with its usually small intervals, repeats throughout the song, like the device of the countermelody (as in m.7) linking phrase periods together. Whereas the first two phrases are short questions, needing only five beats to be semantically complete but with the main word lasting an entire four beats, Herman then (mm.4–7) moves to a more urgent pattern, short phrases joined

Figure 5.13

together (Figure 5.13). He also moves the song forward by hovering on widely spaced chords built on II, on *soft* and *tough,* before beginning a modulation to a dominant seventh in m.6. The harmonic effect is to keep the harmony up in the air while the queries keep coming. The brief bridge in this long song is effective: it opens with a version of the six eighth-notes figure that has been the invariable beginning of each main phrase up to this moment, but then climbs to the upper part of the octave rather than subsiding. The words tell a lot, compactly: "What a shame I never really found the boy / Before I lost him." The end of the song has a four-bar extension that ties back, in terms of semantic reference, to the verse. It is the first Herman song that moves us.

Herman's finest song is another "torch" song, from "Mack and Mabel" (1974), *Time Heals Everything*. It is a song that builds up dramatic force as it goes along, rather than being blatantly emotional from the start. It begins with an unusual verbal pattern—and an unusual emotional mood—that seems to determine the structural choices thereafter. The opening bar, containing the title phrase, is a complete, if minimal, statement, followed by two virtually syntaxless interjections; then a repetition. By the time m. 5 arrives, we suspect that "time heals

Figure 5.14

everything" is some sort of mantra, and the pair of interjections, expressions of doubt or at least skepticism. Mm 5–8, forming a longer unit of thought, try to rise above this sense of dislocation, but what is formally a syllogism is really just a hope (Figure 5.14, 1–8). The musical means are perfectly chosen to advance the developing story line. The first period (of four bars) uses a conventional four-step bass-line progression. The melodic notes of the opening phrase move downward in even half-steps to the key-note, but the interjections hover in doubt beneath it. The first bar is in the principal key, E flat major; the next bar, in the related key, C minor. The second two-bar unit is exact repetition, one step up. Yet the trochaic rhythm of mm.2 and 4 works directly against continuity; the conventional choice would have been two quarter-notes. And the harmony for m.2, blurred minor triads, is kept rather sparse and indecisive, an effect heightened by the fact that m.2 is itself broken in half. It feels as if the song opens in two tempos: a moderate one for the statements (mm.1, 3), and an out-of-time one for the adverbial phrases (mm.2, 4).

The second period (mm.5–8) stretches the melodic range a bit, over a bass-line that is a complement to that of mm. 1–4. Toward the end, there are a couple

Figure 5.14 Continued.

of surprises, the low note on *one*, and the stretched dominant seventh chord on *end* that signals an emotional pivot. Both touches contribute a tincture of yearning. In the second four bars, moreover, the line stretches, and the momentum gathers. The strong reverse dotted (short-long) pattern of mm.2 and 4 is retained but compressed, as if by force of will the singer can transform doubt into confidence.

The ensuing A_2 section follows the same plan: harmonically predictable, semantically ambiguous, rhythmically halting. But it is not a true A_2 section; it does not come to a close. Instead, after only six bars, desperation sets in (mm. 15–20). The adverbial interjections come faster, jammed together; the tenor voice of the chords reveals a rapid, unsettled, progression; and the bass-line becomes urgently chromatic. At this point, where one had expected a smooth transition to a bridge, there is instead a two-bar episode of desperation, with pitch oscillation no longer representing comment, but panic. A half-tone step up in the bass halfway through m.16 increases harmonic tension.

At m. 17, we come to an apparent resolution, as the errant harmony voice and bass-line settle back into the chord of the opening of the song. It appears that we are at the opening of a full A_3. But here is the crux of the song. The resumption of A is only momentary. The setting of *Time* at m. 17 is not as at the onset, but is now set on an assertive note above the key-tone. Immediately, the title phrase is repeated, raised now to the highest pitch reach of the song, as if one more passionate assertion (on a tone that begs to lead up to the tonic) will at last make it true. But it is futile. The song moves into a conventional cadence, in which "but loving you" brings defeat. At m. 19, the brakes go on; the sad truth emerges.

We now realize that the unsettled middle section (prior to m.17) was not just an interpolation, but a special expressive device: musically the equivalent of a piano tremolo or an accelerating drum roll, verbally a hash of adverbs. It propels the song, at the onset of A_3, into a wailing emotional climax. This unusual 20-bar song has no bridge or release. When the manic midsong tremolo arrives, it simply cancels the end of A_2 and jumps the whole structure right into the final A. The achievement of this song is in the shape and pacing of its gestures, which perfectly convey the psychological complexity of the story.

Going back in time, there are good songs from "Dear World" (1968). *Each Tomorrow Morning* has a compelling release, with a graceful rhythmic carryover at the end of it. *And I Was Beautiful* has a persuasive concept, that even remembering being loved, makes one beautiful. *Kiss Her Now* is touching in its conception and in its bittersweet minor melodic movement and poignant ending. *I Don't Want to Know* is a solid waltz that builds up a lot of passion, using unpredictable phrase shapes ("If summer is ** no longer carefree / If children are ** no longer singing / If people are ** no longer happy"), as if the speaker is pausing to think of an example. Reverting to "Mack and Mabel," *I Won't Send Roses* has a sad, verbally surprising ending, as does *I Promise You a Happy Ending*. They are both songs built on a good idea, though neither is remarkable in realization.

SOME OTHER THEATER AND FILM SONGS, 1950–1990

In 1946, David Raksin (also discussed in our jazz-song section) wrote music for a Broadway show, "If the Shoe Fits," lyrics by June Carroll. *I Wish* is a very short song with lyric of simple sentiment set to a melody abstruse enough to have been a motif from a movie background score. On the other hand, *I'm Not Myself Tonight* is a 56-bar song whose chorus is, molecularly, AABBAAC. It's the song of a love-struck hero ("My heart's in danger / I am like a perfect stranger"), in which a relatively uncomplicated melody is made more arresting by Raksin's musicianly chords, including a long chromatic step-down before the first B. *My Business Man* is a pleasantry sung by a girl who is happy with her odd choice of lover: "I've got a charmer, he's my business man" (later, "my tubby tycoon"). The old-fashioned tune fits the lyric: both are a bit cheap, but fun.

Young At Heart (1954), music, Johnny Richards, words, Carolyn Leigh, is the title song of a film, perfect for its purpose. The opening vocal contour is memorable, based just on intervals that narrow, a sixth to a fifth to a fourth to a third, and featuring a lovely easy triplet. The B-sections in this roughly ABAB song bring rhythmic aeration to an otherwise smooth contour. The words couldn't be better: they too get smarter in the B-sections.

Harold Rome's fervent *Wish You Were Here* (1953) was from the show by the same name. We find Rome a most uneven writer, but *Who Knows?* (1962) is a good ballad, with a strong opening built on a ninth interval.

A very nice film song from 1950, by film composer Nicholas Brodsky and Sammy Cahn, is *Wonder Why*. It has a dreamy sort of melodic line, suitable for its inward-looking words.

Kay Swift, an associate of George Gershwin's and a good songwriter on her own (*Fine and Dandy*, 1930), still wrote after 1950. A film song, *Once You Find Your Guy*, from that year, has an effective tune, with a Kern-like continuity, owing to its use throughout of half-tone turns in the voice line, broken by leaps of the seventh. The words are serviceable.

A movie song by Mitchell Parish and Heinz Roemheld, *Ruby* (1953), has a seductive melody line, which keeps reaching up to 6 and 7, sometimes lowered, sometimes not. The words are less striking than the tune.

Richard Adler's score for the Broadway musical "Kwamina" (1961) includes a song with a memorable melody, *Nothing More to Look Forward To*, but the words are too awkwardly set to give the song life. There is also *What's Wrong With Me*, which has a pretty tune, and much more comfortable lyrics, but the harmony for the transitions of the song is stilted. Adler's work was better in his previous collaboration with Jerry Ross for "The Pajama Game" (1954). That show produced the delightful standard *Hey There* and a very funny ensemble, *Think of the Time I Save*, which concerns time-study carried to extremes. There are two amusing duets: one, *Small Talk*, is a good straight ballad with a contrasting patter element; the other, *I'll Never Be Jealous Again*, is a vaudeville-style routine in canon form. The year 1955 brought the wonderful "Damn Yankees," full of comedy and ensemble numbers that are as good as musical comedy gets. (*You Gotta Have) Heart* remains the most widely appealing song.

A composer of colorful orchestral-pop pieces, Leroy Anderson, wrote the music, and Walter and Jean Kerr the lyrics for "Goldilocks" (1956). From this show came *I Never Know When to Say When*, the confession of a girl who loses her heart too often. It has the verve of a vaudeville show-stopper. Unfortunately, the punch line (the title phrase) occurs too early in the chorus. The internal rhymes are a bit self-conscious, as if the lyricists were demonstrating their skills as versifiers.

David Baker, music, and David Craig wrote several fine songs for off-Broadway shows in the 1950s. *Just Love* is a scurrying up-tempo song, and charming: "It wasn't pills or prescriptions or alcohol," but "plain and simple love, that's all." A more substantial song is *A Funny Heart*, a very good ballad from 1955 about someone who uses her comic persona as a shield. The bridge reads, "Another night begins / the moon looks down and grins"; all the words are exemplary, and the tune is touching. *You Walked Out* (1957) is an ABAC lament with such a 4/4 bounce that it hardly seems a lament at all. The main motives of the A- and B-sections are similar: they start on the second beat in the measure and give the whole song a kind of rhythmic unity. The C-section melody starts with a string of quarter-notes harmonized in fourths for, "Now I'm learning fast how mis'rable I'll be."

Ralph Blane is usually identified for his work with Hugh Martin, but he also wrote independently. From "Three Wishes For Jamie" (1952) came a very dramatic song, *It's a Wishing World*. The 18-bar verse, subtler than the chorus, has the sound of an Irish folksong, but with pop-jazz harmony from the very first measure. The verse ends on an octave descent, using flatted tones of the scale, for "My love is waiting over the sea." The chorus stretches the musical range one note beyond an octave, ending with a 9-to-8 climax. It's a big theater ballad, effective if a bit overblown.

The eminent film composer Victor Young (e.g., *A Ghost of a Chance*) continued writing into the 1950s. A song with Ned Washington, *A Woman's Intuition* (1951), is a singers' favorite. It's an old-style, "notey," medium-bounce song, with some effective octave intervals in the voice line; it sounds like something Ethel Waters might have sung, in her confiding way. Another 1951 song with Washington, *You're the One*, is conventional in style but quite subtle, with a suddenly diminished chord in m.2, an unexpectedly arching melody line in m.5, and an elegant, unrhymed end to the bridge. The song, *Where Can I Go Without You* (1954), written with Peggy Lee, is in the same relaxed, far-ranging, style, with chains of thirds moved up through an octave plus a third. The words use the hoary trope of travel that is lonely because the loved one is absent, but it seems to us the best late Young song. Other songs from around 1950 include the well-known *When I Fall in Love*, with words by Edward Heyman. It has a pretty opening strain, but the song as a whole is square. Another song with Heyman, *I Oughta Know More About You* (1949), has a fine lilt with an effective rhythmic shift in m.7.

Johnny Burke is best known as a lyricist, most notably with Van Heusen. In 1961, however, he wrote both music and lyrics for "Donnybrook." This score had a variety of good songs, many with a comic Irish tone, as well as two fine ballads. *I Have My Own Way* (Figure 5.15) has an unusual structure. The main body of the song is 32 measures, ABAC, plus a four-measure coda. There follows a 24-measure interlude, which amounts to a separate song. Both are beautiful, with free-flowing melody lines that modulate slowly at each main section. Within sections, the vocal line and chords are strictly diatonic, except for some telling accidentals and seventh/ninth chords at section ends. The Interlude is in very

Figure 5.15

much the same style, but introduces some slow triplets that yield rhythmic variety. This is a shining, poised theater song that should be far better known.

He Makes Me Feel I'm Lovely describes the happiness and self-assurance the speaker feels from her ability to attract a potential lover. It too has an unusual structure. It is a 48-bar song in the form ABA ABA C AB, plus coda. The B-sections are short four-bar musical and lyrical asides, and each ends with chords slightly outside the expected tonality—chords signaling the possibility that the singer harbors some doubts. The doubts disappear in the coda, which ends firmly in the tonic. We have to believe that Styne had this song in mind when he wrote songs for "Darling of the Day," also with an Irish theme. These songs show Burke to have been a fine composer.

Sammy Fain is best known as a Tin Pan Alley and Hollywood writer. He turned out songs from the 1920s to the 1970s, including the commercially popular *I'll Be Seeing You* (1938) and *Love Is a Many-Splendored Thing* (1955). We find the latter melodramatic. A Fain — Cahn song from the Disney movie "Peter Pan" (1953), *The Second Star to the Right*, is pretty enough but has a desultory bridge. Fain's work for the theater is less well known than his movie music, but produced some better work. From "Flahooley" (1951), lyrics by E.Y. Harburg, the best remembered song is *The Springtime Cometh*—not up to Harburg's best, it suffers from an excess of the cutes. A better song is *He's Only Wonderful*. The verse is musically a bit stiff, but its repeated notes set up Harburg's conceit for the song, which involves sly understatement. The loved one is "only wonderful and not much more," and the singer will have to settle for "pot love," a nice pun. Fain's melody here is full of upward skips of fifths, sometimes augmented, to set adjectives like *wonderful* or *marvelous*. Fain tries a little too hard at the bridge. He has more success with two songs from the Broadway show "Something More" (1964), lyrics by Marilyn and Alan Bergman. The title song has a complicated, disjunctive melody, the construction of which reflects the speech rhythms of the unusual lyric, which itself is full of hesitations: "I want *** well I don't know what I want, but I want ***** something." There is a good musical tension in this sophisticated song, which rockets along in 2/4, interrupted by pauses and second-thoughts. *That Faraway Look* is a simpler song, but has similar interesting syncopated hesitations. After a short introduction, a conscious imitation of children's hide-and-seek doggerel, the main motif relies on up and down leaps in sixths and sevenths, and spins along quite well until it seems to lose energy in the last few bars.

Lilac Wine is a long song from the revue "Dance Me a Song" (1950), music and lyrics by James Shelton. It's an elegant, folklike song, which compares a lover's infatuation with the effects of a magic potion: in the verse, "I made wine from the lilac tree, Put my heart in its recipe, It makes me see what I want to see." There are melodic/harmonic hints of Cole Porter at the close of the 24-bar verse and later. The 46-measure chorus, ABAB, is marked "slowly and dreamily," and this is reinforced by a long-breathed vocal line set over a gentle, rocking habaneralike rhythm. The singer is clearly feeling the effects of romantic self-delusion. *I'm the Girl*, from the same show, is a clear-eyed confession by a girl who knows she's a convenient substitute for someone else. The verse has a folk-tale simplicity, and tells the whole story: "He likes me, yes, no more than that, the one he really loves is you." The chorus uses triplets in an interesting way, sometimes incorporating pauses: (**I** * am the **girl** that he'll **look** at and **smile**"). The triplets become appropriately obsessive in the repeated-note bridge.[11]

Composer and lyricist Bob Merrill wrote an effective score for "Carnival" (1961). *Her Face* is a psychologically complex, fervent ballad about love forsworn. The 1957 show "New Girl In Town" included a very pleasing gentle ballad, *Look At 'er*, which uses a small range above and below the key-tone, has sweet plain words ("I think he's sweet as taffy / He thinks I'm downright daffy"), and comes to a good ending. Merrill wrote both music and lyrics for *Promise Me a Rose*, a short, sweet 20-bar song from the show "Take Me Along" (1959). The lilting dactyl-cum-iamb rhythm of the melodic motif of the A-section carries through almost every measure. One is tempted to call the song a ditty because of this regularity, but the song is too nice to define this way. The lyrics are imaginative without being overly clever.

> If you promise me a rose, I go out and buy a pot.
> My imagination grows Into roses by the plot.
> I've got roses on my doors, On my ceiling and my floors.
> And if you forget to keep your promise, for some reason or another you fail,
> How can the dreamer of such sweet roses be bothered by a slight *** detail?

All three verses of this fine little song are equally charming.

Albert Hague grew up in Germany, his music more influenced by European operetta styles and harmonies than by American jazz-age sensibilities. He had a melodic gift, but his harmonic sense seemed sometimes underdeveloped, as in *Young and Foolish*, the well-known song from "Plain and Fancy" (1955), with Arnold Horwitt. Another song from that show, *Hell of a Way to Run a Love Affair*, moves along smartly and is truly amusing. It's about a hapless boyfriend who "turns Paris into Hackensack." From 1964 is *Someone's Waiting*, a small gem of a song with a lyric by Marty Brill. The song has a satisfying compactness musically and lyrically, mostly owing to chains of thirds in the voice line.

For the off-Broadway musical "The Golden Apple" (1954), the distinguished lyricist John Latouche collaborated with Jerome Moross, a composer of concert music and vernacular opera. *Lazy Afternoon* is very famous. It is a wonder that such a musically sophisticated song became a standard. It's really a multitonal, multimodal song. Every couple of bars, a shift of a fourth or fifth in the bass brings it into a new implied key. The reason it does not sound theoretical, we think, is that it has a hypnotic vocal line made up almost entirely of adjacent steps; other than for some pick-up figures and phrase endings, the voice line just floats from one tone to the next. The other way it holds together, and is easily brought into memory, is that, like another song that lodges in the mind, the Schmidt — Jones *Try to Remember*, the lyrics are extremely well-knit. Locally, they are recursive: successive phrases beginning with *and...and*, but in each phrase of the A-sections triple rhymes occur at the same metrical point (e.g., *zoomin'/bloomin'/human*). At the same time, however, there are key words that are linked an entire phrase or more apart: *lazy* (m.1), *lazy* (m.9), *hazy* (m.26), *lazy* (glancingly, and in a nonsymmetrical position, m.32). This aligns whole sections of the song, instantly. As for Latouche's lyric, this song is perhaps the most purely imagistic of all classic popular songs, to be rivaled only by some of those in the singer-songwriter tradition, notably Joni Mitchell. During almost the entire song, Latouche just points to phenomena to be experienced: (e.g., "a fat pink cloud"). But auditors, being human, don't simply see and hear; they draw inferences—and feel and think, which permits the writer, in the last line, one imperative statement, "Come spend this lazy afternoon with me." The song is so well made that it virtually sings itself, and it's one of the finest achievements of the half-century. A less stunning song from the same show is *It's the Going Home Together*—sweeping and pretty, with a Celtic feel but no surprises.

A gifted composer, Mark (Moose) Charlap, who died young, wrote a good score for a 1958 musical, "Whoop-Up," with Norman Gimbel. *Sorry For Myself* has a striking principal melodic figure that hovers widely around one important note of the triad and then smoothes out; it imparts a nice conversational flavor to the words. The song ends well, despite one now-impolitic moment in the lyric. *Never Before* is a jaunty song, driven along by a strong two-beat rhythm and a tight lyric by Gimbel; for example, "... hopped around for joy, Like some trick wound-up toy...." The best Charlap song, written in 1964 with Eddie Lawrence, is *I'll Never Go There Any More*. It's a slow waltz, with a melody that features a hesitating quality, the opposite of a lilt. This is achieved entirely within mm.3–4, with one harmonic move, G going to A-flat, and one reversed rhythm (Figure 5.16). It is extremely subtle, and it tells the listener that this is not just another graceful waltz. There is a strangely insistent middle section to the song, and then, as the beginning hinted, a heart-stopping surprise in the final A-section. This is a wonderful, sad song. *Tomorrow For Sure* (1952) is a beguiling song of innocent expectation. The melody is graceful in its blend of trochee and dactyl figures.

Figure 5.16

The lyrics, by Buddy Bernier, have just the right touch of hopeful naiveté. There is no bridge. *I Was Telling Her About You* (1956) is marked *Slowly with feeling*, but the main melodic motive, which is like a jazz riff, seems to want to burst out into a sort of fast waltz. Don George's lyric includes a clever apology: "The girl in my arms meant nothing to me, I was telling her about you."[12]

An experienced theater songwriter, Ervin Drake (b. 1919), who wrote both words and music, had his biggest success with *It Was a Very Good Year* (1961). The song has an overt nostalgia, but a surreptitious hard edge. Drake had an opportunity to develop this edge in his score for "What Makes Sammy Run" (1963). *The Friendliest Thing* (Two People Can Do), whose sexual referent lays it right on the line, has a smoky, late-night feel to it. It's ABAC. The melodic motives of all four sections are based on four-note strut-vamps that accompany a straight-forward endorsement: "If you are free / No strings attached / And you're like me, No wings attached." *Something to Live For* is a more-than-competent ballad, less musically elegant but verbally smarter than Ellington's identically titled song. At five points, on first beats, bell-like octaves sound like chiming musical exclamation points. The lyrics are clever, sincere, and hip at the same time, with complex rhymes like "Life's no longer negative for, at last I've something to live for," and "I'm your only raison d'être, to love and honor, et-cet-'ra." *A Room Without Windows* is a swinging song in classic theater style, with lots of forward syncopation. Textually, it's a romantic proposition, but pretty blunt, a more suggestive equivalent to Loesser's *A Slow Boat to China*. The end of the bridge is musically deft, setting "I'd tell them what we're after, is a one-way ticket to * a room without keyholes...." A song of Drake's we like is *Now That I Have Everything*, a ballad with a good concept: "I didn't like myself at all" ... but finally, *you* came.

From a 1961 off-Broadway musical, "All Kinds of Giants," there came an elegant, charming ballad, *Paint Me a Rainbow*, by Sam Pottle and Tom Whedon. It has an opening strain worthy of Jerome Kern, starting on the leading tone and using a glancing raised 4. The first period uses the classic, so-satisfying rhythmic pattern of a light dotted figure followed by a slow triplet. The out-of-scale tone comes in again, to fine effect, at the end of the song, differently harmonized. The words are fine, with a nice play on *wishful/wistful* in the bridge. It's a song worth knowing

There are two good ballads from "I Had a Ball" (1964), by the team of Jack Lawrence and Stan Freeman. *Almost*, about a love affair that never quite started, has an interesting release which plays off graceful quarter- and half-note units in the melody against a tangolike rhythm in the bass. *The Other Half of Me* is a song of wishing for one's love to come along. It has a graceful melody and a lyric with some sweet-sour lines: "Is there a chart for the heart or a graph?"

Laurence Rosenthal is known primarily for his television and film music and for musical theater ballet music. However, he wrote a complete score for a Broadway show, "Sherry" (1967), with lyrics by James Lipton. There are two compelling songs with long melodic lines and rhythmic momentum that build to dramatic endings. *How Can You Kiss Those Good Times Goodbye?* has an insistent rhythm in 2/4, with a very gradual working-through of E minor to its related G major. One hears it as a good dance tune with a Greek flavor, perhaps. The lyrics have nice touches: "...we rode a private rainbow, you and I," and internal rhymes that do not preen: "A simple stroll without a soul became a whole parade." The melody of the last 14 bars is a coda building up to a theatrical finish as it works its way through a series of dramatic key changes. *Maybe It's Time For Me* is similarly constructed, but even better. Its opening, invoking a chord with a raised 5 hanging up on a dissonant 7, is striking. Phrases made up of stately quarter-notes build up and terminate with whole-notes followed by triplets accompanying the title phrase. The release descends in shortening, hesitating units (Figure 5.17). The last version of A is very fine, with another back-and-forth set of anxious sentiments:

Figure 5.17

"Maybe it's time, Why can't it be time, Please let it be time, this time...." It is a very strong theater song.

From the show "Ben Franklin In Paris" (1964) comes *Look For Small Pleasures*, with music by Mark Sandrich, Jr., lyrics by Sidney Michaels. It's a beautiful song with a stately melody that verges on the hortatory, but is not off-putting.. The lyrics offer sound advice: "Look for small pleasures that happen every day / And not for fortune or fame." There are other good songs in the show.

ANDRE PREVIN (b.1929)

The distinguished composer, pianist, and conductor, André Previn, was, at an early stage of his career, a Hollywood studio musician and film scorer. He maintained an active interest in classic popular music for some time, writing for the Broadway musical "Coco" with Alan Jay Lerner in 1969, and songs for another stage musical with Johnny Mercer as late as 1974. As a composer he has turned to opera and to concert music, but continues to express his respect for the genre: since the mid-1990s, for example, he has recorded songs by Harold Arlen and Jerome Kern with the excellent concert singer Sylvia McNair. The songs from "Coco" are competent but uninteresting, as to both music and words. The songs with Mercer amount to textbook examples of decent theater songs; they give evidence of having been designed primarily for the needs of the plot. *Good Companions* is an old-fashioned four-to-the-bar medium-tempo song with a dull lyric by Mercer but a fine main tune.

Previously, however, as a songwriter for films, Previn was more individual in approach. With his then-wife, Dory Langdon, he wrote a song (1967) awkwardly titled *Theme From "Valley of the Dolls."* One sees why it carries this title, since the words to the song are additive, with no phrase that would constitute a title. They are intricate words, somewhat obsessive ("gotta get off/gonna get/have to get/off from this ride"), and they go with a rather niggling tune, with lots of repeated notes, that uses varying numbers of beats in a bar, so that the perceived downbeat constantly shifts. The numbers of beats corresponding to the segmented verbal phrase quoted just above are, in order, four, three, two, four. All in all, an odd but effective song. More (but not entirely) conventional is a film song with Langdon, *You're Gonna Hear From Me* (1965). This one has an unambiguous title phrase occurring, in a familiar pattern, at the end of A_1, A_2, and A_3, the first two times set as remote or direct dominants for partial cadences. What is unusual is that the song changes key abruptly for the first four bars of the final A-section. It is not very convincing, but the chord transitions are sophisticated. This song sounds like an inventive jazz pianist working out a vocal tune. The words are right for the song.

With Langdon, Previn wrote *Where, I Wonder* (1965), a wistful minor ballad with a nice lyric twist at the end. The A-sections are striking, with a series of tonally ambiguous chords set over a long dominant suspension (based on G) to the key of C minor; it is not until m.11 that the basic tonality of the song clarifies into the relative major, E. A very pretty song from 1962, *Second Chance*, has a striking opening that sounds, again, like a jazz pianist feeling out the keyboard. It uses the octave of a fourth below to a fifth above the key-tone, in upward patterns pausing momentarily on 6, 1, 2, and eventually a lowered 7 above. The words are musing, wishful ("Can't I have a second chance / when you've had three or four...?") A 1963 song with Langdon, *Just For Now,* is close to being an art song, the melody, with arpeggiated open harmony, like Fauré, and words drawing an analogy between the cycle of nature and the seasons of love. It would be a bit *raffiné* were it not for a harmonically richer release that reminds us we're in popular America.

An even prettier, soft-jazz song is *Lost In a Summer Night*, lyrics by Milton Raskin. This one starts its opening phrase, "Underneath a willow," on the raised 7, and then climbs up a chain of thirds. There is a very nice second period to the A-material, and the title phrase comes in satisfyingly at the end of sections. The words are bucolic and seasonal ("lyin' on clover," "kiss of June").[13]

A decade earlier, Previn was writing songs with Comden and Green: these are more mainstream, and of high quality. From a 1955 film, "It's Always Fair Weather," there is a lovely medium-tempo ballad, *I Like Myself.* It has a conversational verse that transitions well into a well-made ABAB chorus. The special effect of this delicate song comes mostly for the concept—the speaker likes himself because he finds he is liked—and from finely tuned words ("Feeling so unlike myself / Always used to dislike myself...now my love has got me riding high / She likes me so, so do I"). It's one of the best Comden and Green lyrics. From the same film came one of those defiant bad-girl songs, *Thanks a Lot But No Thanks*, which is a lot of fun. A later novelty song with the same lyricists is *I Said Good Morning.* It's one of the silly fast songs that highly sophisticated urban songwriters contrive to illustrate the simple joys of country life ("Good morning to the chickies and the hens...the piggies in their pens"). It's clever, though Warren and Gordon, Berlin, and others did better ones.

The great film song, to us the best of all Previn's work, is *The Faraway Part of Town* (1960), with Langdon, heard as a voice-over, sung passionately by Garland, for an obscure film. It's a bluesy song, with exquisite chords and a fine pacing. Arlen would have been proud to write it. It opens with a complex chord that sounds like a C-minor chord trying to modulate to B flat, but the strain turns out to be in C major with added 7, the lowered 3 serving just as a quick smudge note, for color. That immediately gives the song a yearning, unstable sound, a feeling emphasized by the second period of the A-section (Figure 5.18) that uses a rocking figure built on a vamp that introduced the song. When the title phrase comes, it uses a perfect, then an augmented sixth interval, where once again the lowered 3 is coloristic. The song is ABAB in form, but the B repeats the brief,

Figure 5.18

rocking rhythm we first heard in A. The final B, extending the song to 36 measures, contains a vocal climax (m. 33) so rich that it makes the range of the song sound far larger than it really is. Langdon's words are beautiful ("... she walked and she wondered / The river reflected her frown."). It's a memorable song.

It would be good to have more Previn songs, but these are ones to be grateful for. Divorced from Previn, Langdon began to write very personal songs, words, and music, in the singer-songwriter style (chapter 7).

Songs for Disney Films

Brothers Richard M. and Robert B. Sherman wrote many successful songs for animated musicals. Although they are pegged as "Disney writers," implying a safe, somewhat trite, approach, many of their songs are less banal than those written for Disney movies by songwriters with wider reputations. *I Wanna Be Like You* (1967) is a neat Dixieland strut, musically very hip for the time, with funny words. *That Darn Cat* (1965) is jazzy and fun, about a hipster feline ("He knows ev'ry trick, doesn't miss a lick"). The pleasant *A Spoonful of Sugar* (1964) "... helps the medicine go down"—a sentiment that could define Disney songs generally, especially the ballads, which generally come to a fortune-cookie conclusion.

Disney film scores loosened up a bit as time went on. Barry Manilow, with lyric-writers Jack Feldman and Bruce Sussman (the team for the huge commercial hit, *Copacabana*) wrote *Perfect Isn't Easy* (1988). The song is one of those time-honored, musical-comedy "me" songs about how hard it is to be a star.

Alan Menken and Howard Ashman, a team responsible for the off-Broadway cult favorite, "Little Shop of Horrors" (1982), also loosened the range of suitable approaches for Disney. *Be Our Guest*, from "Beauty and the Beast" (1991), is a rollicking can-can-like number, with clever words: "If you're stressed, it's fine dining we suggest," or, "... unfold your menu, and then you...." The song's appeal is limited by its talking-plates-and-silverware trope, but it's fun.

Menken, with lyricist David Spencer, wrote a couple of songs in the 1990s that sound like theater songs. *Eyes That Never Lie* has a "notey" melody, harmonized with Chopinesque thirds; the lyric is unusual and effective, focusing on the hidden character of the loved one. *I Can Show You a Thing or Two* starts off with a swung-eighths tune that stakes out a fine terrain. The chords are elegant, and there is a neat progression at the close of the song. But the middle section wanders, and uses some arbitrary dissonance to harmonize a quite-conventional voice line. Neither is fully convincing.

For a non-Disney animated film, the composer James Horner wrote a song with a good melody, *Someone Out There* (1966), Cynthia Weil doing the words. It's an ethereal song, in that it deals with virtual love ("... we might be wishing on the same bright star....").

HENRY MANCINI (1924–94)

Someone has said that Mancini's songs, almost all of them written for films or television, are elegant yet folksy. In a good song by Leonard and George, *Not Exactly Paris*, this intramural point is made in a lyric that goes, "...kisses and linguine set to Mercer and Mancini...." *Moon River* (1961), with perfectly calculated lyrics by Mercer, was both a little folksy and a little elegant. Some find it banal, but it is really quite subtle. We like the 1962 *Days of Wine and Roses* less, thinking it a bit emollient in its lyricism. The film theme song *Charade* (1963) is a memorable little waltz with a French accordion flavor that could have suited Edith Piaf. *Moment to Moment* (1965) has a beautiful melody, sparely harmonized. The vocal line of the melody seems to imply its own harmony. Mercer wrote serviceable lyrics for both of these songs.

Two For the Road (1967), with words by Leslie Bricusse, is 32 bars, ABAC, with a sort of tango beat. The B-section is interesting melodically and rhythmically, with musical hiccups in mm. 14-15. The song, perhaps Mancini's best, is beautifully integrated. It's really a 33-bar song, with a multiple pick-up to the first period, rhythmically and melodically matched by similar long anacruses every two bars in A (Figure 5.19). The B-section begins more evenly, with four strong beats, but the complex pick-up figures re-occur, either in eighth- or quarter-note patterns. Only in the last four bars of the song do we get to steady half-notes, set over conventional, here mighty satisfying, step-down chords for "that's a long, long while."

Figure 5.19

Whistling Away the Dark (1969) was an incidental film song. It's another of Mancini's pretty waltzes. Mercer's lyric starts out describing a child (singular) but awkwardly switches to "they" thereafter, probably to avoid using *he* or *she*. Two earlier songs are worth noting. A television theme song, *Mr. Lucky* (1959), with tightly wound lyrics by Jay Livingston and Ray Evans, is a very smooth job. It opens harmonically on V of the main key, but with a raised 5 going to a 6 in the vocal line, an elegant touch. Mancini uses dissonant leading tones throughout, often to surprising next steps. This song should be better known. The poised *Too Little Time* (1953), with lyrics by Don Raye, is another of Mancini's good movie theme songs. The release has a graceful lyric: "No time for us to live and laugh enough / Summer, Winter, Fall and Spring aren't half enough." Finally, Mancini has a neat up-tempo song, *Dreamsville*, with his own words ("In love in Dreamsville, it's always new"). Mancini was a gifted and very successful writer. We only wish that he had written full scores.

A Note on Bricusse

His best film songs, like *After Today* and *Something in Your Smile*, are good indeed, but they fall outside the scope of this book because Bricusse was English.

Philip Springer has written very good songs with the best lyricists. *Westport*, a 1957 cabaret number with words by the witty Carolyn Leigh, is a gem of a comic song about imaginative forms of adultery in the suburbs. The general take is positive: "The sanctity of wedlock's on the downgrade / But housing is enjoying quite a boom!" The song comes to a funny, Sousa-like ending. At about the same time, Springer and Leigh provided Sinatra with a fine song, *How Little We Know* (1956), which has rather wistful words fitted to a confident beat. In 1956, Springer and Leigh also wrote *You Bring Out the Lover In Me*. The song is marked *swing with drive*, but has a melody that could just as easily be set to a beguine rhythm. The lyric describes the loss of control that accompanies passion; for example, "...these notions that spring out? You bring out the lover in me."

There's Always One Day More (1957) is an extremely accomplished song. It ranks up there with Kern's *All the Things You Are* for the most key changes per measure, but unlike Kern's song it does not have soaring melodic motives to trigger these changes. Instead, the A-section melody is a series of short phrases, each of which falls within the range of a fifth, but each of which is built on a chromatic bass-line moving down by half-steps. These discontinuous phrases perfectly reflect the changing circumstances in Carolyn Leigh's cautious lyric. The release is a beauty. Tonally it moves down, vocally it arches up; the combination creates a strong wistful effect (Figure 5.20).

In a very different style, Springer worked with Yip Harburg on *Time, You Old Gypsy Man* (1980). It would be deeply touching even if one did not know that it was the lyricist's last published song. Musically, the song is kept simple: the design is AABA, plus a two-bar coda. The bridge remains in the same key as the A-sections, with slightly more complex harmonies. The opening figure

Figure 5.20

combines I and ii chords, with a careful hesitation in rhythm on *gy**psy*, a feature that recurs throughout the song. The half-cadences drop down to ruminative low notes. But it is the rueful, self-amused words that tie together and deepen the song. Harburg sustains one long metaphor of nouns, with *gypsy...thief ...rogue...vagabond*, and another long figure of speech depending on verbs: *drugged...tricked...fiddled...silvered* (my hair)...*crinkled* (my eyes)... *turned off...stripped...fled*. The verb *silvered* ends A1, and then begins A2. This is as fine as lyric-writing gets, and a great finale for Harburg.

Walter Marks is known for two Broadway shows for which he wrote both words and music, "Bajour" (1964) and "Golden Rainbow" (1967). The latter contained Marks's best-known song, *I've Gotta Be Me*. From "Bajour," about gypsies in New York, comes *Must It Be Love?*, with a 16-bar verse and a 60-bar chorus. The verse is as musically spare as Rodgers and Hammerstein, with phrases that cascade scale-wise and an enharmonic change after the first eight measures from A flat to C. The chorus has the wide range of a good theater song, and moves along smoothly, though there is a deliberate false scansion whenever the title phrase occurs. *Living Simply* is a waltz with a simple, fresh-sounding melody, also Rodgers-like, and easy harmonies that live up to the title. The lyric is simple and strong: "Living simply, simply living in plain, sane fashion." *Love-Line* is the best of the three. There is no verse. The chorus starts palm-reading straight-off: "Your love-line is straight, your life-line is long." The lovely opening vocal line plays with 5 and raised 5, and the chords are lushly augmented. As the lyrics predict things to come, the harmonies alter tellingly, giving the song an exotic flavor. It's a good late-evening song for a romantic tryst in a dark café.

"Golden Rainbow" was a glitzy show about Las Vegas—with surprisingly classy songs. *For Once In Your Life* struts along in a chorus-line beat of alternating quarter and half notes, with a big syncopation for the title phrase in which the speaker urges his lady to loosen up. *How Could I Be So Wrong?* has the knowing, sharp edges of a Coleman   Fields song, and features little pattering asides: "How could I be so wrong? (I kept telling myself)." *It's You Again* is a more innocent ballad, describing reconciliation with a long-lost love. The musical phrases ascend quietly by one- or two-step intervals ("After all these years of missing you....") until they reach "It's you again," whereupon the line turns gently downward. The melodic line, unusual and pretty, uses stacked pentatonic intervals.

Clark Gesner wrote music and lyrics for the show "You're a Good Man Charlie Brown" (1967), from which comes a little ballad, *Happiness*, a conception as tangible as "two kinds of ice cream," or "pizza with sausage," or "five different crayons." This is not a show song trying to be genuine, this charmer is the real thing. Other songs from this friendly little score, including the hilarious *Book Report*, are equally charming.

Larry Grossman has written music for theater and television. *Play It Again, Sam* (1969), lyrics by Hal Hackady, is a terrific "Broadway blues" number, that is, a song in ABAB pop format (plus extension and fade-out) with an obsessive little vamp, with lowered 3 and 7 for the vocal line. The middle section uses the same cat-chasing-its-tail figure in a new key. The song is like the Arlen — Mercer *One For My Baby* in its scenario. A 1970 Broadway show, "Minnie's Boys," again with Hackady, had two interesting songs. *Where Was I When They Passed Out Luck?* (marked *Funky Gospel Waltz*), is a musically and lyrically witty Broadway anthem concerning a charming loser with chutzpah who lined up to get brains and talent—but when it came time to get luck: "Where was your smart, clever friend? Back, showin' off my talent and brains to the bums linin' up at the end." It's got an alert rhythmic drive. These two songs remind one strongly of Kander and Ebb; they are at least as good. *He Gives Me Love* is a ballad in the form of a meditation, which could be sung equally convincingly by an exasperated but devoted parent or by a lover. "Heartaches he gives me, how can I complain? He gives me love...." The vocal line is underscored by the extensive use of chiming off-octave chords, giving the song a slow, wistful melodic character.

In 1982, Grossman wrote an ambitious score for "A Doll's Life," lyrics by Comden and Green. The score is unusual, with idiosyncratic pieces that have an operatic character and range. *Learn to Be Lonely* is a long song with abrupt, highly curving musical phrases that match lyrics, unlike any others we can cite by Comden and Green, that show an original metaphorical quality (Figure 5.21). The second A repeats the oscillating quarter-note thirds in describing a new star:

Figure 5.21

"twinkling, sparkling, burning, glad to be born," and later a new sun. The title phrase is brought in as an interpolation at the end of the first A-section, and as an after-thought at the end of the song. This elegant piece, as well as the narrative song, *You Interest Me*, from the same show, could be considered art songs. We hope that Grossman is still writing venturesome songs.

Craig Bohmler's work is a fresh take on the sound of traditional twentieth-century musical theater pop-jazz style. From "Gunmetal Blues" (1980) with lyrics by Marion Adler, comes *Jenny*, a song that brings to mind David Raksin's *Laura* (musically, it is very like Wilder's *Ellen*). Jenny appears to be a mystery woman, existing somewhere between reality and illusion. The lovely melody seems to meander from one main key to another by means of chains of thirds extended, à la Debussy, to 5, 7, 9.... Adler's evocative lyrics reinforce the mystery of the subject: "She walks in my sleep on the edges of waking me." The song is gorgeous, though too long for its musical content. Bohmler and Adler also wrote "Enter the Guardsman" (1999). *One Great Love* is also a long song, with something approaching endless melody moving through different keys. The words sound the ecstatic note perhaps too continually. Bohmler's style is rather like Maury Yeston's, in bending strong melody to musicodramatic purpose.

William Finn broke new ground in the New York musical theater with "March of the Falsettos" (1981) and "Falsettoland" (1990). These were written in fairly conventional theatrical form (dialogue, songs, ensembles) on specifically gay plot lines. *What Would I Do* is a ballad with a strong melody and an interesting metrical shift from four to three per bar, but insipid chords. A long song from

1995, *The Music Still Plays On*, uses a few chords with abrupt transitions among them, and a rather wandering voice line in light pop-rock style. It seems to need impactful words to make an effect, but Finn's lyric is constructed of too-consciously poetic, absurdist figures of speech that we find merely strange: "Love is dressed up in a hat / its thighs have gone to fat…."

For a 1982 film, "One For the Heart," the singer and songwriter Tom Waits wrote a set of quite wonderful songs to serve as an alternative to a soundtrack; that is, the songs not sung by the actors, but delineating the emotional landscape. Here Waits is thoroughly comfortable with the pop idiom, writing tunes that invoke the mood of the muted trumpet or the sax but fit the voice as well, while still evincing a post-romantic sensibility by virtue of his topics and words. There are bluesy, Van Heusen-like AABA ballads like *Picking Up After You*, with a provocative triple meaning; and loose, walking-bass, rhythm-and-blues like *Little Boy Blue*, whose lyric rings changes on nursery rhyme lingo ("Little boy blue lost little Bo-Peep…."). *I Beg Your Pardon* is a tight 32-bar song, involving apologies to a lover ("I'll give you Boardwalk and all my hotels"). It has an unbuttoned lyric reminiscent of Bob Dorough. The title winds through the song as both a parenthetical clause in the A-sections and the culmination of the release. All Waits's songs in this score are in standard four- and eight-bar units, but sometimes in unusual patterns. Thus, *This One's From the Heart* is just a riff for the voice with a brief modulation at the end of each unit for the title phrase; it amounts to an additive AAAA, but stays interesting because of the lyric. The most unusual song may be the long and complex *Old Boyfriends*, which moves restlessly between major and minor and in which the speaker recognizes that she carries a lot of baggage ("They look you up when they're in town / To see if they can still burn you down.") It is a song with a deep specific gravity. This score was prefigured in 1977 by an excellent film song, *I Never Talk to Strangers*, with singles-bar reference. These Waits songs in classic pop style sounded as convincing in the 1980s as they would have forty years earlier.

A song by Keith Levenson, music, and Martin Charnin, words, *It Happens At Night* (1996) is a notable example of a long-established type: the glamorous/sleazy, film-noir, paean to New York. Naturally, it uses a pop-blues vamp, and a sexy slow rhythm, as if the "long-stemmed beauties" are patrolling the night. The distinctive rhythmic feature is the use of prominent trochaic patterns, **short**-long, like a hip-swing. Coleman, Strouse, and some of the film composers may have done it also, but this is a sassy instance.

EDWARD KLEBAN (1939–87)

For years, Kleban was known only for his lyrics to "A Chorus Line" (1975), music by Marvin Hamlisch. Because the music in this show was almost continuous, the lyrics were extraordinarily important in revealing the psychology of the characters. Given its narrative nature, there are few entities in the score that fit our chosen genre. The well-known *One*, a dancey two-step number, has had some life outside the show, as has the overblown ballad *What I Did For Love*. While Hamlisch went on to do other successful work, Kleban had very little produced until after his death.

Nevertheless, he was writing words and music to a number of good songs. Some of them were collected and used in the posthumous theatrical production, "A Class Act," in 2000. *Better* is a confident song with witty lyrics, set to a catchy tune that is a series of short and sweet phrases, with slight hesitations between them that set up the punch lines of the lyric (Figure 5.22). The show contained a number of autobiographical songs: the perky, bizarre *Light On My Feet*, a

Figure 5.22

Figure 5.23

projection of one's persona past death; a musical memoir called *Paris Through the Window*; and *Self Portrait*, a musing, intense song of great tenderness, whose bridge is shown in Figure 5.23.

One More Beautiful Song is short, 16 bars then repeated in a different key; it is fairly conventional, but has a pleasant melody and a nice wit: "Let there be one huge laugh before it's over, And maybe one high note to crack the dome!" The very fine *The Next Best Thing to Love* is a double-length song in the form AABBA, the second B extended. It exemplifies melodic restraint: except for the title phrase when it appears, most of the vocal line is contained within less than an octave. The movement of the melody is for the most part in half-steps. The harmonies have at times a bell-like quality that reinforces the dour retrospection of the lyrics. The B-sections are even more melodically restrained, but with a richer, less static harmony.

All these songs by Kleban alone have a dark mood. However, they show how words that might be self-pitying alone can take on a luster when set to music to which one cannot assign a specific emotional meaning. Kleban's words and music are always evenly and movingly matched.

To revert to Hamlisch briefly: he wrote *How Can I Win* (1993), lyrics by David Zippel. The song is noteworthy for its peculiar concept, a kind of catalog of self-blame or perhaps paranoia. The music attempts to provide a dramatic accompaniment for some pretty heavy thought: "I live each day like my emotions are at war...." We wonder how much better this song would have been had Kleban done the lyrics.

Notes

1. Performance: Blossom Dearie, "Once Upon A Summertime," Verve LP 827757.
2. Performance: "Mark Murphy Sings Mostly Coleman and Fields," Audiophile CD 132.
3. Performance: Marlene VerPlanck, "I Like To Sing," Audiophile LP 186.
4. Performance: VerPlanck.
5. Performance: Sally Mayes, "The Dorothy Fields Songbook," DRG Cabaret CD 91410.
6. Performance: If you're willing to forgo the words, a terrific piano version is in "Oscar Peterson Plays Broadway," Verve CD Jazz Masters 37.
7. Performance: Audra McDonald, "How Glory Goes," Nonesuch CD 79580.
8. A reader of our draft protests that the song refers to physical abuse, and contains "sick" lines. It's true, but songs are not credos.
9. Performance: These two songs were wonderfully sung by Charlotte Rae, "Songs I Taught My Mother," Vanguard LP 9004.
10. Billie Holiday should have recorded this. A good performance is Susannah McCorkle, "How Do You Keep the Music Playing?" Pausa LP 7195.
11. Performance: Sylvia Syms, "Lovingly," Atlantic LP 18177.
12. Performance: Carol Sloane, "When I Look In Your Eyes," Concord CD 4619.
13. Performance: June Christy, "Gone For the Day," Capitol LP 902.

6
The Land Where the Good Songs Go

The title is that of a beautiful old song by Jerome Kern and P. G. Wodehouse, from 1917, in which the singer hopes to spend, perhaps end, life in company with the songs she loves. Intimate settings have always been the best place to appreciate songs with delicate melody, subtle chords, or words that require, and repay, close attention, and to enjoy a performance style that uses just a piano with bass or drum-set, rather than the style needed to "project" in a theater. Such ambiences exist only in a few cities, and are sought out by small audiences. The "cabaret crowd"—those who write for, perform in, and enjoy songs in small clubs—are a tight little circle, but they always have been. Those who perform there have huge repertoires of treasures, keeping alive not only deserving songs that were always recherché but songs that have faded from awareness. In such locales, young singers learn that repertoire from their peers. Piano bars and clubs facilitate both conservation and transmission. Here we discuss some of the songs that have found life there.

BART HOWARD (1915–2004)

Normally, he wrote both words and music. His songs are well-turned, the harmony discrete, telling in their effect but not flaunting their means. The songs deal with, not love so much as romance, as something transitory, but beautiful while on the wing. They are small but potent.

One of the authors disliked the song that made Howard a fortune, *In Other Words* (also called *Fly Me to the Moon*; 1954), because it was so often bellowed by drunks in piano bars—some of them customers. But when he sang it, he found that it was supple and beautiful, both in its excellent verse and rather short chorus, masterfully tied together. The secret lies in Howard's well-shaped vocal phrases, which individually have a clear profile but hover together within one vocal register, one tonal area. The words to the chorus start, and for a while remain, in a high-falutin' sort of diction; but then the songwriter says, Who needs metaphor, it can all be said in other words; that is, simply. It is thus the perfect song about popular song.

A partial exception to the small-but-potent characterization is *My Love Is a Wanderer* (1952), an art song in construction, using all the notes of the diatonic major scale in long vocal lines spaced evenly in time and covering almost two octaves. Unusually, the title comes from the opening line of the verse, which uses just one octave for some evocative word-play:

> My love is a wanderer, wand'ring over land and sea,
> And I am a wonderer, wond'ring: does my love love me?

Such a lot of information in just a few words. When the chorus opens out, and the loved one responds, finally, "Meet me in Shannon in the Spring!" at the climax of the song (with *me* set on the peak note), it is a small, joyful victory. The title phrase that opened the verse returns, again unusually, as a hushed, wistful coda.

We continue to cite exceptions first. *Year After Year* (1955) is a moderate tempo song with lot of momentum, owing to its basic rhythmic pattern: one stressed word on a long note, then two quick syllables on the last two parts of a triplet, the latter figure always an up-beat to the next long element. It's a dance figure with an elegant syncopation in it, a sort of beguine. The pattern becomes quite driving at the end of the song, as "Year ** after year...." (*aft-er* being the up-beat element) loops around five times, for a big finish.

Let Me Love You (1954) is a song that works moderately fast or slow, owing to its easy dotted rhythm, shapely phrases, and unobtrusively clever words. The opening phrase is a command, three even, peremptory words and then an octave drop on *you*. Thereafter, in a nice contrast, it eases into a relaxed, swinging dotted rhythm. The lover tells the loved one what she will do for him, if he complies: they're all very charming promises, ending with "I'll buy you the first of May!"[1] Another lightly sprung, lively song is *Who Wants to Fall In Love?* (1953). This one starts with a confiding verse ("Listen to what the cynics say to you"), then moves into a merry summary of why love is a poor bet. Howard opens the chorus while modulating, which gives the tune an immediate élan (Figure 6.1). The release is full of neat rhyme: "You cry, you over-drink / You sigh, you under-think," is one example. In its eccentric abandon, it is comparable to the classic, slightly nutty, *I Like the Likes of You*, by Duke and Harburg.[2]

The song *Perfect Stranger* (1956) is an unusual, shy song, one of Howard's best in implying a dramatic situation. After a candid verse that sketches in the background, the chorus opens in lilting two-syllable half-step phrases, setting the title words, and others. The speaker wants to fall in love, but, as the brevity

Figure 6.1

of phrase suggests, holds back. The bridge finally clarifies the problem: when the other party is no longer a perfect stranger, will he or she turn out to be perfect? "Is the perfect stranger smiling, or is he laughing at me?"[3]

As we have said, the representative Howard song is a graceful, love (or loss-of-love) song. One would swear that *To Be In Love* (1957) was unknown Porter, with its elegant movement, lightly diminished harmonies, and slightly arch lyric with lots of interior rhyme ("You turn my ev'ryday days to a riotous blaze of Red-Letter Nights"). In this long song, the 12-bar bridge is closely related to the A-section material, but leads to a 24-bar C-section that becomes downright rapturous. Another song that deepens as it progresses is *Walk Up* (1956), about a relationship that dissipates. The verse tells the "back story" engagingly, with subtle rhythmic adjustments ("I tho't I'd never learn to cook for looking at you"). The chorus is graver. Its opening words ("There was a time") give it away, and a mournful minor dominant-of-a-dominant chord at the end of that phrase is conclusive: this happiness is in the past. It ends with a throat-closing quietness: "You walked out of the flat, and that was all." It is a sad song, sadder for its understatement.[4]

There are a number of excellent but lighter songs. *You Are Not My First Love* (words by Howard and Peter Windsor) is fairly well-known because it has a lyric twist at the end. *On the First Warm Day* (1951) is a lovely tune, chaste and poised, like a song by Harry Warren. It has a nice feature of allowing the second phrase to repeat the first, but extend it by two beats and two notes, which gives the A-sections a gentle push ahead. The transition into the final A is elegant. *I'll Be Easy to Find* (1958), in its relaxed rhythmic movement, is reminiscent of Porter's *Easy to Love*. The Porter influence is too overt in *Take Care of Yourself*.

The ballad *Alone With Me* (1955) is in slow 3/4 time, with chords that cause the melody line to "hang up" affectively on the second beat. It has a lovely close. *Thank You For the Lovely Summer* (1952) is a song of loving goodbye ("Better luck to both of us next Fall"). A couple of songs written in 1960 are the bouncy *Fantastic* ("...the way a melody becomes a symphony complete with tympani and strings") and the more lyrical *Miracles*. Both are competent; both depend, in these cases rather imaginatively, on the concepts specified by the titles, an approach to songwriting that has its limitations. A 1961 song, *Ev'rybody's Lookin'* (Around For an Angel), is a lot stronger, casual and odd, with a light rock sort of tune and a lyric twist to it. This one holds up through humor. Howard did the lyrics for a neat, bouncy number, music by bandleader Neal Hefti, *Don't Dream of Anybody but Me* (1959). It's a song that depends, effectively, on a missing first beat for the title phrase, and thereafter.

There is a cost for the prolific Howard's grace and fluency. There are many songs that are almost memorable. *One Love Affair* (1955) has a marvelous verse, verbally like Porter once again ("...I couldn't be rude if a nice little nude little genie flew in...."), but the chorus is humdrum. *The Man In the Looking Glass* (1965) has a good concept—someone looking back on his life with wry recognition—but it would have been better in a less trivial rhythm. *Sell Me* (1957) is an up-tempo bluesy number, in a familiar sexy mode. The verse says, "When I go shopping for a love affair," and that sets the mercenary tone. We like it; it's fun; and we think Howard should have taken it even further. To quote a line from the song: "When you sell me your line, make it good, boy!"

The best of Howard's work is exquisite. A number of his works are "about" words or music, or both together, which brings an added pleasure to those who love songs. Most of his songs are like delicious first courses, leaving one hungry, sometimes, for something more.

WILLIAM ROY (1928–2003)

Roy, a singer, pianist, and accompanist in New York clubs, was of the same stylistic generation as Bart Howard, and his work resembles Howard's, being delicate, harmonically insinuating, and literate. It is, on the whole, a bit more heartfelt and direct, less bittersweet or wry, than Howard's. This quality is evident in his fine song, *Look a Little Closer*, which opens with a sinuous rhythmic figure: a long stressed note, followed by several shorter ones and then a slow triplet leading to a final stressed note ("Search ** along a road without end...," *road with-out* being the triplet). There is a tight chromatic descent, and then a slightly more open set of upward intervals, but all within the compass of a fifth. Thereafter the melodic line expands gradually, until at the climax it uses a major seventh. There are very brief chord changes. The song is about looking close to home, for home is where the heart is. It's lovely.

When I Sing Alone (1974) is a more overtly emotional song, with an unusual underlying conception, that of an entertainer—"in front of the world, I sing of me"—who is interiorly singing to a loved one, especially when by himself. The release gets big in scale, and high in pitch. It's a gratifying song for any subtle singer. In a very different style, *Come Away With Me* is a fast café-society waltz, invoking, as many such songs have, glamorous place names, from Capri to the surprising Albanian Sea, as inducements.

Will Roy had the talent to be a theater composer, although his only show, "Maggie" (1953, after J. M. Barrie), was not a success. But *What Every Woman Knows* is a good song, with a strong opening strain and a perceptive overall idea. And *Charm* is a dream of a song. There is a plot-sketching verse from which we understand that a woman feels that she lacks that indispensable quality, charm. The chorus, in medium 4/4, is oddly sprightly and rather folkish in seeming to impart a universal message without great personal angst. The opening melody sounds quite like the Rodgers — Hammerstein *When the Children Are Asleep*, but it moves into more venturesome territory. Many of the phrase endings use a spondee pattern, with the two long notes (e.g., "disarm him") inscribing a half-tone move from 6 to lowered 7, and hanging up there without moving on to the key-tone. It's arresting, as are the citations of some strategic lapses from feminine good taste, like "she just has to charm the pants off him." It should be a favorite with singers who possess true charm.[5]

MARSHALL BARER (1923–98).

For sheer virtuosity and wit, no lyricist of the half-century outdid him. Barer, moreover, had an off-kilter sense of humor that made him more than just brilliant; in this regard, he was a kind of urbane counterpart to the hipper, but more demotic, Dorough or Frishberg (see below). Barer's unique slant may be exemplified by his approach to a song about a social gathering where the men, after retreating for brandy and cigars, ask themselves, *Shall We Join the Ladies?* and, deciding in the affirmative, conclude, "and make one *huge* lady!" This song, written with David Ross in the 1950s, is one outrageous notion after another, including the reference to a relative who weighed several hundred pounds: "But she was tall, *terribly* tall!" A song written with composer Anita Leonard Nye, *Forthebirds*, has an astounding, almost frighteningly glittering, lyric. Many writers achieve cleverly, well-positioned wit in a song, but hardly anyone achieves an entire lyric that is like fireworks on the Fourth of July: they just keep exploding. This one includes, just as a sample, the couplet, "When I see a bonnet with something upon it / That should have been kept as a pet . . . (yes, I have no egret)," and it concludes with a barrage of giddy rhyme about a tropical avian star: "If a toucan can can-can as well as a man can . . . What one toucan can do, two can too." Cole Porter, for his song *Can Can*, would have killed to have found comparable words.

Some of Barer's work will be cited in connection with Ellington. Another important collaborator for Barer was the gifted Mary Rodgers, for the 1959 "Once Upon a Mattress," the off-Broadway comic version of the children's parable about the princess and the pea. The score for this show must bring delight to any child—and delight plus guffaws to any adult, especially in the deadpan numbers that sound like rewrites of musical comedy formulae, except better. There are more or less "straight" ballads, such as the graceful *In a Little While* and *Yesterday I Loved You*, which sounds disconcertingly like a preparody of a love song from "Camelot" while still being quite lovely. The show is parodistic in nature, so its songs do not travel outside it. There is one song, however, with an irresistible sweep, called *Normandy*, which can. Rodgers's melody just dances along, and Barer writes about

> ...a man who knows a man who knows
> a cozy inn, a friendly place,
> with rows of windows facing the sea

with a deft command of concealed rhyme; and then, again,

> This time of year
> the air I hear is rare and clear
> and warm in Normandy.

The other song too good to overlook is a splendid dance number, *Very Soft Shoes*. The tap rhythm is too intricate to illustrate, but it's a steady dotted figure with pauses for footwork right in the middle of words, as in "My Dad was deb * onair...." At the end it works up to a Feet, don't fail me now! finish: "When Daddy * wore his * very * soft * shoes."

For another purpose, Barer wrote a lovely song with Mary Rodgers called *Something Known*, but then put his words at the disposal of the gifted David Ross for an even finer tune (1985). It turned out to be one of the most beautiful songs imaginable, one that demands to be rediscovered. The words are delicate, heart-stopping.

> Something known, but never spoken
> Something natural, but set apart
> Sweet and swift, a glimpse of something shining
> Seen from a corner of your heart....
> Strange and soft like thunder on the mountain
> Heard from a million miles away...a million miles away.

The *million miles* phrase is slightly varied in pitch and contour, as if it could repeat a million times. Ross made the song as AAA, with each A-section opening in a subtly different way. Each section has two periods, the first set low and curving downward, the second arching upwards. In the final section, the second phrase goes even higher, for the climax, and turns into a long coda, tending gently down over the final five bars (Figure 6.2).

Like many witty writers, Barer had a sentimental, vulnerable heart. With William Roy, there is a psychologically complex song, like a Shire — Maltby number,

Figure 6.2

about reluctant fatherhood, *Baby Mine*, that lightens up for a moment with the offhand comment that "...only God can make a trio." There is also, with Lance Ong, a wonderful Caribbean Christmas song, *Christmas Is an Island*, and with Hugh Martin, a song of nostalgia about classic movies, *On Such a Night As This*, which will bring a pang to anyone old enough. With Ross, there is a love song in the diction of English poetry, called *Beyond Compare* (1990), which opens with "How do I love thee? Let me count the ways—one, two, three, four, five, six million (this could take me days and days)." The lyric includes a 24-carat pun concerning songwriter Lorenz Hart.

Finally, with Gordon Connell, there is a slow bossa nova, with a lovely rhythmic hitch in it, *Come What May*. Barer's lyric runs:

> Hold my hand, and I'll have the strength to take a stand
> When push comes to shove—as it will some day—
> And the heavens above all go somewhat grey
> If we have enough love
> Then let come what may…what may…what may.

Other than a couple of songs with Ellington and the work with Mary Rodgers, Barer's songs, almost invariably excellent, remain obscure. A performer could make a career of them.[6]

A Note on Mary Rodgers

Inexplicably, Rodgers withdrew from the limelight. With Sondheim, she wrote several songs, one of which, *The Boy From…*, was once a favorite in clubs; but its suggestiveness palls before it finishes. A 1963 song with Martin Charnin, *Hey, Love!* is a fine one, with a strong opening tone set with swift-changing harmonies and a clever brief bridge. We would write more about Mary Rodgers if we could.

MICHAEL BROWN (b. 1920)

Another songwriter contemporary with Barer and also enjoying a specialist's reputation is Michael Brown, who made a splash as a performer as well as a songwriter in the early 1950s. Brown wrote both words and music, and has also been a successful children's author. Although his sophisticated taste may have limited his fame with the broad public, his first big success (1950) was a long, narrative "country blues" song called *The Swamp Boy*. The words are extraordinary, in a dark Southern Gothic idiom of seduction and death. The song now seems remote, even bizarre, but it was impressive for its artistic daring — a dare that was, alas, lost in Frankie Laine's bawling performance. In total contrast, Brown wrote a knock-out comedy song, in hoedown style, for a 1952 "New Faces" Broadway show, called *Lizzie Borden*. Listeners from that era will never forget the cheeky humor of such lines as "Oh, you can't chop your poppa up in Massachusetts, and then blame all the damage on the mice." More elegant and blithe is the utterly charming *Witchcraft*, from a 1957 revue.

> Have you ever considered witchcraft—I think you might have the knack—
> You could win ev'rybody's marbles, and not have to give them back.…
> It's a wonderful thing to know, my dear—as a hobby or as a whole career—
> And the field isn't crowded at all this year in witchcraft.

The tune is a syncopated delight. It's as good as the Coleman — Leigh song of the same title from the same year.[7]

Brown was highly sophisticated, in both musical and literary aspects, but this did not entail being brittle. Some of his most effective earlier songs were in a surreal sort of traditional ballad style: they include *The Son of a Man and a Mermaid* ("Mother was cool to the touch—I don't know a lot about Father"), and the English-grotesque *The Monkey Coachman*, who drives a bride to her death (both from 1956). They are deeply peculiar but attractive, primarily because they are not camp. Subsequently, Brown wrote a number of songs in a conventional "show" style; a whole set of these are from a Broadway revue-with-story line, "Different Times" (1972).[8] The fascinating thing about excellent but obscure songs such as *I'm Not Through* and *I Dreamed About Roses* is that they are just as good as similarly aimed songs by Bock or Spence (or, with *Roses*, Jerry Herman). Had they been done commercially by a recording star, they might have been big hits. Alternatively, we suppose, had Brown written songs for more ambitious musicodramatic contexts, they might have communicated more memorably, a paradox we touch on in our final chapter.

JOHN WALLOWITCH (b. 1926)

Wallowitch is a pianist, performer, coach, and above all a New Yorker. He writes very superior songs in the classic popular style: the tunes are first-rate, though not harmonically pathbreaking, and the words are often remarkable. In chapter 1, we suggested that, in popular song, funny trumps witty. Almost anyone with verbal skill and some clear-eyed experience of life can be witty at times; the formal constraints of this genre of song help one to achieve it. But seeing the world askew, and surprising the auditor into laughter, is a rare gift. When we say that his tunes are (merely) "first-rate," we allude to the inherent need for a songwriter who creates both words and music to balance them for overall effect. Wallowitch finds that balance as well as anyone. His songs have a wonderful aplomb.

Some of his funniest songs are well known, at least in the New York cabaret world. *Bruce* (1983) is a hilarious (and sweet) song about a cross-dresser. Its effect comes from the way the songwriter manages to create two characters: the man in question and a friend, presumably a woman who is concerned to help him get the details just right. Other laugh-out-loud songs, probably effective only in a club, include *I'm 27*, and the over-the-top *Cheap Decadent Drivel*.[9]

Like many witty but humane persons, Wallowitch has written a number of songs that elicit a smile and a tear together. *Oh Wow* (1972) is an example: it starts hip and ends naïve. *Florida* is a long narrative song about a couple who have been together a very long time, and who fear they've missed a lot—until they think about it. It is a song, written from an amused but not mocking attitude, which could have been created by Randy Newman.

Some of the songs gently celebrate places and times past, and the cycle of life. *And Nothing Ends* (1955) is a short song with a placid tone that darkens toward the end, and a Schubertian melody that moves from minor to major, with the latter somehow sadder than the former. Like any wise romantic, Wallowitch is ambivalent in his nostalgia. *There Used to Be* (1990) salutes a lovelier, more gracious time, and says, "But everything ends." Then he takes it back: "I swear that's not true...'cause baby there's me and baby there's you." *Manhattan Blue* (1991), a long song, disproves the generalization that Wallowitch uses conventional harmony. The chord changes here are worthy of Strayhorn, especially seventh chords that are dissonant, treble against bass. The long verse wanders, but the sad words of the chorus are just right, about twilight over the city.

There are, naturally, ballads of easy elegance about lost or forgone love. *I Live Alone Again* has a good verse and a graceful melodic line, with a turn including a raised 5 on the title phrase. *Here Comes April Again* has good words, including "...here's to cursing the love we knew." *Will There Really Be a Morning?* (1971) sets words by Emily Dickinson: it's not hard to imagine the poet tapping her genteel feet to Wallowitch's soft bossa nova beat.

Wallowitch's noncomedic songs stay within a narrow emotional range, the verbal content expressing tenderness, regret, amusement, resignation, fondness, nostalgia. Even his tempo and expression markings at the beginning of songs read, *thoughtfully and tenderly*, *moderately*, *comodo*, etc. We asserted in chapter 1 (p. 16) that this is the default zone for the classic popular song. After a time, a writer like Wallowitch can seem too well-bred, too reined in. Wallowitch, with his poised and graceful melodies, his adherence to regular and familiar metrical patterns, and his immaculate lyrics, is strikingly like Noel Coward with a completely American range of reference, which is something to admire if not send off rockets for.

However, a conventional song that cuts deep is *I See the World Through Your Eyes* (1983). It is a song about someone who has, presumably, died, but whose presence is profoundly felt. The phonetics of the title phrase are lovely in themselves. The visual (later, auditory) metaphors are handled well: seeing through the loved one's eyes, the notion that memories bring indelible pictures. The A-section melodic line, with its oscillating sixth intervals (with repeated half-step appoggiatura above) and its avoidance of the key-tone, yields a musical sense of being adrift in longing (Figure 6.3). The format is ABAB, and the phrases of B continue longer than those of A: they seem to press ahead, to overcome the sense of being caught in memory—except when that memory floods back, as at the end of the first B (mm.10-13) where *we* and *long* are prolonged so that motion of the song almost stops. The song ends beautifully, with a reiteration, "And I still see the world through your eyes," with the voice dropping one tone to the lowest note of the song.

Figure 6.3

DAVE FRISHBERG (b.1933); BOB DOROUGH (b.1923); BLOSSOM DEARIE (b.1928)

Some singer-songwriters of the period we cover were not of the confessional sort, that is, those whose musical grounding was the guitar and who created poetic, personal, normally self-referential, lyrics (see chapter 7). There were quite different examples, of whom the most original and distinctive include Frishberg, Dorough, and Dearie. It is natural to cover them together, not only for stylistic reasons but because these three wrote songs together (and with others), and performed each other's material. Each creates music or words or both. Each reflects a piano-based jazz tradition (each plays piano), in a concise, spare, light bebop style. Each writes highly individualistic lyrics. As performers they are small-scaled, swinging, funny, sometimes tender: sophisticated troubadours from a slightly exotic culture, one that you wish you had known before the tourists came. Their most congenial environment is the recording studio or the small club, where the musical and verbal fine points, and the off-beat sensibility they share, are fully communicated.

Dave Frishberg

Frishberg's most widely performed songs are probably *Peel Me a Grape* (1962, words and music, Frishberg) and *I'm Hip* (1974, music by Bob Dorough). The first of these has been in Dearie's repertoire for decades. It's in a loping, syncopated rhythm with relaxed triplets on the weak beats. The bridge takes up a crisper dotted rhythm. It's an affable song about gold-digging, in which the speaker (female) runs down the parameters: "Here's how to be an agreeable chap / Love me and leave me in luxury's lap." *I'm Hip* is more satirical and more verbally complex, with several stanzas of self-incrimination in which the speaker demonstrates how cool (thus how square) he is: "I'm in step / when it was hip to be hep, I was hep...." There is an especially nice, brief release.

Several paradoxes attend "word songs" of this sort. First, once you hear Frishberg or Dearie sing them, they seem to belong to that singer, to depend on his or her delivery—yet others perform them to great effect. It depends on attitude. What is needed is to be satirical but not mocking, crisp but not brittle, affectionately amused but not overtly witty. The second oddity is that they date, but don't turn stale. The references may slip away, the language style may fall out of use, and yet the songs still communicate. Frishberg has written several songs about old-time baseball, and a number of fond songs about departed jazz scenes known only to aficionados (e.g., *Zoot Walks In*, 1991, tune by Zoot Sims and Gerry Mulligan). If you know these worlds, the songs have a special meaning, but anyone is likely to know enough to get the point. Many songs refer in passing to older songs in the culture; again, you may only vaguely get the reference, but you know it's there. Cole Porter's most preeningly knowing songs may date; Frishberg's just get blurry around the edges. And much of his slangy style is timeless, as in *Gotta Get Me Some Zzz* (1981). Has anyone else ever used an arbitrary vocable so integrally in a lyric?

Not all Frishberg's songs are precisely affable. A 1984 song, *Blizzard of Lies*, is a cheerfully swinging but barbed number about life as a con game.

> Better watch your step when your old dog Shep
> Can't even look you in the eyes
> You're cold and lost, and you're double-crossed
> When you're marooned in a blizzard of lies.

This one references *You'll Never Walk Alone* in a gently mocking way. It's a song that's effective for a singer, who can slip without effort from the main narrative, which argues the point by exemplification, to the almost manic conclusion, "Marooned, marooned, marooned [nine times repeated, at the end of the song] in a blizzard of lies." Similarly, *Quality Time* (1994) is tough, a delightful medium-swing tune with slyly incriminating words.

> I know a small hotel, remote and quiet
> If they decide to sell, my firm could buy it
> Then we'd develop it and gentrify it—
> We're talking quality time.

Others of the songs are nonaggressive but still contain a sting. *Another Song About Paris* (1980), which incorporates a banal French waltz and a bow to "An American in Paris," raises the question of whether the world really needs any more songs about a topic that's been done to death. Singers take note: if you must do Paris songs, this one's an antidote.

The other direction in which Frishberg's songs depart from a default-point of affability are some sweet nostalgic songs. *Do You Miss New York?* (1980), whose verse (Frishberg writes wonderful verses) opens with the great phrase, "Since I took a left (and moved out to the Coast)." It has a poignant melodic opening that plays with the octave against the major seventh. *Listen Here* (1977), about listening to "that little voice inside," is more romantic in style, with fine chord changes, especially to a recurrent major seventh chord set on IV of the scale, and a flexible melodic line that moves from short to urgent phrases so that the auditor gets the feeling of overhearing someone talking to himself. *Marilyn Monroe* (1981, music by Alan Broadbent) has great chords, sounding like Bill Evans musing at the keyboard.

Sweet Kentucky Ham (1979) is a joy, about being stuck in an uninteresting town and longing for home. It has a time-honored bass-line progression, and sets the title phrase on a wistful chromatic phrase. *Snowbound* (1994) is a sweet song that manages also to sound like a gentle spoof on "sweet band" music. Far beyond that sort of avuncular pleasantness is Frishberg's great lyric to the ballad *You Are There*, music by Johnny Mandel (see p. 271).

To dwell a bit on Frishberg's affiliation with jazz, there is a casual song, *I Want to Be a Sideman* (1996), an example of how this writer, with references ranging from Glen Miller to Lester Young, can poke fun and tender a salute, all at the same time. It's casual, but fresh as new grass. The gist is, "I want to spend all my time with music and musicians."[10] Finally, one of Frishberg's finest, most buoyant songs also deals with a memorable jazz figure, Bix Beiderbecke, the influential 1920s cornet player. On one level, *Dear Bix* (1976) is a perfect AABAB (plus coda) format, in regular eight-bar sections, with a key-change to IV at the bridge, and the melodic climax just before the final B. Thus it is like dozens of other fine classic pop songs. On another level, very audible even to those who aren't jazz-oriented, it's a "take" on jazz patterns of the Kansas City era, heard in bass-line and in the familiar chord-change layout involving I, ii, IV, V. At the bridge comes a rhythmic accompaniment pattern that calls for a broken-octave, stride-piano style. The jazz touches are not just in the substructure, but in the treble and the voice line as well. *Dear Bix* opens with a four-bar piano riff taken from a Bix

Figure 6.4

recording (*In a Mist*), and closes (after the vocal) with a repeat of that figure, followed by another short Bix quotation (*I'm Comin' Virginia*). In fact, the very shape of the opening tune is that of a cornet solo (Figure 6.4), as is the lead-in to the bridge. The medium tempo and the fairly long passages of dotted-eighths (not notated in the music, but assumed) are exactly the right vehicle for a blithe and loving lyric, with casual forms of address ("Bix, old friend," "Bix, old bear," "Bix, old elf") and characterizing statements that could not be more apt for the subject, as in "no...B flat run-of-the-mill-type guy." Where *does* a songwriter get the conception for such a wonderful song, and the "chops" to carry it off?

Bob Dorough

Dorough, like Frishberg (and Bix), is nonpareil. He's off-beat funny, jazz-smart, eccentric in attitude—and obviously doesn't obsess about writing hit songs. Dorough's most stylistically familiar-sounding song, from a decade earlier than *I'm Hip* with Frishberg, may be the excellent *Devil May Care* (1955, words by T. P. Kirk). It's in what we think of as story-telling minor mode (p. 25). Many classic pop songs take this insouciant approach using a nontragic minor; another example is *No More Blues* (Jobim — Hendricks). Dorough's blithe song starts with an octave skip, 5 to upper 5, and rests for a moment on 6 before making its way to the minor-scale key-tone. It has a double-length bridge, nicely continuous with the A-sections. The experience-of-life message is, "For only a fool thinks he can hold back the dawn," with a nice chord built on the leading-tone as a transition back to the A-section.

In *The Winds of Heaven* (1968), lyric writer Fran Landesman constructed a deeper story, tantalizingly obscure, for another narrative-minor song, with more use here of minor to major alteration in a light jazz style. Apparently the lovers need a bit of stimulus: "If the winds of heaven would only blow the roof off...." There is an attractive vocal melisma on the last *winds* as the final minor cadence approaches. Landesman's lyric to *Unlit Room* (1968) is more specific. The story is about a woman at loose ends, "an unknown girl in an unknown town, wishin' I was outward bound...baby, take me to the lost-and-found." It also is in medium-tempo narrative minor. These two 1968 songs are interesting in that they seem to call for a light rock rhythm, probably reflecting the tenor of the times. They sound a little generic. One has the impression of two very talented writers, one with an unusual verbal attitude (see Landesman's songs with Wolf), one with a piano-jazz background, groping toward a middle-of-the-road style that they do not do better than less-talented others.

That is not the case, however, with the finest of the Dorough — Landesman songs, *Small Day Tomorrow* (1966). This one is stunning, with a lyric telling an even more intriguing tale and music that reverts to a classic pop-blues style, minor mode with lowered 3. The lyricist seems to have taken the lead here; for example, after establishing *small day tomorrow* as a rhythmic template, there are small adjustments—"too much * sorrow," or "day after tomorrow" requiring two extra quick notes for *after*—that catch the ear freshly. Dorough does exactly what's needed, without fuss or flashiness. It's a tale of a relationship with limited expectations but some pleasures nevertheless: "Big wheels with their big deals … need their sleep"; by contrast, "We've got a big night / and a small day tomorrow." The lyric is also curious in that it begins with a self-introduction in the first person ("I don't have to go to bed / I've got a small day tomorrow"), then gives some personal background ("I'm a drop-out…I would rather cop out…than run with all the sheep"), and finally includes the other person ("We've got a big night.…"). The success of this song owes both to the distinctiveness of the main idea, of what flows from a small day, and to the reliance on a standard pop-blues format handled in a very sophisticated way.[11]

An earlier song with Landesman, *Nothing Like You* (1961), is built on a few enigmatic chords, a midregister riff figure, a chromatic opening and closing vocal line, and a middle section that plays with back-and-forth sixth intervals. It shouldn't hang together, but it does, partly because the words are subtle, with some pleasant off-rhyme.

One of Dorough's better-known songs is the more lyrical *Love Came On Stealthy Fingers* (1965), for which he did both words and music. This one is in conventional pop style, in the major with a neat chord at the end of the pretty bridge section, and with a long-phrased sax-style singing line. It's about giving in to late love: the words end with the title phrase, followed by "…and stole my heart away."

Another work where Dorough did both words and music is the distinctive *I've Got Just About Everything* (1962). This is a racing, bracing, constantly syncopated song in bop style, with words, lots of words, that are almost continuous—and all very fast. It sounds like a terrific piano solo with words added. It's not to be sung by anyone without great articulation, but to hear it is like being under a confetti shower. Listening to the words of *The Coffee Song* (1999, also known as *Too Much Coffee, Man*), you think that Dorough must be the funniest songwriter alive. This one is a crazy, verbose parody of *The Peanut Vendor Song* and other Brazilian novelties, and you can only wish that Carmen Miranda had lived to perform it. Or Groucho Marx.

There's a brief line in the lyric *I've Got Just About Everything* lyric that runs, "I like the human race." It shows.[12]

Blossom Dearie

As a pianist-vocalist, Blossom Dearie has issued perhaps two dozen excellent records. In the earlier phase of her career, these songs tended to be standards, or little-known, high-quality songs by the great songwriters of the period up to the 1970s. Later, her recordings have tended to feature new or recently written songs by simpatico writers (such as Frishberg or Dorough) or by herself, with a variety of lyricists. She has done regular club dates, mostly in New York, which won her a wide and admiring, if somewhat specialized, audience, the audience that went to hear Mabel Mercer in the 1960s and 1970s.

Thus the listener might have come to know Dearie by her version of, say, a Rodgers or Styne or Coleman song, and then have stayed around to listen to more rarefied material. It is that material that we focus on here. In keeping with her jazz piano style—spare, crisp, clearly voiced, quietly swinging, in an airy bebop mode—and with her singing style, where the same adjectives apply, together with "perfectly enunciated," her songs make a big effect with small means. Not for her songs of passion and angst, or songs with a big range or a take-no-prisoners rhythm. They swing, but do so subtly. Her songs don't go to you; you come to them.

A feature of Dearie's vocal lines is that, while lovely or strongly shaped, they fit right inside the progression of chords of the song, instead of being "harmonized" by chords. You can hear that she started out as a house pianist in New York clubs. An example is one of her loveliest songs, *Inside a Silent Tear* (1973, words by Mahriah Blackwolf; Figure 6.5). The chords are lush but delicate, replete with 7 and 9, and they use strong discords to underline the longing that characterizes the lyric; for example, G against A-flat in m.9; or the suspended A-natural in m.15, which gradually gives way via the steps in the bass-line to a normal A-flat at the start of the next bar. The harmony is rich enough so that some chords are

Figure 6.5

most easily understood as involving two keys simultaneously, as in m. 9. Earlier, in mm.4–5, there is a breathtaking chord change on the word *reality*, from a C-seventh chord to a B-flat chord combined with an F-sharp triad.

The excerpt is from the bridge, which is so closely woven to the opening and closing sections that the song seems like one long line. For example, the rhythmic pattern for the words *follows me* and *find myself* is echoed throughout the song: *silent tear, emptiness, loneliness*. A longer, stressed syllable is followed by two shorter ones always a half- or whole-tone higher, and the second short note is always prolonged. It is a dignified sort of figure: hold, step, step, hold. However, the tempo/expression marking for the song as a whole is *Slow, tender Bossa*, so one would want to sing the two short notes freely, with the first one shortened just a bit. A superb song.[13]

Quite in contrast is the brisk, scampering *I'm Shadowing You* (also 1973), with funny hip words by the great Johnny Mercer. It's a light bop tune, with a lot of notes grouped at the beginning of those bars that end the main phrases (Figure 6.6). That is, *shadowing you* all happens before the third beat of its bar, and then nothing at all happens for another six beats. Anyone else would have

Figure 6.6

placed *you* on the strong third beat. This gives the song its jaunty sprung rhythm; and Mercer contrives to echo the bebop quality of the music by the similarly set phrase, "(the) deed'll be done," which is great fun to enunciate as well as being an amusing snatch of scat syllables using real words. The point of the song, which is about someone affectionately dogging the steps of her beloved, is conveyed by making a virtue of repeated notes. Note the use of *shadowing* rather than the more obvious *following*, and what a difference that makes. Dearie has been fortunate, which is to say discriminating, in her selection of lyricists.[14]

There are two swing-style songs by Dearie that tip their hat to English rock musicians, *Sweet Georgie Fame* (1968, words by Sandra Harris) and *Hey, John* (1973, words by Jim Council), the latter referring to Lennon. Both are delightful; the former is a rare example of a true jazz waltz. Also from 1973, with Mahriah Blackwolf, is a song that only Dearie could have written, *I Like You, You're Nice*.

Its vocal line, in short plain phrases, wanders into strange territories via out-of-the-scale notes, so that the entire song seems improvisatory up to the last six bars, which end firmly on a vocal cadence using a raised 6 to a dissonant 7. The lyric is peculiar and sweet: it appears that she likes him so much that she'll make him "a marvelous, wonderous [sic], and quite notorious cup of Costa Rican coffee," the last phrase set on an out-of-nowhere vocal arpeggio that covers an octave and a half. How's that for a new take on attraction?

In the delicate *Sunday Afternoon* (1973, words by Len Saltzberg), Dearie combines two inherently evocative tone-sets: one, the pentatonic, with its openness, and the triad-plus-6, with its harmonically blurred sound, alternating these throughout the song. She ends with yet another softening device, using the yearning sound of the raised 7, and ending on the floating tone 2. The means are obvious, time-worn; the effect is magical. There are lots of words, all dealing with nostalgia for a purer, easier time.

Owing to the characteristics of her own voice, which is very small and pure, Dearie's songs tend to be inherently small-scaled. They often swing, but are less exuberant than those by Frishberg or Dorough. On the other hand, her melodic gift may be greater. Rogers Whitaker once described her style as ranging from the meticulous to the sublime. Although established by the 1970s as one of the most satisfying songwriters of the period, Dearie continued to create, with a variety of well-chosen lyricists, always interesting, often admirable songs. As was already evident in the 1970s, and more so in the next decade, Dearie wrote some of her songs in an ultra-plain style, normally using entirely diatonic harmony and tunes built squarely on the tones of the triad; sometimes, especially in songs with Saltzberg, she implies a light rock beat. With Johnny Mandel, Dearie wrote words (with Duncan Lamont) for a fine song, *Make Some Magic*, which is as sweetly sexy as one could imagine. ("Our magic carpet-ride is overdue / let's make magic.") The song would be first-rate if only for the extraordinary chord progression on the words *mood I'm in*, in the verse, but there is also a lovely close.

A Note On Duncan Lamont

He is Scots, and so outside our scope, alas, since he clearly adores American classic pop and writes "in the style." His allegiances are clear just from his titles; for example, *Miss You, Mister Mercer*, or *Fred Astaire*, the latter written with Jack Segal. There are a number of other neat songs, which is not such faint praise.[15]

In the later 1980s Dearie wrote a number of songs with Jack Segal. They show an evolution toward a relaxed, word-friendly pop-rock style, in part evinced by her use of electric piano with its pleasant, slightly sappy sound. These are not unpersuasive, and fall within the classic pop style envelope. *You Taught Me Everything I Know*, with a Latin-rock feeling, has a pleasing beat. Even better is *After Me*. which has a hypnotic movement in the way the phrases repeat and circle back. The words are also recursive, with a charming syntactical playing on the word *after*: "They will run after you... after me... after all...." *Stay and Love My Blues Away* is downright seductive, both musically and verbally. It's a nice bossa nova, with a good minor melodic line, avoiding 2 and using 4 a lot, and with a fine chord change at the start of the second phrase. The words tell an endearing story, as one lover urges the other: "You are still in bed, quite ill in bed, I'll stay...." Another slow bossa nova with Segal, *What Time Is It Now?* is lovely, predominantly in the minor mode but with an elegant perfect sixth interval as the bridge begins. The answer to the title question is, "Time for good love... or good-bye." The loveliest of these songs is either *I Don't Remember*, a sweet bossa nova with a fine tune, in which the speaker avers, unconvincingly, that she has no recollection of "... the sultry summer you didn't call, the crying when you said goodbye last fall....," or *Love Is On the Way*, with pure pop chords and a long, elegant melodic line. This lyric is excellent, with rhymes that complete on the penultimate word of the second line of a pair. A 1987 Dearie — Segal song that has received a lot of attention, *Bye Bye, Country Boy*, is too much a short story for our tastes.[16]

It is not clear why Dearie, a prolific and gifted songwriter, seemed largely to abandon her elegant, distaff-Ellington, harmonically grounded style. Perhaps she believed that pop-jazz harmony had in some way dated, and that soft rock was the way to go. We find the songs with Segal in that style worth knowing, but ultimately less endearing than those in classic pop. But we wouldn't be surprised to hear a new song from Dearie, in whatever style, that couldn't be dearier.

TOMMY WOLF (1926–79)

In the early 1950s, St. Louis was an important club locale, owing to residents Wolf and Fran Landesman, his most frequent lyricist. Their often-recorded *Spring Can Really Hang You Up the Most* (1955) remains a great favorite among the more selective singers. In the classic popular song genre, Spring songs fall into two categories, the light-hearted, often silly ones and those speaking of the bittersweet disappointment of lost love. This song is of the latter genre. The words *hang you up* were jazz musician lingo in 1955, and the song was considered daringly hip. Throughout, the lyric flips from rather conventional sentiments ("Morning's kiss wakes trees and flowers") to disillusioned ones ("...I'm on the shelf with last year's Easter bonnets"). The nuanced mixture of moods is especially well handled in the second stanza: "Doctors once prescribed a tonic... Didn't help a bit, my condition must be chronic."

The last phrases of the verse prepare the emotional tone of the remarkable first long phrase of the chorus. That vocal line opens neutrally, on notes of the triad (Figure 6.7, A1). The brief D (m.2) is musically a decoration, but the first sign that not all is unequivocal. The underlying chords are darker: they oscillate

Figure 6.7

between a C-major chord with an added tone and a B-flat major chord (with a hint of G minor), conveying uneasiness from the beginning. A nice discord between B-natural and B-flat contributes also. Mm. 5–6 fill in the rest of the main scale, with descending chains of thirds, so that it's clear that this not a happy song, a message that is underlined by the quick harmonic shifts on main words: *year, feeling, room, ceiling.* By contrast (and borne out throughout the rest of the song), the title phrase takes on an incantatory character because it is barely harmonized, and is always heard as a complete unit. In addition, virtually all the notes of the A-sections hang down from the key-tone, plunging an octave and a half at the extreme.

The bridge (B) reinforces this downward feeling. Via a long and evocative movement to a strong dominant chord, the A material comes back in, but (momentarily) in a lower key, a lovely brooding touch. By bringing back the A material in a surprising, and lower, key (A3), the words here, "Love seemed sure," take on a more momentous quality than the words at the opening of the first A—an unusual effect in this song genre.

Figure 6.7 Continued.

Even the coda opens with new melodic material, achieving a plaintive sort of interpolation ("All alone / The party's over"). There is an especially lovely seventh chord just before the final iteration of the title phrase, which finally ends over a stepwise descent, inviting a jazz pianist's lushest chord progression, to, not the key-tone, but an expressive, unstable, chest-voice low G, locking in the despairing nature of the message.

Landesman's lyric is complex, continually shifting between delicate poetic diction, brief stabs of yearning, occasional whimsy, and self-mocking humor. The pattern is that each long phrase of the chorus begins with rising notes, expressing the more conventional or hopeful words about Spring; then ruefulness comes in, with notes hovering around the lower key-tone; and finally there is a decline into a dark mood. It's easy enough to write a lyric in an entirely bittersweet register, but a mixture like this takes a lot of control, so that the humor doesn't become jokey, or yearning become bathos.

We spend time on this well-known song, because it is so beautifully made. Its ruminative self-pity may make it especially appropriate for cabaret performance, but it is a brilliant song writing, as fresh today as in the troubled 1950s.

Also well-known is *The Ballad of the Sad Young Men*, which showed up in a 1959 Broadway show with a brief run, "The Nervous Set." This is a ballad in an older sense, being written in short phrases of direct recounting. The lyric is morbid, neurotic; it too varies between fancy diction ("slowly dies the heart") and bald gloom. It may be an overinterpretation, but the story told, about "sad young men, sitting in the bars… Trying to forget that they're growing old" seems like a gay narrative. An effective song, but one that now seems dated, even "coded."

From the same show, however, is a marvelous *It's Nice Weather for Ducks*, in a wigged-out idiom and an easy narrative minor mode. The words are too good not to quote:

It's nice weather for eels / I'm sure they find it appealing
'Cause no one wants to go eel-ing / It's nice weather for eels.
The girl and boy ducks love the rain / The she-eel has the he-eel
No one cares when I complain how miserable I fee-eel.…

From the 1950s up to the early 1960s, there are a number of other excellent Wolf — Landesman songs. The first they wrote together, *This Little Love of Ours*, has a poised, telling verse, and then a headlong chorus about the benefits of casual love. ("But emotions cooled, as they sometimes do / How nice for me, how nice for you!") There's no irony here: the melody line purls along with fast little triplets, and the bridge slips into a mock waltz for a moment. *It Isn't So Good It Couldn't Get Better* is even more impressive metrically. The ends of the first A-section phrases, setting the title, last a bit longer than expected, and fall into a complicated pattern of stresses placed two, and then three, unstressed syllables apart. There are some nice forward syncopations, so that the whole song swings. It's as if the songwriters took a light brush pattern from the drummer and turned it into a song. By contrast, the bridge is ultra-simple. A song from 1956, *You Inspire Me*, is notable for some spectacular triple rhymes by Landesman, and some other verbal felicities ("Beguines I'll begin for you.…"). *It Will Only*

Hurt a Minute has a goodvamp, and an up-tempo casualness, with some tricky rhymes (*minute/discipline it/clavichord or spinet*). The lyrics for *Say "Cheese,"* a song about how to stay happy (even when you don't feel like it) are very superior, consistently so through two stanzas. *I Love You Real* is a take on a love song as it might be sung by a macho hipster wanting to score ("Those virile heroes never miss * with dialogue like this"). Wolf's tune is really a string of riffs giving wings to Landesman's breezy accolades to the lover's he-man attributes: "You do for me the same thing spinach does for Popeye." The song is sheer playful fun.

From 1961, the song *There Are Days When I Don't Think of You At All* stretches further. It's a long, contemplative song. In the bridge, the focus switches from self-assessment to speculation about the absent other, a subtle indicator of buried feeling. The opening A-section phrases all come to an end over harmonically strange chord progressions (Figure 6.8), and the song ends up in the air, on a stark tritone interval. Like many in the world of cabaret, these songwriters had the ability to achieve deep and rare shades of emotional meaning using very modest means.

Figure 6.8

Later, Wolf wrote both music and words, or lyrics for others' music. *I'm Always Drunk In San Francisco* (1962, both roles) is memorable mostly for its title, though it has a good tune with a strong flat 7. One admires Wolf's verbal ability, but his rhymes obtrude more than Landesman's (e.g., *things like this go / a lover's kiss go / San Francisco*). The same is true with a song for which Wolf wrote words, *A Face Like Yours* (1975), music by Victor Feldman. It is a slow ballad, using a lovely stepwise melody with partial recursions; but Wolf's end-rhymes are a bit obvious. Somehow, in the classic popular song, the lyric has either to be quite subtle, so that you don't appreciate it fully until you hear the song several times, or utterly up-front, so that you know immediately that the song is word-governed. A tender song, *Boats* (1975), is deceptively childlike. It has a calypsolike rhythm and a simple, up-going stepwise melody in the A-section ("I'm gonna build a little boat and wherever it will float...."), while the bridge reverses the contour, intensifying the rhythm so that it swings charmingly ("Look at this, look at that, what's the difference where I'm at?"). It's easy to become fond of the song.[17]

ROY KRAL (1921–2002)

Roy Kral, composer and pianist, and his wife, singer Jackie Cain, did much to keep alive the classic American popular song of the second half of the twentieth century. They were among the first to recognize the qualities of mid-twentieth-century Brazilian music, which became quite popular in the 1950s. That infusion gave hope, to the lovers of classic American popular song, that elegant melodies and jazz-informed harmonies would survive the onslaught of rock. Kral's *Through the Windows of Cars*, lyrics by Fran Landesman, is a dark song, but with many flashes of melodic and lyrical light. Minor chords underpin a narrative with a "moving-on" theme, alternating between world-weariness and hope: "I've seen rainbows and stars, tattoo parlors and bars, on the way to a dream," and "corn fields and oceans, and odd corners; johnny-come-latelies and long-goners." *A Full Moon* (Niki's Song) has lyrics by Cain. The haunting melody lifts and ebbs to a soft bossa nova beat, suggesting the movement of waves on a beach. The song is written in G major but sounds more like the key of D with a repeated, altered, C-natural. The word *full* is reiterated and emphasized, as the high note in an octave jump to the fifth of the scale. The melody then recedes, on the words "...moon, moving the tide and sand."[18]

Departing from Latin atmosphere, another song with music by Kral, lyrics by Fran Landesman, is *Bogie* (1976), an off-beat tribute to Bogart. The clever lyrics to this "noir" song tell the story of a one-night stand in just a few words: "She's a girl who's in trouble, all her nights are like years." The tune is a simple jazz riff and the minor seventh chords occur in typical jazz progressions, but the voice line includes a slight jazz/rock flavor.

In the 1990s Kral wrote with William Engvick, Wilder's collaborator. *Above Love* is constructed in short units: a tiny phrase on the major triad of the stated key, a tiny response set on the minor third above but with lowered 7 added. Basically it's boogie-woogie until the tag, which doesn't seem to fit the song as much as to lop it off, though the Engvick words here ("Honey, come back down to earth / Join me in a lower berth") make a neat couplet. A more substantial song, *Attitude*, uses the same kind of alternating bitonal structure, with a harmonic filigree of chains of fourths. This is a dimorphic song: the woman has her version of reality, the man his, and they converge at the end where the "attitudes" mesh. Both these songs essentially represent a pianist's playing on the keys, with words.

In 1958 Kral wrote (So You've Had a) *Change Of Heart*, to which Alec Wilder wrote the fine lyrics. It's a beautiful song, in standard 32-bar form, and it's clearly the music of a jazz master, with gloriously messy cluster chords in the A-section, involving modulation every half bar or so. They beautifully accompany the rueful words of a lover who has just been left. Wilder's words say this indirectly, as if the speaker feels the need to be tactful. Although the song begins with the voice line high in the octave, that line soon begins to slip, in a long chain of unusually expressive short phrases (Figure 6.9).

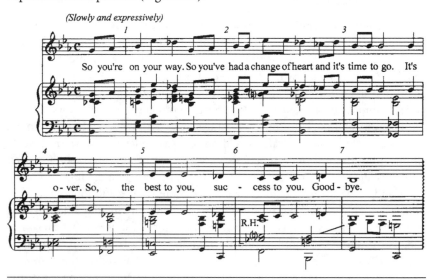

Figure 6.9

An aspect of "jazz songs" is that the harmonic richness is sometimes greater than what the tune or the words support; or, alternately, as with the Kral — Engvick songs, it's the riff that dominates. Neither is true in this song with Wilder, which has strong words and a commanding vocal line. Each downward chord progression, each short verbal phrase—and note the full-stop punctuation—digs deeper. The release, by contrast, stays high, almost in a keening register, which makes the total range for the song more than an octave an a half, very effective for a singer who can handle it.

BILLY VERPLANCK (b. 1930)

VerPlanck is an arranger and song composer. He is an approximate contemporary of Kral's, and like Kral enjoys the benefit of having a fine vocalist wife. In general, his songs are more lyrical, less hiply individualistic, than Kral's. He has written several ballads with Wilder's other important lyricist, Loonis McGlohon. They all possess a clear, calm melodic line combined with chords that are complex enough to color the vocal without derailing it. Two of them are *Instead of Saying Goodbye* (1983) and *Where Is April* (1983). The latter shifts from major to minor and back again very sweetly. *I Like to Sing* (1981) is an up-tempo number, with empty bars for brief vocal doodling. It could have been written as a medium-bounce tune by any of the great 1920s songwriting teams. McGlohon's words are merry ones: "The world is full of people who jog, and in the mountain country they clog. Some folks like lyin' still on a log: but me? I like to sing!" In a more advanced style is the delightful *It's How You Play the Game* (2002), with neat wry words by jazz drummer Joe Cocuzzo: "The rules are just for fools . . . it's how you play your hand, so deal." The main tune is "notey," but saved by the piquant use of the seventh tone and interval to accomplish minute, stinging changes. The B-section is suave — melodically, so with its thirds contrasting with half-steps, and harmonically, with enriching 9, 13, and other tones out of the octave (Figure 6.10).[19]

Figure 6.10

Another lightly swinging song is *What Are We Going to Do With All This Moonlight?* (1997), whose words, by Leon Nock, sustain the blithe tone of the title, as with

> The setting could hardly be apter,
> Soft lighting, sweet music, the wine;
> How perfect for starting a chapter
> That segues to "ours" from "yours" and "mine."

Medium-tempo songs like this remind one of the casual grace and propulsiveness of Matt Dennis (see below), but this is more venturesome musically.

A ballad with words by Frank Grant, *The Day I Found You* (1999), features lots of accidentals in the vocal line. It would be a musically over-ornate were it not for the surprising way VerPlanck brings the sinuous phrases to a dead stop. The lyric is full of rather subtle rhymes.

A feature of VerPlanck's style is that he changes key quickly and frequently, especially in his releases, so that the harmonic pattern of the song unfolds as tonal sections, rather than via elaborate chord sequences. It is a refreshing approach. The trick is to use the key change to re-color the voice and put a new emotional gloss on the words. A haunting song, written in 1988 with Ervin Drake, is *So Long Sadness*, which sounds like a "composed" blues. Each section is unremarkable, but the key changes give a compelling shape to the song as a whole. The lyric seems awkward, especially at the end.

VerPlanck's songs are very well crafted, but not easy to sing. We hope that singers other than Marlene VerPlanck will do them—but only singers with as good a sense of pitch and as clear a vocal production.

SOME OTHER CABARET AND CLUB SONGS

This is an artificial category. It is often not possible to know for what audience songwriters intended a song, but it is sometimes possible to know where it has been heard. Using both *cabaret* and *club* as descriptors reflects the fact that there are locations that specialize in certain musical genres, such as comedy numbers, songs based on jazz material, Afro-Cuban-Brazilian or other ethnic streams. It is generally true that *cabaret songs* suggests something vocally small-scaled and verbally well developed: the audience doesn't come for the beat, but for the fine-tuned emotional experience of words and music working tightly together.

The economics of the club and cabaret scene are such that many of the songs heard there are never officially published or commercially recorded, but lead a fugitive and underground existence, known only to aficionados. We include here certain songs that the reader could in principle find only by going to websites of the creators or performers. We have had to omit a number of attractive songs that have not really been disseminated.

We begin with writers active in the 1950s, such as Matt Dennis, Arthur Siegel, Billy Barnes, Murray Grand, and Charles DeForest, all of them singer-pianists. Dennis is a figure from an era of "jazz clubs." Wilder covers *Angel Eyes* (1953), *Will You Still Be Mine,* and some other pre-1950 songs. We like also Dennis's 1957 song, words by Don Raye, called *Real Love.* It has a rather routine main melodic strain, but a neat bridge.

The pianist-arranger Billy Barnes is the writer of several songs well-known in café society circles, including (I Stayed) *Too Long At the Fair* (1956). It has a dactylic lapping rhythm, and a simple long-phrased melody altered ingeniously in the bridge. There are several stanzas of evocative words, concerning someone who fears she has missed the rewards of life ("The lights of the mid-way are fading above me" or "The merry-go-round is beginning to taunt me…."). The revue, "Billy Barnes' L.A." (1962) had two ballads of interest. *Does Anybody Here Love Me?* is proof that repeated notes can work well, particularly when the lyric reads as though it could be spoken, rather than sung. The 12–bar verse has strings of 15 repeated notes at a time: "Funny, but I've always wanted something all my life…." The tune of this diseuse song is encompassed within seven notes of the scale, but the interesting harmonies and jumps of fifths in the chorus give the song the effect of a much wider range. *Where Was the Music?* has a broader melody that moves along nicely, with rhythmic "dips," building up to a classic eight-bar extension in which the melodic motif is repeated four times with a different harmony each time.

Arthur Siegel was a pianist, singer, and composer best known for his songs, mostly with lyricist June Carroll, for the "New Faces" revues. From the 1952 "New Faces" came an Eartha Kitt signature song, *Monotonous,* an amusing list of the things that failed to impress the singer; for example, "A camel once walked a mile for me." Also from the same show is Siegel's and Carroll's best-known song, *Love Is a Simple Thing.* The song is instantly comprehensible, with a melodic motif as simple as the title implies and a jigging dotted rhythm. It lodges in the mind's ear after just one hearing. (The writers spoofed their own hit in a sequel, *Love Is a Complicated Mess.*) *Tell Her,* from the 1956 "New Faces" (lyrics by Carroll), has an old-fashioned lilt to it, with an A-section melodic motif that climbs one tone per phrase, broken by slower spondaic patterns for the title. The lyric provides an opportunity to change straightforward C major to a harmonically odd couple of measures on the phrase, "suddenly you'll see her change." From this show, *I Want You to Be the First One to Know* is charming, with a rhythm that suggests units of three and four simultaneously. The reiterated title phrase describes ordinary things the singer wants the object of his affection to know, like: "You thrill me," which yields a pleasantly tutti-frutti flavor. *The Other*

One is a less optimistic ballad in which the sophisticated singer suspects that she has a romantic rival. These doubts are presented in waltz time, which seems to lessen the seriousness of the situation. Siegel's utilitarian melody is prescient of a Jerry Herman song that came six years later, *I Don't Want to Know*. Siegel wrote scores for Off-Broadway, among them "Tallulah" from 1995, from which comes a song of great feeling and depth, *I Can See Him Clearly*: it deserves to be discovered by discriminating singers. For sheer good fun, we mention two comic cabaret songs. *Where Is the Melody*? with Siegel's own lyric, bemoans the trend to tunelessness of later pop music; it promises, "I'll come out of my stupor when I listen to Alice Cooper, if they give me melody." The hilarious *Looking For Love*, with lyrics by Tony Lang, is a randy review of a desperate search to find romance in various New York-area venues: "I've been to Jersey twice, but love songs are prosaic in Passaic."[20]

A contemporary, Murray Grand, also wrote songs for "New Faces" revues. He sometimes wrote his own lyrics, as with *Comment Allez-Vous?* (1957), a slight ditty with Porteresque bilingual lyrics ("Cloaks-and-suiters by the oodles / Say it to their cute French poodles"). A cabaret standard is *Guess Who I Saw Today* from "New Faces of 1952," which narrates the discovery of a spouse's infidelity. The A-section tune is casual and light; that of the B-section more ominous, adding to the suspense of the narrative: "The waiter showed me to a dark secluded corner, and when my eyes became adjusted to the gloom...." This is short, but so well-crafted that it seems much weightier than most anecdotal songs. The opening chorus tune of *Hurry*, from the 1956 "New Faces," moves in a stately fashion, featuring whole notes that give it the feel of entrance music for a Ziegfeld beauty parade and contradicts the main message, that "Love passes in a hurry." The song is at odds with itself. On the other hand, Grand's witty style shines in *April In Fairbanks*, from the same show, for which he also wrote the lyrics. It is a parody of Vernon Duke standards. The verse has an elegant Duke-like melody for the words "Autumn in New York and April in Paris are no longer chic." The chorus, marked "with tenderness" (tongue-in-cheek), is hilarious, the melody underlining the verbal absurdity: "You'll never know the charm of spring until you've heard a walrus sighing." Another silly but endearing song is *I Always Say Hello to a Flower* (1958), which incorporates mad little musical *hello*'s. Bea Lillie would have liked this song. There is a blithe salute to a timely love affair, *Not a Moment Too Soon* (1960), with a beguine rhythm and a sophisticated harmonic layout mixing major and minor by using dominants of dominants. As lyricist for Cy Coleman, Grand wrote a beguiling seduction song, *Kick Off Your Shoes* (1965). The words are sly, and the tune, built on a jazz vamp, is irresistible.

Grand is usually thought of as a composer of droll songs, but some of his music had a deeper side. His *Thursday's Child* (1951) goes deep. It starts with a reference to the nursery apothegm—Monday's child fair of face, etc.—set to childlike

Figure 6.11

harmony. The chorus opens with a sinuously gloomy melody, contrasting rising half- and whole-steps (Figure 6.11). There are complex, predominantly minor, chords in virtually every measure.[21]

Thursday's Child is in the tradition of "downer" songs that are musically interesting and melodically attractive. Some of George Cory's and Douglass Cross's songs also come to mind. Their famous song is *I Left My Heart In San Francisco*, but they wrote a number of other songs that range in feeling from pessimistic to black despair. *I'll Always Be Early* (1954) describes painful feelings: the hopeful (hopeless?) lover will always be early; the loved one will always be late—or may never arrive at all. The chorus is a beauty. The melodic motif steps up one note at a time in repeated phrases, while each repeat is echoed in a similar chord transition between phrases. The ending of the bridge is particularly nice, harmonically. *Ivory Tower*, introduced by Mabel Mercer in 1955, takes us further into unhappy territory. It's a long and complicated song. The verse states: "All I have left from a lost love affair / is a home of my own that no one would share." The chorus is mournful, harmonically in D minor, melodically wanting to find F major: "I own an ivory tower / old as the winter moon." The release goes to C flat, the heaviness of which adds to the gloom. This is a song, like some by Gordon Jenkins, where there are too many chord changes for the just-average quality of the melodic line.

Charles deForest's *A Good Man Is a Seldom Thing* (1952) is a fairly standard masochistic plaint ("He rules me like a puppet on a string"); *Don't Wait Up for Me* is more interesting, a slightly blues-tinged, minor-mode song with a good descending voice line and effective lyrics about a woman who knows the man is stringing her along.[22] DeForest's *One Day At a Time* is a textbook example of a good-but-not great popular song. Its melody line is orderly, with top notes that climb step by step; its lyric is literate and meaningful. The climax is well-placed just before the end. The verse is excellent. DeForest's best-known song may be *When Do the Bells Ring For Me?*, a big ballad of romantic yearning. We find it a bit overblown, but it sings well. *I Never Was One For the Blues* (1958) is the happy-go-lucky credo of someone who has decided that the way to avoid heartbreak is to not commit. The main melodic motif skips upwards in carefree sixths and sevenths for "One heartbreak's enough * when the going gets rough." For contrast, DeForest's *Yesterday's Child* (1961) is a cautionary song about this same kind of character, who may not realize it but who will ultimately experience the bittersweet tribulations of true love. This song has just the right number of interesting chords: two circles of fifths in the first eight bars, a nice bass-line stepping down one tone at a time at the start of the bridge, and an alternation of minor and major thirds in the voice-line. The song is full of harmonic tension until the last note of the melody, an unresolved but appropriate 7. It's a very good song.

Perhaps every second song by the writers we have just discussed tends now to sound dated, or even "camp." Many of the "cabaret" songs from earlier decades form a subgenre that might be called theater songs manquées; they hold up less well than those with a jazz feel to them. A group of the major figures we covered earlier—Frishberg, Dorough, Dearie, Wolf, et al.—all reflect the jazz, that is, the "club," sensibility. These songs vary in memorability, but they do not sound dated, and they are not precious. This is a matter not only of theater versus jazz style, it clearly has to do with a change in the cultural universe of songwriters. The songs that follow, from the last quarter of the twentieth century, are formally and technically like those of the earlier period, but they are more contemporary in their subject-matter.

A singer-pianist who composes good songs is Ronny Whyte. He has a good New York song, *A Penny for Your Thoughts, New York*, words by Sheila Astill (1995). It's a long multisection song in which the A-sections begin in slightly varied ways, and the B-material takes off from the second period of A. The words are good, a bit New York-predictable. A very recent ballad, *People, Places, Things*, has a sad, distanced, through-written lyric by Roger Schore. The verse ends, "I rummage through my past," while the words to the chorus all invoke past feelings, and conclude, "Falling in love ends in memories of people, places, things." The tune is minimal and delicate; the last phrase has an especially lovely progression. Whyte provided words and music for the lovely *Warm Goes to Warm* (1987), a song that any of the fine craftsmen would have been proud of. It features a seductive combination of bossa nova rhythm and sinuous melody line. The title phrase bespeaks a deep romantic affinity, as natural as the way "birds fly south for the winter." Whyte lifts the melody line high in the first A-sections, so that the title phrase can ease down gracefully, in the middle of the octave (a, Figure 6.12). At the end of the song, the pattern is reversed so that that phrase drops the octave (b) for a very satisfying finish. Whyte uses the phrase also to begin the B-section, in the same rhythmic pattern, but slightly displaced in terms of meter. It is a lovely song, very subtly made.[23]

Figure 6.12

Robert Miles, music, and Chandler Warren, words, have written several pleasing songs. *Tell Me Softly* (1975) has a pure melody, and might lend itself to a light Latin rhythm. The charming song suggests a lover whispering into one's ear. *If He Knew Me* (1988) is a young-in-character song, a romantic dream. The smooth, Burton Lane-like melody is broken in the middle by a more emphatic contrasting section, involving half notes over a strong chord progression for "...want me, touch me, hold me, love me...."[24] A later song, *The Land of Once Upon a Time*, is a sweet fairytale. A number of songs have been written about humans as players on the stage of life. The lyric by Roger Schore for Miles's *Merely Players* (1993) is unusually good; making a song that could be combined nicely with the Coleman — Comden and Green *Our Private World*.

Richard Rodney Bennett has distinguished himself as a composer and lyricist, as well as a pianist and a composer of film scores and concert music. *I Watch You Sleep*, words by Joel Siegel (1982), has a gorgeous long melody line with phrases that add on and overlap. The words are suitably intimate and tender: "Till I watch you wake, I'll watch you sleep." *I Never Went Away*, words by the composer, has a cool jazz sensibility in its minute modulations and curious wandering form. It's ABAB; the B-sections establish a sequence, but then slip over to the title phrase, sung more than once. The lyric is nicely indirect. On a light note, Bennett has a song with Franklin Underwood, called *Early to Bed*, a blithe little chain-of-thirds waltz about someone who can't stay out late ("Ain't got the energy, ain't got the bread...."). It has a fine extension at the close.

Underwood himself has written *Ain't Safe to Go Nowhere*, a verbally startling light Latin pop-blues about life's disenchantments: "She takes you in, then makes you leave (I told you so!)." It has a Frishberg-like quality: the kicker to the title phrase is, "Not even home." With Stan Freeman, Underwood also wrote the loving ballad, *Be Warmer This Winter*.

Francesca Blumenthal: very New York—wry on the rocks, plus sweet sentiment. The songs are well made, the music seldom venturesome, though pleasing, the chords suitable, the lyrics excellent. In one of her songs she rhymes *languages* with *anguish is*, and gets away with it easily. Her best-known song, *The Lies of Handsome Men*, has a title and concept striking enough to make it memorable, but it's also a really good song. Blumenthal uses compound rhymes that are truncated in the second element, and a chain of strong end-of-line rhymes for *lies*. The rhymes, as an ensemble, are saved from blatancy by the way *lies* slips past as part of the ongoing title phrase: thus, "Someday I'll get wise / But right now I believe the lies of handsome men." More self-mocking and airy is a fine rhythmic song, the sort of song that cries out for brisk sticks and brush drumming, *The Trouble With Love*. It reminds one of Matt Dennis. There is a light wisdom to the message: "...love's always ready to call it a day / to keep it around a person must give it away." Again, the rhymes are improbable but satisfying:

rubble, trouble, and bubble form one set. *Between Men* is a funny song, narrated by a woman who goes in for self-improvement between romances, so that "the next guy who gets me is gonna get more than a 10." Two songs about Paris are hilarious, proving that there is always new word-play for songs: *Marthe of Montmartre* is about a native girl who knew everyone. *On the Streets of Paree* concerns a foreigner who is embarrassed by how Parisians pursue their favorite pastime ("When they pursue...voulez-vous, the *vous* may be one, two, or three"). The tunes here are just serviceable.

One notable thing about "cabaret" songs as a subgenre is that many of the best of recent ones have been written by women, who still rarely get to write entire scores. A recent song by Michele Brourman and Amanda McBroom, is *One of Those Days*. The storyline of the song involves a secret love for a "best friend": the concept is fine, the realization a bit less so.

June Tonkin has a fine romantic ballad (1976), *What a Way to Go*. The title phrase has a nice ambiguity to it; the vocal line is wistful but loving, with a large drop at the end of phrases so that they seem to float away. The B-sections are especially lyrical.[25] *Fancy Meeting You Here* (1987) uses an old song idea—former lovers who meet, at least one of them still carrying a torch, but this is one of the best realizations. It too has expressive vocal drops at the end of phrases and at the climax four bars before the end, but this ballad has a quicker middle section, shifting into the major with the implication of three-beat meter, which adds something extra to the story. *How Will You Remember Me?* (1992), words by Jerome Gray, continues the title with "...when two lovers meet as friends." The song is lovely in the way it alternates chromatic lines with larger, wistful intervals. Tonkin has other good songs, mostly ballads.

In the last two decades of the century, a number of songs presumably written for club performance show a style of elaborated story-telling that clearly reflects the new theater style (chapter 8), as well as the influence of the narrative songs by the singer-songwriters (chapter 7). Such songs tend to sound simple, but their interest comes from minute touches in the working-out. For example, a song by Julie Gold, *Goodnight, New York* (1992), uses contrasting sections of ascending stepwise melodic contour, conveying historical exposition, and larger descending intervals, connoting present-day commentary. The basic rhythm is curiously loose, a sort of slow Charleston pattern, sounding neither like a dance rhythm nor like pointed syncopation but almost like three longish, not quite equal, units in a 4/4 bar. This lends itself to story-telling that seems spontaneous, as if the speaker is letting syllables fall where they may. Indeed, the writer sets unimportant vocables like *the* on the first strong beat, or reverses the stress pattern of *moon-beams*. Sporadically, there is a melismatic moment in the voice line, typical of folk-rock. The narrative itself is partly explicit, partly veiled.

My mother came to America…back in the thirties
All of my yearning, all of my hunger / maybe I'm learning, sometimes I
    wonder.
Goodnight, New York.

The exposition is clear, the commentary less so; and the title phrase is obscure, though it makes poetic sense. It reminds one of the older format of, say, English ballad, with its relaxed rhythm and loose scansion. In the frame of reference of classic popular style, this pleasing song sounds like a very long verse that never leads to a concise chorus. Gold's song, *From a Distance* (1980s), has a satisfying country-folk quality.

A 1992 song, *Have Had,* by Stephen Hoffman and Mark Campbell invokes yet another tradition. Its lyric is imagist in nature, in the sense that the emotion, and the story lying behind it, are inferred from specifics that the writers point to but do not explain. "The sky this evening—you would have loved it": a much-loved person has died, perhaps? That imagist approach is common enough in classic pop; for example, the Rodgers — Hart *Little Girl Blue*, but is even more typical of the singer-songwriter genre. In this song, the shifting 5/4 to 6/4 meter and the discontinuous phrases are closer to that mode.

However, many songs from the recent eras fall into pure classic-pop style. When they are good, they demonstrate that the resources of that style are by no means exhausted. A fine example is *Full Moon At Half Price* (Terry Sampson — Mike Himelstein, 1995). It is a song whose light swing rhythm and basically triadic contoured melody, with occasional "blue" notes, could have been devised by Bix Beiderbecke. The form is 32-bar AABA. The lyric is not an extended narrative, but is in classic-pop metaphoric/aphoristic style on a timeworn topic: the speaker says, You can have the moon and stars—I can't use them anymore because we're no longer in love.

Avoid (1990, Phillip Namanworth) is also in swing style, but with a faster implicit tempo and a comic attitude, so that it sounds a bit like bebop, especially in its intricate and odd B-section. The lyric here is a light-hearted, confiding one: "Why cause problems getting everyone annoyed / when it's so much easier to avoid?"

A lovely ballad by Craig Carnelia, *Just Where They Should Be* (1992), lies halfway between classic pop and singer-songwriter. Its opening strain uses a familiar device: a shifting down by a whole step of the basic chord underlying a purely diatonic melodic line, from a major triad on I to a chord perceived, in the bass-line as going to an altered VII, but harmonically as moving to a minor triad on V. It's a device heard in jazz-influenced songs (e.g., *Spring Can Really Hang You Up the Most*); it's a device used by Sondheim; and it also introduces a modal color, owing to the lowered 7 (Figure 6.13). The ambiguous chord in m.11, just where one expects another whole-step shift, brings the harmonic style back toward pop-jazz. This is a very long song, but in large AABA format. Its

Figure 6.13

fine lyric is closer to the metaphor-imagist approach of classic popular song, but the B-section is direct narrative,

> All year it seemed I was lost, and for all I could tell
> Nothing ever would be good again
> But then just the sound of your key in the door, and all is well.

and in the long coda the story is pinned down touchingly. A Carnelia song from the same period, *Look In My Eyes*, has a minimal melody line, essentially just an element of the horizontal broken chords, triad plus 6, of the accompaniment.

That pattern, and the step-by-step bass-line, sound like someone moving up and down the fingerboard of a guitar.

We have grouped the last seven songs so as to demonstrate the diversity of style of some very good "noncommercial" songs, that is, those songs that call for a face-to-face communicative ambience, of the recent period.[26]

Notes

1. Performance: Blossom Dearie, "Give Him The Ooh-La-La," Verve LP 2081.
2. Performance: Portia Nelson, "Love Songs For A Late Evening," DRG CD 91451.
3. Performance: K.T. Sullivan, "Bart," Painted Smiles CD 114, which includes a number of Howard songs performed by others, including Howard himself.
4. Performance: Joyce Breach, "Remembering Mabel Mercer," Audiophile CD 322.
5. Performance: Joyce Breach and William Roy, "Love Is the Thing," Audiophile CD 314.
6. An all-Barer recording, with such luminaries as Rosemary Clooney and Michael Feinstein, is "The Time Has Come: The Songs of Marshall Barer," Painted Smiles CD 123, and most songs are in the ASCAP database.
7. Performance: Gerry Matthews, "Take Five," Offbeat Records LP 4013.
8. Original cast recording, Painted Smiles LP 1332.
9. Performance: All these funny numbers are included in "Dixie Carter Sings John Wallowitch," DRG CD 91409.
10. Performance: Rosemary Clooney, "At Long Last," Concord Jazz CD 4795.
11. Performance: Irene Kral, "You Are There," Audiophile CD 299.
12. The last-mentioned two songs are included in Dorough's own "Too Much Coffee Man," Bluenote CD 7243, along with other numbers, mostly bebop with words lying somewhere between Jon Hendricks and White hip-hop. Dorough's songs are hard to find; go to Aral Music (Universal)
13. Performance: Carmen McRae, "Velvet Soul," LRC Jazz Classics CD 20027.
14. Performance: "Blossom Dearie Sings," Daffodil Records LP 101.
15. Several from the 1980s are performed by Dearie on "Tweedledum and Tweedledee," Daffodil Records LP 15.
16. Many of the Dearie — Segal songs are on "Tweedledum." Dearie reprises many of her best-known songs on "Blossom Dearie: Blossom's Own Treasures," Daffodil Records CD, 2004.
17. Persuasive performances of many of the songs discussed above, by Ronny Whyte, are included in "Whyte Wolf," Audiophile CD 298.
18. These bossa nova-style songs are heard on "Jackie and Roy Forever," Music Masters CD 1995, and Kral and Cain, "The Beautiful Sea," DRG CD 5866.
19. Performance: Marlene VerPlanck, "It's How You Play The Game," Audiophile CD 325.
20. A number of Siegel songs are included in "Arthur Siegel Sings Arthur Siegel," Original Cast CD 9214, and in "Arthur Siegel At the Ballroom," OC 9526. The "Tallulah" song is on Painted Smiles 1995-1010.
21. Performance: "Barbara Lea," Prestige LP 7065. Grand's more recent work can be heard on "Ruth Canal: Mostly Murray," Commonworth Productions 2003.
22. Performance: "Chris Connor," Bethlehem LP 56.
23. Performance: Ronny Whyte, "All In A Night's Work," Audiophile CD 247.
24. Performances: for Softly, Blossom Dearie, "Positively Volume III," Daffodil Records LP, 1983; for Knew Me and several other Miles — Warren songs, Marion Montgomery, "Sometimes In the Night," Prestige LP 532.
25. Performance: Mark Murphy, "What a Way To Go," Muse CD 5419.
26. It is not a random sample, since most of these have been recorded by a singer who has been ardent in her advocacy of such songs, Andrea Marcovici, "New Words," Cabaret Records CD 5018.

7
Other Voices in Popular Song

SOME COMMERCIAL SONGS

By *commercial* we do not imply that the songs are of lesser quality, simply that they were aimed at reaching an audience via radio and records. New "commercial" pop songs of good quality tended to diminish in impact during the third quarter of the century, since air play and record distribution eventually gave preference to other song styles (chapter 2). Some veteran singers such as Sinatra or Bennett were able, in new LPs, to mix older with newly written songs by such writers as the Bergmans, Lew Spence, or Van Heusen and Cahn. But even those famous singers reached the mass market only when they had huge hits like *My Way* or *I Left My Heart in San Francisco* (and the former was a poor song). Younger singers aiming at a wide reception seldom recorded new songs in classic-pop style.

In what follows, we mention only songs or writers not elsewhere covered in this book, and offer only an arbitrary sampling from a vast universe.

ALAN BERGMAN (b. 1925) and MARILYN (Keith) BERGMAN (b. 1929)

We have often, in this book, insisted that music and words hold coprimacy in a superior classic popular song. This proposition is generally accepted in principle, but somewhat compromised in practice. Radio announcers tend to refer (if at all) to the composer. The general listening public seems to remember composer names more easily. Aficionados of popular songs do better; they may refer to a Rodgers and Hart song because they tend to prefer the work of that songwriting team to the work of Rodgers and Hammerstein, or vice versa. Writers on American popular song, including Wilder, pay more attention to the music, except for those, like Furia, who focus especially on the verbal aspect.

243

Partly to redress an unfortunate imbalance, we organize this section around the lyrics of the Bergmans, who are among the most important of the commercial songwriters of the period. We choose them for a number of reasons. Unlike some distinguished lyricists who wrote primarily with one collaborator—for example, Carolyn Leigh, Fran Landesman, Sheldon Harnick—the Bergmans have written with a number of important composers. The same can be said of other distinguished lyric writers, among whom are Ira Gershwin, Yip Harburg, Johnny Mercer, and Dorothy Fields. We would be tempted to organize sections of this book around their work, but the first three did the bulk of their best work prior to 1950, and after that date Fields wrote only with two important composers, Coleman and Arthur Schwartz.

The team that the Bergmans most resemble is that of Comden and Green. In general, one remembers the lyrics of Comden and Green as literate, and to the composer's point, but not highly individual. This is, to some degree, desirable: lyrics that are too evidently stylish are not good for songs. However, if the present reader will look at the sections on Bernstein, Styne, Coleman, and others, she will find that we often call attention to details of their lyrics that tend to "make" the song. Much the same is true of the Bergmans, whose contribution tends to be modest but admirable. While they can write amusing words, they have a particular ability to provide romantic ones that add to the allure of the music at hand.

As regards their best work, the Bergmans have written most with Johnny Mandel, Michel LeGrand, and Lew Spence. LeGrand is, of course, French. We exclude most of his songs, and consider only that work intended in the first instance for an American audience—almost all of which involved the Bergmans. That work includes many famous film songs from the 1960s to the 1980s: *The Windmills of Your Mind*; *How Do You Keep the Music Playing?*; *What Are You Doing the Rest of Your Life?*; *Summer Me, Winter Me*; *You Must Believe In Spring*; among others. LeGrand's melodies cover a lot of tonal space gracefully. He is too prone to the device of the sequence, that is, setting the same-shaped phrase on first one tone, then another, then another. Partly because of that, we assume, some Bergman lyrics for his songs are overly predictable. The rhymed phrases sound off-the-shelf: *rest of your life / west of your life / request of your life,* from *What Are You Doing?* These big ballads tend also to happen in a rather stately fashion: their regular rhythms in moderate tempo mean that they progress rather than move, and they all tend to express the same emotional quale, perhaps because they were written as title or theme songs for movies. But some very good singers like them. Among these songs, *You Must Believe In Spring* seems to us the finest, in its delicate minor mode and its sweet two-word ending.

A pretty song with LeGrand is *On My Way to You* (1988). It has a big range, and a hypnotic sound owing to the dotted-quarter plus eighth-note figure that runs throughout, except for some descending scale passages. In 1983 the Bergmans wrote, with LeGrand, the songs for the movie "Yentl." They are curious songs, all obviously tied to plot points, and musically rather specialized, sounding like a combination of French accordion tunes and the shtetl. While we find the music odd, the lyrics are all excellent. They define a dramatic situation while generalizing its human meaning, which is what you want a song for a serious "book" to do. These songs include *Papa, Can You Hear Me?*; *A Piece of Sky*; and *The Way He Makes Me Feel*: the last is the most memorable.

By and large, we find the Bergmans's songs with Johnny Mandel more satisfying, probably because of Mandel's richer harmonic sense and greater rhythmic vitality. The Bergman lyrics seem deeper too. *Where Do You Start?* (1987) is a very beautiful song about the breakup of love (Figure 7.1). It is long (40 measures), in AABAC form, in which the A_3 is cut short as a coda begins; the coda itself (C) is an adaptation of A with a more urgent forward motion. In fact, the B-section is closely related to the A-material, but with an elegant key change. The variable phrase lengths of the A vocal line—the first and fourth very short, the second and third spun longer—is what gives one the sense of spontaneous thought on

Figure 7.1

the part of the speaker. The naturalistic impression is reinforced by the use of *last* twice in short succession; those engaged in thought don't stop to rhyme. There is mastery in the way the lyrics are kept relatively neutral, phonetically, at the pause points in the long phrases toward the end of the A-sections; extreme vowels or consonant clusters would have made the line sound sing-song. As the coda progresses, with no long notes or verbal pauses, the writers do use perfect rhyme to mark off units of thought:

> And though I don't know where and don't know when
> I'll find myself in love again
> I promise there will always be a little place no one will see,
> A tiny part deep in my heart that stays in love with you.

On the final five words, the notes become longer, as the thought is completed. Here the lyricists choose not to provide a rhyme for the final word: another effective touch for a song that seems to be overheard, rather than addressed to the auditor.[1]

A 1967 song with Mandel, *Cinnamon and Clove*, has a Brazilian beat and harmonic flavor. It's a gorgeous song with piano chords often dissonant by a half-tone with the voice line. The vocal line, on "cinnamon and clove," keeps coming back to a sweet upward minor sixth interval set on top of a dominant seventh chord. The lyrics are tangy and delicate, speaking of "lemon yellow morning" and "velvet evening." Another stunning work is *A Christmas Love Song* (1988). The bridge to this song is as pretty as one could hope for. The Bergmans's contribution here is not so much in the actual words, which are appropriately plain, as in the conception of the song: "... without bells or mistletoe ** or the tinsel's silver glow.** you just look at me and oh,* Christmas is here!"

The lyricists' plainness is not always an unalloyed virtue. A Mandel song, *Summer Wishes, Winter Dreams* (1973), is vitiated by rhymes about dreams and streams, flowers and hours. A pretty tune, *I Won't Believe My Eyes* (1987), has a good conception, identical with that of the Rodgers — Hart *Wait Till You See Her* (whose refrain ends "You won't believe your eyes"). A song from 1975, *I Have the Feeling I've Been Here Before*, written with Roger Kellaway, has a soft jazz sensibility. The melodic line is Aeolian-modal, with lots of evocative flats. The message is that of having been burned at love ("The joke November makes of May"). It's an unusual and pretty song.[2]

The Bergmans's versatility includes supplying good words for theme or title songs for films, helping to make them standards. The most famous song of this type, in their case, is *The Way We Were* (1973), written with Marvin Hamlisch, adored by singers for its romantic sweep. The way the melody wreathes itself around the raised 5 in the second period is memorable. Other movie songs, written with Hamlisch, Dave Grusin, Johnny Williams, James Newton Howard, all seem underrealized: they have good tunes but a boring bridge, or they end weakly—and they all have words that seem just serviceable. A film song with David Shire, *I'll Never Say Goodbye*, rises above this level, and has an unusual AB design, the B being more substantial.

More interesting than many of the film songs are songs from a television show, "Queen of the Stardust Ballroom" (1978), written with composer Billy Goldenberg. They delineate dramatic situations clearly. The musical elements do not at first seem memorable, but when combined with the Bergmans's words, the songs amount to compressed musical scenes that have great impact. *Fifty Percent* is the song of someone loving not wisely, but as she must ("I'd rather have...any percent of him than all of anybody else at all!"). *I Love to Dance* entrains itself gracefully, with some small tonal and metrical surprises. The lyric is strong: "Tell the band to blow ev'ry tune they know / And throw in a tango or two." *Who Gave You Permission?* is about a spouse suddenly left alone by the death of her husband. *The Job Application* is a stunner about a middle-aged woman finding herself in the job market, and wanting down deep to have her old job back—as a wife and mother. The last two numbers are particularly strong, in that the Bergmans's words, while conditioned by the dramatic purpose, are so compact and telling that the songs can "work" on their own, given the right singing actor.

The first big hit song that the Bergmans enjoyed, thanks to Sinatra, was *Nice 'N Easy* (1960), written with Lew Spence. Among their work, it's perhaps the nearest to a hard swinging song, owing to the persistent syncopation and dotted rhythm, which is often quite subtle. The words are sometimes playful (*of course is* rhymed with *hold your horses*), sometimes amusingly suggestive ("We're on the road to romance, that's safe to say; But let's make all the stops along the way"). The song is sexy and insinuating, especially when sung slowly.

As much as we like the songs with Mandel, there is a sense in which we prize the Spence songs even more. Mandel's extraordinary melodic-harmonic gift would sound well with any set of sensitive lyrics. But in the songs with Spence, the writers are perfectly matched, as if they had found just the partners they needed. One well-known song with Spence, *That Face* (1957), has a terrific, ineradicable tune; the words are exactly apt. Both *That Face* and *Nice 'N Easy* play melodically with half-steps, in a style that almost demands bending the intervals. They also employ, wonderfully well, the "walking beat" that is such an important feature of a wide range of classic popular songs.

With Spence, they also wrote a lovely quiet song called *Lazy In Love* (1961). The tune is delicate, sounding like Hoagy Carmichael crossed with Harold Arlen, with a melody line whose peak notes move up one step at a time in a relaxed

The sun is rest - in'___ its head in the sky___

a breeze is whisp - 'rin', "I'm just pass- in' by"_ a cloud is doz- in'

Figure 7.2

dotted rhythm (Figure 7.2). The Bergman lyric is evocative; the dropped g's support the "lazy in love" conception nicely: "The moon is easin' the sun off the scene…." There are details that make an enormous difference; for example, in the bridge, the placement of *since* half a beat earlier than the ordinary songwriter would have placed it. It's a quiet small song that makes a big effect.

The comfortable match shows itself in a number of lesser songs. *That's Him Over There* (1952), written by Keith and Spence, is a character song, in which a woman admits "…what extremes I have gone to / To prove that I didn't care…." (about him, over there). It's not overdramatized, but indirect, and has some lovely triplets. *I'm a Stranger to Myself* (c. 1952), words by Alan Bergman, is notable for an ear-catching voice-line interval in mm.1–2. The lyric idea, the notion that the singer cannot be complete in herself without someone's loving her, is masochistic, perhaps, but arresting. *Outta My Mind* (1986) is a little like the Styne — Comden and Green *Just In Time*, in how it begins small and then extends bit by bit, both pitchwise and in terms of phrase length. At first the song, "medium bounce" in tempo, seems unremarkable, but then comes a truly clever join between the end of the bridge and the next A-section (on "Boy, was I mistaken!"), and the song gets better and better as it moves toward the end with some satisfying rhyming (*spin—in—been—been*). Though some are very slight, we have never heard a Spence — Bergman song that seemed to us poor.

The Bergmans contributed significantly to the Brazilian wave that invigorated the American pop song genre in the 1960s and beyond, by providing lyrics to some really good tunes. *Like a Lover* (1968), music by Dory Caymmi, is a multistanza ballad (in an older sense) that is essentially bitonal, moving quietly away from F by changing B-flats to B-naturals. The words are sensual and delicate. *So Many Stars* (1967) has a gorgeous melody by Sergio Mendes; it features reiterated, almost hypnotic upward sixth intervals that make for such an aching effect, and the Bergmans set the end of the song with a series of yearning questions: "Which one to choose? Which way to go? How can I tell?..." The song is not so much about love as about a kind of cosmic longing, as the title suggests [3] *The Island* (1981), music by Ivan Lins and Vitor Martins, is a long, dreamy, gently modulating song with the sexiest lyric the Bergmans ever wrote, a beauty. Many of the Brazilian songs, including those by Antonio-Carlos Jobim, suffered a bit, when they were heard in this country, from rather vague lyrics. The Bergmans's effort was thus important. (Another good transplant was the Jobim song, *No More Blues*, with lyrics by the jazz singer and arranger Jon Hendricks: fine ones, even though they reversed the emotional tone of the original.)

There are a lot more Bergman songs. The range of their collaborations is admirable. Their slant is toward romanticism; it would be welcome were they to write with more humor, and did more up-tempo songs. Many of the movie songs seem to have words that skate on the surface of rather ordinary music; but the words for the Goldenberg songs deepen and dignify the music.

LEW SPENCE (b. 1920)

We continue with Spence's songs without the Bergmans. In one case, Spence wrote lyrics for a Burton Lane tune, *A Rainy Afternoon* (1993), a song about remembering making love. The song is so-so, except for how the last A-section turns gradually, effectively into a final C-section.

Among songs with others, *A Wet Night* (and a Dry Martini), 1993, words by Spence and Jerry Gladstone, is fun, in 1940s style with a good bridge. *Susquehanna Transfer* (1954) sounds like a 1940s Warren — Mercer song that would lend itself to big-band treatment. It's good pastiche.

As for songs with words and music by Spence, *I've Never Been So Happy In My Life*, is an adorable, jaunty number that could easily be Jimmy McHugh from the 1930s—or a song from "Sesame Street." It's conventional, but a winner. When we say that a Spence song sounds like someone else, or is in a bygone style, we mean that positively, although the generic tincture may keep it from being "great." But a song written, both words and music, by Spence is, we would say, just that. It's called *What's Your Name?* (1974). It's irresistible in concept and realization. It concerns a hitherto shy person who "falls so head over heels." It includes interior rhyme worthy of Mercer or Nash, like "If you have an itch for ritual" or "knew I need" rhyming with "knew immed (iately)." The flavor of the opening tune is delicious (Figure 7.3). It not only fits the words like a glove, but would make a fine jazz trio number.

This is kind-a sud-den. I a-gree,

What's your name and will you mar-ry me?

Figure 7.3

GORDON JENKINS (1910–84)

Jenkins, an important arranger and studio musician, wrote also some memorable songs. In 1935 he had a big hit with *Goodbye*, which the Benny Goodman band adopted. In the 1950s he wrote several large-scale songs that have mournful lyrics (by Jenkins) and a sax-sounding, big-band harmony rather thickly voiced, with lots of diminished chords and half-step movement. They can be impressive when done by a "big" singer, for drama, or in diseuse style, for pathos. *I Live Alone* (1957) has long chromatic strings of notes that suddenly clarify into a large open-harmony B-section with a yearning feel: "…but still I sent him away… he loved me…I wonder." After 48 bars of this self-report, the words get a bit ridiculous.

That's All There Is (There Isn't Any More), from 1959, is 32 bars plus coda. Again it concerns someone who has sent her lover away; the coda relents, "But if you need me, call me…." This song has a strong opening strain, very much in the musical mood of *Goodbye*; there is a striking chord progression right at the start, and several well-placed climaxes before it ends in dying-fall fashion. These are inherently "women's songs," threnodies about losing love, basically self-dramatizing. They are effective but bathetic, at the extreme of what classic popular style can sustain. A much smaller song, *The Red Balloon* (1959), shows a better balance. It's a pretty waltz, with Jenkins's favorite vocal figure of chromatic lines interspersed with some yearning large intervals; it has a good climax an octave and a half above the lowest vocal tone; and it manages the dying fall gracefully: "Will he hold the string or let it go?…" We prefer this song, no doubt because it looks outward, toward another person. *Blue Prelude*, from the 1940s (with jazz player Joe Bishop), is an exemplary minor, pop-blues song that became something of a jazz standard. It uses flatted intervals that call for a catch in the voice. The rather delicate release asks, "What is love but a prelude to sorrow? . . ." and the song ends in the classic minor-third fall on "Goodbye."[4]

Jenkins's best-known song from the later period (1958) is *This Is All I Ask*, a song about the awareness of aging. The verse is schmaltz, but the chorus opens with a touchingly personal apostrophe: "Beautiful girls, walk a little slower when you walk by me." There is a fine, high climax, and a quiet ending. This one seems entirely satisfying.

MARVIN FISHER (1917–93)

Marvin Fisher was from a family of successful song composers. In 1952 he wrote *Never Like This*, with a serviceable lyric by Roy Alfred. It doesn't explore new territory, but has that comfortable quality of moving along in expected but pleasing melodic phrases and harmonies, with a rhythmic lift in m.3. *Love-Wise* (1959) has a marvelous lyric by Kenward Elmslie, which depends on the slangy use of the suffix *-wise* that makes adverbs out of nouns. This classy song has the quality of not trying to go too far too fast. There is a tenderness in the vocal contour of the first four measures, confirmed by the words thereafter (Figure 7.4). The songwriters draw us gradually into a sort of love-struck reverie, which builds in lyrical and melodic enthusiasm. The release is a gem, in which this enthusiasm is tempered by sly good humor ("[you're] much too nice to break up with . . . you'd be such fun to make up with"). Elmslie provides a subtle touch at the end of the second stanza. All the periods of the song have been end-rhymed. But at the very end he puts the word *prize*, which doesn't rhyme with anything—except, of course, *-wise* throughout.[5]

When Sunny Gets Blue (1956), lyric by Jack Segal, Fisher's most frequent collaborator, is his best-known song. It is an example of a more truly "bluesy" style than most pop songs, with the use of lowered 6 as well 3. The confiding bridge is made on a fine chord progression. *Something Happens To Me* (with Segal, 1960) has a catchy tune and an even better tangolike rhythm. The vocal line stays mostly in one plane, sometimes with strings of seven repeated notes, as with "A strange *kind of chemical change goes* rushing thru me." The repetition is even longer at the end, which brings a clever take on the title. Repeated notes can be a bore; these aren't.[6]

When She Makes Music (with Segal, 1960) is built on long chromatic sequences, in the voice line and with parallel thick diminished chords beneath. The opening is certainly striking, but viscous, like a big-band chart with a vocal added. The song clears, however, in the second period of the A-section, and comes to a beautiful setting for *makes music*, in which the first two syllables lean chromatically onto the longer third syllable, an effect achieved again at the end of the song. One appreciates the songwriters' design, but this song may be better as an instrumental.

Figure 7.4

We found no examples of a Fisher verse. His songs come from a jazz sensibility, not a theatrical one. They swing right into action, with no need to set the stage narratively. The1963 Fisher — Segal *May I Come In?* is an apology to the loved one for a romantic transgression. A burst of chromatic descending eighth-notes ("Speaking of the devil") leads to two calmer short phrases: "well, here I am, * may I come in?" The rhythmic propulsion, together with the initial participial phrase, gives the first lines an utterly natural feel, a fine way to begin a song. The Segal lyrics are subtle throughout.

With the talented lyricist John Latouche, Fisher wrote *Strange* (1953). It's not as jazzy as so many of the other Fisher songs, and there is much less use of obvious chromaticism. The song begins, indeed strangely, on the raised 7 of the scale with the title word, then moves along smoothly, reaching a peak in mm.19-20 of the B-section. Typically for Latouche, there is a lot of compound rhyme ("enjoying with me"/"toying with me") and cross-rhyme ("hum**drum** thing"/"**some**thing"). This is a lyricist's prerogative, and it can be delightful; for this rather slight song, it may be a bit much.

It is instructive to realize that songs by writers like Spence and Fisher may be better—at least the ones that attain recognition—than routine songs by the "great" theater composers. A number of songs in the quite arbitrary selection that follows would meet this standard.

The television personality Steve Allen was a prolific songwriter. His best-known song was *This Could Be the Start of Something* (1956), which one of us views with nostalgia, since it was played at his wedding reception. As rhythmically lively, and less aggressive, is a jaunty song, *I'm Playing the Field* (1956), about the joys of single life. A song from "Sophie," (1963), *They've Got a Lot to Learn*, alternates expectations for love with the letdowns of reality. As the title suggests, reality wins.

Bob Haymes, brother of singer Dick Haymes, wrote one song that became very well known, *That's All* (1952, with Alan Brandt), made famous by Nat Cole and warmly discussed in Wilder. Somewhat later, even better songs of his earned fine treatment by Blossom Dearie, but since then they seem to have faded—undeservedly so. Perhaps the finest is *They Say It's Spring* (1957), written with Marty Clarke. There is a modest verse, expressing impatience with the way "modern cynics" assign the joy of spring to purely natural or seasonal factors. "It may be Spring / But when the robin stops singing you're what I'm clinging to...." These words of the chorus illustrate the special joy of the song, the run-on quality of phrases, with the rhyme completed just before the end of the second phrase. This pattern, of three two-bar phrases followed by one four bars long in length, occurs throughout the song, even (in miniature) in the bridge. The tune is lovely; the chords are conventional; the feeling of a firmly but privately held emotion is distinctive. *A Fine Spring Morning* (1957) has a comparable charm with a similar message, that it's the person, not the season, that counts. This one reverses the pattern of the previous song by opening with a long phrase, continuing with a pair of short ones, and finishing long. ("This is a fine Spring morning / It's ev'rywhere * for us to share / Just look what a fine Spring morning can do.") The bridge here, however, provides a contrast: it's "notey," and features lots of rather daffy rhyme, a common feature of Spring songs; for example, "Chums are getting chummier / and yummy-looking girls are getting yummier." The pleasure of this song comes from the contrast of a gracefully contoured opening melody with the "cuter" middle section. There are several stanzas of words, by Haymes. The way the vowels alter in the title phrase, darker to brighter, is especially euphonious. Another ballad involving Spring is *Now At Last*, with words by Haymes. This one is slower and slightly downbeat in mood ("When the Spring is cold, where do robins go?"). The release, with successive phrases set progressively higher, is grave and lovely. *You for Me* is a "rhythm song," lightly swinging and just barely syncopated. There is a winning enjambment of phrases, especially as the bridge runs right into the last A-section. A song from 1958, *Comin' Home On a Friday*

Night, has more of a 1950s pop feel. It has a good, open-interval tune and one passing, blueslike chord. *Let's Stay Home Tonight* (1955) is similarly conventional in style, but very pretty, with romantic words: "There's a message in your eyes / And if I'm right...." The hallmark of Haymes's songs was a just-perceptibly swinging lyricism, a style in which each phrase seems beautifully poised in and of itself but somehow points ahead.

The singer Mel Tormé was a good songwriter. His 1946 *Christmas Song* with Robert Wells ("Chestnuts roasting on an open fire....") became, of course, a national treasure. A song from 1947 with Wells, *Born to Be Blue*, is excellent. It's closer to real blues style than most pop songs, in that it uses the flatted 3 and 6 a lot, and also has the pattern, roughly, of the blues syllogism: two short declarative phrases followed by one long summative phrase. In the longer phrases, downward half-step glides are prominent, also a blues feature. The lyric is well-integrated, invoking a range of color terms that renders *blue* more poignant. The harmonic approach is sensitive, as it is with *Welcome to the Club*, written with Noel Sherman and R. Wolf. The verse here is beguiling, a sympathetic take on a lover's sadness. The bridge captures the way others try to persuade the speaker to snap out of it, but sympathy resumes, with "Go right on crying in your beer." Tormé alone wrote *A Stranger In Town* (1945), which has a striking melody, involving the raised 7, 8, 9, and then reverses using half-steps. The lyric is evocative and understated. It starts "Just arrived on the seven-ten"; after the speaker looks around, it ends, "Guess I'll leave on the twelve-o-two." It's a mighty sweet song. In the 1950s, Tormé supplied words to an elegant tune by jazz musician Gerry Mulligan, called *The Real Thing*. The tune sounds like a sax line, starting low in the voice, on 5 below the key-tone, and then moving up to the upper 5—but immediately moving on one half-step more, over a lovely chord change. The words describe someone doubting that a new love will amount to anything—but hoping it will.

Robert Wells himself, with lyricist Jack Segal, contributed *When Joanna Loved Me* (1964), a rather notey, noodling tune. The lyric is subtle, in that at the point where Joanna ceases to love (in fact, leaves), the song moves very abruptly through a complex chord progression that puts a good face on things. It's a telling example of mood signaled through music. These two writers also wrote *Here's to the Losers* (1963), an insouciant tribute to those who are unlucky in love. The song is catchy, playing with half-note figures at the beginning; it swings.

The singer Peggy Lee wrote songs in diverse styles, some mentioned elsewhere. She also wrote lyrics with other songwriters. A song written with Sonny Burke, *He's a Tramp*, for a 1955 Disney film, is good, as is *There'll Be Another Spring*, written with Hubie Wheeler (1951). Lee had a unique vocal style that perhaps entailed performing not intrinsically wonderful songs. Both *Fever*, by Otis Blackwell and Eddie Cooley, and the Jerry Lieber — Mike Stoller *Is That All*

There Is? sound like blues riffs organized into light-rock sectional form—which doesn't make them bad, but they are different from the songs this book discusses. By contrast, *Black Coffee*, by Sonny Burke and Paul Francis Webster, is a classy, fully developed pop-blues.

Some of the Lieber — Stoller songs are much more developed. *Some Cats Know* (1966) is in moderate-tempo pop-blues style; it's not about felines, but people who are especially hip about lovemaking, and it's a lot of fun. The last words are definitive: "If a cat don't know…a cat don't know."

My One and Only Love (Guy Wood, Robert Mellin, 1952) was once well-known; its release is quite beautifully handled. A light beguine tune from 1949, *Circus*, by Louis Alter (the composer of *You Turned the Tables On Me*) and Bob Russell, a proficient lyricist, has a good concept, that of the merry-go-round of love ("I was the clown, you were the laughter ** echoing after"), and some interesting chord changes in the bridge, one of which effects a modulation a bar later than one expects.

The famous *Cry Me a River* (1955) by Arthur Hamilton is a good mournful ballad, with a strong bridge melodically. A rhyme at the end of the bridge (*plebian/me 'n*) is forced. *Rain Sometimes* (1965) is a delicate slow ballad about the vagaries of love. Its main rhyme scheme (*rain/champagne/gravy train*, etc.) verges on the precious, but is saved when the writer tweaks the thought at the end. Hamilton has also written a moving post-September 11th song, *It's All Right to Be Afraid*.

To Those Who Wait (1955), by Larry Coleman, lyrics by Carolyn Leigh, is a straightforward song harmonically, but it starts out in a compelling way. There is no verse; the first three measures of the chorus charge right into the main theme with a melody that hovers briefly around the tonic, then above it. The drive to the opening is melodic, not rhythmic. Leigh's lyric includes, "…keep your shirt on, pending * that happy ending…."

(This Is the End of) *A Beautiful Friendship* (Donald Kahn, Stanley Styne, 1956) is a confident, satisfying song with a nice conceit ("…and just the beginning of love"). It works as a ballad, but is better when it swings. Good songs follow natural speech rhythms, except for special effect, and this is exemplary.

A well-known song by David Mann and Bob Hilliard, *In the Wee Small Hours of the Morning* (1955), is a short song, in ABAC form. It is notable for the poise and long line of its main melodic strain. The words are appropriately understated, though the use of *wee* is daring. One can argue that it is too taciturn to be emotionally satisfying, but equally well one can say that, in its brevity and terseness, it is a distillation of sadness.

George David Weiss and Joe Sherman had at least two very successful songs: *What a Wonderful World* (1968, with Robert Thiele) and *That Sunday That Summer* (1963, music, Joe Sherman). We like the latter especially, mostly for its step-down chords under "Go on and kiss her!"

I'm a Fool to Want You, by Jack Wolf and Joel Herron (1951), had an indelible recording by Sinatra. It has a fine opening melody, but otherwise is soggy.

Pianist-composer Eddie Heywood wrote, with Alec Wilder, *You Never Gave It a Try* (1955), an elegant little song using a chaconnelike bass line (starting I-raised I-ii-V-I) under a vocal line that compresses from a major seventh to a "stretched" sixth to a regular sixth. Wilder's words are suitably wistful.

Robert Allen wrote a catchy 1957 song called *Baby Has Gone Bye-Bye*, lyrics by Allan Roberts. The cheerful 2/4 tempo, the old-fashioned first-beat syncopation, and the breeziness of the lyrics ("Oh my, I wonder why, Baby has gone bye-bye") show that the singer isn't all that sad, more befuddled than anything. It's like a Harry Ruby — Bert Kalmar soft-shoe song of the 1920s.

The End of a Love Affair was once a well-known song. It's from 1950, by Edward Redding, a writer otherwise unknown to us, but it seems a model of a song about failed love, with excellent words that are not bathetic, in fact a bit angry ("Do they know, do they care?"). The bridge is good, and the lyric uses identical rhyme, the exact words repeated in corresponding positions.

Jay Livingston and Ray Evans wrote the film song *Buttons and Bows* (1948), and thereafter many widely known ones. *Never Let Me Go* (1956) has a striking, yearning opening to the vocal line, the title phrase hugging the key-tone and coming to rest at the end of the phrase on 2. It also has an effective extension to the bridge, involving a pleading couplet: "You'd never leave me, would you? You couldn't hurt me, could you?" Some stretches of the lyric, however, are unfortunate, as with "...all my bridges burned by my flaming heart." *All the Time* (1958) is a small song, essentially AAA in form. The melodic contour is unusually simple for pop song style, and rather *lied*-like. A 1966 film song, *Maybe September*, plays nicely with *tender/splendor/September*; Percy Faith created a lovely tune in which the third phrase adds a surprising length to the two earlier ones.

The arranger Marty Paich published few songs; a nice one is *I Never Go There Anymore* (1966), lyrics by Rod McKuen. It's about love that fled, creating a void. There is a fine chromatic alteration to the final A-section, and the words are good. (This song will remind aficionados of the Charlap — Lawrence *I'll Never Go There Any More*, a song with far more emotional depth.) McKuen himself wrote quite a number of fairly inert songs, though he also put us in his debt by providing English words to some Jacques Brel material. One song by McKuen alone is especially good, *I've Been to Town* (1963). The sense of the words, which are more powerful than the tune, is that the speaker has been around the cycle of love many times ("...the Milky Way isn't milky white, it's dingy gray"). It's a creative take on an old theme, and pleasant to sing.

For Once In My Life (Orlando Murden and Donald Miller, 1965), made famous by Tony Bennett, Stevie Wonder, and others, has a striking, up-going opening strain; the phrases then climb tone by tone, predictably but effectively.

A subtle, sophisticated song about someone romantically obtuse is *I Haven't Got Anything Better to Do* (1967), by Paul Vance and Lee Pockriss.

The important songwriter Jim Croce wrote in a style different from that of this book, but his well-known song, *Time In a Bottle* (1973) is a close cousin, opening in what we call the narrative minor and moving into graceful major waltztime for the refrain. Roberta Flack's big hit, *The First Time Ever I Saw Your Face* (1971), by Ewan MacColl, is a strong ballad in concept, but somehow generic in realization. Johnny Nash's *I Can See Clearly Now* (1972), made famous by Marvin Gaye, retains its charm, owing to its relaxed rhythm and its invocation of "a bright sunshiny day."

Marvin Hamlisch is a cross-category composer: of the songs for "A Chorus Line," of the excellent, often-recorded ballad, *The Way We Were*, and of the commercial, *Nobody Does It Better*, written with Carole Bayer Sager for a 1977 James Bond movie. We have a guilty fondness for this hands-on-hips song of sexual bliss.

Leon Russell's *A Song for You* was made famous by Ray Charles, justly so. It comes in short units, roughly in AABA form but with lots of repetition, and it has a slight blues quality, hard to pin down. This is a song whose center of gravity is the very short bridge, constructed just with back-and-forth thirds below and above the upper key-tone, sometimes filled in, sometimes plain. This is also the center of gravity emotionally, for the words, "There's no one more important to me / So can't you please see through me?" We also admire the way the lyric moves from the quite poetic, to an achingly direct phrase, slipped in, like "You are a friend of mine."[7]

We find it hard to get a grip on the songs of Burt Bacharach, some written for the theater, others written direct for radio and records. Wilder (235) was perceptive in remarking, "If only one good thing has come out of the experiments of the rock era, it is the natural phrase, whether or not it be an even number of measures," and he acknowledged Bacharach. There is indeed an engaging, pawky quality to his vocal lines. For example, in the famous *Raindrops Keep Falling On My Head* (1969), the upward seventh intervals toward the end of the opening phrase (and equivalent) are delightful. Being inherently hard to sing, they sound like a man-on-the-street making a stab at an octave, and missing. The same is true of the way the phrases last a few beats longer than one would expect. It's writing in the vernacular, for sure.

Much the same applies to *I'll Never Fall In Love Again*, from "Promises, Promises" (1968), with its prolonged *I'll*, as if the speaker were considering what came next. *Knowing When to Leave*, from "Promises" is talky but flexible, with quick octave leaps in the vocal line. On the other hand, the loping off-center rhythm of the title song is like riding a horse with an uneven canter. *Do You Know the*

Way to San Jose? (1968) has great élan, but a thready pulse. *I Say a Little Prayer* (1967) has a broad, lightly syncopated beat to it, and the important harmonies occur rather far apart, so that the song seems closer to the ground, less tightly wound, than most classic popular song.

When one looks at Bacharach's most regularized songs, the ones that fall into familiar patterns, like *What the World Needs Now*, or *The Look of Love*, a complicating factor comes into play. They are fine tunes, especially the latter, but their words—all the songs mentioned here have words by Hal David—seem flat and uncommitted. A 1964 film song, *A House Is Not a Home*, has a pleasant tune, and the bridge contains an unusual segment in B flat (with tritones), modulating to C major, within an overall E flat major tonality. But the lyrics are inept. Logically, one can make the argument that David is also writing in a vernacular, that people talk like this. We can only report that these words convey to us a carelessness that prevents these works from achieving the well-shaped quality we have claimed as a hallmark of the classic popular song. As "lyrics," they lack internal organization. We conclude that Bacharach is a relaxed but venturesome writer, David a lax and clumsy one. The songs linger in national memory, but they are not classic in our terms.

Perhaps the most famous Joe Raposo song is *Bein' Green* (1971), written for children's television. Good singers like it for its artful combination of a message of racial tolerance expressed by verbal indirection in irregular, seemingly casual, musical phrases. It develops a powerful communicative effect gradually. *You Will Be My Music* (1973) is an odd bipartite song, touching at the start but then working to a rather blatant conclusion, musically and verbally. *There Used to Be a Ballpark* (1973) is a gravely pretty song of nostalgia shading into disquiet. Its melodic line is compressed, for the most part circling within the first five tones of the scale. It sounds inhibited, but it does fit the lyrics well. They express a held-in sense of loss and a graying-out of experience, whether it's the performance of the new team ("the old team isn't playing and the new team hardly tries") or, "The sky has gotten cloudy, when it used to be so clear." The biting-the-lip nature of the melodic line is mirrored by the way successive lines of the lyric begin tersely with *and*. It's a subtle, understated song. A theater song written in 1989 with Sheldon Harnick, *I Couldn't Be With Anyone but You*, is a stunner, a ballad that ought to be much better known. It's a long piece that develops in a seemingly offhand fashion, with brief phrases (e.g., "Come over here * [you're] not near enough") that cumulate into more sustained, semantically complex ones. The harmony is open, but bringing an occasional pang. Raposo brings in the title phrase most effectively, by using one tone as a pivot for a modulation. The long release is a confiding, self-effacing song unto itself. Harnick's lyric is excellent, again mixing passionate statement with throwaway interjection: "You're the only one * I can be me with / I know 'cause I've tried. . . ." This is the biggest and most sophisticated of all the Raposo songs.

Jeff Moss also wrote songs for "Sesame Street," but they are equally effective in more sophisticated settings. The gentle melody of *What Do I Do When I'm Alone?* (1971), in the key of C, rarely moves away from a zone between 2 and 6, its simplicity accented by various voicings of a B-flat major seventh chord.

Roger Miller wrote many highly successful songs in a very individualistic style, a bit country, a bit honky-tonk; they are extremely well written and rhythmically subtle. Most have words that move them outside the classic pop register, but there's no reason a pop singer cannot perform them. *King of the Road* (1964) is famous, and has a tight design with complicated syncopation. When Miller wrote, successfully, a Broadway show, "Big River" (1985), his songs continued to be in this personal, verbally idiomatic, style, not in "theater style."

Jimmy Webb is also a highly individualistic, important figure. He was barely out of his teens when he wrote hugely successful songs such as *By the Time I Get to Phoenix; Up, Up and Away; Didn't We?*; and *MacArthur Park*, and has now been writing well since the 1970s. Although his approach is eclectic, we generalize by saying that his songs have interesting and unusual words; shapely tunes that fit their words, whatever the import, very smartly; and rather plain harmony. By and large the chords and tonal patterns could work with light rock or folk-tinged country; it is not surprising that they reflect melodies that use mostly in-the-scale tones. Webb's conceptions for songs are often striking, and the management of the lyric is invariably expert. He sounds to us like someone who consciously decided, in the 1960s, that he would cleave to the dominant idioms of his own day. *Phoenix* (1967) is very plain, with a little glide figure at the end of the first phrase. Its topic is a staple of country rock, but the story is haunting, in a way that country songs about a man ditching a woman are generally not. *Galveston* (1968) is similar musically, but with a seagoing topic. *Up, Up and Away* (1967) is delightful, in its light bossa nova rhythm and its delicate words (e.g., "suspended canopy"); the spaced-apart sequence of *ride-glide*, and later, an expansion to *guide us...hide us...beside us*"; and the inherently buoyant *balloon*, with its upward octave portamento. Structurally the song develops one phrase out of the last, in a rough repeating ABAB design. The nicest effect is the way "Up, up and away, in my beautiful balloon" sounds, while in progress, like the start of a new period in the song, but is actually a closure to the entire first part of the song. This song should not be sung frenetically.[8] *Didn't We* is an ethereal ballad, pure pop in its style and its topic of love that almost worked. ("...almost made our poem rhyme...almost made that long hard climb...."). The melody floats beautifully. An even better, because more original, love ballad is *She Moves and Eyes Follow* (1985), another song with great continuity. This one has a short bridge, so that the form is AABA with excellent transitions. The basic image of the song is the natural beauty and grace of the beloved: "She laughs, and laughter follows like ripples follow a storm," or simply, "She goes, and life follows...." There is an unselfconscious use of both direct and slant-rhyme. The melody is exceptionally pure: it could be a carol tune, except for one brief moment when an inner voice note is lowered so that one sixth-interval chord occurs in the midst of thirds and fifths. *Is There Life After You?* is pleasantly in a light rock style, with a few chords that change directly, without much harmonic modulation. Its lyric is just fine, odd and colloquial; for example, "It's so boring... After the soaring; we were soaring...." Here the word *boring* is right because it is a word that comes automatically to mind for the speaker, who then is struck by the recall of something totally different, *soaring*, and then, after the semicolon, deepens that reflection. This is the way people speak, but it is unusual to find that so directly reflected, including a nongrammatical digression, in a song lyric. There is a reflective song, *Time Flies,* that is notable for a main strain in rather hymnlike, light-rock-chorded style but a bridge with a more harmonically rich underpinning. The words keep coming back to "... and while we were dreaming, time flies," in a tone that is neither sad nor joyful, just ruminative. Webb has the ability to write in slow 3/4 time without seeming insipid. We would mislead if we implied that Webb generally writes in classic pop song style. But anyone who appreciates, for example, Yeston's individualistic theater songs should very much like these "commercial" Webb songs, which are of very high quality.

Billy Joel is an interesting transitional figure between theater style, commercial, and light rock. Most of his songs have compelling vamps, either as an introduction or interstitially throughout the song. *New York State of Mind* (1976) is a lightly bluesy song, a bit Arlen-like, with a strong vamp figure and a lowered 3; it's also slightly Latin with an insinuating rhythm; and finally it has wonderful words. Rhythmically, the song falls within pop style, in that its eighth- and quarter-notes fall naturally into uneven duples, sometimes with triples mixed in, which is a basis for swing. Verbally, it celebrates the city, but doesn't hype it. However, there is a breath of new-style lyric writing in the use of decidedly off-rhyme (e.g., *reality/fine with me*). The 1978 *Just the Way You Are* goes further. The rhythm now is more pliable, more heartbeat in nature, still slightly tangolike, but in the relaxed rock universe, with interpolations (set to the vocable *Mm*) that have the flavor of guitar, not piano. The words are still in pop register, still with pop-jazz chords. The opening tune is ear-catching and convincing. *Piano Man* (1973) works for its story line ("It's a pretty good crowd for a Saturday"), and its old-timey, juke box musical feeling. *I've Loved These Days*, and *And So It Goes* (1993), are songs that good pop singers can do to fine effect. The latter is especially interesting: at first it seems too stripped down, with chordal hymnlike sections alternating with a more linear, pop-harmonized brief refrain (the title phrase), but it gets to one. Joel can write in rock style, evoke blues or country, bring off the quick "strut" song or satisfying ballads. His weakness may be the flip side of versatility, a penchant for pastiche.

Ettore Stratta and Ronny Whyte created a wide-ranging ballad (1986), *Forget the Woman*, in satisfying pop-jazz style. The phrase structure, reminiscent of Styne's *The Party's Over*, consists in a number of short units leading into one very long one, all this repeated, and then a coda. One hears a kind of ABAB form, although the B is closely related to the A. Much of the song is set over widely spaced chords with added 9, which step down one per bar, allowing the melody, which is really a riff, to float above. The words are good, with a nice conclusion.[9]

In covering already, in this section, songs by Lee, McKuen, Joel, Webb, Miller, and others, we have touched on work that edges into the "singer-songwriter" category, but have restricted ourselves to songs that are in a recognizable relationship to classic pop style. Often the affinity is that the words are compact and rhymed, and refer to the subject-matter, the semantic arena, of classic pop, especially with the songs of Webb or Miller. In the last section of this chapter, we discuss songs by singer-songwriters that are not only musically quite formally distinct from classic pop, but that are *about* quite different topics or express different attitudes.

SONGS FROM THE JAZZ SHORE

Elsewhere in this book we have discussed songs by writers with a distinct jazz sensibility, such as Frishberg, Dorough, Wolf, or Dearie. Other songwriters as well have clear affinities with the jazz sound, including Coleman, Arlen, Mandel, or Marvin Fisher.

More broadly, reflecting the fact that "jazz" is an indefinable entity, probably half the songs we cover in this book use what, in chapter 1 and elsewhere, we refer to as pop-jazz stylistic features, such as complex, multilayered rhythms or jazz-inflected harmony; that is, chords with added or altered tones, diminished or augmented intervals, "blue" notes, and so on. All through the central section of this book dealing with particular songs, we repeatedly use such descriptive terms or concepts as *bluesy*, a *bebop* attitude in a lyric, *jazzy* as it applies to a strongly marked rhythm, vamp, or riff, and so on. It is this stylistic trait bundle that accounts in part for the fact that so many classic American popular songs have become jazz "standards."

In what follows, we select some other songs essentially on the criterion that they were written by or performed by figures whose professional identification is that of jazz. Even this is a porous classification. With performers like Lee or Tormé, who have been considered "jazz singers," some of the songs they wrote or recorded are jazz, while many others are classic pop. The same would be true of such singers as Dinah Washington, Anita O'Day, Mark Murphy, and many others.

DUKE ELLINGTON (1899–1974); BILLY STRAYHORN (1915–67)

There is more popular and scholarly writing about Duke Ellington and his music than any other figure in American popular music, Louis Armstrong aside. Here we concern ourselves only with his songs in classic pop style, together with those written by Duke's close collaborator, Billy Strayhorn, a gifted arranger and composer. Some compositions known to be by Strayhorn appeared under Ellington's better-known name. *Take the A Train* is one example. Strayhorn also wrote songs alone, good ones.

A complication is that many Ellington songs started as instrumentals, and had words put to them later (e.g, *Don't Get Around Much Anymore*). One reason the lyrics are sometimes hard to recall is that by and large they are not very good. The beautiful *Solitude* (1934), for example, has strings of banal words about reveries and memories, and the absurd phrase "I sit in my chair / I'm filled with despair." Better that such songs should remain instrumentals.[10]

But one of the perfect songs of the half-century is *Satin Doll* (1953), music by Ellington and Strayhorn, words (later) by Johnny Mercer. It's a famous song, with an incredibly hip lyric, delicate, funny, like water splashing over stones. Would that Ellington and Mercer had been a steady team!

Love You Madly (1950, words by Luther Henderson) became something of a theme-song for Ellington. It's a song that swings hard but keeps its aplomb; the words are not brilliant, but smart all the same. The magnificent *Come Sunday* is not a pop song in form or import, but a hymn based on a tune from the jazz suite, "Black, Brown and Beige," that was set to words, apparently by Ellington, for a recording with gospel singer Mahalia Jackson in 1958. In the same way that all lovers of popular song know and treasure *Summertime* (also not in pop song form), everyone should appreciate this gorgeous and moving song, whose refrain ends, "Please look down and see my people through." *Paris Blues* (1961), from a film about the American jazz scene in Paris, has a great luscious melody and those fat Ellington chords underneath. It's a fascinating song, in that the more striking tune begins with the second eight bars. Ellington works a piano right-hand riff into the vocal line in the release. The so-so words are credited, sometimes to Ellington, sometimes to Strayhorn. This song, with its added seventh and ninth chords, reminds one (except for the frequent lowered 3) of how close American popular/jazz harmony is to the style of French nineteenth-century salon and instrumental music.

In the late 1940s and the 1950s, Ellington attempted some shows for Broadway. "Beggar's Holiday" (1947) has a number of songs with John Latouche. They sound contrived for mass success. There are two shining exceptions. One is the romping *Take Love Easy*. Latouche's words are smug, conceited: "And if you can't take love easy, take it while you can," or "Let your heart break oh so slightly, when your lover

Figure 7.5

says goodbye." The song opens with incisive on-the-beat chords, which the voice lags or anticipates; the second phrase is one of those wonderful step-down affairs, with each successive chord sounding juicier than the last (Figure 7.5). Note how gracefully the phrase pivots, by one half-step, at *easy* The other, exuberant, song is *Tomorrow Mountain*, where Ellington's somewhat jagged tune takes second place to Latouche's glitteringly sophisticated words: "... the gutters I think are lined with mink / and the diamond bushes thrive." (The lyric, we would say, pays droll homage to the Appalachian fiddle tune, *The Big Rock Candy Mountain*.) The high-spot of the song is the release, where Ellington smoothes out into a little piano-riff-like vocal line for Latouche's one-of-a-kind words: "Pigs trot around already roasted... marshmallows bloom already toasted...."

About 1959 there was another unsuccessful show, "Jump For Joy," which included a curious song, *Within Me I Know* (words, Sid Kuller). It is a sort of prefigured torch song, in that the words state hypothetically that all would be lost if the lover left—including anxious touches in the lyrics suggesting that the singer expects it. The main verbal thought is nicely expressed, with internal rhyme: "Within me I know that without you I'd go right out of my mind." The voice line, which opens in a disconcertingly exact reminder of *You Go to My Head*, is hypnotic in that, in the entire first 16 bars, the voice sings only G, the 5 of the key, C. The chord changes underneath arc elegant: ii, V^7, ii, lowered ii^7, I^7, preceding a modulation onto IV and a circle of fifths. But the studied effect is one of neurotic anxiety ("For no matter how closely you hold me, it's never close enough").

From 1964 to 1966 Ellington was still trying for Broadway exposure, this time with the supremely clever lyricist Marshall Barer. "Pousse-Café" lasted three nights. There are some very good things in it, including a song, *If I Knew Now* (What I Knew Then), which is actually a version of an Ellington — Latouche song (*Maybe I Should Change My Ways*) from "Beggar's Holiday." The new Barer lyrics are touching, about someone growing old enough to know how little he knew when young. The title song is an easy pop-blues, with an inviting lyric that the writers must have hoped would be prophetic: "You can sip, you can sup, but the curtain goes up / and you're lost for the rest of the show." A fine Ellington jump tune is *Let's*, with complicated and funny words: "The only lover that can leave me blue / Is the shy one, who wants to but won't," or "My only regrets are regrets / To rue what we do is absurd." Ellington ends the song with some jubilant upward intervals, narrowing by half-steps but all pegged to the upper key-tone. The entire song is fun. A superb ballad is *Someone to Care For*. It's one of Ellington's most beautiful melodies, and it's full of brilliant melodic touches, like *care for* (and *therefore* and *wherefore*) at the end of phrases set alternatively on tender downward glides on major and minor thirds, finally with an octave drop that attains great emotional power. Inevitably the song reminds one of the famous Ellington — Strayhorn songs, *Something to Live For* (1939), not only in the title but in the radiant sweetness of the contour of the song.

A charming small song, *Thank You, Ma'am*, depicts a shy lover who's overwhelmed with gratitude. The lyrics are technically stunning: *lion* rhymes with *I envisioned*, but you hardly notice. There are some pleasantly dirty songs in the show: a ditty called *Up Your Ante*; a pastiche, Kander — Ebb type of song about a good-time girl, *Follow Me Up the Stairs*, which includes a great couplet about what the client *expects to see* and *ecstasy*; and a kick-up-your-heels 1920s romp called *Goodbye, Charlie*, whose verses fill in a familiar sad-but-wise "back-story" in a most hilarious fashion. (It turns out Charlie was more of a cad than one would expect.).[11]

An Ellington 1950s instrumental melody was given words by Lawrence Brown, and called *On a Turquoise Cloud*: the words anodyne, the tune memorable. Another gorgeous song, *Pretty Girl* (1957), credited to Ellington and Strayhorn jointly (as an instrumental it is known as *The Starcrossed Lovers*) ought to be famous. It's very quiet; the release is so minimal and tender, the song almost evanesces right there. The opening line, "Pretty girl, you with the eyes," captures your heart with one note: it is scalar, except that *you* is set on a raised 5, to enormous effect. The highly chromatic song draws to a close with a melismatic movement that stabs the heart (Figure 7.6).

You with the eyes, won't you sur- prise me one fine day?

Figure 7.6

Strayhorn wrote more than he was credited for. By far the most famous song is *Lush Life* (1949), a quintessential late-night-in-your-cups dirge. The song attains an almost uncanny calmness, an alcoholic slowness, by the continuity of a bass-line that simply oscillates (except for the release, and the remarkable last three bars) around chords that change only by a half-step. After reflection, we cannot help but think that Strayhorn's lyric is so "poetic" that it falls into mawkishness and some fairly bizarre verbiage ("Life is awful again / a troughful of hearts...."). One can argue that the situation demands this high-keyed diction, but it didn't seem to do so when Mercer wrote *One for My Baby*.

A Strayhorn composition from 1955 has a characteristically wrenching melody, with a range over an octave and a half, perfect for a long-lined sax, difficult for a vocalist. With words added much later by Roger Schore, it became *Bittersweet* (2000). The opening strain is remarkable because it involves two crucial minor sixth intervals separated by an interval just a half-step short of an octave, with the underlying harmony kept quite spare so that the vocal tension is foregrounded. The transition into the bridge is abrupt, and the bridge itself includes an unprepared key change, so that the song as a whole seems both delicate and blunt. Schore's words appropriately combine some heavy emotion with gentler recall: "No more charades, the feeling fades to bittersweet"—or, as he puts it, "that mixture of both hurt and love."[12]

A good up-tempo tune is *Maybe*, words and music credited to Strayhorn (1961). It has a wise little verse, and then a sassy dotted-rhythm chorus ("Maybe, but then again, maybe not...and maybe is a long long time"). The song sounds like an Arlen — Koehler tune written for Lena Horne at her slyest.

The Last Light of Evening, words by Dominique Eade, is a song to be heard with reverence. It is Strayhorn's last composition, written while dying. Even if one did not know that, it would seem terribly sad, for it bespeaks fear in the sick. The melody is slow-moving, with many calm octave intervals. The words speak for themselves: "Setting sun and falling night...tomorrow's light seems so far away...deep in my heart...I think about you...."[13]

In the framework of this book, the particular importance of Ellington and Strayhorn is harmonic. Much of pre-1950 pop song harmony exists on the sophisticated functional level, as in Berlin or Gershwin, which when well handled can be very satisfying. Porter, using "Latin" styles, or Duke, in his most romantic mood, or Arlen, in pop-blues mood, vary between functional and nonfunctional (p. 30), depending on the needs of the song. Sondheim has a full mastery of functional harmony, but often goes beyond it in order to achieve a color or mood. Ellington, Strayhorn, and Johnny Mandel (below) move among the three levels: functional, coloristic, and emotional. Sometimes with Ellington, one feels that the melodic shape is not that interesting (and the sometimes banal lyrics for his songs do not help); in such a case, we may perceive the harmonic texture as the foreground element. Strayhorn and Mandel are great melodists, so that seldom happens, though Strayhorn's harmony is often so complex and lustrous that it is hard for a listener to "hear" the melody directly.

A number of jazz songs involve lyrics set to well-known jazz instrumentals. *Cottontail*, by Ellington with later words by Jon Hendricks, is a delightful example. Others are *Everyday I Have the Blues* (Basie — Hendricks) or *My Leopard*, based on the Ellington — Strayhorn tune *Isfahan*, or *Waltz for Debbie*, with minimalist words by Gene Lees to a famous tune by Bill Evans. These are songs written for special performance situations or in homage to great jazz composers, and we must pass them by.

In what follows we deal very selectively with the residual category, "jazz song." Often such songs are recognizable essentially by their distinctive harmonic or melodic–harmonic traits. To oversimplify, in some of them the interest is in "the chords" or "the color." This is a nontrivial consideration. When one looks at the written-out music for most "jazz songs," one sees the voice line with words and rhythmic notation plus chord symbols. In keeping with the improvisatory character of jazz, this leaves considerable freedom to the performers. By contrast, Harold Arlen, with a deep affinity for blues and the 1920s jazz forms of his youth, never let his songs be published without written-out specification, that is, voice line plus two piano "hands." It was crucial for him to hear the inner parts as he conceived them, with his voice-leading and chord inversions. He was not a "jazz songwriter," but a song composer.

An example of a "jazz song" depending primarily on color is *Midnight Sun*, with a lyric added in 1954 by Johnny Mercer to an instrumental composed earlier by Lionel Hampton (J. Francis Burke also credited). The main melodic strain here is a very long chromatic scale, followed by a shorter phrase involving a striking major seventh interval. This pattern then repeats. The underlying harmonic treatment is lush and sinuous. It does not really make a "melody": it is in fact a chromatic arabesque, a perfect figure for an instrument (specifically, the vibes), probably not the voice. To set words to this, even so fine a writer as Mercer came up with fancy verbiage like "red and ruby chalice" and "aurora borealis." It's striking, but it's pseudopoetic.

Consider, by contrast, a wholly successful popular song that uses basic jazz means: *No Moon At All* (1953), words and music credited jointly to Redd Evans and Dave Mann. This is a fine, buoyant song whose A-sections, in the minor, are constructed over a simple bass progression, familiar in jazz: VIII-raised VII-VII-VI-lowered VI-V-I. The bridge, in a new major key, uses standard V-to-I moves. What makes it a good song is the shapely, singable melody built on minor intervals with a few spicy accidentals, and set with both forward and normal syncopations. The bridge is a bit notey, as Wilder would say, but the melodic line permits a clever lyric; for example, "...it's so dark ** even Fido is afraid to bark." It's a gamboling sort of song for a singer with finesse—to us it's unmistakably a jazz song in classic pop mode.[14]

Misty, a tune by Erroll Garner, was originally a piano solo, but with a well-contoured, easily sung, tune. Unhappily, its 1954 words by Johnny Burke are banal. *Something Happens* (1960) was written by Garner with lyrics by Sammy Cahn; it is 32 bars, ABAB. The opening A-section motif has a range of only four contiguous eighth notes ending with two half notes: "I see or hear you * something happens." The eighth-note runs in the voice line balance chromatic runs in the bass under the two longer syllables, *hap-pens*. The B-sections also juxtapose three-beat notes with running eighths. The second B ends chromatically and quietly, with "...happens each and ev'ry time." The words again are careless.

At quite a different point in the jazz/pop overlap, Billy Barnes's *Something Cool* (1957), though it has jazz chords, is fundamentally a pop ballad falling into a large category of lost-lady songs ("I don't ordinarily drink with strangers"), effective in its rather bathetic way.

More lithe and playful is *Love Turns Winter to Spring*, by Matt Dennis and Frank Killduff. The deft lyric is a bit predictable from the title ("I'll never wonder at lightning and thunder...old weatherman don't mean a thing"), but the tune is an effervescent one. From the 1940s, not mentioned by Wilder, is Dennis's big-band-sounding *Let's Get Away From It All* (words by Tom Adair), swinging and hip ("Let's go again to Niagara / This time we'll look at the Fall"); it ought to be revived. *That Tired Routine Called Love* (1953) was written by Dennis with lyrics by Ted Steele. It's a long song (54 bars) in the form $A_1A_2BA_1CA_1$. The A_1 material opens the song with an in-air harmonic feeling, on a chord that's an appoggiatura to a V chord; the tonic is not reached until m.7. This indecision fits the speaker's apparent lack of enthusiasm for love: "...those same old tags to broken down gags." But the release is a nicely structured musical shot in the arm, with a wider-ranging tune that sounds like what would normally be A-section material. A nice job, though again the words sound forced.

Two older, very good songs by Joe Greene are in blues layout. *Don't Let the Sun Catch You Crying* (1946) is closer to a true blues, ending each short stanza with the long line, "...I don't need you no more." *Soothe Me* (1947) has specially fine chords, and a melody line that wanders from major to minor; it's an erotic song ("Mellow me, baby, way down inside"). Both Greene songs have excellent short releases, which do not negate the impression of a blues.[15]

Bernard Hanighen was responsible for the fine lyric for Thelonious Monk's famous tune, *'Round About Midnight*, which may well be the best, and clearest, example of a superb jazz song—even more so than *Satin Doll*, which is tongue-in-cheek bop. *'Round Midnight* has a melody line at the edge of being inherently instrumental; it has a big range, a soaring profile, and a harmonic intensity that reflects Monk's blues-gospel background, yet it is still singable. The words for the song are correspondingly intense; they manage to be mournful and angry simultaneously.

Cy Walter, a fine jazz and club pianist, wrote a number of very good songs in an advanced harmonic style. He was fond of bitonal chords and dissonant or "stretched" fifths and ninths; his ballads thus have a yearning quality, as with the gorgeous *Time and Tide* (with a very strong lyric by Alec Wilder, 1961) and *See a Ring Around the Moon* (with Chilton Ryan, 1961).[16] Another song with Ryan, *You Are There* (1960), plays with off-octave intervals. *When a Man Has Done You Wrong* is a clever variation on a bad-love theme. These are a pianist's tunes; the interest is ultimately harmonic. Walter could also do more obviously catchy, up-tempo tunes: *Some Fine Day* (1953) has a brisk opening (using 5-9-6), easing into a swinging rhythm. Walter did the neat words.

Pianist Walter Gross had a gift for songs whose jazz feel is in the beautifully voiced chords. His most famous song was *Tenderly* (1945), but we like *Please Remember* (1953) better. It is in the same harmonic style—diminished chords, major sevenths, dominant sevenths with added 9 or 11—but with a more graceful lyric, in this case by pianist/composer Bobby Troup. The same melting, late-night-club feeling marks Gross's *Once We Were Young* (1956), with his own words. The songs are very 1940, and very pretty.

In much the same style harmonically and melodically are some songs by club pianist/accompanist Joey Bushkin, from the 1950s. The best all have striking opening melodic strains. *Boy Wanted*, an insinuating beguine, sets the title to (unusually) an octave jump on 5 for *boy*, then *wanted* as a half-step down (diminished chord underneath) and a half-step back to a familiar V chord. The pattern then repeats a tone higher: the key tone is not heard clearly in the voice line until m.9. The octave leap plus dip is effective, and the words by playwright Garson Kanin are clever, as if the speaker is advertising for a lover. *When You Walked By*, lyrics by Johnny Burke, has a very similar opening figure, and a pretty, calm, up-the-scale ending. *Something Wonderful Happens In Summer*, lyric by John DeVries, is perhaps the best of these three. Here too the poised, sweet melody departs from the tonic quickly, for V and then IV. There is a gorgeous chord progression just before the second period of the final A, for the words "But when it does, you'll feel wonderful."

The sax player Gerry Mulligan wrote *What's the Rush* (1958, words by Judy Holliday). It's a small, relaxed song, ABAB in form, with some pointed advice: "You'll never get away from you."

David Raksin (1912–2004), the composer of the sublime *Laura* (1945), is a figure comparable in his gift and style to another film writer, Johnny Mandel, a generation later. In both cases, the excellent, far-ranging voice lines combined with extraordinarily lush chords make their songs formally equivalent to songs by, say, Vernon Duke, on the popular side, or Billy Strayhorn, on the jazz shore. In trying to draw such stylistic distinctions, close attention should be given to the lyrics. Raksin's melodies are so broad and expressive that they can sound "instrumental" or even distended unless they have fine words attached to them. For *Laura*, Mercer did the job beautifully. For another film song from 1945, *Slowly*, Raksin provided a beautiful vocal line, but the words by Kermit Goell are pedestrian, concerning the moon "smiling above" with "wond'rous light," and "eyes hazy with mist." Such a song, musically lambent, can sound phony when sung.

Located somewhere in between is *Suddenly*, an incidental film song from 1956. The A-section tune is very strong and pleasing, with its overall arching shape broken by tiny out-of-scale reversals. The transition from the second B back to A (Figure 7.7) is beautifully handled in a mighty satisfying chromatic progression along the bass-line leading to m. 21. The words, by Milton Raskin,

Figure 7.7

are so-so. This disjunction may be especially problematic when the melody is so strikingly contoured. A far-ranging line with big, fervent intervals is inherently gestural, and calls for bold words. As we have suggested, the relative frequency of this disjunction supports our generalization that "jazz songs" are not always satisfactory as unified entities.

In the same sort of club-jazz style is a 1964 song by Benny Carter called *Only Trust Your Heart*. The best moment is in a little eight-bar coda, in which a rising vocal motif trades off with a diminished-harmony descending piano echo. The Sammy Cahn words are good.

JOHNNY MANDEL (b. 1925)

With the work of Mandel, we move well past songs that are primarily "about the chords." Like Arlen's, Mandel's songs are carefully and beautifully composed in all respects. Mandel is an arranger and film score composer, with a strong jazz affinity, and a songwriter with a superb melodic–harmonic gift. Some of his songs, like *The Shadow of Your Smile* and *A Time for Love,* are among the most widely known of the half-century; yet his name is less familiar to the broad listening public than those of a number of lesser talents. His songs with the Bergmans are covered elsewhere. Here we examine songs of his with other lyricists.

The two songs mentioned were written in 1965 and 1966 with Paul Francis Webster, who supplied words for a number of movie "theme songs." Theme songs (and "title songs") are more than background music (though the melody may also be integrated into the background score and be heard many times), but they are not foregrounded either: they are not normally songs where a character in the film finds a dramatic reason to sing. Their presence is intended to express or deepen the emotional gist of the film. Often the words turn out to be journeyman work, since the viewer is not supposed to attend to them as verbal artifacts. Accordingly, many of the best tunes become used as "elevator music"—the lyrics drop away. However, *Shadow* has a very good lyric, with a verse that refers to the story of the film and then sets up the loving message of the chorus, intimating that memory of the lover's smile may outlast the love affair. There is a delicate chain of rhyming phrases, set on a musical sequence: "Now when I remember Spring, all the joy that love can bring, I will be remembering...." *A Time for Love* has an even more beautiful melody, with poised short phrases in the A-sections, moving down the scale, and longer ones in the lovely bridge. The song ends beautifully, with the only large interval used for the title phrase. In this case, the lyric strikes us as stilted ("...leaning out of window-sills, admiring the daffodils....").

With Johnny Mercer, Mandel wrote an exquisite film song, *Emily* (1964). Mercer's words are very fine. "As my eyes visualize a family / They see, dreamily, Emily too" is an extraordinary piece of lyric-writing, with its delicate off-rhyming and unobtrusive internal rhyme as well. The words *family, dreamily, Emily* are all set to a melodic figure, an upward fifth and downward third, used throughout but harmonized in varying ways. It gives a wistful character to sounding the name, but the figure also includes a top tone that is discordant: it is a raised 7, which seems to want to lead always to the upper key-tone but never does. This almost-triadic device might pall, but Mandel keeps the rest of the song moving through and around the basic triad, so that one hears a combination of yearning and completion.

With Dave Frishberg, himself a wonderful songwriter, Mandel has written several notable songs. *El Cajon* (1981) is a goofy number that demonstrates

Mandel's feeling for Latin jazz. It's bossa nova, with a funny story about loving and losing ("… without a car, without a phone … with just a whiff of her cologne.…") in, of all places, El Cajon, CA. As deft as the words are, the song works just fine as an instrumental.

Not so, however, with *You Are There* (1987), one of the most beautiful love songs of the half-century. The vocal range covers an octave and a third: *explores* would be a better verb, because the great feature of this song is the conversational pace and flexible rhythms in the voice line (Figure 7.8). The ad lib instruction is hardly necessary: it is all in the music and the words. First, a short phrase, to tell us where the speaker is. Then the thoughts spin out in phrases that run on, that butt up against each other, even as the voice climbs and falls back and climbs again. Ballads tend to come in even, well-contoured phrases and periods. But this one involves a welling-up of emotional thought, so full of momentum that it eases into triplets once in a while. Once it gets going, the vocal line hardly pauses. This is true also throughout the bridge, which does not bring in contrasting thought but simply changes key briefly. The final A-section has the same urgent pattern,

Figure 7.8

now extended from four bars to six-plus, with words on which a sensitive singer will hold for just a moment more. But the song is about remembered love, and near the end the writers slow the song down, as if the speaker is resting on his memories: "There's just one thing to do…pretend the dream is true…and tell myself that you are there," the word *you* glowing with emotion. The heartbreak comes in the word *pretend*, as the speaker admits what the reality is. It is one of the greatest endings we know; the song as a whole is, we dare to say, *sublime*.[17]

There are other Mandel songs nearly as beautiful. One is *Lovers After All* (1987), with words by the sometime-composer Richard Rodney Bennett. The opening melodic line uses eighth-notes in an open minor triad set on a weak tone of the main scale to lead to a lambent chord progression, ii-V-I. Mandel uses the spaced-apart triad figure throughout the song, both up and down. There is a full interlude, more than a bridge. The finest touch in the song occurs when Mandel sets "…our summers shade into fall" so that *shade into* happens on a slow triplet moving in half-tones: it is breathtaking.[18]

A 1966 song written with Peggy Lee, *The Shining Sea*, has a deceptively plain lyric with quite morbid undertones. The A-section vocal line uses another spread-apart triad plus the 6 and the 2, and there is a Strayhorn-like bridge with intervals of the sixth in odd juxtaposition. *Close Enough for Love* (1978), lyrics by Paul Williams, has a minor-mode theme-song-like melody, a big compass filled with little sequences; that is, melodic patterns shifted from tone to tone in the scale. The harmonic movement is exceptionally rich. The bridge ends gracefully. The verbal concept is interesting, "…not perfect yet, but close enough for love…," but the words render the song slightly soggy.

Mandel in a hard bop style is evident in the brilliant *Harry's House*, with bitter, cutting words by Jon Hendricks.

Among singers, especially, Mandel songs are greatly prized. Had he written full scores for theatrical productions, yielding sustained exposure over the years, rather than individual songs with a number of lyricists, Mandel would no doubt have had even more standards. His melodic gift, while controlled, is so stunning that one takes for granted the sophistication of the harmony—until one thinks of how many another composer might have squandered the first by failing at the second. He is the Vernon Duke of his era.

The beauty of Thad Jones's *To You* (1961) is basically in the chords, unlike his gorgeous song, *A Child Is Born*, with Wilder (p. 135). This probably reflects its origin as a Basie band instrumental for which Jon Hendricks later wrote good words.

Jazz pianist Tommy Flanagan's *The Bluebird* is a gorgeous but risky song, some phrases sounding like A-flat pentatonic, but most turning out to be in E-flat minor, with both 6 and 7 lowered; risky to sing because the melody line simply outlines these scales, and there is nothing in the harmony to ground the indeterminacy. The delicate, musing lyric, written in 2002 by Jay Leonhart, a distinguished bass player, which concerns a wished-for reassurance in love, uses just the right amount of rhyme—and nonrhyme, as with "Whisper near in my ear / gimme the good news," where *good news*, the last words of the song, stand by themselves. The fine-gauged quality of the lyric saves the song from seeming essentially instrumental in nature. This song inevitably brings to mind the Carmichael — Mercer *Skylark* (1942).[19]

A dark, introspective song by jazz pianist Patti Linardos, *There Is No Reason Why* (1982), is interesting in the way it threads the title phrase throughout the song, both as a phrase that leads forward to a completion and as a phrase that resignedly sums up observations just made. It hangs on the edge of being lugubrious. Less drastically gloomy is Jeremy Lubbock's *Not Like This* (1992), which has to do with how to end a love affair ("Did our feelings die the moment our love was over?").[20]

Peggy Lee wrote the lyric for *In the Days of Our Love* (1979), music by pianist Marian McPartland. It's a short song whose B-section takes up half the length. The wistful words, about remembering a bygone love, are written in three long thoughts, and the music is constructed correspondingly. It's a pretty wisp of a song.

Alan Broadbent's 1991 song, *Heart's Desire*, is as beautiful an example of a song "all about the chords" as any we know. The opalescent lyrics by Dave Frishberg, about the risk of seeking love but the overcoming need to do so, push the song further, into an emotional alembic. The coda is especially moving (Figure 7.9).[21]

Figure 7.9

The Singer-Songwriters

The usual short explanation for the supposed decline of the classic American popular song, beginning in the 1950s, is that rock came onto the scene, so songwriters stopped writing in the older style. This is too simple a model. In terms of radio play and record sales, rock and related song forms certainly captured "the market," but that market was new, younger, and larger. Rock certainly succeeded classic pop as dominant in our musical culture, but it did not necessarily replace it, any more than the development of opera in the 1500s eliminated the motet.

In chapter 2, we called attention to the huge impact of technology on the very conception of the "popular song" and on its reception in society. At the extreme, the hard-rock "song" was completely different, the avatar of mass technosonic primitivism, and incommensurable with the classic song. Classic pop continued to exist, but it adapted to a narrower niche.

There was, however, another development in popular music that did, we believe, have a direct effect on classic pop song. The songs of the singer-songwriters of the 1960s and 1970s were in mixed styles, sometimes "light rock" but sometimes folk, country, blues, or jazz idioms or blends thereof. They had words that could be heard, and accompaniments that required only one or a few instruments. Thus there was considerable formal continuity with classic pop. However, the "attitude" of the songs tended to be different.

There had been "singer-songwriters" in the classic pop period, such as Mercer, Frishberg, or Dearie. But the songs of Joni Mitchell, James Taylor, Janis Ian, Carole King, and their cohort clearly fall outside the scope of this book. Bob Dylan, Bruce Springsteen, and others lying toward the hard-rock pole fall further outside it, while the songs of certain other singer-songwriters we mention below lie closer. We offer here only some differentiating generalizations.

In terms of formal aspects, Mitchell et al. created songs that tended to be much longer, less compact, more sectional. The typical songs of this genre are not in arch, closed, or binary format, but progress by repeating and adding-on. Where, musically speaking, classic pop is *intensive*—short, shapely, contoured, closed—these songs are *extensive*, improvisatory in feel, linear and sectional in form. It is perhaps like listening to a reading of a poem versus that of a short story. The impression is often that of a reversion to much older folk or ballad songs, where the song goes on until it stops. Very often the songs have many stanzas: the story line is complicated, though the main message can be often reiterated. Some sections will sound rather like verses in classic pop, sketching in some background, while other sections will take on a more urgent communicative quality.

The songs are more horizontal, flatter in shape than classic pop. Normally, the voice line is less contoured, and less functionally tied to chord changes. The chords may stay the same for a number of bars. Key changes also seem arbitrary: they may, or may not, occur with each new section. Thus the melodic-harmonic texture is more porous. The rhythmic pulse may be changeable and loose, including bars with a different number of beats or phrases that have no regular scansion. If the typical pace of a medium-tempo classic pop song is the even, brisk walk, the movement of these later songs can be irregular or shambling.

The sense of a vocal line working its way to set points (half-cadences, for example), and of familiar transitional chords (dominant sevenths, perhaps) leading into and out of a "middle section," is often missing. A classic popular song turns in tonal space, it pivots on chord changes. The singer-songwriter's song moves linearly, more nearly in one plane.

The vocal range will be narrower, the intervals smaller. On the whole, less "voice" is needed, and the singing style is less presentational, more seemingly inward, than in classic pop. This may reflect the case that the singer-songwriters were often untrained as vocalists; or that they did not want their songs to sound "sung."

The small range and unsteady pace may also reflect that they typically sang while accompanying themselves on the guitar. By and large, it is harder to sound harmonically complex chords, to move very quickly from chord to chord, to effect big dynamic shifts while playing the guitar, which is slower to "speak" than a piano moderately well played.

Generally speaking, the words are fitted less exactly to the voice line, with no great premium put on point-to-point alignment of voice to musical element. Some syllables stretch over several notes, and there are little throwaway or commenting verbal elements that are essentially unpitched. Most lyrics deliberately use "faint rhyme" or loose lexical parallelism of a kind that would be considered inept in classic pop, though it is actually the norm in some folksong traditions. Moreover, many of these songs use modal melody and harmony, with a downplaying of 3 as a crucial tone.[22] Of course, all this is a matter of degree, which is why the classic pop genre and the singer-songwriter genre are not totally incommensurable. Joni Mitchell's *Both Sides Now* is very close to 32 bars, diatonic major, regular eight-bar periods, and AABC format.

These comments are not intended to hold the singer-songwriters to an irrelevant set of standards, or to deny that their songs are artful, but to point out some intrinsic stylistic differences. As yet we have only touched on the most obvious aspect of singer-songwriter songs. The entire verbal and topical universe is distinctly different. Joni Mitchell and Bob Dylan are among the important folk-poets of the half-century,[23] comparable in importance to Allen Ginsberg or Charles Olson, and songwriters like Janis Ian or Dory Langdon are not far behind. Although weak specimens often sound unedited, the best lyrics are a pleasure simply to read. The words are of governing importance: they have primacy over other elements of the song, and they call attention to themselves in a way that classic pop words do not. As to topic, the words are highly personal, often political—and here, the personal is often the political. Autobiographical implications are understood, and detailed revelations about drug use, the particulars of sex, mental distress, suicide, anger at or emotional distance from society, are the norm. These are not the subject matters of classic pop.

Some of the songs are confessional, recounting experiences that may evoke empathetic responses or elicit a fascinated but alienated effect (e.g., Mitchell's *California,* many of Laura Nyro's early songs). They can be defiant, like Langdon's antisexist *tours de force.* At other times, especially with Mitchell, the words are highly imagistic, amounting to sets of figures of speech that, taken together, construct a mood or attitude by clouds or chains of metaphor.

On both the verbal and the musical levels, it is a matter of balance. James Taylor's *Secret O' Life* opens with 11 repetitions of one note, the 5, preceded and followed by a minor third, setting an assertion: "The secret of life is enjoying the passage of time." Harold Arlen's and Johnny Mercer's classic pop song, *Come Rain or Come Shine,* opens with 13 repetitions of one note, the 3, followed by a major third: it sets a promise: "I'm going to love you like nobody's loved you...." Both have the same loose, pattering rhythm, maybe dactylic, maybe trochee/ iamb blended, with a slight hint of something beguine-like. Although the Arlen phrase develops over a set of audible chord changes, one per bar, while the Taylor phrase has only one harmonic event, the two songs make a similar effect—for a while. Then they diverge. The Arlen song moves into a second period of A, almost identical with the first, and thence into a release, as classic pop format dictates. Taylor's first phrase is succeeded by a couple of short, rifflike comments, and then moves into a long phrase that is intriguingly like, but different from, the first. Moreover, the "speech register" is different; Mercer's involves an *I–You* form of address, Taylor's a generalized observation.

We have claimed (p. 17) that the play of identification between singer and hearer, in classic pop songs, is crucial. No doubt that process takes place in these songs of the 1960s and 1970s, but the relationship is different. Many of the songs seem to involve the speaker in relation to some Other, with the listener a privileged auditor. Carly Simon's *You're So Vain* is a famous example. The genius of the verbal aspects of the songs lies in their "authenticity," an aesthetic and moral personal goal common to the period. When a singer sings a song he has written about himself, when he lays it all out, confesses, reveals—one attends, as one does to anyone in distress or exaltation. In an important sense, these song words are more naturalistic, in regard to both topic and illocutionary style, than is the case with classic popular song.

There is a gain, but also a cost. An excess of highly worked imagism can become precious, and serve simply to signal that something "poetic" is happening. There can be a narrowness of cultural reference: the urban White folk-style of some of the writers we mention here is as culturally circumscribed as the urbane White pop world of earlier eras. There is a danger in making "authenticity" the hallmark of "good" song: the notion of artistic correctness can become an aesthetic straitjacket. We often wish that even the best of these songs would move along more quickly, more tersely, with more rhythmic bite; but they cannot, because they have a lot of told / felt experience to get through. Finally, let's face it, what seems revelatory at age 17 can seem tiresome at 30.

We readily concede the large degree of stylistic variation in the songs of "singer-songwriters." Many of Mitchell's songs sound like jazz to us, especially when she began to play her own piano. Most of Phoebe Snow's do. Some of Janis Ian's songs are essentially AABA pop in form (like *Jesse*, AAB plus a tiny C), and very nice for that. Paul Simon's *Bridge Over Troubled Waters* is clearly related to gospel or hymn style, while *Still Crazy After All These Years* is closer to classic pop. The songs of Harry Nilsson or Harry Chapin sound to us like inert pop, while some of the songs of Tom Waits sound like very good pop (see p. 201). We like the ebullient or tender songs of Stevie Wonder, such as the fizzy *Isn't She Lovely?*, the eloquent *Blame It On the Sun*, or the beautiful, deep, *All In Love Is Fair*.

If Joni Mitchell is the finest poet of this cohort, Randy Newman may be, overall, the finest songwriter. His words are laconic, evocative; his musical forms are versatile, often sounding tried-and-true yet innovative. A few are pleasant pastiche, like *Dayton, Ohio—1903*), harking back to the parlor song tradition. Others, like *I Think It's Going to Rain Today* (1966), mix styles: triadic and diatonic in most passages, pentatonic and harmonically ambiguous in the bridge. *Louisiana* (1974) and *Short People* (1977) are in ironic barbershop style. Most Newman songs seem at least like relatives of the classic pop song. But they are not really in that genre, owing to the pervasive irony evident in the texts. The beautiful *Sail Away* (1972) is about the slave trade; *Suzanne* (1970) is the song of a rapist; *Short People* is about bigotry.

To recapitulate: It was not the onset of rock that directly threatened those who wrote in classic popular style, though that may have disheartened them. The work of the singer-songwriters, however, faced those writers with a real dilemma. These new songs were strikingly communicative, and often of high quality, especially poetic. Almost any young professional working around 1975 or later, we suspect, must have wondered down deep whether writing in any way other than "like that" was now old-fashioned or artificial. We offer here two different cases.

John Bucchino has written theater scores and film songs but, since the 1990s, has enjoyed most success with individual songs. His songs are post-classic pop in style, showing a narrative approach in flexible, light-rock rhythms, the repetition of rather minimal chord patterns, and a basically diatonic vocal line. Typically, the form is some version of ABA but with this pattern often repeated, so that the songs feel long without seeming to cumulate. Thus they continue the singer-songwriter tradition, and, like those songs, often deal with unusual, naturalistic subject matters. There is a male hustler and a good-time girl who meet on a bus as they "run away to another skin" (*Sweet Dreams*); instant sexual attraction ("I know you're kissable for grinning up that spark," from *That Smile*); a woman going through with a quick encounter she doesn't seem to want ("We do what we have to"), and then going upstairs to kiss her sleeping husband's bald head (*Sepia Life*). Bucchino's interpretive directions at the top of his songs tell one that he wants to achieve small dramas in these songs; for example, *lightly, with neuroses*. Sometimes the stories are compelling, as with *Not a Cloud In the Sky* (to be sung *with clenched precision*). When they are, it is mostly due to Bucchino's gift for expressing (in nonformal syntax) the ordinary texture of ordinary lives, usually in interior monologue; for example, from the last-named song, "White-knuckle grip on the slip of a thought." When such thought patterns emerge in natural speech rhythm, they sound veridical; but very often the voice line is set in what seems to us an artificially casual metrical texture, with the important words falling off the beat, for reasons we do not understand, unless it is to suggest that the speaker is making up the words as he goes along—an effect that works the first time but is not convincing when the song is heard again. Some of Bucchino's songs, like *In a Restaurant By the Sea*, attain a moody imagistic poetry: "...for a moment eyes collide / and the world's periphery...on a liquid afternoon." Or, from *This Moment* (1999), "Curve of face, warmth of hands, butterfly / Pin in place when it lands ** Try!" Musically, however, he often seems to us unambitious.

By contrast, the 1990s songs of Canadian singer-songwriter K. D. Lang, written with Ben Mink, are in a superromantic popular song style and in familiar formats. *Save Me* is ABAB, plus coda, *Miss Chatelaine* is AABA, while *Still Thrives This Love* is an unusual AABAB in which each section is organized into units of three elements. There is little that is innovative but much that is satisfying, melodically, harmonically (there are dazzling jazz-style voicings), and rhythmically. The popularity of Lang's songs toward the end of the twentieth century may have been due to the beauty of her singing voice, but the songs also reflect a post-classic-pop sensibility in their concepts and lyrics. The personal approach to life and love must remind one of the singer-songwriter generation of the 1960s and 1970s; for example, "Clouds of qualm burst into sunshine," from the second song, or "Earnings of labor may ever show," from the third, or "I've been outside myself for so long," from a good song called *Outside Myself*. There is a poetic approach, in these songs, where the figure of speech overrides normal syntax, but not arbitrarily so and not so as to work against the musical movement. The material is old, yet new again.

Notes

1. Performance: Nancy LaMott, "My Foolish Heart," Midder CD 003.
2. Performance: Sandra King and Richard Rodney Bennett, "Making Beautiful Music Together," Audiophile CD 268.
3. Performance: Susannah McCorkle, "Sabia," Concord CD 4418.
4. Performance: Judy Garland, "Alone," Capitol LP T835.
5. Performance: Mabel Mercer, "Merely Marvelous," Atlantic LP 1322.
6. Performance: Shirley Horn, "Collectibles," Columbia CD 5618.
7. Performance: As good as Charles's is Shirley Horn, "I Love You, Paris," Verve CD 314523486.
8. Performance: Michael Feinstein, "Only One Life," Concord CD 2203.
9. Performance: Tony Bennett, "The Art of Excellence," Columbia LP FC40344.
10. An enlightening discussion of the later-lyrics issue is given by Furia. Wilder covers some of the songs from the 1930s and 1940s.
11. There are other fine unpublished songs that could be located through the Ellington office, Tempo Music, New York. Fortunately, "Pousse-Café" has been recorded as a sort of retrospective original cast album featuring Barer, the estimable singer Barbara Lea, and the wonderful jazz pianist Ellis Larkins (Audiophile CD 263).
12. Performance: Daryl Sherman, "Born To Swing," Audiophile CD 316.
13. Performances of this song and of *Pretty Girl*, Andy Bey, "Shades of Bey," Evidence CD 22215.
14. Performance: Nancy LaMott, "My Foolish Heart," Midder Music CD 003.
15. Performances: Shirley Horn, "You Won't Forget Me," Verve CD 847482.
16. Performance of *Time and Tide*: Buddy Barnes, "Talkin' With My Pal," Audiophile CD 294.
17. Performance: Irene Kral, "You Are There," Audiophile CD 299.
18. Performance: Rosemary Clooney, "Girl Singer," Concord CD 4496.
19. Performance: Marlene VerPlanck, "Speaking Of Love," Audiophile CD 320.
20. Performances of these two songs: Mark Murphy, "I'll Close My Eyes," Muse CD 5436.
21. Performance: Joyce Breach and Richard Rodney Bennett, "Lovers After All," Audiophile CD 282.
22. A crude definition of "modal" would be, involving scales neither major nor minor.
23. Mitchell's importance is more strictly poetic, more a matter of means. Further out on the spectrum, Dylan's style is more nearly that of an altered musical discourse reflecting a new literary stance in pop music, comparable to that of Woody Guthrie's in relation to country-folk.

8
Sondheim and After

STEPHEN SONDHEIM (b. 1930)

Sondheim has been producing songs of quality for fifty years. We have waited to discuss his work, for several reasons. In a sense, his work brackets that of Frank Loesser's, with whom we opened chapter 4. Loesser was the first songwriter in the second half of the twentieth century to secure his place in the top echelon of classic American popular song creators, while Sondheim is the last composer indisputably to gain that rank. And each wrote both words and music.

The great period of Loesser's career lasted only about fifteen years, being finished by about 1960, while Sondheim's noteworthy work had begun by the mid-1950s. By our criteria, Sondheim arguably ceased working in classic popular style sometime in the late 1980s—but his is the much longer run. There is another sense in which the two are not alike. Loesser is understood as a culmination of a long tradition of popular song; he had no obvious followers. Sondheim, beginning about midcareer, had a very strong influence on younger songwriters, in two ways.

First, in terms of his fundamental commitment to musicodramatic innovation and to finding a contemporary style for theater songs, he is not like Loesser but more like Kern and Hammerstein (with "Show Boat") or Rodgers and Hammerstein (with "Oklahoma!" and "Carousel").[1] Some aspects of this influence on the field of those writing for the theater will be touched on in the next section. Second, his mature songs *as songs* have, as a group, a unique character that some have found so distinctive as to cause them to distinguish Sondheim from all other great writers in the tradition. Like Kern, the first in the pantheon, Sondheim's particular combination of melodic and harmonic originality is new.

There are those who find Sondheim's songs unromantic, cynical, alienated, overly worked; others find the same songs intelligent, trenchant, moving in their honesty, brilliant in their literary and musical sophistication. Our attitude will be evident as we discuss Sondheim's songs; we simply note here that songwriters of the last quarter of the twentieth century no doubt regarded Sondheim's range of reference and style as "modern" or psychologically true to life in a way that went beyond the excellence they heard in, say, Cy Coleman.

When some who love the song tradition that joins Kern to Yeston say that they just don't care for Sondheim, they often mean that they do not respond to the topics or situations of his songs, as expressed most obviously in the lyrics. But there is, perhaps, a more strictly musical disquiet. In general, Sondheim's harmony tends to be complex, in using added tones to color the main line, and in avoiding standard chord changes simply to achieve variety. His approach, sometimes called nonfunctional harmony (p. 30), is very evident in his most famous ballad, *Send In the Clowns*, which has very few important chord changes per se, but many subtle harmonic colorations. After a point, the use of "added tones" in harmony results in a sort of compound tonality, that is, the presence of two basic triads at once, and often the impression of the song's being in the stated key but also a little bit in another key at the same time. The net effect is, perhaps paradoxically, to direct attention away from the harmonic structure and toward the note-by-note progress of the melodic line. It is not that harmony becomes less important, but that it becomes less semiotic in its implications. Moving a song through a familiar sequence of tonal centers is no longer that interesting—to Sondheim, and to those who like him. Others may disagree.

Although his first great successes came as a lyricist (for "West Side Story" and "Gypsy," whose songs are covered elsewhere), Sondheim always intended to write both words and music. Five years out of college, he came within a whisker of having a musical produced on Broadway, providing both. At least two of these songs, from 1954, hold up beautifully. *What More Do I Need?* is a song about being young, happy, and in love—in New York. It has a modest but poised melodic compass, and a marked lilt, especially in its exultant pause after *more* in the title phrase, often repeated. In addition, already fully evident with this writer, there is a rueful kind of wit built on the limitations of modern or urban life: "I can see * half a tree," or "Hear the lovely pneumatic * drill." *So Many People* is a love song of quality. A stand-alone song from 1956, *The Girls of Summer*, is an insinuating pop-blues, with an upward-going first phrase balanced nicely by a falling last phrase in each stanza; in it, the singer combines a yearning for sexual experience with just a bit of relief that she has missed it.[2]

The songs from the farce, "A Funny Thing Happened on the Way to the Forum" (1962), are in a grab-bag of Broadway styles, as if proving Sondheim's versatility. The ballads are slight. The memorable songs are rough-and-tumble comedic ones. *Comedy Tonight* is self-defining: "Something appealing / something appalling... Nothing portentous or polite," all in a rollicking mazurkalike rhythm. *Everybody Ought to Have a Maid* is a brilliant piece of male chauvinism. The tune, in its lively dotted tap-dance rhythm, with fast triplets on strong beats, may be effective only when staged like vaudeville. But the lyrics as lyrics are outrageous without being offensive: three old guys holding off senescence by talking dirty, and glorying in it. What should be emphasized about the funny, complicated words is that they are technically perfect in terms of scansion and ease of pronunciation. If one simply says the words at a normal speech tempo, what results are the exact rhythms that Sondheim specifies.

Two of Sondheim's loveliest early songs are from an original television show, a fantasy called "Evening Primrose" (1966). A beautiful soliloquy, *I Remember*, is a long (62-bar) song of troubled recollection. It has two B-sections and five A-sections, three of which are extended to be a little longer than expected, as if the speaker needs just a bit more time to complete the moment's thought. The lyric is built throughout on similes, where the speaker ponders how *x* was like *y*. The delicacy of the figures of speech are noteworthy: as one example, "I remember trees / Bare as coat-racks / spread like broken umbrellas"; so is the musical setting. The recurring opening musical motif (Figure 8.1) uses intervals of mixed minor and major thirds for very short phrases, each ending on a whole note, as the speaker pauses to think further, and the thought in progress does not complete until the fourth bar. The beginning of that bar is where one hears

Figure 8.1

where one first perceives the key. The use of thirds, and the short phrases over a simple harmonic progression, vi-ii-V-I and its variants, evoke a pervasive hesitation, reinforced in the A$_2$ and A$_4$ sections by stretching them to 10 bars, over a long dominant in the bass. But all the recollections are fading: by the end of the song: "I remember days / or at least I try / but as years go by / they're a sort of haze." Much of the pathos of the song comes from the way in which the apex notes ("rememb-*er*") in successive phrases are lifted gradually up, and then down, in intervals that can sound ambiguously major or minor.

From the same source comes the magnificent ballad, *Take Me to the World*. In this great song, all of Sondheim's strengths are already present. The writer begins, before the words start, with a distinctive composed figure, in the upper part of the tenor register, occurring over six beats (and two bars), with a midpause. This might be called a "vamp," except that it does not exactly recur in the song; call it an expressive element. It sets out close relations of tones 1, 2, and 3 of the main key, and by diminishment (the use of a D-flat against C) yields a brief very strong dissonance within the weaker dissonance of D against the key-tone C. Before the words begin, this aurally mesmerizing figure establishes the harmonic (which is to say, emotional) color to be heard throughout.

It is, moreover, an anticipation of the opening melodic phrase, not only tonally but in rhythm. One of Sondheim's characteristic gestures involves, to use a spatial metaphor, a pattern of rock and step. The first five notes and words are in an oscillating pattern, back and forth; then there is a step and a step, involving two longer notes; then, a return to the back-and-forth. Or one could think in terms of small steps and small retreats, then a more confident move, then a bigger retreat. Note that the rocking eighth-notes are not simply a complex upbeat, but start on the beat, which gives them force. The pattern is like that of a late Renaissance court dance (Figure 8.2). That rock-and-step pattern is an important "horizontal" feature of how the song moves through time. The D/E oscillation as the words begin also imparts a sense of underlying triads alternating quickly (G major, C major), and this too lasts throughout.

Within the first four measures there are at least two other notable elements. Under the first long-held word is a lovely "French" chord which does not at all change the main tonality, but dots it with a touch of color. It is an instantaneous harmonic change without implying anything about key change. And at the end of m.3, we hear what amounts to a countermelody in the tenor, which involves a new rhythm, a dotted-eighth on the uppermost tone, and uses for the first time tones in the upper part of the tonic octave. Sondheim uses similar upper-octave countermotives throughout the song.

The song is in perfect ABAB form. At m.9 Sondheim moves the melody to the upper portion of the octave, now with downward steps, brings in his countermelody very prominently (in the left hand), and uses an elegant chord progression, a circle of upward fourths and downward fifths, to return to the opening of

Figure 8.2

A_2. In the B-section, Sondheim uses another of his now-familiar features, chords that use the common triads but spaced so that the tones are inverted and wide apart. Sondheim seems to like intervals of the sixth, supporting the voice, for their open ring. It is a style that serves him well in many songs.

As is normal in an ABAB song, the climax of the song comes at the end of the final B, where Sondheim not only lifts the line to its tonal apex but uses a very prominent Scotch-snap rhythmic figure, an eighth followed by a dotted-quarter, the stress on the first short note. After 30 bars of the rocking figure, it is a stunning effect.

The lyric of this song is plain but wistful. The title phrase (with variants) is often repeated in the song, at the beginnings of phrases, thus underscoring the longing of the speaker, never assuaged.[3]

In the title song from "Anyone Can Whistle" (1964), one hears the same rhythmic gesture, small steps then retreat, or move/pause, as in the opening phrase: "Any-one can whistle [six syllables] / that's what they say [four] / easy." The interjection *easy*, minute but forceful, is also a feature of Sondheim's work, and an important one: it brings a natural vernacular tone to the speech and it puts air into a musical line without derailing it. Its effectiveness is clear when, at the end of the song, the writer avoids it, at a corresponding point, in favor of a sustained four-clause, 18-syllable statement. Many of Sondheim's best songs begin hesitantly, move here and there, circle around, and then come to an emotionally strong conclusion. Musically, this can be seen as a method of gradual motivic development; it is also true to life in dramatic terms. Sondheim rarely uses introductory verses to set scenes or sketch character, but builds psychological development and revelation of character into the body of his songs.

From the same show comes an exultant song, *There Won't Be Trumpets*. It starts with a by-now typical small-compass melodic phrase, but the highest tone of the phrase is shifted, as the song goes along, from tone to tone, going generally higher until it ends one tone above the upper key-tone—a big-finish device that many have used rather blatantly, but that works commandingly here. The song has some tiny dotted-rhythm surprises in its longest lines, at the end of stanzas, and a brief middle section set in an entirely new rhythm. The burden of the words is: Who needs trumpets, when the right person comes along?

With So Little to Be Sure Of is a wonderfully made, touching, nonmaudlin ballad that should be considered by anyone who finds Sondheim obscure. It opens with another instance of a few oscillating quick notes, a turn, followed by two longer ones, the phrase coming to rest with a nice grammatical challenge, the preposition *of* ending the phrase. The phrases get longer and longer, with expressive chords occurring at phrase ends, the intervals get wider, up and down, and the emotional impact accumulates, with some fine lines like, "Being sure enough of you / Makes me sure enough of me." The final A-section brings back the title phrase, but now with *of* set on a low note, touchingly, before the words "in this world [on a fine diminished chord] is you."[4]

"Company" (1970) contained a couple of songs that, for Sondheim, were hits, including the brilliantly mordant *The Ladies Who Lunch*, whose title phrase is nicely set, so as to avoid triplet monotony, and *Being Alive*, the latter of which seems to us rather grandiose in its text and musical layout, especially at the end of its B-section. *The Little Things You Do Together*, however, is a witty song that manages to be dense (in its compound rhymes) and airy (in its rhythms) simultaneously. As for the former: "pursue together... accrue together... misconstrue together," as well as many other examples. As for the rhythm, the song sounds in a very strong two beats per measure, but heaviness is avoided by the use of midbar syncopations and by truncating phrases with a series of short notes, followed either by long rests or by an immediate resumption of the text, without the kind of time-out (empty beats) between phrases characteristic of most songs. The absence of notes where expected, contrasted with the enjambment of words at other junctures, is extremely sophisticated and inherently witty. Though the B-section is short, regular, and driving in rhythm, there is also an interlude, almost manically vaudevillian, that functions as another B-section.

With regard to the tone of the text, it is lyrics like, "Neighbors you annoy together, Children you destroy together, that keep marriage intact," which may underlie the widely held opinion that Sondheim's songs are "cynical." True, a song like this lays about with a swingeing vehemence. We simply point out that some of Sondheim's theatrical subjects are inherently bitter in the nature of the plot and the situation of the characters. Sondheim puts the demands of drama ahead of the lure of writing hits. Later in his career, his subject-matter tended to change: certainly, "Pacific Overtures," "Into the Woods," and "Passion" haven't a whiff of cynicism to them, though there is sometimes anger and always wit.

Also apparent, by the time of "Company," is the fact that Sondheim often writes fast songs with lots of words that are too verbally intricate to be easily comprehended. To be sure, *Another Hundred People* is fast and furious because it limns the quality of life in New York City, while (Not) *Getting Married Today*, with its amusing churchy interludes, depicts a person on the verge of breakdown. But *You Could Drive a Person Crazy*, with its looping, indeed loopy, rhythms, is at once terribly funny, truly revealing of the character of the person being addressed—and almost impossible to "hear" the first time through. "When a person's personality is personable" is a great line, but is not really audible in the song, at tempo. This leads some auditors to call Sondheim "too clever."

Can a songwriter be too clever? Of course; W. S. Gilbert was often overall-literative and verbose. As we have said, Sondheim has generally put dramatic function first. Pragmatically, it means that numbers like the three just mentioned make a highly stimulating effect in the theater, but will be little heard outside it. On the other side of it, Sondheim can come up with a sure-fire, almost cheekily deft, ensemble number like *Side by Side ** By Side* (the ellipsis is the point of the song), by taking an old formula, the togetherness song, and tweaking it so that it refers not to a duo but to a trio (or more): "One's impossible, two is dreary / Three is company, safe and cheery."

That Sondheim can write in any established Broadway style is evident in the songs from "Follies" (1971), a show whose songs are mostly in pastiche. *Broadway Baby* is a razzle-dazzle, Broadway-blues strut, heavy on the strong beats, full of insider lore in the lyrics, of the sort that show-biz dames have stopped the show with for a half-century or more. *I'm Still Here* is very superior pastiche, in an unusual and supple meter, 12/8. The very well-known *Losing My Mind* is, of course, a torch song, and a fairly grim one. It has a memorable gestural pattern of distinct short phrases across which the speaker's thoughts connect. It's in a "sad major" mode, which is unusual. We find it a bit *tragique*.

The most remarkable song in the show is *Too Many Mornings*. It is a difficult song, taking the approach and attitude of *Take Me to the World* into emotionally darker and harmonically deeper territory. It too has a composed brief introduction (again, not a "vamp") that signals the harmonic essence of the entire song, chords with 7 and 9 prominent, sometimes vertically, sometimes spread horizontally over several beats, as in m.21 below (Figure 8.3). The song tends to linger in a given key despite the presence of tones foreign to that scale, e.g., the E-sharps in m.23. Yet the song does change key, at fairly long intervals, by means of a slightly prolonged note over a complex bitonal chord, as at the end of m.24 (and later, over the similar words "All the nights" and "All those times"). Such chords are characteristic of mature Sondheim. They are in part "functional," in that they change the key, at least transitorily, but they are at the same time specifically expressive of the emotional import of the text at that moment, by virtue of their color and density. In the end, the song comes abruptly into a last new key, in clear diatonic harmony without added tones and without complex chords. It's an old technique, common to Richard Strauss and many others: achieving a final radiance by entering at last into a zone of harmonic simplicity.

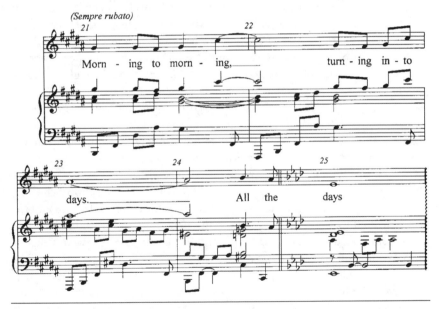

Figure 8.3

Another fine feature of this song is the asymmetry of the opening period. The first phrase, "Too many mornings," lies over two strong beats, the next phrase, "waking and pretending I reach for you," stretches over four, including an anticipatory syncope. Any possible banality of the ending is avoided by a sequence of passionate parallel phrases: "Someone standing at the door / Someone moving to the bed / Someone resting in my arms...." Not the usual popular song, in sense or sound, but all the finer for that.

"A Little Night Music" (1973) is Sondheim's sophisticated and brilliant homage to operetta, and to Ingmar Bergman's famous film, "Smiles of a Summer Night," with its sheen of moonstruck romantic delirium. The entire score is in rapturous but crisp triple rhythms: the waltz, the mazurka, the scherzo, depending on what is appropriate in tempo and verbal emphasis.

The show was a tour de force, with words—lots of words, of the most accomplished quality. But the music does not take second place. Those who carelessly say that Sondheim doesn't write great tunes need only listen to the opening instrumental slow waltz (cum mazurka), known by the title of the show. It is the equivalent of anything written by Rodgers, famous for his fine waltz tunes. The opening strain is subtly harmonized with major seventh dissonances and a momentarily raised 5. The next strain brings the focused ringing of tight-third intervals, but they are, as a set, highly chromatic, with an acid sound to them. Then there is an obvious dip and bow in the line. The composer did provide fine words for vocal performance, including the incomparable phrase, "The hands on the clock turn, but don't sing a nocturne...."

The beautifully integrated score, including much ensemble work, yielded no hit songs. With one big exception: *Send in the Clowns*, Sondheim's biggest hit as a composer-lyricist. The song, we think, became so popular because of the traditional diatonic nature of the melody, with strong reliance on both 4 and 6, so that the entire scale is used more or less evenly; the relaxed steady 12/8 meter without rhythmic interruption; and the spread-out, harplike horizontal nature of the underlying harmony, which is always moving somewhere, but gradually. Given the troubled words, it is a curiously soothing song. The E-flat major tonality gives way imperceptibly to a G-minor bridge that still retains the even triplet character in the voice line. The finest touch in the song is the use of big *Luftpausen*, carving out short phrases, as at "Sure of my lines ** no one is there." Otherwise, the song seems to us a bit monotonous in its unbroken rhythmic movement through just two main keys.

With "Sweeny Todd, the Demon Barber of Fleet Street" (1979), Sondheim set himself the challenge of a show in the louche style of Grand Guignol. His version of British melodrama was at once funny and terrifying, and contained several fast multistanza numbers with complicated and brilliant lyrics, most famously, *A Little Priest*, as funny a song as any ever written. For our purposes there are three songs to note. *Green Finch and Linnet Bird* begins with a simple, predictable melody that creeps along the scale of the main key (sounding all the tones in the first long phrase) and then sounds its triad. The accompaniment softens the scalar effect by including fourth, sixth, and raised seventh intervals. But then, as so often with Sondheim, the song struggles to stay in the home key. In m.4 the bass slips down a tone, then a half-tone, then another half, even while the "home" key of D flat is still arguably present. But only arguably: the G-natural of the melody in m.5 and the E-natural in the next bar send the song briefly into nondiatonic modes. By m.9 we seem to be in the key of B flat dominant to E flat, but it misleads. In m.10 notes foreign to the scale are present again in the voice line, while the bass shifts up a half-tone. In sum, there is plenty of "modulation" in the song, but it is always to local effect (Figure 8.4). The combination of conventional scalar voice line with ambiguous harmonies beneath it is a familiar aspect of the classic popular song. In Sondheim's case, the complex harmony has always been there, but not with the scalar tune. As for the words, the "altered" notes in *jubilate, cages, beckoning* are superbly expressive of the notion of something beautiful but caged, yearning to break free, a sense first heard as an observer's question at the up-going triad for "how is it you sing?" and then in the acidic musical touch that undercuts the formal, positive word *jubilate.* The lyric includes a number of words, such as *whence* and *damask,* that impart a period tone. This is song writing of the most sensitive, subtle quality.

The song is formally interesting in its layout. As befits a meditation or an apostrophe to a bird that is caged—and to the speaker's self, also caged—the song is made up of two basic musical patterns, organized in paragraphs that get longer and longer, but broken by questioning interludes; for example, "Are you crowing... Are you screaming?" The form of the song is not an arch but a systole–diastole alternation.

Another ballad, *Not While I'm Around,* is one of Sondheim's gravest and loveliest. It does move in functional harmony through conventional tonal centers, but in an entirely fresh way. It begins with the Sondheim trademark of four hesitating steps followed by two deliberate ones, set over the familiar interval of the sixth: "Nothing's gonna harm you," with the first four syllables on eighth-notes, the last two on half-notes. It includes his brief-phrase interjections ("No, sir" and "I don't care") that keep the language in the vernacular. At the climax of the song, he manages a powerful linguistic effect. He writes, "But in time... Nothing can harm you, not while I'm around." *Time* and *I'm* are both set on high notes, and of course they rhyme. But they involve different parts of speech: *time* is a common noun, relevant to the overall meaning of the song; *I'm* is a contraction, of the all-important pronoun *I* and the basic verb *to be.* Such unexpected rhymes take on tremendous force, through the effect of surprise. Phonologically they are pure rhymes, but, syntactically, psychologically, they are off-rhymes: they do not occupy parallel grammatical "slots." They momentarily shake up thought.

Figure 8.4

There is an important category, unnamed, of popular song that expresses an uncomplicated appreciation of desire: not torch songs, not empty-bed laments, not songs of sexual innuendo, like many of Porter's—but not naïve songs, either, just naturalistically sexy. In our cultural conditioning, they tend to convey a male attitude toward women. The character of *Pretty Women* is given by the expressive marking *Languid*, and by the nature of the first melodic figure. It is a quick turn, involving half-steps like sensual caresses, flirting with the tonic tone. The figure is also set firmly on the first beat in each measure, and is kept terse, as is typical of Sondheim's style. This imparts to the rhythm a masculine, proud quality, as in a Spanish dance. The song, though in 3/4 time, is no waltz.

As is so often the case with Sondheim, the entire song is constructed on the opening short motif and its underlying chords, major going to minor and back. All the chords are enriched with 7 and 9 and 11, infusing quite stable triads with color (surprising in the chord under -*ing* in m.4). Principally, the hearer is aware of the basic figure set at different pitch zones—and of the proud forceful rhythm (Figure 8.5, mm. 1–7). In terms of format, the song is highly repetitive. There is no contrasting middle section. The structure is $A_1 8$, $A_2 8$, $A_1 8$, $A_2 8$, $A_{1+2} 8$, with

Figure 8.5

Figure 8.5 Continued.

an interpolated measure after the final A$_2$ and a three-bar tag added to the end, for a total of 44 bars. To conclude the song Sondheim brings in the turn figure (m.34), with the expected words but with an anticipatory *Ah*. Rhythmic excitement is generated by the simplest of means (Figure 8.5, mm. 34–35). Instead of an isolated figure of four sixteenth-notes, followed by rests or longer notes, the songwriter intensifies the movement of the song by using long strings of sixteenth-notes, three sets at a time reiterating the same opening pitch. Here the absence of longer notes and rests means also that the verbal material is thicker and more elaborate. At the tag end of the song, he finishes by simply setting *pretty women* four times in a row on an exactly repeating figure, ending the vocal line on dissonant tone 9 as if the figure could go on until the intended goal, possession, were reached.

It would be hard to isolate the most telling aspects of the masterful lyric. The writer uses exact rhyme very sparingly. The word *dancing* in m.4 is rhymed with *glancing*, but not until m.20, and then again with the two words *man sing*, but not until m.38. The latter rhyme would jar if that separation were not present.

In the end it is the combination of casualness (the turn motif, the opening short phrases) with insistence (the repetition of the melodic pattern, the climactic intensification of the rhythm toward the end) that makes this song self-confidently sexy. Some songs make a proud gesture through time, rather than filling a harmonic space. This is one of them.

"Merrily We Roll Along" (1981) was a show, like "Company," concerned with American middle-class disillusionment. *Good Thing Going* is one of Sondheim's

Figure 8.6

best bitter (really, regretful) ballads (Figure 8.6). The opening melodic phrase uses the upper reach of an F octave, but comes to rest one tone higher, which brings a tension of mild dissonance that will continue throughout. The opening phrase is moderately hard to sing accurately, which also evokes tension immediately. The writer groups the next thoughts into smaller units; they are telling because of the way the words so closely hug the notes. For emphasis of meaning, he inserts a surprise tone, a raised 5, for the word *surprise*, and then does the same for *realize*: "realize what?" the listener asks, and the answer comes in the title phrase. Under *realize* he flirts briefly with modulation, but comes to rest on a mildly dissonant 6 of the main key.

The release uses an aggressive rhythm of quick-step eighth-notes, with a "talky" lyric that conveys a whole romantic history in a very few words, with telling pauses:

> And if I wanted too much,
> Was that such

A mistake
At the time?

You never wanted enough,
All right, tough,
I don't make
That a crime.

"All right, tough" is another of this writer's interjections, which not only reveals an attitude but introduces some welcome extra beats into the line. Normally a song lyric that ends with a "surprise ending" is risky, for the surprise is visible well in advance. This song ends with "We had a good thing * going * going * gone." It is not predictable, and the "twist" happens fast, with two stepwise descents on *going*, each involving a tonal tension (from 6 "leaning" on 5, then 3 to 2, "leaning" to 1 of the scale). It is the minimal, but also the most effective, solution possible.[5]

In the same show, Sondheim wrote another Broadway-style number, *Old Friends*, a sort of crisp march built on a little vamp figure. As usual, it's more subtle than it seems at first glance. The opening melody lines go from 8, the upper tonic tone, down to the leading tone and then back to 8, thus insisting on a clear key-tone in the vocal line. But meanwhile the harmony is avoiding the tonic for a good eight bars, arguably for the entire song until the very end. The lyrics are terrific. "But us, old friends, what's to discuss, old friends? Here's to us * Who's like us? * Damn few!" Note the general avoidance of bright vowels, so that *here* and *like* stand out, and how *to* and *few* are rhymed almost subliminally, instead of slammed for a big rhymed finish. The lyric is full of such elegance.

For us, the most beautiful song from "Sunday in the Park with George" (1984) is the almost title song, *Sunday*. Sondheim is now working noticeably often with big, striking motives. The first interval one hears is his favorite open sixth, a carefully spaced partial sounding of the triad of the main key, A major. As the first sung interval, it has a clarion effect. By the middle of the song, Sondheim sounds, very prominently, a two-note dissonant appoggiatura figure, that is, the F-natural (not in the scale) leaning down to an E, which is the second-strongest scale tone. The climax of the song is achieved with another upward sixth to a high A, no surprise, but approached by a nondiatonic path involving lowered 6 and 7 tones; further, the climax rests over a dominant harmony, so that the song ends without a full resolution. The song is beautifully simple: a distinctive interval, a strong dissonance, and a suspended ending. Sondheim's style has simplified, in a sense, but become more daring. The same can be said about poetic style.

Sunday,
By the blue
Purple yellow red water
On the green
Purple yellow red grass,
Let us pass
Through our perfect park
Pausing on a Sunday
By the cool
Blue triangular water
On the soft
Green elliptical grass

There is, first of all, pleasurable oddity in word choice, depending so much on words having to do with color and shape. The words are mostly short, common ones—but then, *triangular* and *elliptical*! Rhyme is almost by pure repetition: *Sunday/Sunday, grass/grass. Pass/grass* is hidden away musically. The next rhyme for *grass* is achieved 11 bars later, a rhyme for *park* after 17 bars. What could be simpler? Or more evocative? It seems minimalist, and yet it is beautiful to sing and knits the song together.

The motif of an upward sixth interval, placed irregularly and filled in by various means, runs through the entire show and integrates it. Most of the songs are long and in arioso style, employing decorative rather than functional harmony imparting local color to the line or the word. There is only one song that could perhaps stand alone, the final anthem, *Move On*. Corresponding to the questing upward sixth interval of the opening *Sunday*, this long final song uses the more settled, conclusive upward fifth over and over again, and terminates over a definite tonic chord. Within the song are some lovely passages of Debussyesque diminished seventh harmony and some bracing sudden changes of key, both of which contribute to the avoidance of sententiousness. The song has a big range, a full octave and a fifth, which automatically gives it grandeur. The words are plain and moving, and yet their particular emotional impact is embedded in the drama. When Rodgers and Hammerstein wrote concluding anthems of affirmation, like *You'll Never Walk Alone* or *Climb Ev'ry Mountain*, they took pains to come up with stand-alone songs. Sondheim, tellingly, doesn't.

Sondheim in fond pastiche mode is evident in his songs from the movie "Dick Tracy" (1990). *Sooner or Later* is Broadway blues in slow triplets, amusingly contrived in the lyric, while *More* is a go at a sexy gold-digging number, also in a mild blues mode with some really clever words: "Something's better than nothing, yes, But nothing's better than more...except all." *What Can You Lose?* is a fine ballad: the conflicted message, so typical of Sondheim, is "with so much to win /

there's too much to lose." There is also a rather haunting song, the theme music to the film "Reds" (1981), words written subsequently as *Goodbye for Now*. It opens with Sondheim's often used, inherently wistful, upward sixth interval, set so as to bracket the upper octave tone. The melody is unremarkable but poised, set over a bass figure that oscillates between two tones a whole-step apart, which gives the song a floating character. The words are appropriate, a vacillation between letting go and wanting to reclaim a love.

In 1987 Sondheim took on yet another established theatrical tradition, with "Into the Woods," an enchanting olio of fairy tale and song. At this point, we are losing Sondheim as a songwriter, though not as a brilliant force in musical theater. The score is full of radiant song, but not songs. It includes metrical background narrative, much like rap; rhymed patter; lots of arietta, often in three or six beats, like some of the astringent waltzes from "Night Music"; clever rhyming that goes one element longer than you would think possible. The title music has a fine skipping/striding quality, a little like some of the music from "The Wizard of Oz," and throughout there are beautiful melodies, often with the motif of an upward seventh interval followed by a descending third (variously, major and minor), as in the phrases about "Children must [won't/will] listen." Sondheim avoids shaping his material into closed-form song. Very often he will begin with what amounts to two parallel A-passages, but will turn what might be a B-section into a long, complex interlude, so that when A comes back, the song form has been loosened. There are passages that could be segmented into songs, by pruning and rearranging, and they might be satisfying to listen to: for example, *Children Will Listen*, which would have no B-section. The beautiful *No More* (riddles, jests, quests...) is in song form, with a quick-moving middle section ("Running away, we'll do it") whose material is related to the opening bars of *Children Will Listen*. It has the familiar Sondheim tone of resignation: "The further you run, the more you feel undefined.") *No One Is Alone* is indeed a song, and a gorgeous one with delicately complex words: "While we're seeing our side, maybe we forgot...someone is on our side...no one is alone.")

But beyond a point, shaping ongoing material from the later work into "songs" would be disrespectful of Sondheim, who clearly chose to move on to longer, stretched forms. His last Broadway show of the century, "Passion" (1995), is beautiful, dark chocolate in sound, dramatically gripping—but the writer gave up song form entirely, in favor of a version of verismo opera employing arioso, motivic repetition, and parlando style. *No One Has Ever Loved Me* could be treated as an integral song, but was intended to serve a larger function in the general dramatic plan. The move away from deliberately shaped songs was hardly unexpected. As early as "Pacific Overtures" (1976) Sondheim had written enormously long numbers that are entire scenes, like the multicharacter *Someone In a Tree*, which distributes mostly triadic bits of the scale across different pitch zones, and intensifies into a Puccini-like ecstatic culmination.

Sondheim is still active. Even if he never returns to discrete songs, we are greatly in his debt for the many spectacular ones from his career.[6]

DAVID SHIRE (b. 1937) and RICHARD MALTBY, JR. (b. 1937)

The many songs by this team of songwriters are somewhat hard to deal with in a book that, as we have reiterated, does not concern the musical theater but songs considered as separate communicative entities.

Shire (music) and Maltby (words) have, since the 1960s, created dozens of songs of high quality. Most of them appeared in shows taking the form of a dramatic revue or ballad-opera; that is, individual songs ordered, paced, and integrated within a loose overall story line in which the singers, through their songs, become characters—something more than types, something less than participants in a plot—who move through a dramatic/emotional arc. The songs themselves are the events, and tend therefore to be long and complex. They also tend to be ensemble numbers, in which the "characters" interact.

There is nothing unique about this metadramatic approach. In its simpler, legend-telling way, the Schmidt — Jones "The Fantasticks" is constructed in much this way. At the other extreme of complexity, many Sondheim shows, with their fractured time lines and action distributed across several characters, take a similar approach. But the Shire — Maltby songs are so specific to their original narrative-dramatic purpose that they may seem obscure outside that context. A performer must probe the meaning of the number (the concept of "back story" in acting may be useful here) to get it across.

An example, from the show "Closer Than Ever" (New York production, 1989) is *Miss Byrd*. This begins as a comedic show song. But it evolves into a complicated scene that gradually reveals the interior life of a secretary, includes a full recounting of several rich sexual fantasies, and in the end conveys a person's existential assessment of the advantages of seeming repressed to others—while little do they know![7]

There are other important ways in which most Shire — Maltby songs lie a bit outside the parameters of the popular song. They are often sectional, as additional stanzas effect more of the action. Maltby's words are invariably excellent, but they are copious—suitable to the narrative—and involve a level of internal allusion that cannot be appreciated in one hearing. Shire's vocal lines and his control over long transitions and near-repetitions are very accomplished, and the sound is American, but American oriented toward European song or opera. Syncopation, pop-blues vocal lines, "jazz harmonies" are largely missing, though the composer uses these when he wishes. Functional harmony (p. 30) is often absent, because the large song structure that is in play demands something more gradual or incremental. Moreover, the relative absence of pop-jazz and "show" rhythms make Shire's songs seem like precursors of the rhythmic style of composers later in the century. That is to say, his songs, written after all from the 1960s on, move and are full of rhythmic incidents, but tend to stay within a loose and adaptable meter sometimes reminiscent of lyrical rock.

Having described how Shire's work generally deviates a bit from mainline style, we cite a film song that does not. *It Goes Like It Goes* (1979), words by Norman Gimbel, is a deliberately simple song intended to underpin the tone of the film. But it is very rewarding. There is, first, a striking introduction with a modal-sounding pattern of open, slightly altered intervals of the sixth over broken triads (mixed with oscillating augmented fourths), a pattern that recurs during the song as a sort of chord riff. There is then a 16-bar section that serves as a verse, setting out the premise ("Ain't no miracle bein' born...growin' up...."). It moves very simply, the bass-line going in eight bars in seven scalewise steps, ending with dominants on IV, II, V, leading to I. That's a pop-style progression, but otherwise the harmonic feeling, from the introduction on, is in a folk-rock guitar style, emphasized by the regular pacing of the words and the casual dropping of the final *g*. The 16-bar refrain, "It goes like it goes," invokes the flow of time, the never-ending accretion of experience. It brings to mind, musically and in its verbal references, some dimly remembered Appalachian folk song, or perhaps a slow rag. The sense of remote origin comes also from the modal quality of the introduction; the slow-rag echo comes from a reversal of rhythmic stress on the word *river* in m.3 of the chorus. A telling chord is on *flows* in m.4: as a pure triad it would be folk, as it is, a minor triad plus 7, it is raglike. The relaxed grammar of the title phrase is exactly right.

The refrain ends with a lambently beautiful open-interval passage over a calm descending bass-line, with pop-style chords restricted to the occasional half-step. The voice line here, with its upward intervals, has an odd, pleasant echo of a European café waltz, even an Argentine tango (Figure 8.7). The overall

Figure 8.7

format is just AB, for two stanzas; this too is folklike. The song can be done by a pop singer, a folk singer, a country singer. It will convey great warmth, as long as it's done simply.

Now we move to the songs with Maltby that can be considered as stand-alone songs. The title song from the show "Starting Here Starting Now" (1965) is too regular and aphoristic in approach to interest us much, though the ending is touching. In other numbers, Maltby's words often construct the course of an entire relationship, as in *Crossword Puzzle*, and Shire uses "broken" chords, notes that would not mean much harmonically if sounded together, but which, as a repeated horizontal pattern in the bass, provide a foundation for the vocal line. *Autumn* has this Alberti-style bass, like a Mozart sonata, in its bridge section, surrounded by pop-jazz "vertical" harmonies in the A-sections. The entirety is unusual and pleasant, and the words are good, with subtle interior rhyme.

Effective songs in other styles include *Barbara*, which demonstrates that these writers can do a fine ABA song with traditional pop-jazz harmony. It's an exceptionally pretty melody with a melodic (and verbal) twist at the final cadence. Clearly reflecting the characters and situations of the show, but also a strong song independently, is *Flair*. This long number starts as a fast vaudeville pastiche, with the speaker clowning to himself about being stuck in a rut of "ordinary, ev'ryday humiliation." Then the tempo and rhythm and speech register all change, to "Where, where is flair... where's the skill to produce an effect but not look like you tried?"

Taken as a group, the songs from a later (1989) revue-with-plot, "Closer Than Ever," seem stronger as integrated, dramatically shaped songs. *Next Time* is a good waltz in AB form, *Fandango* a sly exposition of the tensions over child care in a yuppie marriage ("maybe ** you take the baby"). There is also a delightful tribute to the bass fiddle, *Back On Base*: blithe words in a standard blues format over a "walking" bass-line, a sure-fire club number for a singer and bass player. *It's Never That Easy* is a sweet song about marital devotion. The complex *There* limns the hypocrisies of marriage in a Gertrude Stein-like fashion, using *there* as an adverb of place or time and as an interjection *(there there!)*. Taken as a group, these songs strike one as good songs, but at the same time as good examples of *types* of songs.

There are at least three distinctive exceptions to that generalization. *Like a Baby* is conventionally in AABA form, but with a lyric that throws off nakedly psychosexual implications. The lover likens himself to a baby "alive with brand-new feelings," and goes on to say, "I'm hungry till you feed me / I just want you to need me...." Not your usual trope for a love-song. *If I Sing* is a tribute to a musician father, now grown old. It's a beautiful long song with an interesting construction involving continuous melody. There are two minisongs, 16 bars each, the second strain growing integrally out of the first, with a repetition throughout the song of these two sections. No passage is remarkable in itself, but the song is moving in its format, pacing, and words, and it comes to a very tender close.

The song we intensely admire is *One of the Good Guys*. This long narrative song concerns an upright, well-adjusted man looking back, with something more than longing, almost panic, to an opportunity he had to break out emotionally. His failure to do so both reassures and scares him about himself. The song has a strongly profiled first strain in the melody, using familiar means, a contrast between a rocking rhythm using the interval of the sixth and an even, linear one built on thirds (Figure 8.8, mm. 1–4). Then there is a disturbed interlude at a faster

Figure 8.8

tempo ("But there was a night...."), with a larger range, and restless rhythmic figures for reiterated, almost obsessive, note patterns (mm. 18–20). The two sections alternate, one urgent and specific, the other resigned and philosophical. It all comes together at the very end with a splendid climax on the highest note of the song, and a deeply felt conclusion:

> ...which life you pick to live in / Whichever choice you make,
> The longing is a given. / And that's what brings the ache...
> That only the good guys know.

This is a song that will have a deep, troubling resonance for many.

Like a number of the Shire — Maltby songs, the last two exist on two levels: the narrative-biographical, in the present, and the distanced or reexperienced. They open vistas beyond the everyday world.

Figure 8.8 Continued.

CLAIBE RICHARDSON (1929–2003) and
KENWARD ELMSLIE (b. 1929)

Richardson's gift was far more traditional. He was a melodist in the tradition of Kern and Arthur Schwartz, and he had the good fortune to write songs with the poet Kenward Elmslie, whose sophisticated lyrics are very strong.

An early Richardson — Elmslie collaboration for one of Ben Bagley's "Shoestring Revues" of the late 1950s, was a clever, strange, lyric-driven song, "*They,*" which could be describing extraterrestrials but, the more one listens to it, seems to be describing the gradual coarsening and insensitivity of modern-day people. "In the old days we'd stroll around the city and the people we'd meet were our type ... Now they walk with a radio clutched to one ear when they go to the park for some sun." The precision of the lyric and the purposely monotonous melody, along with the ominous beat and the refrain, "They are known as *They,*" make this song both amusing and unsettling.

Richardson's and Elmslie's best-known songs were written for the "The Grass Harp," a show based on Truman Capote's story, brought to Broadway in 1971. From the 1966 version comes a bittersweet (but mostly bitter) song *I Trust the Wrong People*. The range of the simple melody is barely more than one note above an octave, the high point reached in the plaintive phrase "one more bitter ending," describing yet another disappointment. The title phrase sets the pace with two quarter-notes, then two eighth-notes, then two half-notes, a standard rhythm. But that rhythm, repeated throughout the song, emphasizes the weariness and inevitability of the situation. Two very nice harmonic sequences occur in the transition into and out of the B-section, which is closely related to the A material.[8]

This score includes many excellent songs, ranging in style from a rousing nineteenth-century-sounding march, *Yellow Drum*, which sweeps through four upward-moving keys, to a very catchy Latin-style number, *Marry With Me*. There are three fine ballads, all suffused with a touching vulnerability. In *What Do I Do Now He's Gone?*, a kind of torch song in sectional arietta form, the title phrase is set to the rhythm of those words as they would be spoken; this is repeated in the following phrases "Wander through a silent house" and "Waiting for a friendly sound." The naturalistic voice line happens over a steady four-to-a-bar vamp figure, which gives the words an extra prominence, as does the alternation of major triads under the words with diminished chords between phrases. Mm. 1–11 can be considered a verse, starting on tone 7, to "Nobody home, come spring." The main strain begins at m.12, with the title words. At m.25 of the main section, the singer proclaims a sudden determination: "I won't give up! I'll start again; Right here and now!"; but this fades within seven bars, the title phrase is repeated, and the song comes full circle back to the opening figure, with one important text change: "Nobody home...at all."

The One and Only Person In the World burns with the steady glow of the certainty of one person's love for another. In the first seven measures of the A-section the main melodic theme is limited to the first five notes of the A flat scale, yet has an intensity that gives the impression of a more dramatic range. Richardson keeps the melody flowing by moving to the dominant briefly between melodic periods. Throughout the A-sections of the song, the composer harmonizes the vocal line with intervals of the fourth, a rather unusual effect. The B-section introduces a new, restrained melodic theme. The A-section is repeated once more, then a modified B-section builds to the climactic C-section: "I've someone to share my heart with, It's never to late to start with * the one and only person in the world."

Perhaps the best known ballad is *If There's Love Enough*. It is a fine example of catharsis in a song. The lyrics are so genuinely conceived that any incipient sentimentality is transformed into a satisfying emotional impact. The melodic phrases in each A-section are repeated three times, with the apex note in each successive phrase climbing by one tone of the basic scale (Figure 8.9, mm. 1–12). This scalar movement upward continues to the climax of the first A-section, on *house*, and then descends to a dominant chord with one momentarily suspended tone, preparing the next A. It is an elegant half-cadence, using the standard chord but keeping it slightly up in the air, thus avoiding the routine. Note also how the accompaniment chords under the opening two words include direct half-step dissonance, emphasized by the composer's prolonging of those two words. The A-sections are indeed 12 bars long, but they consist of the usual

Figure 8.9

eight-bar units plus four-bar extensions, which amount to short A_2 units (mm. 25–36). There is an eight-bar B-section in a contrasting key (mm. 25–32), but even this ends with a version of the four-bar extension; in fact, it is the climax of the song, in which the words beginning "Be still" reach the highest notes, set over forcefully voiced, slightly dissonant chords.

The first-stanza lyric concerns caring for a house, but the second stanza repeats the melody with a lyric about caring for a person: "If you feed a man, and you mend his shirts, If there's love enough in you to kiss away his hurts, that man is yours...." In the final A-section, the charge is to love a "stray," a child not one's own; this builds to yet another melodic highpoint, as the speaker urges that one need only "Provide, provide, don't measure what you do," set here over chords less dissonant than before—and so this affecting song comes to its resolution. The composer provided a lovely written-out coda, which recapitulates the harmonies of the body of the song.

Richardson and Elmslie collaborated on another show, "Lola" (1982), referring to the notorious Lola Montez. This flamboyant nineteenth-century celebrity inspired Richardson to write gorgeous music, and Elmslie exotic and erotic

Figure 8.9 Continued.

lyrics. In *Beauty Secrets*, an aging paramour assesses her chances of continuing to attract the young men she desires, while feeling contemptuous of their inexperience: "Naked in the dawn, a handsome devil of a lad…a self-appointed Galahad." It has a beautiful melody with an operatic range, well-suited for the introspection of a diva: "After we've kissed and kissed, and kissed / Don't let him wrinkle up his nose at the wrinkles on my wrist." *Staying In* is a languid waltz that captures the feeling of lazy, insouciant lovemaking. The three notes of the title phrase start 3-5-2; then the tune moves to 6-9-5. "Staying in" is followed by "lying down" and "making love." In *Mirrors and Shadows*, the speaker describes his obsession with an older woman. The lyric is suitably lavish: surrounded by "mirrored halls…vermilion shadows…velvet walls," he is "face to face with a maze of mirages [he] can't explain."

These unusual songs would be effective scaled down to a club setting.[9]

MICHAEL LEONARD

His birth year appears to be a secret, but a Broadway show from 1964, "The Yearling," brought work by Leonard and Herbert Martin to attention. One ballad, *Why Did I Choose You?*, caught on with good singers right away. It has an expressive, singable vocal line throughout, first lying low in the octave and tending upwards, where the title question is posed, then displaced to high, at or slightly above the octave, with strongly contoured downward-going phrases that answer the question. What is unusual about the song, satisfyingly so, is that while the basic layout of keys is normal — a key-change in m.8, a return to the home key in m.16, marking roughly eight-bar units—the melodic line follows a different pattern. The second period of the first A begins at m.5 and flows right into mm. 9–16. Thus, in the first 16 bars, the harmonic and key layout is 8+8, but the segments of the vocal line are 4+12. The pattern is complicated slightly in the second half of the song, where the second "thought" has an extra four bars, starting at m.29, which sounds like a coda but is actually a vocally graceful interlude ("I lost it lovingly and willingly to you"). The relative weighting of the segments of the song seems to expand constantly, within the first 16 bars and throughout the song as a whole.

Another notable song is *I'm All Smiles*, which has a formal oddity that seems to be the hallmark of the song. To oversimplify: the song opens with a distinctive rhythm but in an indecipherable key. The rhythm is strong, mazurkalike. In the entire first 16 bars, only the word *dar-ling* (set as a Scotch-snap, **short**-long) deviates from a one-syllable-, one-word-per-bar pattern: very simple, very effective. However, the notated key does not sound clearly until mm. 13–16. Prior to that, if you focus simply on the voice-line notes, the song is changing key constantly (or implying chains of keys), and if you look at the chords it is even more ambiguous. The form of the song is AABAC. The release, after the first 16 bars are repeated, is fairly conventional in all respects, as is a coda growing out of the last A-section in which the voice line falls into a more urgent, one-syllable-per-beat pattern (thus seeming to speed up by a factor of three), and climbs in range to a big climax on "Someone to live for, to laugh with and cry for."

It's a song that jazz players should like, for its instantly riveting opening 3/4-time tune and its juicy chords in the opening section. Curiously, the words are rhythmically and semantically incisive, yet the harmonic texture for the first half of the song is unsettled, doubt-producing. It is a remarkable song: whether it is a good song depends on one's weighting of clarity versus complexity.

Spring Is a New Beginning is long, fast, exuberant, given the urgency of new life, new hope by an urgent, rustling accompaniment figure and by quick transitions into sections with off-balance meters or underlying triplets. There are also clashing major/minor seventh chords and abrupt modulations, but a basically lyrical melody line that ranges through almost two octaves. It is an art song, but it sounds harder to sing, owing to complex inner lines, than it is. Quite by contrast, *Growing Up Is Learning to Say Goodbye* is short and simple, both vocally and in its message, which concerns moving on gracefully in life. The excellent verse is 12 measures; the chorus is only 20, and even those 20 measures include a two-measure insertion (mm. 15–16) delaying the last phrase. The chorus consists in four long thoughts that sound musically integrated, but in fact use different material: the third sounds like a "bridge" only because the vocal contour reverses. In both verse and chorus, there are chords that are *almost* diminished chords, or *almost* dominant sevenths or major sevenths, but with extra tones so that they sound fresh but ambiguous. It is a touching, truthful song.

The Kind of Man a Woman Needs is as good, and unusual, as *I'm All Smiles*. It too has a fine, poised melody line, often using (as did *Growing Up*) a Debussyesque stacking of thirds, for a subliminal sense of multitonality (Figure 8.10). But measure by measure, the vocal line is clear and elegant, with just an occasional out-of-scale tone for emotional emphasis. The harmonic basis for the

Figure 8.10

chorus is normal, but for the verse it is extraordinary. The verse changes apparent key often and rapidly; "apparent" because even the briefly perceived keys include out-of-scale tones. There are also false implications: midway through the verse, which begins in B, a dominant-seventh shift to B flat is delayed for a bar, and at the end a clear dominant seventh (a D chord going to G) leads instead to the key of E flat for the chorus. This harmonic restlessness gives the verse a powerful improvisatory character, which makes the chorus sound more considered or conclusive. It is a pattern shown in many classic popular songs, done especially well here. The Martin words are allusive for the verse, plain for the chorus. This song should be far better known.

As we suggested above, some of Leonard's work is odd enough to put some people off. His habit of stretching tonality slightly in the voice line, thus giving it a certain buoyancy, and moving from chord to chord more rapidly than is true of most progressions in this genre, give his work a sound that is a little out of the vernacular, perhaps recalling "European" song style but not in a musty way.

In 1983, in *Don't Let a Good Thing Get Away*, Leonard wrote a neat medium-bounce song that is perfectly conventional, in both senses of the adjective. It has delightful words by lyricist Carolyn Leigh, in her usual style of amused cynicism: the verse ends, "I'm a fool, but don't you be one," and the chorus advises dryly that "Love sometimes lasts for years." The song is a pleasure.[10] An utterly charming, clear-eyed song, *Not Exactly Paris* (1992, words by Russell George), concerns a love that, mysteriously, lingers, ("It was not exactly marriage / didn't have the longest run"). The verse is especially good.

STEPHEN SCHWARTZ (b. 1948)

He is an important theater composer, who pioneered light rock musical style on Broadway with "Pippin," "Godspell," and others in the 1960s and 1970s. The librettos to these musicals were episodic and free-form, incorporating aspects of what might be called contemporary oratorio, which may account for the diffuseness and lack of contour, as we see it, of the songs from the scores. Schwartz has written much of his music in a format where sections are sequenced in an unpredictable way. Sometimes this has a naturalistic effect, but often an open-ended, meandering quality: one has the impression that the song could have been half again as long or a third shorter. We do find Schwartz the best of the "rock musical" theater writers from this period, more interesting, for example, than Gail MacDermott, whose songs from "Hair" (1967) and "Two Gentlemen of Verona" (1972) devolve to a tonal pattern of three triads alternated, in the first case, or an odd protorock in the second.

That Schwartz can write strong autonomous songs is clear, however. In the numbers from "The Baker's Wife" (1990), he creates songs roughly in classic format, some version of ABA shape, but incorporates them within sectionalized ariettas or linearly composed scenes. Here his style is to set long, shapely vocal phrases over an accompaniment of broken chords, that is, spread out in time, which oscillate directly, without modulation per se, between compatible tonalities. He will go in one move from, say, A major or D major to G major, a key that has some, but not all, of the same tones. This shifting results in an overall "modal" tonality to the piece as a whole. The sustained melody over arpeggiated accompaniment is an art-song sound, while the harmonic movement is redolent of guitar-based light rock. Schwartz also likes phrase units (both musically and verbally) of 10 or 12 bars, with implicit division into 5 or 6 (or longer) bars, which yields a stretched feeling to a basically lyrical line.

This is an interesting and generally appealing approach. *If I Have to Live Alone* is close to classic pop. The message is a familiar one: that life continues after a lover has gone. *Where Is the Warmth?* is similar in layout, with a more unusual story line to it: being attracted to someone but knowing that the lover is sealed off emotionally (as the title phrase indicates) so that, at the end, the speaker says, "With a little laugh *** and a smaller sigh, my beautiful man, goodbye." The vocal line in this song is pretty, with a number of expressively altered tones.

Since I Gave My Heart Away, from a television musical (2000), is an attractive pop song, with two stanzas and a familiar message: "...the more of your heart you give to someone else / the fuller... it gets." The song builds to a fine climax at the end, but the tune is, finally, square. Pretty as these songs are, the lyrics tend to be fairly bromidic (*Warmth* being the least so); we cannot get excited about them.

In contrast, we find Schwartz's *Life Goes On* (1992) stunning. It demonstrates that a long narrative song in new-theatrical style need not be formless. By *new-theatrical* we mean that the song is sectional, recounting a complex story while transitioning from pop-jazz harmony to light-rock mode and back again. The verbal control is perfect, hence the emotional impact is deep. The lyric seems at first highly situational, prosaic, with references to driving to a hospital; to "bruises and tubes in your chest"; and to returning home and having a meal of franks and "watching the Yanks stink up the diamond." But even within this presentation of seemingly arbitrary quotidian events, there is great poetic resonance, for example, emanating from the word *diamond(s)*: the tears in relatives' eyes "glittered like diamonds"; "bones through the skin, brittle as diamonds"; the observer, carefully keeping his detachment "...like a counterfeit diamond that used to be real." There are widely separated off-rhymes that produce just a scintilla of recall; for example, *numbness* and *mumbled* some 19 bars apart, and some stinging echoes, like "keep controlled... a little cold." The lyric concludes with a detail that is moving in its simplicity. Throughout the song, the speaker has been saying, with resignation, "...and life * goes on." Now a moment of self-realization obtrudes, as he realizes, "And a slightly smaller part of my life *** goes on." There is much more in the lyric that could be cited; suffice it to say that it is an intensely moving story, not at all bathetic.

This song is lyric-driven, but fortunately the writer has created a beautiful opening, then often-repeated, melodic figure. As one hears the first phrase, centered on tone 5 but with the immediate clash of the raised 5, as one registers the dissonance of the E-flat and E-natural (F-flat) octaves and the very complex opening chord, an A-flat seventh with two strong dissonances, one intuits the mysterious emotional import (Figure 8.11). There is a moment of tonal clarity

Figure 8.11

in the third phrase, and then a return to the nameless but expressive out-of-key musical figure. This alternation turns out to permeate the whole song. It also develops that the striking diminished sixth interval of m.1 threads through the song; for example, all the *diamond* tropes use this interval. The song could have been mawkish, but through artistic judiciousness achieves something deep, subtle, and new. It is dark without being morbid. Harold Arlen might have written the melody, but no lyricist of that day could have done this lyric. Is the song in classic popular style? Allowing for secular change in subject matter, yes.[11]

Schwartz's expertness as a lyricist is evident in a song written with Alan Menken, *Cold Enough to Snow* (1993). This is, one could say, a formula song in pure classic pop style: it uses a charming "moderate shuffle" dotted rhythm, a cheerful diatonic melody with a well-placed "smudge" tone, and normal pop-jazz chords. Schwartz's words, about the chill that lost love brings, are euphonious, with slangy diction and cleverly managed vowels, dark against light. It is a song that is nothing special, but extremely likeable—though the very end is a bit banal in its string of longer notes.

It seems to us that the closer Schwartz comes to classic pop style, writing either words or music or both, the more banal the result. The looser and more harmonically unsettled his work, the more interesting.

MAURY YESTON (b. 1946)

Yeston is one of the few contemporary composers of songs for whom direct melody is of prime importance. His compositional style can be compared to Kern's in its use of the flowing melodic line. The songs are in no way calculated for easy listening: his songs have real depth and an awareness of character and situation. This combination of the emotional and the intellectual perhaps explains the variety of musical genres one can recognize in his songs. The Yeston works we mention here come from various sources, including Broadway musicals, song cycles, and stand-alone works. They are all so well crafted that the listener is able to enjoy them on their own, whatever their origin.

From a show, "In The Beginning" (1975), comes *New Words*. In this gentle song a parent teaches a child words: the moon is "like a cookie" and as "white as milk." The mystery of distant objects in the sky is likened to an object closer to the child—the parent's face, illuminated by love. The melody achieves a feeling of yearning by having phrase beginnings return over and over to 3 of the scale. Intensity grows as the melody builds upwards from 3 to 5 on the word *love* in the phrase, "we call it 'love.'" An octave jump up to 5 resolutely expresses the added force of the word *harder*, as the speaker warns, "So hard to say, my son—it gets harder." The song is an emotional *tour d'horizon*, expressed by someone who cares.

Another song featuring parent and child, but with the roles reversed, is from the 1982 musical "Nine." *Getting Tall*, sung by the boy in the past to the man he has actually become, is a gentle song with a pretty, Rodgers-like melody. It serves as a sort of homily for grown-ups, but is likely to have a cathartic effect on anyone.

Knowing you have no one if you try to have them all,
is part of tying shoes / part of starting school,
part of scraping knees if we should fall.
Part of getting tall.

Two other songs from "Nine," which centered on the idea of Fellini's making a sequel to "8½," are evocative of the Italian pop music of that period. *Only With You* moves along easily in a slightly Latin-sounding rhythm of four beamed eighth-notes followed by a single eighth and a quarter-note: "**Being just me** is so * **easy to be**, When I'm * **only with you.**" The words ring changes on the title phrase—and there is a surprise at the end. In a way, the listener, like the speaker, is "taken for granted, completely enchanted." A curious song, *Unusual Way*, alternates passages in the narrative minor ("In a very unusual way one time I needed you") with phrases in the major ("In a very unusual way you were my friend"). The listener hears a blend of classical and soft-rock feeling. In a different style, *Be On Your Own* is a bitter song, a plain melody over angry broken chords. In it, a lover is sent packing, with a good deal of rancor, but it softens at the end: "You'll take with you all you own...and all of me."

You're There Too (1988) shows another side to Yeston. This delightful song is a wry, loving tribute to a faithful companion who shares life's hard knocks with the speaker. The casual tune and the friendly words are consistently interesting, phrase by phrase, with a light touch that pleases.

> When evil omens fill the sky
> I notice with a downcast eye
> That there's a small other foot adjacent to my shoe,
> And I'm not surprised to find I'm leaning
> On the person it belongs to, meaning
> You're there too.

The speaker goes on to say he's frequently at a loss to cope with life, but his partner's companionship makes it better.

> But look who's falling on her face beside me,
> You're there too.

Danglin' (1978) is a lament, set to a soft compelling beat, with a James Taylor feel to it, but it is a sophisticated song with nice unexpected upturns in the melody, as well as some neat country-style vocal turns. It's an example of Yeston's versatility and ability to write short, emotionally effective songs in any style. By contrast, *I Had a Dream About You*, from a song cycle, "December Songs" (1991), is long and unusual. The speaker dreams of a happy relationship and a happy time driving in the Maine woods. We know this must be imaginary because they see two orange moons overhead, but the melody is driven by a consistent rhythmic beat that repeats and repeats, and the listener almost begins to believe, along with the speaker, that this could be reality. Sadly, it is not, and there is a dark ending in the last words: "I had a dream about you, but of course it was only a dream." This is a "talky" song, but with a lyric whose every clause falls right into place.

From the musical "Grand Hotel" (1989) there's a clever song, *I Want to Go to Hollywood*, in a sense Yeston's tribute to a whole category of songs in which someone in a backwater (in this case, Friedrichstrasse, where "if things get broken, they stay broken") dreams about fame. This long song sounds like a tongue-in-cheek version of a Kander — Ebb show-stopper, complete with a good vamp, but the words are more subtle. The song is amusing, sweet on account of its youthful naiveté, and appalling underneath.

Yeston's version of "The Phantom of the Opera," entitled "Phantom," predates the British import based on the same material. From his first version of this show (1983) comes what is perhaps the most gorgeous and expansively written of Yeston's songs, *Home* (revised, 1991). This joyous celebration of love for music, theater, and opera soars, and stays aloft throughout its length. After a confiding verse with a pentatonic-sounding voice line, the main section opens with a long melody, clear-eyed like a Robert Burns tune (Figure 8.12). The harmonic feeling is also classical (though using the 6, so common in pop style) until the seventh chords of mm.8–9, with their lovely easing from dissonance to consonance, a strong, slow appoggiatura in an otherwise chaste line. The importance given to *and* makes the song sound as if it were extruding itself.

Figure 8.12

Yeston's "Titanic" score (1997), which had to compete with the film of the same name, has a number of overlooked gems. *Autumn* is a pretty waltz with a proper Edwardian air, while *Still* is a soaring, heartbreaking melody (the words perhaps a bit stentorian) sung as a duet for an elderly couple who will go down with the ship. *Still* could be Kern in his closest-to-art-song style, including the use of many enharmonic modulations where the same note is the pivot for modulation. *We'll Meet Tomorrow* is as close to operetta style as Yeston comes, and seems trite, but from the same score is *No Moon*, a quiet, Chopinesque waltz that could be a metaphor for life's mysteries: "We go sailing, sailing, ever on go we."

Those who appreciate the kind of songs this book is about, but who fear that the genre will disappear, can take heart in the fact that Yeston is only in his late fifties as of this writing.[12] That said, there is a sense, in his work thus far, of writing songs "in the style of," without revealing a strong personal profile. His unfailingly excellent lyrics do not raise this issue, since they lie perfectly poised between prosaic and poetic: we would guess that normally, for Yeston, creating a song is triggered by some words or verbal concept. We have the feeling that Yeston has not yet done his very best work. His essaying of long forms (as in *Still* or *By the River*, 1991) may promise songs that will blend the classic popular song and the aria. Indeed, many of his songs are vocally too demanding for most pop-song singers, and his typical, though not invariable, avoidance of pop-jazz harmony would seem to provide a springboard for some version of "popular" lyric opera.

STEPHEN FLAHERTY (b. 1960) and LYNN AHRENS (b. 1948)

Ahrens (lyrics) and Flaherty (music) have been writing together since the early 1980s. With "Ragtime" (1996), they reinvigorated the tradition of the Broadway show with a big sound and big numbers, but they also have written songs on a smaller, sophisticated, and more intimate scale. An early collaboration, "Lucky Stiff" (1988) had two songs of this description. *Times Like This* is humorous and touching at the same time. It is a lyric-driven song; the music serves to provide a setting for such clever lines as: "…unlike certain people, you can teach him how to stay," or "…gazing at the views, his head upon your shoes…." (Guess to whom the song is addressed.) It's "special material" of a high order. *Lucky* swings with a soft-shoe beat but with a definitely off-beat situation (a stage note in the music reads, "He looks at Uncle's body."). Happily, the song can be performed outside of this context. The melody is built on infectiously pleasant little seven-note riffs which set phrases like, "Think of how I made it through" and "All of this and also you," connected by some chromatic noodling. Ahrens' lyrics are delightful ("…we'll both find out how living feels…my life will be a hell ** on wheels"). They lead us ultimately to a grand pun (given the stage context): "You're one lucky stiff and so am I." The short-breathed layout of the tune and the use of vamp figures between phrases remind one inevitably of Kander and Ebb at their most vital.

For those who believe that there is a surfeit of pop Christmas songs, we recommend *All Those Christmas Clichés* (1993). The short verse starts out with weary cynicism, but ends with a sentimental confession, documented in the chorus by a well-crafted combination of music and lyrics that could hold its own with any of the seasonal pop alternatives. The lyric is a list of overused holiday images, but these are given sentimental legitimacy by a straightforward but original melody without harmonic clichés. A witty reference to Tormé's *Christmas Song* serves as a key-change transition. In the final section the lyric adds emotional depth as it develops into a statement of personal yearning:

> I want the bells and the drums, mistletoe and sugarplums and kids to tuck in tight.
> And as for that guy in the bright red outfit, instead of flying off, he stays.

Much of Flaherty's music has an essential American character, evinced in the elegant simplicity of his melodic phrases. The music from "Ragtime" is full of American themes. There is, of course, the ragtime rhythm itself, threaded through the score. In the very strong title song, the compelling, seemingly rigid rhythmic figure allows for words with considerable sweep and depth.

> It was the music of something beginning,
> An era exploding, a century spinning.

There are also the melodic and harmonic strains of gospel ('Till We Reach That Day) and folk music anthems. The "big" songs in "Ragtime" are the anthems *Back to Before*, in which the uncertainties of a new era are contrasted to the comfortable past, and *Wheels of a Dream*, in which a father sings of his hopes for his young son to enjoy future freedoms, while he himself cannot. These are big melodies with inspiring but not overfervent lyrics. They have the reach and spaciousness of good old American tunes like *Shenandoah*. Also from "Ragtime," *Your Daddy's Son* is a bluesy lullaby, the main melodic phrase of which is built on a movement of thirds in G minor from the key-tone to the octave above it, using a lowered 3 and 6 and a pure 7. Echoes of Gershwin's "Porgy" linger here.

New Music is another example of Flaherty's striving for, and reaching, the essential American sound of the early decades of the twentieth century. The main strain, with its strong expanding intervals, has the classic ragtime rhythm, and the layout of the song reflects the tradition of ragtime and marches: there are two "trio" sections, so that the overall form is ABBA, basically all in the same key. The chords are open and simple, but the chord progressions are quite complicated: for example, the raised 5 in m. 2 gliding into to the V-I move. Ahrens's lyric plays to the catchy, syncopated, pianistic feeling of the melody: "His fingers stroke those keys and ev'ry note says 'Please.'" A lesser lyricist would, given the layout of the main theme, overrhyme; she does not, but provides elegant interior rhyme throughout. *New Music* is written as an ensemble piece; it could be adapted into a solo song, but might become monotonous without the intended vocal textures. Flaherty himself has said that, "In the creation of this song I was just as inspired by the music of Jerome Kern and Irving Berlin as I was by the music of Scott Joplin."

From "Once On This Island" (1990) comes a gently calypso-flavored song, *Come Down From the Tree*. It achieves its light rhythmic effect by setting strong syllables alternately on strong and weak beats, for a shifting-meter effect, and by using brief, two-move chord changes that go nowhere but make a nice side-step. Verbally, it's a sweet little homily, pleasantly harmonized: "When your heart knows what it needs, you must go where it leads. Leave the nest." The song seems simple, but has an insinuating charm.[13]

Another instance of the quintessentially American feel of Flaherty's melodies comes from the musical show "Suessical" (2000). The song *How Lucky You Are* is a happy tune with a shuffle rhythm and a tune that calls to mind the Eubie Blake — Andy Razaf *You're Lucky to Me* (1930), but which takes off in an un-sentimental direction. The lyrics are fun, full of light-hearted cynicism: "When the fates are unkind [and you] get kicked from behind." "Suessical" included another of this team's most lyrical ballads, *Alone In the Universe* (Figure 8.13). The title words are set to a simple eight-note melodic strand, covering only the

Figure 8.13

interval of a fifth: it repeats like a bell theme throughout the song. A very great deal is achieved just by prolonging the first syllable of *a-lone*. The harmonization is pellucid: single tones, placed judiciously, keep chiming the third, fourth, fifth intervals, like stars twinkling at different frequencies. The words are correspond-ingly clear and delicate.

> My own planets and stars are glowing…
> Not one person is listening
> They don't have any way of knowing.…

The effect is one of awe, yearning, hope, faith. It is a wonderful song, an art song in character, contemporary but with an age-old import.

From "My Favorite Year" (1993) is a stunning song called *If the World Were Like the Movies*. It limns character as it goes along; in this case, that of a star who is not happy with himself as a person. There is a simple upward scale for the main theme, subtly varied with brief downward hesitations as the speaker ponders his human failures ("We'd correct our little blunders *** and select our better takes," and "Love preserved on film forever *** all the battle scenes removed.") It's a song about truth-telling, and the exceptional lyrics express that truth dry-eyed, right up to the bitter conclusion. The song demands a plain performance; done properly, it is memorable, like Sondheim songs of comparable depth.

Ahrens and Flaherty are comparatively young, perfectly matched, and highly sophisticated without showing off. A constant in their work, evident in the music but also reflected in the words, is a predilection for an open, often radiant harmony. In this, they seem to hark back to the style of much of Kern, and bypass the more "chewy" harmony of later great American songwriters. They have shown the ability to create songs in the classic Broadway tradition, as well as the ability to investigate new, more contemporary approaches linked to that tradition. As with Yeston, if one has any concern, it is that their elegant eclecticism, reflecting the demands of their dramatic material, might work against their reaching a unique profile as songwriters. However, one could have said this about most of the pre-1950 great songwriters at midcareer. As excellence accumulates, individuality takes shape.

Some Songs of the 1990s

In this section we examine some songs by writers who became known in the last decade of the century or a little earlier. We do so, not to provide extensive or even balanced coverage—these writers have just begun, and can be expected to develop and change—but to try selectively to identify some signficant trends.

In this period, there are obvious differences between songs written for musical-dramatic contexts and autonomous songs written, presumably, for performance in clubs or for recording. One difference is evident in the actual mode of presentation of the song. Songs written for the theater (or as deliberate song cycles) are *published*, if they win some attention. Songs written for more casual purposes, especially by writers whose work is heard primarily through recording, tend to go unprinted; one obtains them from the writer's website or from a singer who includes the song in her or his repertoire. This is a telling change. Earlier, if one heard a song on the radio or a record and wanted to get to know it, one bought the sheet music and learned it at the piano at home. Now one buys a recording.

Another change is obvious in the form in which printed music appears. In the heyday of classic popular song, the sheet music or the piano-vocal score was represented on the page in three-stave form. There were two staves for piano and a separate staff for the vocal line, with words shown under it. Sometimes the vocal element was incorporated into the right-hand piano part, as the top strand in two staves.. Either way, one heard the tune as one played the piano. By the middle of the century, chord symbols, normally for guitar, appeared over the voice line, for those who played "by ear." Even when chord symbols were included, the serious composers in classic pop insisted on a full piano accompaniment because they wanted to specify, not just the main chords, abstractly, but the precise vertical spacing and balance of those chords; for example, in which pitch range the chord should sound, and with which note on top, which on the bottom, and so on. The printed music also showed inner lines that connected the chords or that created subsidiary patterns: transitions, accompanying figures, countermelodies, and so on.

Toward the end of the century, "occasional" songs became represented, normally, by the "lead sheet"—the vocal line, words underneath, plus indications of chords. This means, inevitably, that the composer no longer specified the precise color and texture of the harmonic underpinning of the song, no longer designated certain inner details. Perhaps this more abstracted form of notation opens the door to greater freedom of realization, on the part of experienced musicians. It did with "jazz songs," which had been normally published in this format for several decades. But for those whose skills are rudimentary, it results in a vaguer, stripped-down realization—a sort of Platonic sketch for a song.[14] This convention of notating music must reflect the assumption that it is the recording that fully realizes the song; the written-out music is just a rough guide.[15]

In an interesting differentiation, one sees the opposite trend in the published music for songs for the theater or concert presentation. Such vocal music is now shown on the page with a full, written-out accompaniment in two staves, *not* including the voice line: that is shown separately above, words underneath. The piano parts are often quite difficult to play, generally more so than older classic pop. This style of music printing was infrequent until the 1960s. It has become the norm with writers like Flaherty, Yeston, and the later Sondheim. Chord symbols may or may not be included; if so, they are pro forma and inaccurate. For the amateur "consumer," say someone sight-reading at the piano at home, it means that one cannot realize the song—voice line and accompaniment—all at once, since the "tune" is not given in the piano right hand. One has to focus on the vocal line separately, and fit it to the piano parts. Few sight-readers can do this with ease.

Such an approach to on-the-page representation is the hallmark of the art or concert song, where the composer definitely wants to specify as much of the total aural effect as possible. The degree of specification implies that if a song is to be recorded, it should sound as the composer intended, including pitch relationships, interior figures, vamps, rhythmic fillips, chord texture, tonal color, and the like.

To summarize, by the end of the century, "commercial" songs intended for recording or "occasional" songs intended for a club are notated skeletally, while theater songs are fully specified.

There is a further, important differentiation between theater songs and independent or "occasional" songs toward the end of the century. The latter remain separate entities: they may be complex, but they have a beginning and an end, and a lyric that is complete unto itself.

Instead of "theater songs," however, we need now to say, vocal music written for the theater. By the 1990s, the traditional "book musical" was seldom being written by mainstream theater composers, at least not successfully—children's musicals or regional theater pieces being exceptions. We touch on some of the possible explanations for this trend in chapter 2. Beginning with writers such as Coleman ("City of Angels") and some of the work of writers like Finn or Stephen Schwartz, Strouse or Schmidt and Jones, and fully evident in later Sondheim (e.g., "Passion"), Flaherty and Ahrens, or Yeston, theater songs do not happen as separate units—verse, chorus, perhaps reprise. On all levels in the musical theater, the demarcating signals, in earlier eras, of an impending song—a new tempo from the orchestra, a change of lighting or scenery, the actor facing front—have disappeared. To one degree or another, songs now are part of a much more fluid, larger musical flow, in which nonvocal orchestral interludes, speech-song, free recitative alternate with more tightly bounded passages (i.e., *songs*). Throughout the work, motives associated with a mood or a character or an event may recur, as with opera; the same melodic fragment may happen in the orchestra, then in a "song," then in parlando passages, all of this linear integration designed for dramatic purpose. (The interesting work of Shire and Maltby, in which sets of individual songs are threaded through an overall story line, can be seen as another approach to the same integrated effect for the musical theater.)

One reason why theater scores now are published in the quite tightly specified form we have described is that the continuity and interrelationships in the musical/dramatic whole cannot otherwise be indicated on the page. If, for example, a specific vocal pattern occurs throughout the piece, associated with a character or a mood, or if a chord with a distinctive color or a brief rhythmic figure is used to signal a recurring event, these obviously must be precisely given in "the score." As one evaluates theater songs of the 1990s, it must be kept in mind that they likely have a different formal character, texture, and purpose from those of earlier eras, and that a difference will be audible when the "song" is lifted out of the dramatic context.

It now makes sense to say that Ricky Ian Gordon, for example, is a song *composer*, no matter who writes the lyric, while Richard Rodgers wrote the music to songs, with Hart or Hammerstein or Sondheim in partnership or even in mind. Steven Lutvak, on the other hand (below), is a *songwriter*, not simply because he writes his own words but because his songs, as he presents them to the public, offer a greater freedom of interpretation and aural realization in performance. Neither attitude is intrinsically superior to the other. But it has been about one hundred years since the distinction has been so obvious in "popular" music.

Finally, we must point out one other major shift in style, toward the end of the century. As we discussed in the previous chapter, the verbal universe of the "singer-songwriters" of the 1960s and 1970s changed the norm of the popular song lyric. This was a matter of topic, range of cultural reference, poetic register, and point-by-point coordination with the music, all of which amounted to a new approach to the lyric. We believe that this change in the setting-point, as it were, for song lyrics has had a distinctive effect, on *both* theater songs and autonomous songs since around 1980. Crudely stated, it is a new kind of naturalism.[16] The new shift is not much evident in Sondheim, who continued to write in his own tight, brilliant, literate verbal style. It is audible in Yeston, we think, or Ahrens, and in many of the songs we discuss in this chapter. The longer-range implications of this change in verbal–literary style we will take up again in our final chapter, in connection with the question of whether "classic popular song" is still a meaningful conception.

We begin this brief survey with some theater writing. Jonathan Larson's songs from the show "Rent," a great success in 1996, have, for us, mostly topical freshness to recommend them. The musical style is loose, basically triadic, usually in the "moderate light rock" beat and tempo specified by the writer. The vocal lines often include melismas that seem to be intended to decorate or aerate the vocal line. Larson's words sometimes seem new, but syntactically peculiar: "A new lease * you are, my love, on life." In any case, the songs are not close to classic pop in style.

Andrew Lippa definitely did write in pop-jazz style for his songs from "The Wild Party" (1999). For dramaturgical reasons we have touched on, some of these "songs" are embedded in long and complicated scenes, and yet can be carved out from the ongoing flow of plot and character. For example, the long number, *Out of the Blue*, begins with a disillusioned woman singing, in a "verse," about needing a change in her love life. The tune and the chords (a) could be Cy Coleman; the lyric has a tiny touch of Sondheim (Figure 8.14). There is a cat-and-mouse vamp (b) leading into the "chorus." Unusually, the title phrase occurs first on the vamp. At m.41 (c), the B-section brings in a new rhythm and style of address. The harmony is full and splashy, with widespread dominant

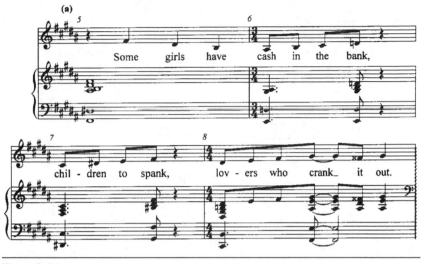

Figure 8.14

sevenths and a tune that now covers more than half-steps. The song continues in roughly repeating AABA form, in 32-bar units, arriving at the end with some complex bitonal chords.

It's Kander and Ebb, but less obvious; clearly a pop-jazz number, on an old familiar theme. Is it for real? is it pastiche? is it written like this to fit the plot? The other songs do not clarify matters. *An Old-Fashioned Love Story* is definitely in parodic Broadway strut style, following a mock-Latin verse, though this

Figure 8.14 Continued.

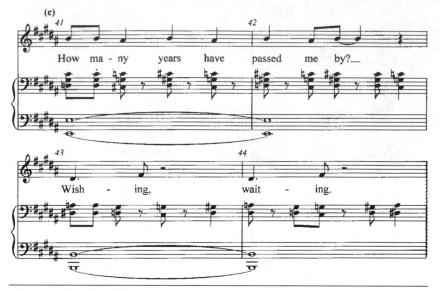

Figure 8.14 Continued.

happens to be a lesbian love story. *I'll Be Here* could be a Rodgers and Hammerstein devotional love song, though with a "get groovy" middle section and an interesting Arlenesque closing progression. The ballad *How Did We Come to This?* is like a Sondheim song, with terse phrases setting rhetorical questions and asides, whose emotional flavor become more and more bitter: eventually, "Filling up with frenzy / Killing with a kiss... Time goes by, plans grow stale / people die and parties fail...."

By our criteria, these Lippa songs are surely *good*. His lyrics are impeccable as to diction and scansion, and often trenchant. He uses interesting "functional harmony" economically and to good effect. Does this set of songs sound "derivative" on purpose? We suspect so: there are clues throughout: a tired set of chords is tied to a banal thought, or, in *I'll Be Here*, the words seem to be deliberately insipid. Can Lippa write as well, but in a fresher mode? Time, we hope, may tell.

The songs we know from two shows by Michael John LaChiusa ("Hello Again,"1994, and "Marie Christine," 1999), are art songs, interesting mostly for their musical texture: chord spacing, inner figures, and the like. *Tom*, from the former, is made up of mostly paired lines, each with a somewhat new tonal thrust, and a rhapsodic middle section. *Lover, Bring Me Summer*, from the latter, has an evocative mood. These are artful songs, but very composed, almost in the sense of a *salade composé*.

The songs from Jason Robert Brown's musical theater piece, "Parade" (1999), are too plot-specific to stand alone, but he is a lyrical writer, with a subtly modal French harmonic sense. A 1996 song, *Stars and the Moon*, is very effective. It is a long song that recounts a personal history, that of a girl who sells out for care and comfort, and then wakes up: "…it never changed…it never grew…I never dreamed…." The format is not that different from the popular song norm: a triple A, a triple B, and a tiny repeat of A—and then more stanzas.

Ricky Ian Gordon is a versatile and impressive composer. His concert works for chorus, for example, are very rewarding. He has also written song cycles, including "Only Heaven" (1997, words by Langston Hughes) that constitute "art song," in this case with some use of a most attractive gospel-blues style. An autonomous song, *A Horse With Wings* (1993), with his own words, has been performed by popular singers. It is a long and touching song, basically triadic, with a poised vocal line that explores the triadic intervals by wreathing itself around tones 6, 4, and 2. It's the song of an as-yet unspoiled spirit wanting life to be as beautiful as it's supposed to be.

As of this writing, we do not know how to assess Adam Guettel (b. 1965), except that he is a major new talent in the musical theater—and that he can, but does not normally, write songs in classic popular style. His opera, "Floyd Collins," from the 1990s, established him as a technically accomplished composer in long form. The opera is in semiparlando style, with much use of broken triad and other ostinato figures, frequent major/minor alternation, and some chordal bitonality. It steers far away from pop-jazz harmonies, particularly avoiding use of tone 6. There is much ensemble writing, but often a loose, lovely solo vocal line. "Songs" can be detached from this tightly integrated whole. *How Glory Goes* is big and melodically sweeping, and *Through the Mountain* has the shape of a popular song, though it is much longer, and a pretty melody.

An ambitious song cycle, "Myths and Hymns" (2000), has a mythic and mystic import, switching between American vernacular and a sort of Blakean symbolism. There are here many elements in extended ABA, as opposed to aria layout. One piece, *How Can I Lose You*, is in classic pop form, AABA, uses popular song harmonies, notably chains of dominant sevenths to move from key to key, and has a well-worn pop song theme, self-destructive romantic anxiety. It sounds quite like a Sondheim song without a dramatic crux.

Among free-standing songs of Guettel's, there is a luminously lovely love song, *The Allure of Silence* (1996, words by Lindy Robbins). It is not harmonized as a normal popular song, but may be the better for that: in this respect, and in the way the vocal line lies, Sondheim again comes to mind. The format is a big ABA, with the tender, repeating B-section more prominent than most. Our only cavil is that the word *allure* seems linguistically out of key. Another Guettel — Robbins song, *Was That You?* (1996), is in perfect classic pop style, so well constructed that it avoids any hint of stylistic self-consciousness. It's an AABA bossa nova, with an unusual harmonic transition from the B, and polysyllabic rhymes that sneak into the lines without disrupting them. The A-section structure is especially nice in the way short phrases begin and end, bracketing longer, rhythmically supple phrases in between.

As of this writing, the greatly gifted Guettel seems to be headed toward writing lyric theater pieces or vernacular operas comparable to those of Aaron Copland or Carlisle Floyd.[17]

We move now to independent songs, many of which might be best heard in club settings. Steven Lutvak's attractive songs are distinctive in their tonal-harmonic sense. We mean that his chords have a way of moving along in a fairly normal sequence, and then sidling into a new tonal center half a step off from what is expected. This involves both horizontal and vertical relationships. As to the former, the songs glide from key to key, across successive sections, in a gentle, pleasing way. As to the latter, Lutvak is fond of, for example, seventh chords (with flatted 7) that prove not to be traditionally "dominant" to the next key center. His scales, as heard most clearly in the voice line, are often five-tone: not pentatonic but Debussyesque in involving combinations of whole steps and minor thirds, so that the song seems to wander from major to minor. Finally, these are songs with a lot of sectional repetition. All these characteristics add up to an overarching sweetness; there is a lot of space in his music, even when the lyrics are intense. Lutvak normally writes his own words: typically, they are complicated emotionally, but not passionate; there is an observer outside the words, learning how he feels from what he says.

After You (2002) is an example, a plangent ballad about a broken love affair. Lutvak uses a mixture of rhyme and assonance here, as in other songs, and he likes to prolong a thought: "...I cannot pretend, it's just that I didn't think we'd end this way ** I didn't think we'd end...." There is a Cole Porter song called *After You, Who?*, and the Lutvak song opens with exactly these words. For a neat across-generations contrast: the Porter song is more compact, and one gets the point more quickly, but it is also more contrived and less touching. *Guide Me* (1991), from a regionally produced musical, is more like a classic pop song harmonically, but it uses another device that keeps the song up in the air. It has alternating bars of six and seven beats, in which the "extra" beat is also the stressed element of the next thought, so that the sense of a bar-line is minimized. Instead of creating a bump in the flow, it causes that flow to eddy. (Figure 8.15).

Lutvak does sometimes depart from his ultra-smooth style, and then he writes in a more familiar way musically. Even then, his lyrics are dense, technically deft, and true. *My View of You From the Piano* (1992), perfect for club performance, is a relaxed, dotted-rhythm show song with an amusing text. It's like an act of

Figure 8.15

love between parties separated by space and role, and collegial respect. *Beware the Anger of Soft-Spoken Men* (1991) is a bitter beguine. *The Dinner Party* (1998) is a Noel Coward creation, if Coward had been New York and Jewish. Perhaps most delightful of all is *I Just Wanted You to Know* (1996), which is exuberant, loving, with a Stevie Wonder beat.

Lutvak's delicately oblique tonal sense, and the excellent balance of words to music, remind us a little of Yeston. As yet, Lutvak's honest, personally appealing songs do not blaze like some of Yeston's moments, but we suspect that if Lutvak is able to write full scores for the theater, an added intensity will come into his work.

Those who love the classic popular song may well, on principle, dislike the songs of Stephin Merritt. But his songs are worth listening to anyhow, for they are brilliant realizations of an anti-classic-pop stance. Significantly, they were written for, realized through, recording.[18] Virtually all Merritt's songs overtly or by implication undercut or deconstruct the formulas and attitudes of the songs that this book celebrates. There are direct hits on Irving Berlin, for example, with songs like *A Pretty Girl Is Like*...(completed by, "a minstrel show"); the words go on to say, "A melody is like a pretty girl / who cares if it's the dumbest in the world...." A similar song, *Nothing Matters When We're Dancing*, takes off dancing songs, that staple of American pop: "...among the dreadful tunes / the awful songs we don't even hear...."

These songs are not parodies; they are real songs, except that they subvert classic pop songs. Musically, they are suave, though of little complexity; if they were complex, the deadpan camp element would be lost. The format is that of brief stanzas, with repeating elements or refrains. The most characteristic metrical aspect is constantly changing scansion, within and across text lines, with empty beats that break and restart the line. The vocal elements are contrived to bring the words forward, clause by clause—and the words are brilliant. We cite here just a grab-bag of examples:

I don't believe in the sun / How could it shine down on everyone and never shine on me

You said you were in love with me
Both of us know that that's impossible

Let abbots, Babbitts and Cabots / say Mother Nature's wrong

The book of love is long and boring

Must we really waltz / Drag another cliché / howling from the vaults

Merritt's words are not exactly angry, but hostile; more aggressive than cheeky, sometimes cheerfully obscene, and yet brisk and speedy, without overkill. Self-mocking humor and an individual slant are constants, so that one cannot "tune out." Some songs, like *Blue You*, amount to emotional love songs. There is a plethora of remote rhymes and assonances. Some lyrics are compact enough to amount to aphorisms; usually, they are constructed of parallel sets of moderately long sentences, stanza by stanza. They amount to takes on human relationships and emotions that matter-of-factly demolish old verities. As such, we would comment that they are as much clichés as the expressed sentiments they cancel: they have no more depth than that, but they deserve an equivalent attention, as the negation of a song genre that the writer has deep in his consciousness.

Notes

1. In the former case, it was Hammerstein who sought a newly forceful dramatic subject and style, as he did often thereafter.
2. Performances of the first and third: Dawn Upshaw, "I Wish It So," Nonesuch CD 79345.
3. Performance: Upshaw
4. Performance: Joyce Breach, "This Moment," Audiophile CD 293.
5. Performance: Nancy LaMott, "My Foolish Heart," Midder Music 003.
6. In fact, in "Bounce," as produced in Washington in 2003, songs are indeed present, notably The *Best Thing That Ever Has Happened.*
7. Compare this to a song with a similar subject, *Miss Marmelstein*, from Harold Rome's show "I Can Get It For You Wholesale" (1962). Rome's song is a funny but crude jape, while Miss Byrd is like overhearing a therapy session.
8. Performance: Elaine Stritch, "Kenward Elmslie Visited," Painted Smiles LP 1339.
9. The songs from "Lola" are not published but there is an original cast recording, and *Beauty Secrets* has been recorded by Barbara Cook, "Kenneth Elmslie Visited."
10. Performance: Joyce Breach. "Love Is The Thing," Audiophile CD 314.
11. Performance: Andrea Marcovici, "New Words," Cabaret CD 5018.
12. Many of the songs mentioned can be found in "The Maury Yeston Songbook," PS Classics CD 310.
13. Performance: Audra McDonald, "How Glory Goes," Nonesuch CD 79580.
14. That this thinning-out bothers some writers can be seen by anxious directions on the lead sheet: Sound the D in this register, or, Put the F-sharp on top of the chord.
15. Kenneth Hymes points out that the extended use of speech rhythms and a very approximate approach to sung pitch makes printed music inherently inadequate. Singers like Billie Holiday deviated from notated pitch, but it was clear what was being deviated from.
16. To be sure, the great lyricists of the 1920s and 1930s represented a new kind of naturalism vis-à-vis Harbach or Wodehouse or early Berlin.
17. Performances: Audra McDonald offers persuasive renditions of LaChiusa, Brown, Gordon, and Guettel on Nonesuch CDs 79482 and 79580. For *A Horse With Wings*: Andrea Marcovici, "New Words."
18. As gathered in a three-CD set, "69 Love Songs," issued by Merritt's group, The Magnetic Fields, as Merge 169; all songs copyright 1999.

9

Classic American Popular Song at the End of the Twentieth Century

Did the classic popular song cease, or enter a terminal decline soon after 1950? Certainly not. In this book we identify an Indian Summer of songs, largely in the 1960s, by writers who had grown up listening to the work of the great figures from the first half-century and who wrote very much in that established style. We also report on a new generation, whom we see as Restocking the Songbook, in a period from the 1960s into the 1980s. Here too one recognizes the classic style, but detects the influence of alternative song styles, especially jazz and rock, and can discern a new sense of what "musical theater" was all about.

Two of the great innovators (in Wilder's terms), within the entire tradition that began about 1920, made their careers in this second half-century. Loesser, active before 1950, produced his best work thereafter, until his early death in 1969. Sondheim, who became well known in the 1960s, is still productive.

Some insist that, nevertheless, the Golden Era of classic popular song ended shortly after the midcentury. This requires one to argue either that the intrinsic quality of songs in this genre declined, or that such songs became less popular. The first claim is not supportable. The second claim is true enough if one means that they ceased to be *uniquely* popular. In chapter 2, we discussed how the classic song, primarily fed from Broadway and Hollywood, ceased to be the *dominant* popular song, a trend reflecting technological, commercial, and societal factors.

Wilder, drafting his book around 1970,[1] acknowledged that the 1950 line of demarcation was artificial by including some of the late songs of Arlen, Rodgers, Lane, Arthur Schwartz, and others. He discussed those songs with conviction, but covered that work less thoroughly than the earlier work by the same writers, as if he believed that he was dealing with the trailing edge of a dying tradition. We find it mysterious that Wilder barely mentioned Loesser, who by 1970 had completed a spectacular career. We suspect that he could not deal with an obviously important case that did not fit his mental model, and that, had he composed the book ten years later, faced with a decade or more of very superior work by Coleman and Leigh (later, Coleman and Fields), Bock and Harnick, Strouse and Adams, early- to midcareer Sondheim, and the work to that date of a number of others, he might have abandoned the model.

Wilder was not alone in a premature drawing of a boundary. James Maher's Introduction to Wilder's book (xxxvii) refers ominously to a sense of irreversible change: "The rock era was about to begin." A number of songwriters, around 1970, are on record as regarding "rock" with fear or loathing, decrying its few chords, inaudible words, and overwhelming loudness. From our vantage-point today, we believe that other factors were also involved, which demoralized both the writers of and listeners to classic popular song.

The first was the actual emergence of an array of diverse, widely popular song styles competing for attention after midcentury. As described in chapter 2, all of a sudden, after 1955 or so, "everybody" was listening to rock and roll, rhythm and blues, country and western, gospel and soul, English rock, the revived American folk song, Cuban and Brazilian rhythms, and the singer-songwriters. The hegemony of the classic pop, 1920 to 1950, had depended on a set of static circumstances, including a rather narrow pattern of transmission by which familiarity bred familiarity. That pattern was now over.

Still, by our standards enumerated in chapter 1, the classic popular song genre displays a vital continuity from before 1925 to 1975 or 1980, something close to sixty years. As popular song genres go, this was a long run. The heyday, in popular culture, of songs from operettas in central Europe lasted perhaps fifty years, up to the 1920s. The most familiar period of English music hall songs was late Victorian through Edwardian. The French street and café chanson, from the Belle Epoque up to Aznavour, gave way after World War II to a grittier, more existential style (and an assimilation of Weimar Germany style.). Brazilian *musica popular brasileira* began in the 1930s as samba-based carnival music; in the 1960s one of its forms, the softer, nondance bossa nova, emerged and had a major influence on North American pop, but by 1980 or so the Tropicalia movement had adopted a soul-rock fusion. While it was natural for Wilder and others to feel discomfort, by 1970, at the efflorescence of new American song genres, it would have been more remarkable had such a development not occurred.

All popular culture, by definition, expresses cohort-based change. There is always the desire for the new. We discussed in chapter 2 how attenuated the cultural attitude of "pop" seemed, as early as the mid-1950s. Romantic heartbreak and start-each-day-with-a-song were no longer news. However, the desire for the new also has a retroflexive aspect. Those who recognize and espouse what is new look back and explicitly devalue what came before. Thus:

> If Joe Jackson had been born a few decades earlier, he would have been writing show tunes:... *Luckily*, Mr. Jackson grew up in the punk-rock era ... he (has) cut away pop sentimentality and revved up the beat.[2]

A writer in 2004 offers examples of white-bread and bourgeois pop as Mel Tormé and Ella Fitzgerald, in her recorded *Songbooks*.[3] It is one thing to recognize that, within popular traditions, the cultural frame of reference alters. "Silver threads among the gold" gives way to "Molly and me, and baby makes three," then to "I get no kick from cocaine," then to "Oh what a beautiful morning," and so on. But these comments show an active hostility to something that was once widely admired, and an attempt to legislate what currently attracts admiration. The second way in which classic popular song writers became demoralized must have been the awareness that journalists and those in charge of "the business" held them in something close to disdain.

Disdain for classic pop is not entirely a revisionary dogma. We have no hard evidence, but there was a period around 1970 when the commercial facet of the pop-song enterprise seemed to be depending on sheer insistence to win the day. We suspect that, had a discriminating twenty-year-old investigated classic pop for the first time then, and found that the most prominent exponents of the style were Liza Minnelli, late Sinatra, Bobby Darin, Bob Fosse, Kander and Ebb—each (whatever their virtues) representing a blatant, in-your-face presentational style—she would have said, I want no part of it.

Our particular interest, however, has not been in charting the course of popularity, but in the intrinsic aspects of the classic pop song tradition over a period of sixty years or more. One obvious question is: Were classic pop songs of the thirty-year period following 1950 comparable in invention and quality, as well as in surface "style," to those of the thirty-year period preceding that date? Our answer, at the end of this long book, is *yes*, in terms of technical features, individuality, and emotional force. A large number of the songs we cover are among the best songs of the entire classic popular genre.

Before we set about doing the research for this book, our answer to the question was, *conceivably yes*. It was an opinion that often startled most of our friends. They were convinced, somehow, that the tradition had crashed. We believe that the evidence in chapters 3 through 8 supports our conclusion. We would urge skeptics not to confuse popularity and longevity with quality. It is true that the fine songs of the first thirty years, 1920 to 1950, remain, as a group, better known. After all, they have been with us longer; and in the earlier period they received far more exposure. We all respond to popular music most deeply when we are fairly young. As time goes on and we hear the songs again and again, recognition imparts a mnemonic luster. Exposed for the first time to a recent song, we may think, That's a terrific song!—but nevertheless, for those now in their sixties, the prototypes, the canonical exemplars were established long ago. Younger listeners probably came to them through their use as jazz standards, or through occasional theatrical revivals, and their attachment to such songs will be more recent, perhaps more shallow.

The present book selects about 1200 songs for at least brief examination.[4] Their dates, when known, are distributed as follows across the decades.[5]

Prior to 1950:   85
        1950s: 350   1980s: 100
        1960s: 300   1990s: 90
        1970s: 115   2000s: 20

The songs we cover from the 1940s are those Wilder missed. Songs from the 2000s all date from the first year or two of the decade, and could stylistically be just as well grouped with songs from the 1990s.

We cannot know for certain how many songs Wilder chose to ignore. Most of the classic pop songs the present authors chose to omit (among those known to us or called to our attention) were not dreadful, but hackneyed. They sounded as if they had been written before, better.

In terms of *positive* instances, however, we found roughly as many in our five decades as Wilder did in his three or four. Looking simply at frequencies, the numbers for the 1970s, 1980s, and 1990s (with those from the 2000s included) are roughly even. The 1950s and 1960s yielded the bumper crops. The 1950s total represents a confluence of "late-harvest" songs by long-established writers with new songs by new writers. Taking that into account, we would say that the classic pop-song endeavor continued essentially unchanged until some time in the late 1960s, when there was a stepping-down to a lower plane.

Our selection from just prior to 1950 through the 1970s yielded, for three decades, about as many notable songs as Wilder found for his three decades. The reduction beginning after 1970 could represent a drop in the actual number of superior classic pop songs created, perhaps owing to demoralization among songwriters and a narrowing number of opportunities. Or it might be that fewer superior songs reached a wide public, because commercial priorities lay elsewhere.

It is conceivable that, following 1970 or so, the superior songs became subtly less good in intrinsic quality, so that we found relatively fewer of them. It is impossible to calculate an average-goodness measure across decades, but we see no evidence for an insidious dilution of quality as time goes on. As a rough indicator of an intersubjective validity for judgment of a "really good" song, we can say that the two of us, when we examined candidate songs, almost always coincided in our independent judgments: this one is really good, that one is okay. In addition, each of us had known most of the songs selected and discussed by Wilder for many years, and only infrequently did we disagree with his judgments. We believe that, had he covered the post-1950 period, his judgments would have been much like ours.[6]

We find, then, that the "Golden Age" to which some allude should refer to the entire second *and* third quarter of the twentieth century. To be sure, we are sensitive to a certain fatigue that set in as the decades went on, not so much in the songs themselves as in auditors' responses. We have noted, among some commentators, the sense that the whole enterprise became old-fashioned. We ourselves were not always immune to that sense of *vieux jeux*. Occasionally, in chapters 3 through 8, we say that a song is attractive and well-made, but shop-worn. We also mention at times that the conception (as to situation or subject-matter) or execution (as to diction or harmonic moves) of a particular song resembles an earlier one. Priority counts in popular arts. Finally, we have had occasion to say that a song deserved to be a "standard"—had it been written earlier and recorded more often.[7]

The power of the American classic popular song has always come from its being a well-turned cliché. One can turn the cliché freshly only so many times before the process becomes artificial. The best way to use cliché is to leave it plainly stated—and not state it too often. With regard to the "turning" itself, we find a wonderful melodic/harmonic freshness in Mandel, Sondheim, Yeston, Richardson, Leonard, Marvin Fisher, and a number of others—all different, all remarkable. The "commercial" songs of Lew Spence are quite as good as those of Jimmy McHugh. In terms of verbal "turning," it strikes us that the overall achievement of lyricists in the second half-century is, if anything, more impressive than that of the earlier period. It is remarkable how Fields changed her style to write with Coleman. Loesser, Sondheim, and Harnick are certainly among the most brilliant and versatile lyricists of the entire tradition. No one was funnier than Barer, more deft and delightful than Dearie or Wallowitch; no one more insouciantly original than Leigh or Landesman.

As diction shades into subject-matter, things become more complex. The particular worldview of Frishberg, Dorough, or Wolf with Landesman could not have been comunicated prior to World War II. These are contemporary sensibilities. The dry-martini wit of Porter and the bourbon-and-branch-water humor of Mercer are everlasting treasures of the great tradition; but so is the wit, fuel unknown, of these later writers. These new lyricists are not necessarily more sophisticated, but they are sophisticated about modern things. The complication is that the earlier writers were culturally mainstream, and their work resulted in hits. These later writers, at least, were appealing to more specialized tastes. They do address themselves to the core subjects—love and loss, leaving and coming home, happiness and pain—but often obliquely. Sometimes their explicit topics are baseball players, jazz musicians, or the interactional games people play. On the one hand, they bring a particular strain of very American humor into the popular song, as if Mark Twain or John Cheever were writing songs. On the other hand, it sometimes seems that they are like birds building a nest with whatever materials are handy. How eccentric can songs be and still remain in a "classic" tradition?[8]

Most songwriters, including those writing for the theater, still wrote, following 1950, with high technical competence about the canonical verities. It is they who risked seeming tiresome to the listening public. We need not proffer superficial generalizations about cultural change in American life in the third quarter of the century. We do claim that the stepping-down in numbers of superior classic pop songs, apparent in our table (p. 332) beginning in the 1970s, has to reflect, not the challenge of rock but the preference, among young listeners, for the topics and style of discourse characteristic of the singer-songwriters. We argue this point on pp. 274. In popular genres, style of discourse is crucial. The classic popular song had been a Keatsian sonnet. The new song was a Byronic personal epic. It was often self-centered, as opposed to being a concise symbolic construction depending on the play of identification between speaker and listener. It was narrative, not metaphorical; it was musically sectional, not closed in form; it was metrically loose. In terms of both musical form and semantics, it rejected the compact, well-turned character of the classic popular song.

Were classic pop songs after 1970 or so essentially *different* from those in the 1950 to 1970 period? Often they seemed to take account of changes in the old neighborhood, as we discuss just above in terms of range of reference. From time to time we have also noted the presence of a light-rock rhythm.[9] Toward the end of the century, the mixing of modal and traditional pop-jazz harmonies, evident as far back as the Beatles, became an accepted, almost expected, feature, so that songs written in diatonic major or minor seemed old-fashioned to some.

A prevalent type of classic pop song, in earlier decades, had been the light, medium-tempo, almost throwaway song whose hallmark was charm: the sort of song that sneaks up on you and gives a light caress. Such songs became less and less common, or at least less successful,[10] even while dramatic songs, pure love songs, and songs depending upon propulsive rhythmic means continued to be written.

Increasingly, in the last decades of the century, songs did without verses. Traditionally, "verse" introduction to songs established, by means of a brief background or *tour d'horizon*, the situation from which the metaphor of the body of the song emerged. Now, as the body of the song became more personalized and more narrated in direct presentational voice, there was no need for scene-setting before the song got under way. Many of the songs we most admire from the last quarter-century are "stretched" traditional songs: a bit bigger, a bit longer, a bit more complex. The departure from a modest two-part form (statement, then inference; background, then foreground) meant that some songs became less transportable. It is harder for a singer in a club to establish a mood, a situation, a role for the speaker (and one for the listener) when the song simply starts.

The dropping out of verses surely reflected an alteration in dramaturgy, as well. We have summarized (p. 319ff) the way in which musical theater works became more fluid in form and more linearly integrated and recursive, involving an ongoing flow of musical events giving way occasionally to heightened expression. Even when the older dialogue/song distinction was preserved, the range of topic or the tone of discourse changed. In some of Yeston's beautiful theater songs, it is not entirely clear who are the dramatis personae or what is the situation. Here too the songs are less transferable to other presentational contexts. At a point in the 1980s, Sondheim veered away from the dialogue/song/dialogue format, even when working with a traditional "book." With regard to his songs, no one can trot out the old charge (about pop songs generally) that they are verbally banal. A listener may not like what the lyrics address, but the songs are fresh. They omit verses, by and large, but supply the relevant information about context and attitude in the body of the song. They are psychologically astute, but perhaps "alienated" in attitude. Some of Sondheim's excellent songs from "Merrily We Roll Along" or "Company," where modern, realistic fictional situations are involved, deal (respectively) with wasted self-deluded lives (the former) or a desperately alone antihero, who cries, in *Being Alive*, "Somebody force me to care." As songs they are fascinating, but empathetically distant. It is hard to identify with someone who is disgusted with himself.

Back in 1961, with "How to Succeed In Business," Loesser, we think, was writing theater songs that succeeded communicatively but that concurrently expressed a judgmental commentary, most obviously in *I Believe In You*. It is very hard to make songs convey irony.[11] How Loesser would have faced some of the dramaturgical challenges that Sondheim took up is unknowable. Shire and Maltby took the step of changing the terms of the challenge of how to write songs that are true to a dramatic purpose but that communicate directly outside the show. They said, Let us first imagine characters, then devise songs, lyrical or dramatic, that these characters would voice, and then have the singers find themselves in a "plot" that they discover through the accumulation of what the songs recount.

The plot-by-induction device cannot be used very often. Unlike the case with light and charming songs, which tended to disappear, theater composers of the later period continued to write passionately lyrical and strongly dramatic songs in familiar ways. We find many of the songs of Kander and Ebb or Herman rather retrograde in style. However, *I Want to Be With You* (Strouse — Adams), *Alone In the Universe* (Flaherty — Ahrens), *The Kind of Man a Woman Needs* (Leonard — Martin), or *Heart's Desire* (Broadbent — Frishberg) are fine dramatic songs in a new vein, easily exportable, and fine fresh love songs from this period are too numerous to list. Though some of Yeston's songs are ambiguous in their reference, his songs (especially those for "Nine") are perfect for a stream-of-consciousness medium—autonomous enough to catch the attention without stopping the flow of incident and action in the theater.

There is a tricky calculus having to do with the specific versus the generic in songs. Wilder believed that, in the end, songs originating in the theater or films were more satisfying than stand-alone songs. Often it seems that there is some enriching residue in theater songs, traceable to the original dramatic context or character. A songwriter addressing the representative listener, via radio or record, avoids any distraction that might come from references to particular places, people, or situations. That is why such songs are so often built around a figure of speech in ordinary language. In songs from the theater, there is sometimes a reference whose precise meaning is unclear to the listener but which deepens rather than deflects the impact of the song. The Rodgers — Hammerstein *I'm In Love With a Wonderful Guy* would not, we think, have been popular had it not seemed to refer to a "real" person: someone from Kansas, naïve and bromidic in attitude. In Sondheim's beautiful *Take Me to the World* the lyric mentions "a world that smiles / with streets instead of aisles." Why *aisles*, and why, for the speaker, would streets *smile*? If you know "Evening Primrose," you have the answer. Otherwise, the lyric tantalizes by its slight strangeness, rather than putting us off.

In the theater, ad hoc elements are present in a song because the writer wants to convince the listener that *these* characters would express *these* sentiments at *this* juncture: that this is not just a song that could be sung by anyone in any show.[12] But conversely, for it to be persuasive for the character to move into song at all, the writer needs to achieve a certain level of generality; otherwise, the character might just as well get on with dialogue and incident.

Whatever its origin, a memorable song cannot be utterly generic (unless it is memorable for its fatuity). A good song needs to suggest that it captures real experience that could have been. It is paradoxical—but if you catch the deeper emotional context, the song takes on additional overtones; if not, you sense them there anyhow. We have mentioned in this chapter that many of the songs of the second half-century are odd, off-beat, or idiomatic: more so, on average, than earlier songs. Wilder was right, empirically: for his classic period, the deeper songs did tend to come from shows. But apparently it is not a necessary relation. Songs can have a satisfying degree of characterological impact outside a dramatic situation.[13]

A number of recent songwriters have made good careers outside the theater: Billy Joel, Tom Waits, Jimmy Webb come to mind as gifted "commercial" writers. Some very recent writers like Lutvak seem in effect to be creating, incrementally, song cycles whose common thread is their creator's own personality and experience. Perfect, pure love songs are still achievable: for example, the Mandel — Frishberg *You Are There,* or the Ross — Barer *Something Known.* Some stand-alone songs tell compelling dramatic stories, like Stephen Schwartz's *Life Goes On* or Julie Gold's *Goodnight, New York.* We are not recommending that new songwriters avoid the theater. In fact, several times in this book we have wished that writers had been challenged in that way, because we found their songs a bit generic or underambitious. But nothing would have been gained had they written for the theater of the tired businessman or the spectacle-lover. In the end, there is a *theater of the mind* that will always involve song, including song that has nothing to do with plot points but that conveys a special meaning from within interior monologue. The best songwriters will always find ways to represent such moments.

If we who appreciate the classic popular style still expect superior songs to begin in the theater, be disseminated by original-cast recordings, then be adopted by singers of high merit, then taken up by jazz trios, then heard in clubs—in other words, to make their way to being "standards" by the old pathway—we are doomed to disappointment. Does it then follow that the best new songs will be heard only in cabaret? How are truly superior songs ever to become *popular* songs if they reach only coterie audiences?

If "cabaret" signifies a place where listeners go to hear old show songs together with some new songs that sound like distillates of a vanishing substance, then indeed we are talking of a largely antiquarian enterprise, like hand-printed books, or daguerreotype, or going to hear Gilbert and Sullivan. But the experience can be far more than this. The discriminating singer Andrea Marcovici says:

> Cabaret is an intensely personal evening of song and stories, delivered in a simple honest way in an intimate space that shatters the fourth wall. The audience participates in a direct, emotional conversation with the artist and leaves feeling contacted and personally touched.

If the term *cabaret* suggests preciousness, a kind of Preservation Hall for the cognoscenti of a bygone music, let us just change the term. All over our country, people seek out clubs in order to hear their favorite dance music, "roots music," or other "world music" of personal significance to them. One sense of *club* is that you and I know about it, but others don't. In such a locale, you are not just a spectator, you come to pay special attention. There is no reason why listeners will not find clubs in which to hear new work by writers of classic popular song.

Such clubs can also be virtual.[14] Surely today, given Web streaming and cable TV with good sound, performers can "put over" a meaningful sequence of songs, perhaps equivalent to a "concept album." In a song club, actual or virtual, the crucial element is that the performer advocate good material, old or new. Ultimately, a fine song is a figure of sound, an island of order in a sea of sound.

> How did we change, caught in this strange new music? . . .
> Just like that tune, simple and clear, I've come to hear new music.[15]

In our Introduction, we raised the possibility that songwriters of the late part of the twentieth century might be seen as moving the genre in a distinctly new direction, which would prove eventually to be the new classic popular style. As of about the year 2000, we do not see any such clear direction. Among the significant songwriters active at the end of the twentieth century (Sondheim aside), there is no clear direction for modifying or going beyond the classic popular song style. One writer, Merritt, writes neatly in that style but rejects it by mocking the enterprise. Otherwise, Schwartz seems convincing with an admixture of light, guitar-based rock style, though this blend by no means represents a victory of the rock over the pop genre. Yeston and Guettel seem to incline toward adapting the classic pop style to the art song cycle or the lyric opera, while Flaherty and Ahrens are comfortable marrying it with other twentieth-century popular traditions. Lippa sticks close to the classic style but dresses it up with some musical complexities that are not entirely convincing, while Lutvak shows a freedom of approach whose implications are not yet clear. Our overall assessment is that, among today's writers, the classic pop style is thoroughly viable, though no longer widely popular. The question is, how vital is it?

Commercially speaking, it is living on reduced rations. A lot depends, for the future, on the songwriter's understanding the cultural expectations of what a song should be *about*. A lot depends on satisfying a need for musical-cultural diversity and for a variety of styles of discourse in song. Songwriters should be listening to griot, hip-hop, chanted or choral speaking, and metered speech from a wide range of cultural roots. There is a vast potential in the amazingly various Afro-American idiom, whether Cape Verdean, Senegalese, Afro pop, Cuban, Brazilian, South African.[16] The bossa nova influence of the 1960s had a fine stimulating effect on American popular song.[17] Any musical vernacular, so long as it combines (to Western ears) strong melodic profile, rhythms that spring or swing, plangent instrumentation, a clear tonality, and a lyric in ordinary but artful English—all in a compact, concise, elegant package—can generate the next classic style in our society.

Such an envisioning of the future (it is not a prediction) may seem like a routine invocation of multiculturalism. It is not. There is a far more persuasive example to point to than bossa nova. In the United States of the twentieth century, classic popular song was syncretic in its deep structure. The classic style, it turned out, was a Creole of Euro-American tunes, African rhythms, blues patterns, Celtic and East European scales, French harmony, and predominantly Anglo-American verse diction. Successful Creoles are generative. Early hybrids were sometimes perceived at first as absurd or barbaric. But by the time Berlin and Gershwin had finished, they had formed an irresistible style that not only dominated in our own society, but swept most of the world. Why would one assume that it will not happen again?

Notes

1. Alec Wilder, with James T. Maher, "American Popular Song: The Great Innovators, 1900-1950." (New York: Oxford Univ. Press, 1972.) Hereafter, Wilder.
2. Jon Pareles, "New York Times," April 16, 2003. Emphasis added.
3. James Gavin, "New York Times" Book Section, March 7, 2004.
4. See Introduction, pp. xxii–xiv, for more detail.
5. The book mentions two hundred or so songs whose dates we could not determine. These tend to be from the 1980s and 1990s, as "publication" became somewhat ill-defined (see p. xviii, note 7). We also mentioned (p. xiv) we were less systematic in our search for good songs written at the very end of the century. For these reasons, the true numbers for these decades may be a bit larger.
6. Wilder did temper his doom-laden view before his death in 1980. Listening to some new recordings, he is reported to have said, "All of this is a revelation to me...I assumed that lights were fast going out all over the place...it isn't over." The quotation comes from the liner notes for Irene Kral's CD, "You Are There."
7. There is a factor of bad luck in timing: as one poignant example, the very fine songs of Hugh Martin, which we would not do without but wish had been created twenty years earlier, when they would have become better known.
8. We would say, very. Our concern here is more for audience "penetration," rather than technical quality.
9. Light rock in classic pop sometimes feels perfunctory. In some songs by Stephen Schwartz and many songs by John Bucchino, we have commented that by slightly regularizing the meter or by adding a little to the vertical complexity of the harmony, classic pop emerges: but it is still weak rock and thin pop.
10. A few distinguished examples from the post-1950 period would include *Real Live Girl, Nice 'n Easy, Two for the Road, Dance Only With Me, Love-Wise, A Fine Spring Morning,* and *I'm All Smiles.*
11. Randy Newman's *Short People* (Got No Reason to Live) is a counterexample that may prove the point.
12. There are analogous considerations on the musical level, as regards the conventionality or strangeness of chord progressions and harmony, or the degree of predictability of the tune.
13. Compelling examples would include the Shire — Maltby *One of the Good Guys*, the Springer — Harburg *Time, You Old Gypsy Man*, or the Wilder — McGlohon *'Sgonna Be a Cold Cold Day*.
14. And listeners will get used to finding songs electronically, not on the printed page.
15. From *New Music*, by Flaherty and Ahrens.
16. In this regard, we do not give up on the musical theater as a source for innovation. Arlen and Capote, Arlen and Harburg, Flaherty and Ahrens, and Paul Simon made promising forays, but obviously a much wider range of backgrounds and talents is needed. Perhaps "musical theater" of the future will not be found within four walls, but in the streets, clubs, television, films, where "the action" does not stop for songs but incorporates them as part of the setting.
17. The reason why bossa nova failed to have an even larger impact is that strong English-language lyrics were generally not forthcoming. If only Caetano Veloso, seeking political exile, had chosen North America!

Permissions

Songs Licensed by the Hal Leonard Corporation

(I'll Marry) The Very Next Man from the Musical FIORELLO! Lyrics by Sheldon Harnick; Music by Jerry Bock. © 1959 (Renewed 1987) MAYERLING PRODUCTIONS LTD. And JERRY BOCK ENTERPRISES for the U.S.A. All rights for the World excluding the U.S.A. Administered by ALLEY MUSIC CORP. and TRIO MUSIC COMPANY INC. All rights reserved.

Another Autumn from PAINT YOUR WAGON Words by Alan Jay Lerner; Music by Frederick Loewe. © 1951 by Alan Jay Lerner and Frederick Loewe. Copyright Renewed. Chappell & Co. owner of publication and allied rights throughout the world. International Copyright Secured. All Rights Reserved.

I Don't Want To Know from DEAR WORLD Music and Lyric by Jerry Herman.
© 1968, 1969 (Renewed) JERRY HERMAN. All Rights Controlled by JERRYCO MUSIC CO. Exclusive Agent: EDWIN H. MORRIS & COMPANY, A Division of MPL Music Publishing, Inc. All Rights Reserved.

I Was Telling Her About You Words and Music by Mark Charlap and Don George.
© 1955 (Renewed 1983) EMI FULL KEEL MUSIC All Rights Reserved. International Copyright Secured Used by Permission.

Ivory Tower Words and Music by George C. Cory, Jr. and Douglass Cross © 1955 (Renewed 1983) COLGEMS-EMI MUSIC INC. All rights reserved. International Copyright Secured. Used by Permission.

Joey, Joey, Joey from THE MOST HAPPY FELLA By Frank Loesser © 1956 (renewed) FRANK MUSIC CORP. All Rights Reserved.

Let's See What Happens Words and Music by E.Y. Harburg and Jule Styne © 1967 by Chappell & Co. Copyright Renewed. International Copyright Secured. All Rights Reserved.

Lilac Wine Words and Music by James H. Shelton © 1949 by Chappell & Co. Copyright Renewed. International Copyright Secured. All Rights Reserved.

Merry Little Minuet Words and Music by Sheldon Harnick © 1958 by Alley Music Corp. and Trio Music Company, Inc. Copyright Renewed. All Rights for Trio Music Company, Inc Administered by Windswept. International Copyright Secured. All Rights Reserved. Used by Permission.

I Want To Be With You from GOLDEN BOY. Lyric by Lee Adams; Music by Charles Strouse. © 1964 (renewed) Charles Strouse. Worldwide publishing by Charles Strouse Music, Helene Blue Musique Ltd. administrator, www.CharlesStrouse.com. All Rights Reserved. Used by Permission.

I'll Never Go There Any More Words by Eddie Lawrence; Music by Moose Charlap. © 1964 by Chappell & Co. Copyright Renewed. International Copyright Secured. All Rights Reserved.

I've Got You Under My Skin from BORN TO DANCE. Words and Music by Cole Porter. © 1936 by Chappell & Co. Copyright Renewed, Assigned to John F. Wharton, Trustee of the Cole Porter Musical and Literary Property Trusts. Chappell & Co. owner of publication and allied rights throughout the world. International Copyright Secured. All Rights Reserved.

I've Just Seen Her (As Nobody Else Has Seen Her) Lyric by Lee Adams; Music by Charles Strouse. © 1962 (Renewed) Charles Strouse. Worldwide publishing by Charles Strouse Music, Helene Blue Musique Ltd. administrator,www.CharlesStrouse.com. All Rights Reserved. Used by Permission.

I've Never Been In Love Before from GUYS AND DOLLS By Frank Loesser. © 1950 (Renewed) FRANK MUSIC CORP. All Rights Reserved.

If He Walked Into My Life Music and Lyric by Jerry Herman. © 1966 (Renewed) JERRY HERMAN. All Rights Controlled by JERRYCO MUSIC CO, Exclusive Agent: EDWIN H. MORRIS & COMPANY, A Division of MPL Music Publishing, Inc. All Rights Reserved.

The Kind Of Man A Woman Needs from THE YEARLING. Lyric by Herbert Martin; Music by Michael Leonard © 1966 (Renewed) HERBERT MARTIN and MICHAEL LEONARD. All Rights Throughout the World Controlled by EDWIN H. MORRIS 7 COMPANY, A Division of MPL Music Publishing, Inc. and EMANUAL MUSIC CORP. All Rights Reserved.

Long Before I Knew You from BELLS ARE RINGING. Words by Betty Comden and Adolph Green; Music by Jule Styne. © 1959, 1960 by Betty Comden, Adolph Green and Jule Styne. Copyright Renewed. Stratford Music Corp., owner, and Chappell & Co., Administrator of publication and allied rights for the Western Hemisphere. International Copyright Secured. All Rights Reserved.

Love Wise Words and Music by Marvin Fisher and Kenward Elmslie. © 1958 Sony/ATV Tunes LLC. Copyright Renewed. All Rights Administered by Sony/ATV Music publishing, 8 Music Square West, Nashville, TN 37203. International Copyright Secured. All Rights Reserved.

Love Look Away from FLOWER DRUM SONG. Lyrics by Oscar Hammerstein II; Music by Richard Rodgers. © 1958 by Richard Rodgers and Oscar Hammerstein II. Copyright Renewed. WILLIAMSON MUSIC owner of publication and allied rights throughout the world. International Copyright Secured. All Rights Reserved.

Luck Be A Lady from GUYS AND DOLLS By Frank Loesser. © 1950 (Renewed) FRANK MUSIC CORP. All Rights Reserved.

Married Life from NICK AND NORA.; Lyric by Richard Maltby, Jr. Music by Charles Strouse. © 1992 Charles Strouse. Worldwide publishing by Charles Strouse Music, Helene Blue Musique Ltd. administrator, www.CharlesStrouse.com. All Rights Reserved. Used by Permission.

Maybe It's Time For Me Words by James Lipton; Music by Laurence Rosenthal. © 1967 by Chappell & Co. Copyright Renewed. International Copyright Secured. All Rights Reserved.

Nobody Told Me from NO STRINGS. Lyrics and Music by Richard Rodgers. © 1963 by Richard Rodgers. Copyright Renewed. WILLIAMSON MUSIC owner of publication and allied rights throughout the world. International Copyright Secured. All Rights Reserved.

Ohio from WONDERFUL TOWN. Lyrics by Betty Comden and Adolph Green; Music by Leonard Bernstein. © 1953 by Amberson Holdings LLC, Betty Comden and Adolph Green. Copyright

Whatever Time There Is from CHARLIE AND ALGERNON. Lyric by David Rogers; Music by Charles Strouse. © 1979 Charles Strouse. Worldwide publishing by Charles Strouse Music, Helene Blue Musique Ltd. administrator, www.CharlesStrouse.com. All Rights Reserved. Used by Permission.

Where Did Everyone Go Words and Music by Jimmy Van Heusen and Mack David. © 1963 Sony/ATV Tunes LLC. Copyright Renewed. All Rights Administered by Sony/ATV Music Publishing, 8 Music Square West, Nashville, TN 37203. International Copyright Secured. All Rights Reserved.

Words Without Music Words by Ira Gershwin; Music by Vernon Duke. © 1935 by Chappell & Co. and Ira Gershwin Music. Copyright Renewed. All Rights for Ira Gershwin Music Administered by WB Music Corp. International Copyright Secured. All Rights Reserved.

Your Cheatin' Heart Words and Music by Hank Williams. © 1952 Sony/ATV Songs LLC and Hiram Music in the U.S.A. Copyright Renewed. All Rights on behalf of Hiram Music Administered by Rightsong Music Inc. All Rights outside the U.S.A. Controlled by Sony/ATV Songs LLC. All Rights on behalf of Sony/ATV Songs LLC Administered by Sony/ATV Publishing, 8 Music Square West, Nashville, TN 37203. International Copyright Secured. All Rights Reserved.

We Don't Matter At All from IT'S A BIRD, IT'S A PLANE, IT'S SUPERMAN. Lyics by Lee Adams; Music by Charles Strouse. © 1966 (Renewed) Strada Music. All Rights Controlled by Helene Blue Musique Ltd. All Rights Reserved. Used By Permission.

While The City Sleeps from GOLDEN BOY. Lyrics by Lee Adams; Music by Charles Strouse. © 1964 (Renewed) Strada Music. All Rights Controlled by Helene Blue Musique Ltd. All Rights Reserved. Used By Permission.

Golden Boy from GOLDEN BOY. Lyrics by Lee Adams; Music by Charles Strouse. © 1964 (Renewed) Strada Music. All Rights Controlled by Helene Blue Musique Ltd. All Rights Reserved. Used by Permission.

Is There Anything Better Than Dancing from NICK AND NORA. Lyrics by Richard Maltby, Jr.; Music by Charles Strouse. © 1991 Charles Strouse publications. All Rights Controlled by Helene Blue Musique Ltd. All Rights Reserved. Used by Permission

Look Who's Alone Now from NICK AND NORA. Lyrics by Richard Maltby, Jr;. Music by Charles Strouse. © 1992 Charles Strouse. Worldwide publishing by Charles Strouse Music, Helene Blue Musique Ltd. administrator, www.CharlesStrouse,com. All Rights Reserved. Used by Permission.

Songs Licensed by Cherry Lane Music Company

And Then You Kissed Me Words by Sammy Cahn; Music by Jule Styne. © 1944 by Producers Music Publishing Co., Inc. and Cahn Music Co. Copyright Renewed. All Rights for Producers Music Publishing Co., Inc. Administered by Chappell & Co. Worldwide Rights for Cahn Music Co. Administered by Cherry Lane Publishing Company, Inc. International Copyright Secured. All Rights Reserved.

Home from PHANTOM. Words and Music by Maury Yeston. © 1991 Yeston Music Ltd. (BMI). Worldwide Rights for Yeston Music Ltd. Administered by Cherry River Music Co. International Copyright Secured. All Rights Reserved.

Getting Tall from NINE. Words and Music by Maury Yeston. © 1982 by Yeston Music Ltd. (BMI). Worldwide Rights for Yeston Music Ltd. Administered by Cherry River Music Co. International Copyright Secured. All Rights Reserved.

New Words Words and Music by Maury Yeston. © 1975; Renewed 2003 Yeston Music Ltd. (BMI). Worldwide Rights for Yeston Music Ltd. Administrated by Cherry River Music Co. International Copyright Secured. All Rights Reserved.

New Words Words and Music by Maury Yeston. © 1975; Renewed 2003 Yeston Music Ltd. (BMI). Worldwide Rights for Yeston Music Ltd. Administered by Cherry River Music Co. International Copyright Secured. All Rights Reserved.

Only With You from NINE. Words and Music by Maury Yeston. © 1982 Yeston Music Ltd. (BMI). Worldwide Rights for Yeston Music Ltd. Administered by Cherry River Music Co. International Copyright Secured. All Rights Reserved.

Unusual Way (In A Very Unusual Way) from NINE. Words and Music by Maury Yeston. © 1975; Renewed 2003 Yeston Music Ltd. (BMI). Worldwide Rights for Yeston Music Ltd. Administered by Cherry River Music Co. International Copyright Secured. All Rights Reserved.

You're There Too from IN THE BEGINNING. Words and Music by Maury Yeston. © 1994 Yeston Music Ltd. (BMI). Worldwide Rights for Yeston Music Ltd. Administered by Cherry River Music Co. International Copyright Secured. All Rights Reserved.

Songs Licensed by Warner Bros. Publications

All Those Christmas Cliches by Lynn Ahrens and Stephen Flaherty. © WB Music Corp., Warner-Tamerlane Publishing Corp. All Rights On Behalf of Hillsdale Music, Inc. Administered by WB Music Corp. All Rights On Behalf of Dormont Music Administered by Warner-Tamerlane Publishing Corp. All Rights Reserved. Used by Permission. WARNER BROS. PUBLICATIONS U.S. INC., Miami, FL 33014.

Alone In The Universe by Stephen Flaherty and Lynn Ahrens. © 2001 WB Music Corp. (ASCAP), Pen and Perseverance (ASCAP) and Hillsdale Music, Inc. (ASCAP). All Rights Administered By WB Music Corp.(ASCAP). All Rights Reserved. Used by Permission. WARNER BROS. PUBLICATIONS U.S. INC., Miami, FL 33014.

Being Good Isn't Good Enough by Betty Comden, Adolph Green and Jule Styne. © 1967 (Renewed) Chappell & Co. All Rights Reserved. Used by Permission. WARNER BROS. PUBLICATIONS U.S. INC., Miami, FL 33014.

A Christmas Love Song by Alan and Marilyn Bergman and Johnny Mandel. © 1988, 1991 Threesome Music Co. and Marissa Music. All Rights Reserved. Used by Permission.
WARNER BROS. PUBLICATIONS U.S. INC., Miami, FL 33014.

Come Down From The Tree by Stephen Flaherty and Lynn Ahrens. © 1994 WB Music Corp. (ASCAP), Pen and Perseverance (ASCAP) and Hillsdale Music, Inc. (ASCAP). All Rights On Behalf Of Pen and Perseverence (ASCAP) and Hillsdale Music, Inc. (ASCAP) Administered By WB Music Corp. (ASCAP). All Rights Reserved. Used by Permission. WARNER BROS. PUBLICATIONS U.S. INC., Miami, FL 33014.

Fifty Percent by Alan and Marilyn Bergman and Billy Goldenberg. © 1978, 1979 Threesome Music Co. and Izzylumoe Music. All Rights Reserved. Used by Permission. WARNER BROS. PUBLICATIONS U.S. INC., Miami, FL 33014.

Flair by David Shire and Richard Maltby, Jr. © Fiddleback Music Publishing Co., Inc. (BMI) and Revelation Music Publishing Corp. (ASCAP). All Rights On Behalf Of Fiddleback Music Publishing Co., Inc. (BMI) Administered By Warner-Tamerlane Publishing Corp. (BMI). All Rights On Behald Of Revelation Music Publishing Corp. (ASCAP) Administered by WB Music Corp. (ASCAP). All Rights Reserved. Used by Permission. WARNER BROS. PUBLICATIONS U.S. INC., Miami, FL 33014.

Foggy Day by George Gershwin and Ira Gershwin. © 1937 (Renewed) George Gershwin Music (ASCAP) and Ira Gershwin Music (ASCAP). All Rights Administered By WB Music Corp. All Rights Reserved. Used by Permission. WARNER BROS. PUBLICATIONS U.S. INC., Miami, FL 33014.

Good Thing Going by Stephen Sondheim. © 1978 Rilting Music, Inc. (ASCAP). All Rights Administered by WB Music Corp. (ASCAP). All Rights Reserved. Used by Permission. WARNER BROS. PUBLICATIONS U.S. INC., Miami, FL 33014.

Gotta Dance by Hugh Martin. © 1948 (renewed) Chappell & Co., Inc. All Rights Reserved. Used by Permission. NER BROS. PUBLICATIONS U.S. INC., Miami, FL 33014.

Green Finch And Linnet Bird by Stephen Sondheim © 1978 Rilting Music, Inc. (ASCAP). All Rights On Behalf Of Rilting Music, Inc. (A SCAP) Administered by WB Music Corp. (ASCAP). All Rights Reserved. Used by Permission. WARNER BROS. PUBLICATIOONS U.S. INC., Miami, FL 33014.

Highly Emotional State (From "Sweet Charity") by Cy Coleman and Dorothy Fields. © 1965, 1969 Notable Music Co., Inc. and Lida Enterprises, Inc. Copyrights Renewed. All Rights Administered WB Music Corp. (ASCAP). All Rights Reserved. Used by Permission WARNER BROS. PUBLICATIONS U.S. INC., Miami, FL 33014.

How Can You Kiss Those Good Times Goodbye by James A. Lipton and Laurence Rosenthal. © 1967 (Renewed) Chappell & Co., Inc. (ASCAP) All Rights Reserved. Used by Permission WARNER BROS. PUBLICATIONS U.S. INC., Miami, FL 33014.

How Will He Know by Betty Comden, Adolph Green and Jule Styne. © 1951 (Renewed) Chappell & Co., Inc. (ASCAP).All Rights Reserved. Used by Permission WARNER BROS. PUBLICATIONS U.S. INC., Miami, FL 33014.

Hurry It's Lovely Up Here by Burton Lane and Alan Jay Lerner. © 1965 (Renewed) Chappell & Co., Inc. (ASCAP). All Rights Reserved. Used by Permission. WARNER BROS. PUBLICATIONS U.S. INC., Miami, FL 33014.

I Got Rhythm by George Gershwin and Ira Gershwin. © 1930 (Renewed) WB Music Corp. (ASCAP). All Rights Reserved. Used by Permission. WARNER BROS. PUBLICATIONS U.S. INC., Miami, FL 33014.

I Have My Own Way by Johnny Burke. © 1961 (Renewed) Warner Bros. Inc. All Rights Reserved. Used by Permission. WARNER BROS. PUBLICATIONS U.S. INC., Miami, FL 33014.

I Got Out Of Bed On The Right Side Music and Lyrics by Johnny Mercer and Arthur Schwartz. © (Renewed) EMI Robbins Catalog Inc. All rights Reserved. Used by Permission. WARNER BROS. PUBLICATIONS U.S. INC. Miami, FL 33014.

I Like Myself Music and Lyrics by Betty Comden, Adolph Green, and Andre G. Previn. © (Renewed) EMI Robbins Catalog Inc. All Rights Reserved. Used by Permission. WARNER BROS. PUBLICATIONS U.S. INC., Miami, FL 33014.

If The World Were Like The Movies by Stephen Flaherty and Lynn Ahrens. © 1993 WB Music Corp. (ASCAP), Pen and Perseverance (ASCAP) and Hillsdale Music, Inc. (ASCAP). All Rights On Behalf Of Pen and Perseverance (ASCAP) and Hillsdale Music, Inc. (ASCAP) Administered by WB Music Corp. (ASCAP). All Rights Reserved. Used by Permission. WARNER BROS. PUBLICATIONS U.S. INC., Miami, FL 33014.

I'm The Girl by James H. Shelton. © 1949 (Renewed) Chappell & Co. All Rights Reserved. Used by Permission. WARNER BROS. PUBLICATIONS U.S. INC., Miami, FL 33014.

I Walk A Little Faster by Cy Coleman and Carolyn Leigh. © 1958 (Renewed) Notable Music Co., Inc. (ASCAP) and Carwin Music Inc. (ASCAP). All Rights On Behalf Of Notable Music Co., Inc. Administered By WB Music Corp. All Rights Reserved. Used by Permission WARNER BROS. PUBLICATIONS U.S. INC., Miami, FL 33014.

Normandy by Mary Rodgers and Marshall Barer. © 1967 (Renewed) Chappell & Co. (ASCAP) All Rights Reserved. Used by Permission. WARNER BROS. PUBLICATIONS U.S. INC., Miami, FL 33014.

Not While I'm Around by Stephen Sondheim. © 1979 Rilting Music, Inc. (ASCAP). All Rights Administered By WB Music Corp. All Rights Reserved. Used by Permission. WARNER BROS. PUBLICATIONS U.S. INC., Miami, FL 33014.

Ohio by Leonard Bernstein, Betty Comden and Adolph Green. © 1953 (Renewed) Chappell & Co. (ASCAP) and Leonard Bernstein Music Publishing Co. LLC (ASCAP). All Rights Administered By Chappell & Co. Inc, All Rights Reserved. Used by Permission. WARNER BROS. PUBLICATIONS U.S. INC., Miami, FL 33014.

On A Clear Day (You Can See Forever) by Alan Jay Lerner and Burton Lane. © 1965 by Alan Jay Lerner and Burton Lane. Copyright Renewed. All Rights In The U.S. Administered By WB Music Corp. and Chappell & Co. By Agreement With The Heirs of Alan Jay Lerner and With Burton Lane. Publication and Allied Rights Elsewhere Assigned To Chappell & Co. All Rights Reserved. Used by Permission. WARNER BROS. PUBLICATIONS U.S. INC., Miami, FL 33014.

On Second Thought by Cy Coleman and Carolyn Leigh. © 1965 (Renewed) All Rights On Behalf Of Notable Music Co., Inc. Administered By WB Music Corp. All Rights Reserved. Used by Permission. WARNER BROS. PUBLICATIONS U.S. INC., Miami, FL 33014.

One Day We Dance by Cy Coleman and Carolyn Leigh. © 1958 (Renewed). All Rights Reserved. Used by Permission. WARNER BROS, PUBLICATIONS U.S. INC., Miami, FL 33014.

One Of The Good Guys by David Shire and Richard Maltby, Jr.© 1984 Progeny Music (BMI), Fiddleback Music Publishing Co., Inc. (BMI), Long Pond Music (ASCAP) and Revelation Music Publishing Corp. (ASCAP). All Rights On Behalf Of Progeny Music (BMI) and Fiddleback Music Publishing Co., Inc. (BMI) Administered By Warner-Tamerlane Publishing Corp. (BMI). All Rights On Behalf Of Long Pond Music (ASCAP) and Revelation Music Publishing Corp. (ASCAP) Administered By WB Music Corp. (ASCAP). All Rights Reserved. Used by Permission. WARNER BROS. PUBLICATIONS U.S. INC., Miami, FL 33014.

One More Walk Around The Garden by Alan Jay Lerner and Burton Lane. © 1979 by Alan Jay Lerner and Burton Lane. All Rights In The U.S. Administered By WB Music Corp. and Chappell & Co. By Agreement With The Heirs of Alan Jay Lerner and With Burton Lane. Publication and Allied Rights Elsewhere Assigned To Chappell & Co. All Rights Reserved. Used by Permission. WARNER BROS. PUBLICATIONS U.S. INC., Miami, FL 33014.

Our Private World by Cy Coleman, Betty Comden and Adolph Green. © Notable Music Co., Inc. and Betdolph Music Company. All Rights Administered By WB Music Corp. All Rights Reserved. Used by Permission. WARNER BROS. PUBLICATIONS U.S. INC., Miami, FL 33014.

Pretty Women by Stephen Sondheim. © 1978 Rilting Music, Inc. (ASCAP). All Rights Administered By WB Music Corp. (ASCAP). All Rights Reserved. Used by Permission. WARNER BROS. PUBLICATIONS U.S. INC., Miami, FL 33014.

Ragtime by Stephen Flaherty and Lynn Ahrens. © 1997 WB Music Corp. (ASCAP), Pen and Perseverance (ASCAP) and Hillsdale Music, Inc. (ASCAP). All Rights On Behalf Of Pen and Perseverance (ASCAP) and Hillsdale Music, Inc. (ASCAP) Administered By WB Music Corp. (ASCAP). All Rights Reserved. Used by Permission. WARNER BROS. PUBLICATIONS U.S. INC., Miami, FL 33014.

Real Live Girl by Cy Coleman and Carolyn Leigh. © 1962 (renewed) Notable Music Co., Inc. and Carwin Music Inc. (ASCAP). All Rights On Behalf Of Notable Music Co., Inc. Administered By WB Music Corp. All Rights Reserved. Used by Permission. WARNER BROS. PUBLICATIONS U.S. INC., Miami, FL 33014.

Roundabout by Vernon Duke and Ogden Nash. © 1946 (Renewed) Warner Bros. Inc. and Kay Duke Music. All Rights Reserved. Used by Permission. WARNER BROS. PUBLICATIONS U.S. INC., Miami, FL 33014.

The Shadow Of Your Smile by Johnny Mandel and Paul Francis Webster. © 1965 Metro-Goldwyn-Mayer Inc. © Renewed 1993 EMI Miller Catalog Inc. All Rights Controlled By EMI Miller Catalog Inc. (Publishing) and Warner Bros. Publications U.S. Inc. (Print). All Rights Reserved. Used by Permission. WARNER BROS. PUBLICATIONS INC., Miami, FL 33014.

She Loves Me by Sheldon Harnick and Jerry Bock. © 1963 (Renewed 1991) Mayerling Productions Ltd. and Jerry Bock Enterprises. All Rights Reserved. Used by Permission. WARNER BROS. PUBLICATIONS U.S. INC., Miami, FL 33014 (Licensed by Carlin America).

So Many Stars by Alan and Marilyn Bergman and Sergio Mendes. © 1967 (Renewed) WB Music Corp. (ASCAP), Threesome Music (ASCAP). Administered By WB Music Corp. (ASCAP). All Rights Reserved. Used by Permission. WARNER BROS. PUBLICATIONS U.S. INC., Miami, FL 33014.

Sunday by Stephen Sondheim. © 1984 Rilting Music, Inc. (ASCAP). All Rights On Behalf Of Rilting Music, Inc. (ASCAP) Administered By WB Music Corp. (ASCAP). All Rights Reserved. Used by Permission. WARNER BROS. PUBLICATIONS U.S. INC., Miami, FL 33014.

That's For Children by Dorothy Fields and Arthur Schwartz. © 1950 (Renewed) Chappell & Co. All Rights Reserved. Used by Permission. WARNER BROS. PUBLICATIONS U.S. INC., Miami, FL 33014.

Times Like This by Stephen Flaherty and Lynn Ahrens. © 1991 WB Music Corp. (ASCAP), Pen and Perseverance (ASCAP) and Hillsdale Music, Inc. (ASCAP). All Rights On Behalf Of Pen and Perseverance (ASCAP) and Hillsdale music, Inc. (ASCAP) Administered By WB Music Corp, (ASCAP). All Rights Reserved. Used by Permission WARNER BROS. PUBLICATIONS U.S. INC., Miami, FL 33014.

Tomorrow Mountain by Dale Wasserman and Duke Ellington. © 1947 (Renewed) WB Music Corp. (ASCAP) and Famous Music Corporation (ASCAP). All Rights Reserved. Used by Permission. WARNER BROS. PUBLICATIONS U.S. INC., Miami, FL 33014.

Tonight At Eight by Sheldon Harnick and Jerry Bock. © 1963 (Renewed 1991) Mayerling Productions Ltd. and Jerry Bock Enterprises. All Rights Reserved. Used by Permission. WARNER BROS. PUBLICATIONS U.S. INC., Miami, FL 33014 (Licensed by Carlin America).

Two For The Road by Henry Mancini and Leslie Bricusse. © Northridge Music Company and WB Music Corp. Copyright Renewed. All Rights Reserved. Used by Permission. WARNER BROS. PUBLICATIONS U.S. INC., Miami, FL 33014.

Wait Till We're Sixty-Five by Burton Lane and Alan Jay Lerner. © 1965 (Renewed) Chappell & Co., Inc. (ASCAP). All Rights Reserved. Used by Permission. WARNER BROS. PUBLICATIONS U.S. INC., Miami, FL 33014.

Where Am I Going by Cy Coleman and Dorothy Fields. © 1965 (Renewed) Notable Music Co., Inc. (ASCAP) and Lida Enterprises, Inc. (ASCAP). All Rights Administered By WB Music Corp. All Rights Reserved. Used by Permission. WARNER BROS. PUBLICATIONS U.S. INC., Miami, FL 33014.

Where Do I Go From Here by Sheldon Harnick and Jerry Bock. © 1959 (Renewed 1987) Mayerling Productions Ltd. and Jerry Bock Enterprises. All Rights Reserved. Used by Permission. WARNER BROS. PUBLICATIONS U.S. INC., Miami, FL 33014.

Where Do You Start by Alan and Marilyn Bergman and Johnny Mandel. © 1987 Threesome Music Co. And Marissa Music (ASCAP). All Rights Reserved. Used by Permission. WARNER BROS. PUBLICATIONS U.S. INC., Miami, FL 33014.

Sepia Life by John Bucchino. © 2000 by John Bucchino. Art Food Music owner of publication and allied rights throughout the world. (administered by Williamson Music). International Copyright Secured. All Rights Reserved. Used by Permission.

Not A Cloud In The Sky by John Bucchino. © 2000 by John Bucchino. Art Food Music owner of publication and allied rights throughout the world. (administered by Williamson Music). International Copyright Secured. All Rights Reserved. Used by Permission.

In A Restaurant By The Sea by John Bucchino. © 2000 by John Bucchino. Art Food Music owner of publication and allied rights throughout the world. (administered by Williamson Music). International Copyright Secured. All Rights Reserved. Used by Permission.

This Moment by John Bucchino. © 1999 by John Bucchino. Art Food Music owner of publication and allied rights throughout the world. (administered by Williamson Music). International Copyright Secured. All Rights Reserved. Used by Permission.

Songs Licensed by Carlin America

What Are Little Girls Made Of written by Alec Wilder, William Engvik.Used by permission of Edward B. Marks Music Company.

The Little Things You Do Together written by Stephen Sondheim. Used by permission of Herald Square Music, Inc. on behalf of Quartet Music, Jerry Leiber Music, Mike Stoller Music, and Rilting Music, Inc.

Merry Little Minuet written by Sheldon Harnick. Used by permission of Alley Music Corporation [and additional information supplied by co-publishers].

(I'll Marry) The Very Next Man from "Fiorello" written by Jerry Bock, Sheldon Harnick Used by permission of Alley Music Corporation [and additional information supplied by co-publishers].

Where Was I When They Passed Out Luck written by Larry Grossman, Hal Hackady Used by permission of Alley Music Corporation [and additional information supplied by co-publishers].

Tonight At Eight from "She Loves Me" written by Jerry Bock, Sheldon Harnick Used by permission of Alley Music Corporation [and additional information supplied by co-publishers].

Songs Licensed by The Richmond Organization

The April Age Lyric by William Engvik; Music by Alec Wilder. TRO © 1976 (Renewed) Ludlow Music, Inc., New York, NY. Used by Permission.

Blackberry Winter Words and Music by Alec Wilder and Loonis McGlohon TRO © 1976 (Renewed) Ludlow Music, Inc., New York, NY. Used by Permission.

Ellen Lyric by William Engvik; music and Arrangement by Alec Wilder TRO © 1954 (Renewed) 1968 (Renewed) Ludlow Music, Inc., New York, NY. Used by Permission.

I Know Your Heart By Hugh Martin and Timothy Gray. TRO © 1964 (Renewed) Cromwell Music, Inc., New York. Used by Permission.

Mimosa And Me Lyric by William Engvik; Music by Alec Wilder.TRO © 1964 (Renewed) 1968 (Renewed) Ludlow Music, Inc., New York, NY. Used by Permission.

The Result Was Dad Lyric by William Engvic; Music by Alec Wilder. TRO © 2004 Ludlow Music, Inc., New York, NY. Used by Permission.

'S Gonna Be A Cold Cold Day Lyric by Loonis McGlohon; Music by Alec Wilder. TRO © Copyright 1990 Ludlow Music, Inc., New York, NY. Used by Permission.

While We're Young Words by Bill Engvic; Music by Morty Palitz and Alec Wilder. TRO © Copyright 1943 (Renewed) 1944 (Renewed) Ludlow Music, Inc., New York, NY. Used by Permission.

Who Wants to Fall in Love (Aye, Aye, Aye) by Bart Howard. TRO © 1953 (Renewed) 1958 (Renewed) Folkways Music Publishers, Inc., New York, NY. Used by Permission.

A Child Is Born Words by Alec Wilder; Music by Thad Jones TRO © 1997 Ludlow Music, Inc. and D'Accord Music, Inc., New York, NY. Used by Permission.

My Love Is A Wanderer Words and Music by Bart Howard TRO © 1952 (Renewed) Hampshire House Publishing Corp., New York, NY. Used by Permission.

Small Day Tomorrow Lyric by Fran Landesman; Music by Bob Dorough TRO © 1972 (Renewed) Cromwell Music, Inc., New York, NY. Used by Permission.

(So You've Had A) Change Of Heart Lyric by Alex Wilder; Music by Roy Kral TRO © 1958 (Renewed) Hollis Music, Inc., New York, NY. Used by Permission.

Through the Windows of Cars Words and Music by Roy Kral and Fran Landesman TRO © 1994 Hampshire House Publishing Corp., New York, NY. Used by Permission

Unlit Room Lyric by Fran Landesman; Music by Bob Dorough TRO © 2004 (renewed) Ludlow Music, Inc., New York, NY. Used by Permission.

Walkup Words and Music by Bart Howard TRO © 1956 (Renewed) and (1958) Renewed) Folkways Music Publishers, Inc., New York, NY. Used by Permission

Songs Licensed by Others: Chapter 3

Cocoanut Sweet Lyrics by E.Y. "Yip" Harburg; Music by Harold Arlen. Published by Glocca Morra Music (ASCAP) and SA Music (ASCAP) Glocca Morra Administered by Next Decade Entertainment, Inc. All Rights Reserved. Used by Permission.

He Had Refinement Lyrics by Dorothy Fields; Music by Arthur Schwartz. Zak' a tak Music Productions, Nyack, NY 10960.

Alone Too Long Lyrics by Dorothy Fields; Music by Arthur Schwartz. Used by Permission. Aldi Music c/o Songwriters Guild, New York, NY 10036.

Small World Words and Music by Vernon Duke (unpublished) Used by Permission. Kay Duke Ingalls, Santa Fe, NM.

I Wanna Be A Dancin' Man Lyrics by Johnny Mercer; Music by Harry Warren. Used by Permission. Four Jays Music Company, Los Angeles, CA 90013.

Songs Licensed by Others: Chapter 4

Stay In My Arms Music and Lyrics by Marc Blitzstein. Used by Peermission. Blitzstein Music Company, Tiverton, RI 02878.

I Wish It So Music and Lyrics by Marc Blitzstein. Used by Permission. Blitzstein Music Company, Tiverton, RI 02878.

Songs Licensed by Others: Chapter 5

Promise Me A Rose Words and Music by Bob Merrill. Used by Permission. Golden Bell Songs, Los Angeles, CA 90069.

The Friendliest Thing Two People Can Do Words and Music by Ervin Drake. Used by Permission. Songwriters Guild of America o/b/o Lindabet Music, Weehawken ,NJ 07087.

A Room Without Windows Words and Music by Ervin Drake. Used by Permission. Songwriters Guild of America o/b/o Lindabet Music, Weehawken, NJ 07087.

Something To Live For Words and music by Ervin Drake. Used by Permission. Songwriters Guild of America o/b/o Lindabet Music, Weehawken, NJ 07087.

Too Little Time Lyrics by Don Raye; Music by Henry Mancini. Used by Permission. Big Four Music Company, Las Vegas, NV 89120.

Old Boyfriends Music and Lyrics by Tom Waits. Used by Permission. Fifth Floor Music Co. Los Angeles, CA 90038.

Songs Licensed by Others: Chapter 6

Goodnight New York by Julie R. Gold. © 1993 by Irving Mills Music, Inc. on behalf of itself and Julie Gold Music [BMI] Used by Permission. International Copyright Secured. All Rights Reserved.

Just Where They Should Be Written by Craig Carnelia. Published by Big A Music LLC. Administered by A. Schroeder International LLC. Used by Permission, International Copyright Secured.

Witchcraft Words and Music by Michael Brown. Used by Permission of the composer.

I See The World Through Your Eyes Words and Music by John Wallowitch. Used by Permission of the composer.

Inside A Silent Tear Words by Mahriah Blackwolf; Music by Blossom Dearie. Used by Permission of the composers.

I'm Shadowing You Words and Music by Blossom Dearie. Used by Permission of the composer.

I Don't Remember Words by Jack Segal; Music by Blossom Dearie. Used by Permission of the composers.

Spring Can Really Hang You Up The Most Words by Fran Landesman and Music by Tommy Wolf ©1955 assigned to Wolfland 1987 renewed 1989. Wolfland administered by Fricout Music. Used by permission. All rights reserved.

There Are Days When I Don't Think Of You At All Words by Fran Landesman and Music by Tommy Wolf © 1953 Thomas Joseph Wolf, Jr. renewed 1984. Wolfland administered by Fricout Music. Used by permission. All rights reserved.

It's Nice Weather For Ducks Words by Fran Landesman and Music by Tommy Wolf © 1961. Wolf-Mills Music assigned to Wolfland 1987 renewed 1989. Wol fland administered by Fricout Music. Used by permission. All rights reserved.

Ballad Of The Sad Young Men Words by Fran Landesman and Music by Tommy Wolf © 1959 renewed 1987. Wolfland administered by Fricout Music. Used by permission. All rights reserved.

I Love You Real Words by Fran Landesman and Music by Tommy Wolf © 1955 Thomas Joseph Wolf, Jr. renewed 1983. Wolfland administered by Fricour music. Used by permission – All rights reserved.

This Little Love Of Ours Words by Fran Landesman and Music by Tommy Wolf © 1953 Thomas Joseph Wolf, Jr. renewed 1981. Wolfland administered by Fricout music. Used by permission. All rights reserved.

Boats Words and Music by Tommy Wolf © 1975. Wolfland administered by Fricout Music. Used by permission. All rights reserved.

I Like To Sing Words by Loonis McGlohon; Music by Billy VerPlanck. Mounted Records, Inc. Used by permission of Billy VerPlanck and the Loonis McGlohon Intellectual Property Trust.

It's How You Play The Game Words by Joe Cocuzzo; Music by BillyVerPlanck. Mounted Records, Inc. Used by permission of the composers.

What Are We Going To Do With All This Moonlight? Words by Leon Nock; Music by Billy Ver-Planck Mounted Records, Inc. Used by permission of the composers.

(I Stayed) Too Long At The Fair by Billy Barnes © 1956-57, renewed 1984-85 Tylerson Music (ASCAP). Administered by Criterion Music Corp. All Rights Reserved. Used By Permission. International Copyright Secured.

Comment-allez Vous Words and Music by Murray Grand. Used by Permission of the composer.

Where Is The Melody by Arthur Siegel. © 1978 Helene Blue Musique Ltd. All Rights Reserved. Used by Permission.

Warm Goes To Warm Words and Music by Ronny Whyte. Used by permission of the composer.

People, Places, Things Words by Roger Schore; Music by Ronny Whyte. Used by permission of the composers.

Ain't Safe To Go Nowhere Words and Music by Franklin Roosevelt Underwood. Used by permission of the composer.

The Lies Of Handsome Men Words and Music by Francesca Blumenthal. Used by permission of the composer.

Between Men Words and Music by Francesca Blumenthal. Used by permission of the composer.

On The Streets Of Paree Words and Music by Framcesca Blumenthal. Used by permission of the composer.

The Trouble With Love Words and Music by Francesca Blumenthal. Used by permission of the composer.

Blizzard Of Lies (Dave Frishberg and Samantha Frishberg) © 1983 Swiftwater Music. All Rights Reserved. Used by Permission.

Dear Bix (Dave Frishbergh) © 1985 Swiftwater Music.All Rights Reserved. Used by Permission.

Quality Time (Dave Frishberg) © 1994 Swiftwater Music. All Rights Reserved. Used by Permission.

Songs Licensed by Others: Chapter 7

What's Your Name? Words and Music by Lew Spence. © 1974 by Lew Spence Music. Used by permission of the composer.

They Say It's Spring Words and Music by Bob Haymes. By permission: Jatap Publishing Co. c/o Irving Mills Music.

A Fine Spring Morning Words and music by Bob Haymes. By permission: Jatap Publishing Co. c/o Irving Mills Music.

There Used To Be A Ballpark Words and Music by Joe Raposo. By permission Instructional Children's Music, Inc. New York NY 10017.

I Couldn't Be With Anyone but You from "A Wonderful Life" Music: Joe Raposo; Words: Sheldon Harnick © 1989 by Wizzybus Music, Inc. and Mayerling Productions Ltd. Used by permission.

Up,Up and Away by Jim Webb. By permission: Jonathan Three Music Co. c/o Lastrada Entertainment Company, Ltd., Hewlett, NY 11557.

Pretty Girl by Billy Strayhorn. © (Renewed) by Tempo Muisc, Inc. (ASCAP) International Copyright Secured. All Rights Reserved. Reprinted by Permission.

Bittersweet by Billy Srrayhorn and Roger E. Schore. © (Renewed0 by Tempo Music, Inc. (ASCAP) International Copyright Secured. All Rights Reserved. Reprinted by Permission.

Last Light Of Evening by Billy Strayhorn. © (Renewed) by Tempo Music, Inc. (ASCAP) International Copyright Secfured. All Rights Reserved. Reprinted by Permission.

Pousse Café by Duke Ellington and Marshall Barer. © (Renewed) by Tempo Music, Inc. (ASCAP) International Copyright Secured. All Rights Reserved. Reprinted by Permission.

Let's from POUSSE CAFÉ by Duke Ellington and Marshall Barer. © (Renewed) by Tempo Music, Inc. (ASCAP) International Copyright Secured. All Rights Reserved. Reprinted by Permission.

Love Turns Winter To Spring Words and Music by Matt Dennis. Maxey Music. Used by Permission.

Heart'sDesire (Dave Frishberg and Alan Broadbent) © 1991 Swiftwater Music. All Rights Reserved. Used by Permission.

You Are There (Dave Frishberg and Johnny Mandel) © Swiftwater Music and Marissa music. All Rights Reserved. Used by Permission.

Suddenly Words by Milton Raskin; Music by David Raksin. © 1956, Madrigal Music Company (ASCAP) Van Nuys, CA 91406.

Song Licensed by Others: Chapter 8

"They" Lyrics by Kenward Elmslie; Music by Claibe Richardson. Used by Permission of Kenward Elmslie.

What Do I Do Now He's Gone? Lyrics by Kenward Elmslie; Music by Claibe Richardson. © 1971 Thackeray Falls Music Co. Used by Permission of Kenward Elmslie.

The One And Only Person In The World Lyrics by Kenward Elmslie; Music by Claibe Richardson. © 1971 Thackeray Falls Music Co. Used by Permission of Kenward Elmslie.

If There's Love Enough Lyrics by Kenward Elmslie; Music by Claibe Richardson. © 1971 Thackeray Fallsmusic Co. Used by Permission of Robbie Hickman and Kenward Elmslie.

Beauty Secrets Lyrics by Kenward Elmslie; Music by Claibe Richardson. Used by Permission of Kenward Elmslie.

General Index

Song Index

Songwriters' Index

Index of writers of songs in classic popular style
(Songwriters in other styles are listed in the General Index)